Kaplan Publishing are constantly finding new ways to make a difference to your studies and our exciting online resources really do offer something different to students looking for exam success.

This book comes with free MyKaplan online resources so that you can study anytime, anywhere. This free online resource is not sold separately and is included in the price of the book.

Having purchased this book, you have access to the following online study materials:

CONTENT	ACCA (including FFA,FAB,FMA)		FIA (excluding FFA,FAB,FMA)	
	Text	Kit	Text	Kit
Electronic version of the book	✓	✓	✓	✓
Check Your Understanding Test with instant answers	✓			
Material updates	✓	✓	✓	✓
Latest official ACCA exam questions*		✓		
Extra question assistance using the signpost icon**		✓		
Timed questions with an online tutor debrief using clock icon***		✓		
Interim assessment including questions and answers	✓		✓	
Technical answers	✓	✓	✓	✓

*   Excludes F1, F2, F3, F4, FAB, FMA and FFA; for all other papers includes a selection of questions, as released by ACCA
**   For ACCA P1-P7 only
*** Excludes F1, F2, F3, F4, FAB, FMA and FFA

How to access your online resources

Kaplan Financial students will already have a MyKaplan account and these extra resources will be available to you online. You do not need to register again, as this process was completed when you enrolled. If you are having problems accessing online materials, please ask your course administrator.

If you are not studying with Kaplan and did not purchase your book via a Kaplan website, to unlock your extra online resources please go to www.mykaplan.co.uk/addabook (even if you have set up an account and registered books previously). You will then need to enter the ISBN number (on the title page and back cover) and the unique pass key number contained in the scratch panel below to gain access.

You will also be required to enter additional information during this process to set up or confirm your account details.

If you purchased through Kaplan Flexible Learning or via the Kaplan Publishing website you will automatically receive an e-mail invitation to MyKaplan. Please register your details using this email to gain access to your content. If you do not receive the e-mail or book content, please contact Kaplan Publishing.

Your Code and Information

This code can only be used once for the registration of one book online. This registration and your online content will expire when the final sittings for the examinations covered by this book have taken place. Please allow one hour from the time you submit your book details for us to process your request.

Please scratch the film to access your MyKaplan code.

Please be aware that this code is case-sensitive and you will need to include the dashes within the passcode, but not when entering the ISBN. For further technical support, please visit www.MyKaplan.co.uk

D0943455

KAPLAN PUBLISHING

ACCA

Strategic Professional

Strategic Business Reporting (INT & UK) (SBR)

EXAM KIT

British Library Cataloguing-in-Publication Data

A catalogue record for this book is available from the British Library.

Published by:
Kaplan Publishing UK
Unit 2 The Business Centre
Molly Millar's Lane
Wokingham
Berkshire
RG41 2QZ

ISBN: 978-1-78740-115-0

Acknowledgements

These materials are reviewed by the ACCA examining team. The objective of the review is to ensure that the material properly covers the syllabus and study guide outcomes, used by the examining team in setting the exams, in the appropriate breadth and depth. The review does not ensure that every eventuality, combination or application of examinable topics is addressed by the ACCA Approved Content. Nor does the review comprise a detailed technical check of the content as the Approved Content Provider has its own quality assurance processes in place in this respect.

The IFRS Foundation logo, the IASB logo, the IFRS for SMEs logo, the "Hexagon Device", "IFRS Foundation", "eIFRS", "IAS", "IASB", "IFRS for SMEs", "IFRS", "IASs", "IFRSs", "International Accounting Standards" and "International Financial Reporting Standards", "IFRIC" and "IFRS Taxonomy" are Trade Marks of the IFRS Foundation.

Trade Marks

The IFRS Foundation logo, the IASB logo, the IFRS for SMEs logo, the "Hexagon Device", "IFRS Foundation", "eIFRS", "IAS", "IASB", "IFRS for SMEs", "NIIF" IASs" "IFRS", "IFRSs", "International Accounting Standards", "International Financial Reporting Standards", "IFRIC", "SIC" and "IFRS Taxonomy".

Further details of the Trade Marks including details of countries where the Trade Marks are registered or applied for are available from the Foundation on request.

This product contains material that is ©Financial Reporting Council Ltd (FRC). Adapted and reproduced with the kind permission of the Financial Reporting Council. All rights reserved. For further information, please visit www.frc.org.uk or call +44 (0)20 7492 2300.

CONTENTS

Section

This document references IFRS® Standards and IAS® Standards, which are authored by the International Accounting Standards Board (the Board), and published in the 2018 IFRS Standards Red Book.

Key features in this edition

In addition to providing a wide ranging bank of real past exam questions, we have also included in this edition:

- Paper specific information and advice on exam technique.

- Our recommended approach to make your revision for this particular subject as effective as possible.

    This includes step by step guidance on how best to use our Kaplan material (Study Text, Pocket Notes and Exam Kit) at this stage in your studies.

- Enhanced tutorial answers packed with specific key answer tips, technical tutorial notes and exam technique tips from our experienced tutors.

- Complementary online resources including full tutor debriefs and question assistance to point you in the right direction when you get stuck.

You will find a wealth of other resources to help you with your studies on the following sites:

www.MyKaplan.co.uk

www.**acca**global.com/students/

UK GAAP focus

The majority of the UK syllabus exam will be the same as the international exam, which is based on International Financial Reporting Standards (IFRS® Standards and IAS® Standards). The UK exam will also test some differences between UK GAAP and International Financial Reporting Standards. There could also be a focus on the requirements of Companies Act. It is anticipated that the differences will account for no more than 20% of the SBR UK paper.

UK syllabus students should refer to the list of examinable documents for the UK examination. This document is available on the ACCA web site at www.accaglobal.com

To assist UK syllabus students, additional questions and answers based on examinable UK content are included in this Exam Kit.

Quality and accuracy are of the utmost importance to us so if you spot an error in any of our products, please send an email to mykaplanreporting@kaplan.com with full details.

Our Quality Co-ordinator will work with our technical team to verify the error and take action to ensure it is corrected in future editions.

INDEX TO QUESTIONS AND ANSWERS

KEY TO THE INDEX

PAPER ENHANCEMENTS

We have added the following enhancements to the answers in this Exam Kit:

Key answer tips

All answers include key answer tips to help your understanding of each question.

Tutorial note

All answers include more tutorial notes to explain some of the technical points in more detail.

Top tutor tips

For selected questions, we 'walk through the answer' giving guidance on how to approach the questions with helpful 'tips from a top tutor', together with technical tutor notes.

These answers are indicated with the 'footsteps' icon in the index.

ONLINE ENHANCEMENTS

 Question debrief

For selected questions, we recommend that they are to be completed in full exam conditions (i.e. without your notes).

In addition to the examiner's technical answer, enhanced with key answer tips and tutorial notes in this Exam Kit, online you can find an answer debrief by a top tutor that:

- works through the question in full

- points out how to approach the question

- how to ensure that the easy marks are obtained as quickly as possible, and

- emphasises how to tackle exam questions and exam technique.

These questions are indicated with the 'clock' icon in the index.

 Online question assistance

Have you ever looked at a question and not know where to start, or got stuck part way through?

For selected questions, we have produced 'Online question assistance' offering different levels of guidance, such as:

- ensuring that you understand the question requirements fully, highlighting key terms and the meaning of the verbs used

- how to read the question proactively, with knowledge of the requirements, to identify the topic areas covered

- assessing the detail content of the question body, pointing out key information and explaining why it is important

- help in devising a plan of attack

With this assistance, you should then be able to attempt your answer confident that you know what is expected of you.

These questions are indicated with the 'signpost' icon in the index.

Online question enhancements and answer debriefs are available on MyKaplan:

www.MyKaplan.co.uk

SECTION A QUESTIONS

Group financial statements

SECTION B QUESTIONS

			Page number		Past exam
			Question	**Answer**	**(Adapted)**
29	McVeigh		53	230	Dec 18
30	Mehran		55	234	Sep 18
31	Carsoon		56	238	
32	Skye		58	240	
33	Whitebirk		59	243	
34	Aspire		60	246	
35	Business combinations		61	250	
36	Margie		63	255	
37	Kayte		64	259	
38	Verge		65	261	
39	Aron		67	265	
40	Alexandra		68	269	
41	Klancet		69	273	
42	Emcee		71	277	
43	Gasnature		72	281	
44	Janne		73	285	
45	Evolve		74	292	
46	Artwright		76	293	
47	Lucky Dairy		77	296	

UK GAAP focus

			Page number		Past exam
48	Fill		79	299	Dec 18 (A)
49	Skizer		80	301	Sep 18 (A)
50	Bobarra		80	303	
51	Harris		81	305	
52	Rowling		81	307	
53	Toto		82	308	
54	Howey		82	309	
55	Loki		82	311	

EXAM TECHNIQUE

- **Divide the time** you spend on questions in proportion to the marks on offer:

  Whatever happens, always keep your eye on the clock and **do not over run on any part of any question!**

- If you **get completely stuck** with a question:

  – move on

  – **return to it later.**

- Stick to the question and **tailor your answer** to what you are asked.

  – pay particular attention to the verbs in the question.

- If you do not understand what a question is asking, **state your assumptions**.

  Even if you do not answer in precisely the way the examiner hoped, you should be given some credit, if your assumptions are reasonable.

- You should do everything you can to make things easy for the marker.

  The marker will find it easier to identify the points you have made if you leave plenty of space between the points that you are making.

- **Discursive questions**:

  Your answer should have a clear structure. Use headings and paragraphs to provide focus.

  Be concise and stay on topic. You will score no marks if you do not answer the question.

- **Workings**:

  It is essential to include all your workings in your answers – method marks are available even if your final answer is incorrect.

PAPER SPECIFIC INFORMATION

THE EXAM

FORMAT OF THE EXAM

	Number of marks
Section A: Two compulsory questions	50
Section B: Two compulsory questions of 25 marks each	50
	——
	100
Total time allowed: 3 hours 15 minutes.	——

Note that:

- The first question in Section A will test group accounting. In addition to the consideration of the numerical aspects of group accounting (max 25 marks), a discussion and explanation of these numbers will be required. This question will also test other areas of the syllabus.

- The second question in Section A will require consideration of (i) the reporting implications and (ii) the ethical implications of specific events in a given scenario. Two professional marks will be awarded in this question for the application of ethical principles to the scenario.

- Section B consists of two questions, which may be scenario or case-study or essay based and will contain both discursive and computational elements. Section B could deal with any aspect of the syllabus but will always include either a full question, or part of a question, that requires the appraisal of financial and/or non-financial information from either the preparer's or another stakeholder's perspective. Two professional marks will be awarded in the Section B question that requires analysis.

PASS MARK

The pass mark for all ACCA Qualification examinations is 50%.

The UK exam

The Examiner has indicated that Section B questions in the UK exam will be adapted to assess UK specific content. This question may be based on either a single entity or a group and will be worth 15-20 marks. It may have discursive and/or numerical content and requirements, and could cover the following syllabus areas:

- The financial reporting requirements for UK and Republic of Ireland entities (UK GAAP) and their interaction with the Companies Act requirements

- The reasons why an entity might choose to adopt FRS 101 or FRS 102

- The scope and basis of preparation of financial statements under UK GAAP

- The concepts and pervasive principles set out in FRS 102

- The principal differences between UK GAAP and International Financial Reporting Standards.

Note that the UK syllabus exam will be denominated in dollars (identified as $); this Exam Kit adopts the same notation and style for UK syllabus content.

DETAILED SYLLABUS

The detailed syllabus and study guide written by the ACCA can be found at:

www.accaglobal.com/student

KAPLAN'S RECOMMENDED REVISION APPROACH

QUESTION PRACTICE IS THE KEY TO SUCCESS

Success in professional examinations relies upon you acquiring a firm grasp of the required knowledge at the tuition phase. In order to be able to do the questions, knowledge is essential.

However, the difference between success and failure often hinges on your exam technique on the day and making the most of the revision phase of your studies.

The **Kaplan Study Text** is the starting point, designed to provide the underpinning knowledge to tackle all questions. However, in the revision phase, pouring over text books is not the answer.

Kaplan Online progress tests help you consolidate your knowledge and understanding and are a useful tool to check whether you can remember key topic areas.

Kaplan Pocket Notes are designed to help you quickly revise a topic area, however you then need to practice questions. There is a need to progress to full exam standard questions as soon as possible, and to tie your exam technique and technical knowledge together.

The importance of question practice cannot be over-emphasised.

The recommended approach below is designed by expert tutors in the field, in conjunction with their knowledge of the examining team and their recent real exams.

The approach taken for the Applied Skills exams is to revise by topic area. However, with the Strategic Professional exams, a multi topic approach is required to answer the scenario based questions.

You need to practice as many questions as possible in the time you have left.

OUR AIM

Our aim is to get you to the stage where you can attempt exam standard questions confidently, to time, in a closed book environment, with no supplementary help (i.e. to simulate the real examination experience).

Practising your exam technique on examination-style questions, in timed conditions, is also vitally important for you to assess your progress and identify areas of weakness that may need more attention in the final run up to the examination.

In order to achieve this we recognise that initially you may feel the need to practice some questions with open book help and exceed the required time.

The approach below shows you which questions you should use to build up to coping with exam standard question practice, and references to the sources of information available should you need to revisit a topic area in more detail.

EXAMINER'S COMMENTS

We have included many of the examiner's comments to the examination questions in this kit for you to see the main pitfalls that students fall into with regard to technical content.

However, too many times in the general section of the report, the examiner comments that students had failed due to:

- 'misallocation of time'

- 'running out of time' and

- showing signs of 'spending too much time on an earlier question and clearly rushing the answer to a subsequent question'.

Good exam technique is vital.

STRATEGIC PROFESSIONAL CBE

For September and December 2019 exam sessions, all Strategic Professional exams will be assessed by paper based examination. From March 2020, these exams will become available by computer based examination. The exam format may impact upon your approach to revision. For more information regarding what is available in your market, we therefore advise consulting the ACCA Global website.

Remember that in the real examination, all you have to do is:

- attempt all questions required by the exam

- only spend the allotted time on each question, and

- get them at least 50% right!

Try and practice this approach on every question you attempt from now to the real exam.

For additional support with your studies please also refer to the ACCA Global website.

THE KAPLAN SBR REVISION PLAN

Stage 1: Assess areas of strengths and weaknesses

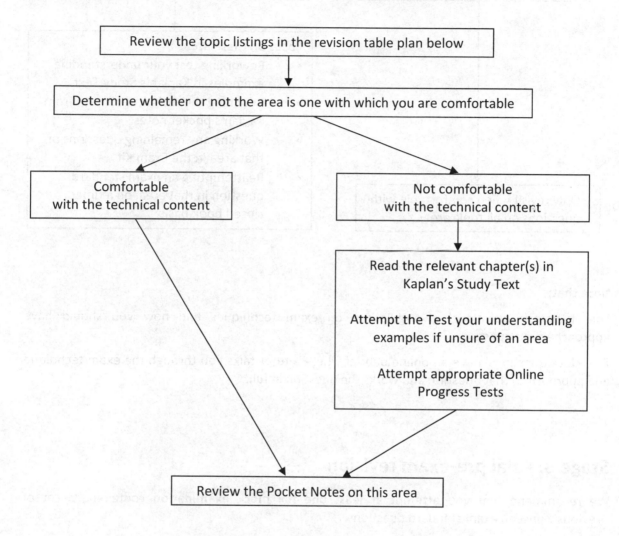

Stage 2: Practice questions

Follow the order of revision of topics as recommended in the revision table plan below and attempt the questions in the order suggested.

Try to avoid referring to text books and notes and the model answer until you have completed your attempt.

Try to answer the question in the allotted time.

Review your attempt with the model answer and assess how much of the answer you achieved in the allocated exam time.

Fill in the self-assessment box below and decide on your best course of action.

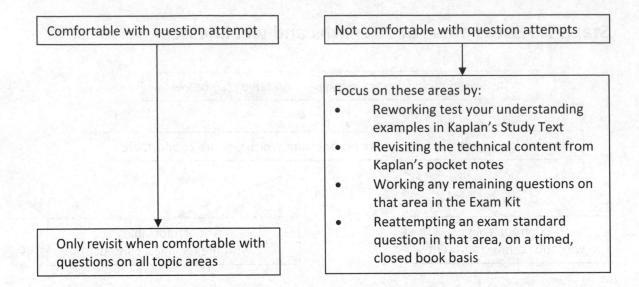

Note that:

The 'footsteps questions' give guidance on exam techniques and how you should have approached the question.

The 'clock questions' have an online debrief where a tutor talks you through the exam technique and approach to that question and works the question in full.

Stage 3: Final pre-exam revision

We recommend that you **attempt at least one full mock examination** containing a set of previously unseen exam standard questions.

It is important that you get a feel for the breadth of coverage of a real exam without advanced knowledge of the topic areas covered – just as you will expect to see on the real exam day.

Ideally this mock should be sat in timed, closed book, real exam conditions and could be:

- a mock examination offered by your tuition provider, and/or
- one of the specimen exams.

KAPLAN'S DETAILED REVISION PLAN

Topic	Study Text Chapter	Pocket Note Chapter	Questions to attempt	Tutor guidance	Date attempted	Self-assessment
The financial reporting framework	1	1	Q23 Q25(a) Q44(b)	Ensure that you know the contents of the *Conceptual Framework* and that you are able to apply it to transactions.		
Ethical and professional principles	2	2	Q15 Q16	Ensure that you can apply the ACCA *Code of Ethics and Conduct* to practical scenarios.		
Reporting financial performance						
Fair value measurement	1	1	Q30(a)	You must know the definition of fair value and be able to apply it. Make sure that you know the markets used to measure fair value and the levels of inputs to fair value measurement.		
Performance reporting and revenue	3, 4	3, 4	Q19 Q31(a)	This could include revenue recognition or the presentation of discontinued activities.		
Non-current assets, agriculture and inventories.	5, 6	5, 6	Q37 Q42 Q47	There are several reporting standards within this heading. In particular, issues around property, plant and equipment, and intangible assets, and impairment are regularly examined.		

Topic	Study Text Chapter	Pocket Note Chapter	Questions to attempt	Tutor guidance	Date attempted	Self-assessment
Foreign currency transactions	7	7	Q34(a)	Ensure that you know how to account for exchange differences arising on overseas transactions within an individual company's financial statements.		
Leases	8	8	Q21 Q22	Ensure that you know how to determine when a contract contains a lease. You must be able to account for leases from the perspective of the lessee and the lessor.		
Employee benefits	9	9	Q29	Ensure that you understand how to account for defined benefit and defined contribution schemes.		
Share-based payment	10	10	Q36(a)	Ensure that you understand how to account for both cash-settled transactions and equity-settled transactions.		
Provisions and events after the reporting period	11	11	Q30(b)	Ensure that you know when a legal or constructive obligation arises, and that you can apply the definition of an adjusting and non-adjusting event per IAS 10.		
Financial instruments	12	12	Q39 Q46	Ensure that you understand and can apply recognition, measurement and classification rules relating to financial instruments per IAS 32 and IFRS 9.		

Topic	Study Text Chapter	Pocket Note Chapter	Questions to attempt	Tutor guidance	Date attempted	Self-assessment
Income taxes	13	13	Q24(b)	The main focus is likely to be the recognition and measurement of deferred tax assets and liabilities.		
Segment reporting	14	14	Q38(a)	Ensure that you can define a reportable segment and apply the definition to information provided. It is also important to know whether two segments can be aggregated.		
Related parties	15	15	Q20	Ensure you can identify related parties per IAS 24, and the implications for any transactions which they may enter into.		
Small entities	17	17	Q33(a)	Ensure that you know the key differences between full IFRS Standards and the IFRS for SMEs Standard.		
Changes in accounting regulation	16, 23	16, 23	Q2(b) Q9(b) Q28(b) Q33(b)	You must be able to discuss the implications of adopting new accounting regulation. You should also ensure you are up-to-date with current issues in the profession.		

Topic	Study Text Chapter	Pocket Note Chapter	Questions to attempt	Tutor guidance	Date attempted	Self-assessment
Group financial statements						
Basic groups, including associates and joint arrangements	18	18	Q2 Q9	Ensure that you understand the standard workings required for subsidiaries in group financial statements, as well as key definitions – such as 'control', 'joint control' and 'significant influence'.		
Changes in group structure	19	19	Q5 Q6	Ensure that you know how to account for share transactions where control is either gained, lost or retained.		
Foreign currency subsidiaries	20	20	Q3 Q10	Ensure that you can consolidate a foreign subsidiary and can calculate the exchange differences that arise on its net assets, profit and goodwill.		
Statements of cash flows	21	21	Q1 Q4	Ensure that you know the format of a statement of cash flows and can deal with changes in group structure within the statement.		
Interpretation for stakeholders	22	22	Q26 Q37(b) Q38(b) Q40(b)	Ensure that you are happy with the interpretation of financial and non-financial information, including additional performance measures. You must also be able to discuss the framework for integrated reporting.		

Note that not all of the questions are referred to in the programme above. The remaining questions are available in the Kit for extra practice for those who require more questions on some areas

Section 1

PRACTICE QUESTIONS

SECTION A QUESTIONS – GROUP FINANCIAL STATEMENTS

1 **MOYES (DEC 2018)** *Walk in the footsteps of a top tutor*

Background

The following are extracts from the consolidated financial statements of the Moyes group.

Group statement of profit or loss for the year ended 30 September 20X8:

	$m
Revenue	612
Cost of sales	(347)
Gross profit	265
Operating expenses	(123)
Share of profit of associate	67
Profit before tax	209

Extracts from the group statement of financial position:

	30 September 20X8	30 September 20X7
	$m	$m
Inventories	126	165
Trade receivables	156	149
Trade payables	215	197

The following information is also relevant to the year ended 30 September 20X8:

Pension scheme

Moyes operates a defined benefit scheme. A service cost component of $24 million has been included within operating expenses. The remeasurement component for the year was a gain of $3 million. Benefits paid out of the scheme were $31 million. Contributions into the scheme by Moyes were $15 million.

Goodwill

Goodwill was reviewed for impairments at the reporting date. Impairments arose of $10 million in the current year.

Property, plant and equipment

Property, plant and equipment (PPE) at 30 September 20X8 included cash additions of $134 million. Depreciation charged during the year was $99 million and an impairment loss of $43 million was recognised. Prior to the impairment, the group had a balance on the revaluation surplus of $50 million of which $20 million related to PPE impaired in the current year.

Inventory

Goods were purchased for Dinar 80 million cash when the exchange rate was $1:Dinar 5. Moyes had not managed to sell the goods at 30 September 20X8 and the net realisable value was estimated to be Dinar 60 million at 30 September 20X8. The exchange rate at this date was $1:Dinar 6. The inventory has been correctly valued at 30 September 20X8 with any expense correctly included within cost of sales.

Changes to group structure

During the year ended 30 September 20X8, Moyes acquired a 60% subsidiary, Davenport, and also sold all of its equity interests in Barham for cash. The consideration for Davenport consisted of a share for share exchange together with some cash payable in two years. 80% of the equity shares of Barham had been acquired several years ago but Moyes had decided to sell as the performance of Barham had been poor for a number of years. Consequently, Barham had a substantial overdraft at the disposal date. Barham was unable to pay any dividends during the financial year but Davenport did pay an interim dividend on 30 September 20X8.

Discontinued operations

The directors of Moyes wish advice as to whether the disposal of Barham should be treated as a discontinued operation and separately disclosed within the consolidated statement of profit or loss. There are several other subsidiaries which all produce similar products to Barham and operate in a similar geographical area. Additionally, Moyes holds a 52% equity interest in Watson. Watson has previously issued share options to other entities which are exercisable in the year ending 30 September 20X9. It is highly likely that these options would be exercised which would reduce Moyes' interest to 35%. The directors of Moyes require advice as to whether this loss of control would require Watson to be classified as held for sale and reclassified as discontinued.

Required:

(a)   Draft an explanatory note to the directors of Moyes which should include:

    (i)   a calculation of cash generated from operations using the indirect method; and

    (ii)   an explanation of the specific adjustments required to the group profit before tax to calculate the cash generated from operations.

    Note: Any workings can either be shown in the main body of the explanatory note or in an appendix to the explanatory note.   **(12 marks)**

(b)   Explain how the changes to the group structure and dividend would impact upon the consolidated statement of cash flows at 30 September 20X8 for the Moyes group. You should not attempt to alter your answer to part (a).   **(6 marks)**

(c)   Advise the directors as to whether Watson should be classified as held for sale and whether both it and Barham should be classified as discontinued operations.

(6 marks)

(d)   The recognition criteria in the 2010 *Conceptual Framework* stated that a flow of economic benefits must be probable before an element can be recognised in the financial statements. However, IFRS and IAS Standards were criticised for applying this probability criterion inconsistently. The 2018 *Conceptual Framework* addressed these concerns.

Required:

Explain how the probability criterion has been inconsistently applied across accounting standards. Illustrate your answer with reference to the measurement of assets held for sale, provisions, and contingent consideration transferred in a business combination. Your answer should discuss the Board's revised recognition criteria in the 2018 *Conceptual Framework*.

(6 marks)

(Total: 30 marks)

2   BANANA (SEP 2018) *Walk in the footsteps of a top tutor*

Background

Banana is the parent of a listed group of companies which have a year end of 30 June 20X7. Banana has made a number of acquisitions and disposals of investments during the current financial year and the directors require advice as to the correct accounting treatment of these acquisitions and disposals.

The acquisition of Grape

On 1 January 20X7, Banana acquired an 80% equity interest in Grape. The following is a summary of Grape's equity at the acquisition date.

	$m
Equity share capital ($1 each)	20
Retained earnings	42
Other components of equity	8
	—
Total	70
	—

The purchase consideration comprised 10 million of Banana's shares which had a nominal value of $1 each and a market price of $6.80 each. Additionally, cash of $18 million was due to be paid on 1 January 20X9 if the net profit after tax of Grape grew by 5% in each of the two years following acquisition. The present value of the total contingent consideration at 1 January 20X7 was $16 million. It was felt that there was a 25% chance of the profit target being met. At acquisition, the only adjustment required to the identifiable net assets of Grape was for land which had a fair value $5 million higher than its carrying amount. This is not included within the $70 million equity of Grape at 1 January 20X7.

Goodwill for the consolidated financial statements has been incorrectly calculated as follows:

	$m
Share consideration	68
Add NCI at acquisition (20% × $70 million)	14
Less net assets at acquisition	(70)
	———
Goodwill at acquisition	12
	———

The financial director did not take into account the contingent cash since it was not probable that it would be paid. Additionally, he measured the non-controlling interest using the proportional method of net assets despite the group having a published policy to measure non-controlling interest at fair value. The share price of Grape at acquisition was $4.25 and should be used to value the non-controlling interest.

The acquisition and subsequent disposal of Strawberry

Banana had purchased a 40% equity interest in Strawberry for $18 million a number of years ago when the fair value of the identifiable net assets was $44 million. Since acquisition, Banana had the right to appoint one of the five directors on the board of Strawberry. The investment has always been equity accounted for in the consolidated financial statements of Banana. Banana disposed of 75% of its 40% investment on 1 October 20X6 for $19 million when the fair values of the identifiable net assets of Strawberry were $50 million. At that date, Banana lost its right to appoint one director to the board. The fair value of the remaining 10% equity interest was $4.5 million at disposal but only $4 million at 30 June 20X7. Banana has recorded a loss in reserves of $14 million calculated as the difference between the price paid of $18 million and the fair value of $4 million at the reporting date. Banana has stated that they have no intention to sell their remaining shares in Strawberry and wish to classify the remaining 10% interest as fair value through other comprehensive income in accordance with IFRS 9 *Financial Instruments*.

The acquisition of Melon

On 30 June 20X7, Banana acquired all of the shares of Melon, an entity which operates in the biotechnology industry. Melon was only recently formed and its only asset consists of a licence to carry out research activities. Melon has no employees as research activities were outsourced to other companies. The activities are still at a very early stage and it is not clear that any definitive product would result from the activities. A management company provides personnel for Melon to supply supervisory activities and administrative functions. Banana believes that Melon does not constitute a business in accordance with IFRS 3 *Business Combinations* since it does not have employees nor carries out any of its own processes. Banana intends to employ its own staff to operate Melon rather than to continue to use the services of the management company. The directors of Banana therefore believe that Melon should be treated as an asset acquisition but are uncertain as to whether the International Accounting Standards Board's exposure draft *Definition of a Business and Accounting for Previously Held Interests ED 2016/1* would revise this conclusion.

The acquisition of bonds

On 1 July 20X5, Banana acquired $10 million 5% bonds at par with interest being due at 30 June each year. The bonds are repayable at a substantial premium so that the effective rate of interest was 7%. Banana intended to hold the bonds to collect the contractual cash flows arising from the bonds and measured them at amortised cost.

On 1 July 20X6, Banana sold the bonds to a third party for $8 million. The fair value of the bonds was $10.5 million at that date. Banana has the right to repurchase the bonds on 1 July 20X8 for $8.8 million and it is likely that this option will be exercised. The third party is obliged to return the coupon interest to Banana and to pay additional cash to Banana should bond values rise. Banana will also compensate the third party for any devaluation of the bonds.

Required:

(a) **Draft an explanatory note to the directors of Banana, discussing the following:**

    (i) **how goodwill should have been calculated on the acquisition of Grape and show the accounting entry which is required to amend the financial director's error** **(8 marks)**

    (ii) **why equity accounting was the appropriate treatment for Strawberry in the consolidated financial statements up to the date of its disposal showing the carrying amount of the investment in Strawberry just prior to disposal** **(4 marks)**

    (iii) **how the gain or loss on disposal of Strawberry should have been recorded in the consolidated financial statements and how the investment in Strawberry should be accounted for after the part disposal.** **(4 marks)**

Note: Any workings can either be shown in the main body of the explanatory note or in an appendix to the explanatory note.

(b) **Discuss whether the directors are correct to treat Melon as an asset acquisition and whether the International Accounting Standards Board's proposed amendments to the definition of a business would revise your conclusions.** **(7 marks)**

(c) **Discuss how the derecognition requirements of IFRS 9** *Financial Instruments* **should be applied to the sale of the bond including calculations to show the impact on the consolidated financial statements for the year ended 30 June 20X7.** **(7 marks)**

(Total: 30 marks)

3   BUBBLE *Walk in the footsteps of a top tutor*

Background

The following extracts from draft financial statements relate to Bubble, a public limited company, and Tyslar, a company in which it has an investment.

Extracts from draft statements of financial position as at 31 October 20X5

	Bubble $m	Tyslar Dinars m
Assets		
Non-current assets		
Property, plant and equipment	280	390
Investment in Tyslar	46	–
Financial assets	122	98
Total non-current assets	448	488
Equity		
Equity shares ($1 each)	80	210
Retained earnings	230	292
Other components of equity	40	–
Total equity	350	502

The following information is relevant to the preparation of the consolidated statement of financial position as at 31 October 20X5.

Tyslar

Bubble owns 60% of the equity shares of Tyslar, a company located overseas which has presented its financial statements in dinars. The shares in Tyslar were acquired on 1 November 20X4.

At the date of acquisition, retained earnings were 258 million dinars and Tyslar had no other components of equity. On this date, non-depreciable land was carried in the financial statements of Tyslar at 50 million dinars but it had a fair value of 70 million dinars.

The non-controlling interest at acquisition is to be calculated at fair value by reference to the quoted share price of Tyslar. At the acquisition date, the quoted share price was 2.62 dinars per share.

An impairment review of goodwill was undertaken as at 31 October 20X5. The goodwill of Tyslar is to be impaired by 20%. Tyslar has not issued any equity shares since acquisition.

The following exchange rates have been provided:

	Dinars to $
1 November 20X4	8
1 May 20X5	9
31 October 20X5	9.5
Average for the year to 31 October 20X5	8.5

Overseas property

Bubble wished to expand its overseas operations and on 1 May 20X5 acquired an overseas property with a fair value of 58.5 million dinars. In exchange for the building, Bubble paid the supplier with land which Bubble had held but for which it had yet to determine its use. The carrying amount of the land was $5 million but it had an open market value of $7 million. Bubble was unsure as to how to deal with this transaction and so has transferred $5 million from investment properties to property, plant and equipment. The transaction has commercial substance.

In addition, Bubble spent $0.5 million to help relocate staff to the new property and added this amount to the cost of the building. Bubble has made no other entries in its financial statements in relation to the property. Bubble has a policy of depreciating properties over 35 years and follows the revaluation model under IAS 16 *Property, Plant & Equipment*. As a result of a surge in the market, it is estimated that the fair value of the property is 75 million dinars as at 31 October 20X5.

Required:

(a) (i) **Calculate, with supporting explanations, the value of goodwill arising on the acquisition of Tyslar that should be reported in the consolidated statement of financial position as at 31 October 20X5.** **(7 marks)**

(ii) **Explain why foreign exchange differences arise on the retranslation of Tyslar and how they are accounted for in the consolidated financial statements. As part of your answer you should calculate the balance on the group translation reserve as at 31 October 20X5.** **(10 marks)**

(iii) **Advise the directors of Bubble on how to correct the accounting treatment of the overseas property, showing the adjustments needed, and calculate the 'property, plant and equipment' balance as it would appear in the consolidated statement of financial position as at 31 October 20X5. (7 marks)**

(b) **Functional currency**

Tyslar operates a mine. Its income is denominated and settled in dinars. The output of the mine is routinely traded in dinars and its price is determined initially by local supply and demand. Tyslar pays 40% of its costs and expenses in dollars with the remainder being incurred locally and settled in dinars. Tyslar's management has a considerable degree of authority and autonomy in carrying out the operations of Tyslar and is not dependent upon group companies for finance.

Required:

Discuss and apply the principles set out in IAS 21 *The Effects of Changes in Foreign Exchange Rates* in order to determine the functional currency of Tyslar. **(6 marks)**

(Total: 30 marks)

4   JOCATT   *Walk in the footsteps of a top tutor*

Background

The following draft group financial statements relate to Jocatt, a public limited company, with a reporting date of 30 November 20X2.

Jocatt Group: Extracts from statement of financial position as at 30 November

	20X2 $m	20X1 $m
Non-current assets		
Property, plant and equipment	502	412
Investment property	8	6
Goodwill	40	68
Financial assets	4	–
Current assets		
Inventories	105	128
Trade receivables	62	113
Non-current liabilities:		
Long-term borrowings	67	71
Deferred tax	32	41
Defined benefit pension deficit	25	22
Current liabilities:		
Trade payables	144	55
Current tax payable	33	30

Jocatt Group: Extract from statement of profit or loss and other comprehensive income for the year ended 30 November 20X2

	$m
Profit from operations	52
Finance costs	(8)
	____
Profit before tax	44
Income tax expense	(11)
	____
Profit for the year	34
	____
Other comprehensive income after tax – items that will not be reclassified to profit or loss in future accounting periods:	
Changes in revaluation surplus (PPE)	(4)
Net remeasurement gain on defined benefit plan	8
Tax on the above	(1)
	____
Other comprehensive income for the year	3
	____

Jocatt Group: Statement of changes in equity for the year ended 30 November 20X2

	Share capital	Retained earnings	Revaluation surplus (PPE)	Total	Non-controlling interest	Total equity
	$m	$m	$m	$m	$m	$m
Balance at 1 Dec 20X1	275	328	16	619	36	655
Share capital issued	15			15		15
Dividends		(5)		(5)	(11)	(16)
Acquisitions					20	20
Total comp inc for year		32	(5)	27	10	37
Balance at 30 Nov 20X2	290	355	11	656	55	711

Additional information

The following information relates to the financial statements of Jocatt:

1   On 1 December 20X1, Jocatt acquired 8% of the ordinary shares of Tigret for $4 million and recorded it as a financial asset at the cost of purchase. This investment was designated to be measured at fair value through other comprehensive income.

On 30 June 20X2, Jocatt acquired a further 52% of the ordinary shares of Tigret and gained control of the company. The purchase consideration transferred on 30 June 20X2 comprised cash of $15 million and shares of $15 million. The fair value of the non-controlling interest in Tigret on 30 June 20X2 was correctly determined to be $20 million. The fair value of Tigret's identifiable net assets at the acquisition date, excluding deferred tax, was $45 million and included:

	$m
Trade receivables	5
Trade payables	6

Jocatt has calculated and accounted for goodwill arising on the acquisition of Tigret of $5 million ($30m + $20m − $45 million). However, the following has not been taken into account:

- At 30 June 20X2, the fair value of the 8% holding in Tigret had risen to $5 million. In the consolidated statement of financial position as at 30 November 20X2, this investment is still classified as a financial asset and is measured at $4 million.

- The tax base of the identifiable net assets of Tigret was $35 million at 30 June 20X2. The tax rate of Tigret is 30%.

2   Goodwill relating to all subsidiaries had been impairment tested in the year to 30 November 20X2 and any impairment correctly calculated and accounted for.

3   Jocatt operates a defined benefit scheme. The service cost component for the year ended 30 November 20X2 is $16 million. The net interest component of $2 million is included within finance costs.

4   Jocatt uses the fair value model for measuring investment property. No investment properties have been purchased or sold in the current period.

5   Jocatt sold property, plant and equipment with a carrying amount of $10 million for cash of $19 million. Depreciation for the period was $27 million.

Required:

(a) (i) Discuss, with calculations, how goodwill arising on the acquisition of Tigret should have been calculated. Show the adjustments which need to be made to the consolidated financial statements. **(7 marks)**

(ii) In accordance with IAS 7 *Statement of Cash Flows*, prepare:

- Cash flows from operating activities (using the indirect method)

- Cash flows from financing activities.

Note: Ignore deferred taxation other than where it is mentioned in the question. **(17 marks)**

(b) Direct and indirect methods

The directors of Jocatt have commented that the indirect method of reporting cash flows from operating activities is more useful and informative to users of financial statements than the direct method.

Required:

Discuss the extent to which the directors' comment is valid. **(6 marks)**

(Total: 30 marks)

5 ZIPPY *Walk in the footsteps of a top tutor*

Background

Zippy is a manufacturing company with a reporting date of 30 June 20X6. It has a wide portfolio of investment properties, as well as investments in many other entities. The draft statement of profit or loss and other comprehensive income for one of those entities, Ginny, is provided below

Draft statement of profit or loss and other comprehensive income for the year ended 30 June 20X6

	$m
Revenue	132
Cost of sales	(76)
Gross profit	56
Investment income	19
Administrative costs	(12)
Other expenses	(18)
Operating profit	45
Net finance costs	(6)
Profit before tax	39
Income tax expense	(7)
Profit for the year	32

	$m
Other comprehensive income	
Items that will not be reclassified to profit or loss	
Gains on property revaluation	16
Total comprehensive income for year	48

The following information is relevant to the preparation of the group statement of profit or loss and other comprehensive income:

Ginny

On 1 July 20X4, Zippy acquired 60% of the equity interests of Ginny, a public limited company. The purchase consideration comprised cash of $90 million and the fair value of the identifiable net assets acquired was $114 million at that date. Zippy uses the 'full goodwill' method for all acquisitions and the fair value of the non-controlling interest in Ginny was $50 million on 1 July 20X4. Goodwill had been reviewed annually for impairment and no impairment was deemed necessary.

Zippy disposed of a 20% equity interest in Ginny on 31 March 20X6 for cash consideration of $44 million. On the disposal date the remaining 40% holding had a fair value of $62 million and Zippy was left with significant influence over Ginny. Zippy accounts for investments in subsidiaries at cost and has included a gain in investment income of $14 million within its individual financial statements to reflect the disposal. The net assets of Ginny had a fair value of $118 million at 1 July 20X5 and this was reflected in the carrying amounts of the net assets. All gains and losses of Ginny have accrued evenly throughout the year. The disposal is not classified as a separate major line of business or geographical operation.

Office blocks

Zippy holds properties for investment purposes. At 1 July 20X5, Zippy held a 10-floor office block at a fair value of $90 million with a remaining useful life of 15 years. The first floor was occupied by Zippy's staff and the second floor was let to Boo, a subsidiary of Zippy, free of charge. The other eight floors were all let to unconnected third parties at a normal commercial rent. When Boo vacates the property next year, it will be let out to third parties. It was estimated that the fair value of the office block was $96 million at 30 June 20X6. Zippy has a policy of restating all land and buildings to fair value at each reporting date. The only accounting entries for the year ended 30 June 20X6 in relation to this office block have been to correctly include the rental income in profit or loss. It can be assumed that each floor is of equal size and value. Depreciation is charged to administrative costs.

During April 20X6, an explosion at a different office block caused substantial damage and it was estimated that the fair value fell from $20 million at 30 June 20X5 to $14 million at 30 June 20X6. Zippy has estimated that costs of $3 million would be required to repair the block but is unsure whether to carry out the repairs or whether to sell the block for a reduced price. The property has been left in the financial statements at a value of $20 million. A provision of $3 million for the repair costs was charged to other expenses.

Required:

(a) (i) Explain, with suitable calculations, how the investment in Ginny should be accounted for in the consolidated statement of profit or loss and other comprehensive income of the Zippy group for the year ended 30 June 20X6.

(11 marks)

(ii) Explain, with suitable calculations, how the two office blocks should be accounted for in the consolidated financial statements of the Zippy group for the year ended 30 June 20X6. (8 marks)

(iii) Explain why the accounting treatment of the 10 floor office block in Zippy's individual (non-consolidated) financial statements will differ from the treatment in the consolidated financial statements of the Zippy group. Calculations are not required. (4 marks)

(b) **Other comprehensive income**

The directors of Zippy are unsure as to the differences between other comprehensive income and profit or loss and the rationale as to why some gains can be and others cannot be reclassified to profit or loss. Zippy has a defined benefit pension scheme and the directors have heard that local GAAP in some countries allows actuarial gains and losses (the remeasurement component) to be deferred using an applicable systematic method rather than being recognised immediately.

Required:

Discuss the differences between other comprehensive income and profit or loss and the rationale as to why some gains and losses can be and others cannot be reclassified to profit or loss. Include in your answer a brief discussion of the benefits of immediate recognition of the remeasurement component under IAS 19 *Employee Benefits*. (7 marks)

(Total: 30 marks)

6 ASHANTI *Online question assistance*

Background

The following financial statement extracts relate to Ashanti, a public limited company, and its investments.

Extracts from the statements of profit or loss for the year ended 30 April 20X9.

	Ashanti $m	Bochem $m	Ceram $m
Revenue	810	235	142
Cost of sales	(686)	(137)	(84)
Gross profit	124	98	58

The following information is relevant to the preparation of the group statement of profit or loss.

Sale of shares in Bochem

On 1 May 20X7, Ashanti acquired 70% of the equity interests of Bochem, a public limited company. The fair value of the identifiable net assets at that date was $160 million. The share capital and retained earnings of Bochem were $55 million and $85 million respectively and other components of equity were $10 million at the date of acquisition. The excess of the fair value of the identifiable net assets at acquisition is due to an increase in the value of plant, which is depreciated on the straight-line method and has a five year remaining life at the date of acquisition. Depreciation is charged to cost of sales.

Ashanti disposed of a 10% equity interest to the non-controlling interests (NCI) of Bochem on 30 April 20X9 for a cash consideration of $34 million. The carrying amount of the net assets of Bochem at 30 April 20X9 was $210 million before any adjustments on consolidation. Goodwill arising on the acquisition of Bochem was $44 million but had reduced in value by 20% before the sale of the equity interest to the NCI.

Sale of shares in Ceram

Ashanti acquired 80% of the equity interests of Ceram, a public limited company, on 1 May 20X7. The purchase consideration was cash of $95.2 million. Ceram's identifiable net assets were fair valued at $115 million and the NCI of Ceram attributable to Ashanti had a fair value of $26 million at that date. On 1 November 20X8, Bochem disposed of 50% of the equity of Ceram for a consideration of $90 million. Ceram's identifiable net assets were $160 million and the fair value of the NCI of Ceram attributable to Bochem was $35 million at the date of disposal. The remaining equity interest of Ceram held by Bochem was fair valued at $45 million. After the disposal, Bochem can still exert significant influence. Goodwill had been impairment tested and no impairment had occurred. Ceram's total profit for the year ended 30 April 20X9 was $14 million and can be assumed to have accrued evenly.

Additional transactions

Ashanti sold inventory to both Bochem and Ceram in October 20X8. The sale price of the inventory was $10 million and $5 million respectively. Ashanti sells goods at a gross profit margin of 20% to group companies. At the year-end, half of the inventory sold to Bochem remained unsold but the entire inventory sold to Ceram had been sold to third parties.

At the year end, Ashanti sold goods on credit to Spice, an unrelated company, and recognised revenue of $5 million. Before the date of the sale, the customer had made an announcement that it would be restructuring its debts. At the date of the sale, it was deemed improbable that Ashanti would recover the amounts outstanding.

Required:

(a) (i) **Explain, with suitable calculations, how Ashanti should deal with the sale of the equity interests in Bochem in the consolidated financial statements.**

(6 marks)

(ii) **Explain, with suitable calculations, how Ashanti should deal with the sale of the equity interests in Ceram and its remaining investment in Ceram in the consolidated statement of profit or loss.**

(8 marks)

(iii)   Taking into account all of the information presented, calculate the 'revenue' and 'cost of sales' figures that would appear in the consolidated statement of profit or loss. Your answer should include an explanation of the correct treatment of Ashanti's sale to Spice.   **(9 marks)**

(b)   **Night**

The directors of Ashanti are considering acquiring 49.9% of the equity shares of Night. The next biggest shareholders will be Night's two original founders, who will hold 21% and 8% of the equity shares respectively. The original founders are not related. The remaining 21.1% of the shares will be held by 11 shareholders, who are acquaintances of the original founders but whom have a remote relationship to one another. There has not been complete owner representation at the last three annual general meetings of Night. Ashanti will have the ability to appoint four of the six members of Night's Board of Directors ('the Board'). The Board of Night have overall responsibility for decisions that affect the entity's operations.

Required:

Discuss whether the proposed share purchase will lead to Ashanti obtaining control over Night.   **(7 marks)**

(Total: 30 marks)

 Online question assistance

7   **TRAILER** *Walk in the footsteps of a top tutor*

Background and financial statement extracts

Trailer, a public limited company, operates in the manufacturing sector. Trailer purchased an investment in part during the reporting period. Extracts from the draft statements of financial position at 31 May 20X3 are as follows:

	Trailer	Park
	$m	$m
Equity:		
Share capital	1,750	1,210
Retained earnings	1,240	930
Other components of equity	125	80
Total equity	3,115	2,220

The following information is relevant to the preparation of the group financial statements:

Loan to charity

Trailer has made a loan of $50 million to a charitable organisation for the building of new sporting facilities. The loan was made on 1 June 20X2 and is repayable on maturity in three years' time. The interest rate on the loan is 3%, but Trailer assesses that an unsubsidised rate for such a loan would have been 6%. The first interest payment was made on 31 May 20X3. Trailer initially recorded a financial asset at $50 million and reduced this by the interest received during the period. The loss allowance has been correctly dealt with.

Restructuring plans

Trailer has announced two major restructuring plans. The first plan is to reduce its capacity by the closure of some of its smaller factories, which have already been identified. This will lead to the redundancy of 500 employees, who have all individually been selected and communicated with. The costs of this plan are $14 million in redundancy costs and $4 million in retraining costs. The second plan is to re-organise the finance and information technology department over a one-year period but it does not commence for two years. The plan results in 20% of finance staff losing their jobs during the restructuring. The costs of this plan are $10 million in redundancy costs and $6 million in retraining costs. No entries have been made in the financial statements for the above plans.

Acquisition of Park

On 1 June 20X2, Trailer acquired 60% of the equity interests of Park, a public limited company. The purchase consideration comprised cash of $1,250 million.

On 1 June 20X2, the fair value of the identifiable net assets acquired was $1,950 million and retained earnings of Park were $650 million and other components of equity were $55 million. The excess in fair value is due to plant and machinery with a remaining useful life of 7 years as at the acquisition date. It is the group's policy to measure the non-controlling interest (NCI) at acquisition at its proportionate share of the fair value of the subsidiary's net assets.

The goodwill of Park was impairment tested at 31 May 20X3. The recoverable amount of the net assets of Park was $2,083 million. There was no impairment of the net assets of Park before this date.

Required:

(a) (i) **Discuss, with suitable workings, how the loan to the charitable organisation should be dealt with in the consolidated financial statements for the year ended 31 May 20X3.** **(6 marks)**

(ii) **Discuss how the restructuring plans should be dealt with in the consolidated financial statements for the year ended 31 May 20X3.** **(5 marks)**

(iii) **Prepare the equity section of the consolidated statement of financial position as at 31 May 20X3.** **(12 marks)**

(b) **NCI at fair value**

It is the Trailer group's policy to measure the NCI at acquisition at its proportionate share of the fair value of the subsidiary's net assets. The directors of Trailer have used this policy for several years and do not know the implications, if any, of accounting for the NCI at fair value. The fair value of the NCI of Park at 1 June 20X2 was $800 million.

Required:

Explain to the directors, with suitable calculations, the impact on the financial statements if goodwill arising on the acquisition of Park had been calculated using the fair value of the NCI. **(7 marks)**

(Total: 30 marks)

8   WESTON *Walk in the footsteps of a top tutor*

Background

Weston has appointed a new financial controller. Weston calculates 'cash generated from operations' using the indirect method. The following information relates to the financial statements of the Weston Group:

Extracts from Weston Group: Statement of financial position as at 31 January

	20X6	20X5
	$m	$m
Non-current assets		
Property, plant and equipment	389	413
Goodwill	4	19
Investment in associate	102	–
Current assets		
Inventories	108	165
Trade and other receivables	106	104
Cash and cash equivalents	39	43
Non-current liabilities		
Retirement benefit liability	60	72
Net deferred tax liability	14	15
Current liabilities		
Trade and other payables	36	41
Current tax payable	47	92

Extracts from statement of profit or loss and other comprehensive income for the year ended 31 January 20X6

	$m
Continuing operations	
Profit from operations	167
Share of profit of associate	16
	———
Profit before tax	183
Income tax expense	(40)
	———
Profit for the year from continuing operations	143
Discontinued operations	
Loss for the year from discontinued operations (see note 2)	(25)
	———
Total profit for the year	118
	———

Other comprehensive income for the year (after tax) which will not be reclassified to profit or loss in future years

Remeasurement gains on defined benefit plan	3
	___
Total comprehensive income for the year	121
	___

Notes:

1   On 31 July 20X5, Weston disposed of its entire 80% equity holding in Northern for cash. The shares had been acquired on 31 July 20X1 for a consideration of $132 million when the fair value of the net assets was $124 million. This included a fair value uplift of $16 million in relation to plant with a remaining useful life of eight years. Deferred tax at 25% on the fair value adjustment was also correctly provided for in the group accounts and is included within the fair value of net assets. The fair value of the non-controlling interest at acquisition was $28 million. Goodwill, calculated under the full fair value method, was tested annually for impairment.

     At 31 January 20X5, goodwill relating to Northern had been impaired by 75%. A goodwill impairment charge has been included within administration expenses for the current year but does not relate to Northern.

     The carrying amounts in the individual accounts of Northern at disposal are listed below. The fair value adjustment and subsequent deferred tax were not incorporated into the individual accounts of Northern.

	$m
Property, plant and equipment	80
Inventories	38
Trade receivables	23
Trade and other payables	(10)
Deferred tax liability	(6)
Bank overdraft	(2)

2   The loss for the period from discontinued operations in the consolidated statement of profit or loss and other comprehensive income relates to Northern and can be analysed as follows:

	$m
Profit before tax	6
Income tax expense	(2)
Loss on disposal	(29)
	___
	(25)
	___

3   Weston purchased a 40% interest in an associate for cash on 1 February 20X5. The associate paid a dividend of $10 million in the year ended 31 January 20X6.

4   The retirement benefit liability relates to Weston as other companies in the group operate defined contribution schemes. The latest actuarial valuation is as follows:

	$m
Net obligation at 1 February 20X5	72
Service cost component	11
Contributions to scheme	(19)
Remeasurement gains	(4)
Net obligation at 31 January 20X6	60

The benefits paid in the period by the trustees of the scheme were $7 million. Weston operates in a country which only allows tax relief when contributions are paid into the scheme. The tax base was therefore zero at 31 January 20X5 and 31 January 20X6. The tax rate paid by Weston is 25%. The service cost component is included within administrative expenses.

5   There were no disposals of property, plant and equipment during the year except on the sale of Northern. Depreciation for the year was $20 million and is included within cost of sales.

Required:

(a)   (i)   In accordance with IAS 7 *Statement of Cash Flows*, prepare:

- **Cash flows from operating activities (using the indirect method)**

- **Cash flows from investing activities.   (18 marks)**

(ii)   Using your answer to part (a) (i), explain how to calculate cash generated from operations using the indirect method.   (5 marks)

(b)   Manair

Weston is considering purchasing equity shares in a regional airport called Manair. It would be one of three shareholders. The majority shareholder would hold 60.1% of voting shares, the second shareholder would hold 20% of voting shares and Weston would hold 19.9% of the voting shares. The board of directors consists of ten members. The majority shareholder will be represented by six of the board members, while Weston and the other shareholder will be represented by two members each. A shareholders' agreement will state that certain board and shareholder resolutions require either unanimous or majority decision. There is no indication that the majority shareholder and the other shareholders will act together in a common way. Weston will provide Manair with maintenance and technical services and will send a team of management experts to give business advice to the board of Manair.

Weston does not propose to account for its investment in Manair as an associate. Weston believes that the majority owner of Manair will use its influence as the parent to control and govern it.

Required:

Discuss if Weston's proposed accounting treatment for its investment in Manair is in accordance with International Financial Reporting Standards.   (7 marks)

(Total: 30 marks)

9 JOEY *Walk in the footsteps of a top tutor*

Joey, a public limited company, operates in the media sector. Joey has investments in a number of companies. The draft consolidated statement of financial position at 30 November 20X4 is as follows:

	$m
Assets:	
Non-current assets	
Property, plant and equipment	6,709
Goodwill	40
Investment in associate (Margy)	700
	7,449
Current assets	2,011
Total assets	9,460
Equity and liabilities:	
Equity attributable to owners of parent	
Share capital	850
Retained earnings	4,086
Other components of equity	258
	5,194
Non-controlling interest	908
Non-current liabilities	2,770
Current liabilities	588
Total liabilities	3,358
Total equity and liabilities	9,460

The following information is required to correct the draft consolidated financial statements:

Acquisition of Hulty

On 1 December 20X3, Joey acquired 80% of Hulty's 600 million $1 equity shares in exchange for cash of $750 million. The carrying amount of Hulty's net assets at the acquisition date was $960 million. Joey determined that the fair value of the 20% non-controlling interest in Hulty at that date was $250 million. It is group policy to measure the non-controlling interest at fair value. Joey recorded a goodwill asset arising on the acquisition of Hulty of $40 million ($750m + $250m – $960m).

However, shortly after the acquisition date, the accountant of Joey realised the following:

- Deferred cash consideration of $50 million arising on the acquisition of Hulty had not been recorded by Joey. This payment is due on 30 November 20X5. An appropriate discount rate is 10%.

- The fair value of Hulty's identifiable net assets had been calculated to be $980 million as at 1 December 20X3. The excess in the fair value of the net assets over their carrying amounts was due to an unrecognised franchise right with a remaining useful life of four years at 1 December 20X3. No entries have been recorded in respect of this franchise right.

Acquisition of Margy

On 1 December 20X1, Joey acquired 30% of the ordinary shares of Margy for a cash consideration of $600 million. Joey treated Margy as an associate and has equity accounted for Margy up to 1 December 20X3. Joey's investment in Margy as at 1 December 20X3 is still included in the draft consolidated statement of financial position. At 1 December 20X3, the fair value of the 30% equity interest in Margy held by Joey was $705 million.

On 1 December 20X3, Joey acquired a further 40% of the ordinary shares of Margy for a cash consideration of $975 million and gained control of the company. At 1 December 20X3, the fair value of Margy's identifiable net assets was $2,250 million. The fair value of the non-controlling interest was assessed as $620 million. A gain on bargain purchase of $655 million ($975m + $620m – $2,250m) has been recorded in profit or loss.

Additionally, buildings with a carrying amount of $200 million had been included in the fair valuation of Margy at 1 December 20X3. The buildings have a remaining useful life of 20 years at 1 December 20X3. However, Joey had commissioned an independent valuation of the buildings of Margy which was not complete at 1 December 20X3 and therefore not considered in the fair value of the identifiable net assets at the acquisition date. The valuations were received on 1 April 20X4 and resulted in a decrease of $40 million in the fair value of property, plant and equipment at the date of acquisition. This fair value decrease, which does not affect the fair value of the non-controlling interest at acquisition, has not been entered into the financial statements of Margy or the draft consolidated statements. Buildings are depreciated on the straight-line basis.

Agreement with CP

Joey is looking to expand into publishing and entered into an arrangement with Content Publishing (CP), a public limited company, on 1 December 20X3. CP will provide content for a range of books and online publications.

CP is entitled to a royalty calculated as 10% of sales and 30% of gross profit of the publications. Joey has sole responsibility for all printing, binding, and platform maintenance of the online website. The agreement states that key strategic sales and marketing decisions must be agreed jointly. Joey selects the content to be covered in the publications but CP has the right of veto over this content. However on 1 June 20X4, Joey and CP decided to set up a legal entity, JCP, with equal shares and voting rights. CP continues to contribute content into JCP but does not receive royalties. Joey continues the printing, binding and platform maintenance. The sales and cost of sales in the period were $5 million and $2 million respectively. The whole of the sale proceeds and the costs of sales were recorded in Joey's financial statements with no accounting entries being made for JCP or amounts due to CP. Joey currently funds the operations. Assume that the sales and costs accrue evenly throughout the year and that all of the transactions relating to JCP have been in cash.

Required:

(a) (i) Explain, with suitable workings, how to correct the errors that have arisen when accounting for the acquisition of Hulty. Show the adjusting entries required to correct the consolidated statement of financial position.

(8 marks)

(ii) Explain, with suitable workings, how to correct the errors that have arisen when accounting for the acquisition of Margy. Show the adjusting entries required to correct the consolidated statement of financial position.

(8 marks)

(iii) Discuss, with suitable workings, how the agreement with CP should have been accounted for in the consolidated financial statements. (6 marks)

(b) **Shares**

Joey's share capital is comprised of 'A' class shares. These shares have been correctly classified as equity. Joey is considering issuing the following instruments:

- 'B' class shares that are not mandatorily redeemable but contain a call option allowing Joey to repurchase them. Dividends would be payable on the B shares if, and only if, dividends are paid on the A ordinary shares.

- Share options which will give the counterparty rights to buy a fixed number of ordinary shares for a fixed amount of $10 million.

The directors of Joey require advice as to whether these financial instruments should be classified as debt or equity in accordance with IAS 32 *Financial Instruments: Presentation*. Moreover, they wish to know if the Board's proposals, as outlined in the recent Discussion Paper DP/2018/1 *Financial Instruments with Characteristics of Equity* would change the classification of these two instruments.

Required:

(i) In accordance with IAS 32 *Financial Instruments: Presentation*, discuss whether the 'B' class shares and the share options should be classified as financial liabilities or equity. (4 marks)

(ii) Discuss whether the Board's proposals in DP/2018/1 *Financial Instruments with Characteristics of Equity* would change the classification of the 'B' class shares and the share options. (4 marks)

(Total: 30 marks)

10   PARSLEY *Walk in the footsteps of a top tutor*

 Question debrief

Background and draft financial statements

Parsley, a public limited company, has investments in Sage and Saffron. All three companies prepare their financial statements in accordance with International Financial Reporting Standards. The presentation currency of the group is the dollar ($). Saffron's functional currency is the Franc (FR). The draft statements of profit or loss for the year ended 30 April 20X4 are presented below:

	Parsley	Sage	Saffron
	$m	$m	FRm
Revenue	143	68	210
Cost of sales	(61)	(42)	(126)
Gross profit	82	26	84
Distribution costs	(10)	(6)	(14)
Administrative expenses	(23)	(10)	(29)
Operating profit	49	10	41
Investment income	1	2	–
Finance costs	(2)	(4)	(3)
Profit before taxation	48	8	38
Taxation	(11)	(2)	(8)
Profit for the period	37	6	30

The following information is relevant to the preparation of the consolidated financial statements:

Sale of shares in Sage

Parsley acquired 70% of Sage's one million $1 ordinary shares for $6 million many years ago. At the acquisition date, the carrying value of Sage's net assets was $5 million, and this was deemed to be the same as their fair value. The non-controlling interest was measured using the proportion of net assets method. Goodwill arising on the acquisition of Sage has never been impaired. On 31 October 20X3, Parsley sold 300,000 of its shares in Sage for $6.5 million. The fair value of the interest retained was $9.5 million. The retained earnings of Sage were $9 million as at 30 April 20X3. The only entry posted in Parsley's individual financial statements is to record the cash received and to credit these proceeds to a suspense account.

Acquisition of Saffron

On 1 May 20X3, Parsley purchased 60% of Saffron's one million FR1 ordinary shares for FR71 million. The non-controlling interest at acquisition was valued at FR29 million using the fair value method. At 1 May 20X3, the carrying value of Saffron's net assets was FR60 million but the fair value was FR70 million. The excess in fair value was due to an unrecognised brand with a remaining useful economic life of five years at the acquisition date.

At 30 April 20X4, it was determined that goodwill arising on the acquisition of Saffron was impaired by FR4 million.

The following exchange rates are relevant:

	FR: $1
1 May 20X3	5.0
30 April 20X4	4.0
Average for year ended 30 April 20X4	4.6

Lease

On 1 May 20X2, Parsley signed a lease to use an item of machinery. The useful economic life of the machine and the lease term were both five years. Lease payments are due annually in advance. The lease payment for the first year was $1.2 million. Parsley's rate of borrowing is 10%. The present value of the lease payments, excluding the payment made on 1 May 20X2, was $3.8 million.

Lease payments increase annually by the rate of inflation over the previous 12 months. On 1 May 20X3, inflation for the prior 12 months was 8%.

The lease was correctly accounted for in accordance with IFRS 16 *Leases* in the year ended 30 April 20X3. The only entry made in the current year is to record the cash payment made to the lessor within cost of sales.

Required:

(a) (i)   Discuss, with calculations, how Parsley should account for Sage in the consolidated statement of profit or loss and other comprehensive income for the year ended 30 April 20X4. **(8 marks)**

(ii)   Discuss, with calculations, how Parsley should account for Saffron in the consolidated statement of profit or loss and other comprehensive income for the year ended 30 April 20X4. **(8 marks)**

(iii)   Explain how the lease agreement should be accounted for in the consolidated financial statements for the year ended 30 April 20X4. Show the adjusting entries required. **(8 marks)**

Related parties

Related party relationships are a particularly key concern when preparing financial statements for group entities. The objective of IAS 24 *Related Party Disclosures* is to ensure that financial statements contain the necessary disclosures to make users aware of the possibility that financial statements may have been affected by the existence of related parties.

Required:

(b)   Describe the main circumstances that give rise to related parties and explain why the disclosure of related party relationships and transactions is important.

(6 marks)

(Total: 30 marks)

 Calculate your allowed time and allocate the time to the separate parts

11   MARCHANT *Walk in the footsteps of a top tutor*

Tutorial note

This question requires the preparation of a consolidated statement of profit or loss and other comprehensive income. The examining team have said that the preparation of full consolidated financial statements is unlikely to appear in the Strategic Business Reporting exam. However this question still provides important revision of a range of consolidation issues.

The following draft financial statements relate to Marchant, a public limited company, and companies it has investments in.

Marchant Group: Draft statements of profit or loss and other comprehensive income for the year ended 30 April 20X4.

	Marchant $m	Nathan $m	Option $m
Revenue	400	115	70
Cost of sales	(312)	(65)	(36)
Gross profit	88	50	34
Other income	21	7	2
Administrative costs	(15)	(9)	(12)
Other expenses	(35)	(19)	(8)
Operating profit	59	29	16
Finance costs	(5)	(6)	(4)
Finance income	6	5	8
Profit before tax	60	28	20
Income tax expense	(19)	(9)	(5)
Profit for the year	41	19	15
Other comprehensive income – revaluation gains	10	2	–
Total comprehensive income for year	51	21	15

The following information is relevant to the preparation of the group statement of profit or loss and other comprehensive income:

1   On 1 May 20X2, Marchant acquired 60% of the equity interests of Nathan, a public limited company. The purchase consideration comprised cash of $80 million and the fair value of the identifiable net assets acquired was $110 million at that date. The fair value of the non-controlling interest (NCI) in Nathan was $45 million on 1 May 20X2. Marchant wishes to use the 'full goodwill' method for all acquisitions. The share capital and retained earnings of Nathan were $25 million and $65 million respectively and other components of equity were $6 million at the date of acquisition. The excess of the fair value of the identifiable net assets at acquisition is due to non-depreciable land.

Goodwill has been impairment tested annually and as at 30 April 20X3 had reduced in value by 20%. However at 30 April 20X4, the impairment of goodwill had reversed and goodwill was valued at $2 million above its original value. This upward change in value has already been included in above draft financial statements of Marchant prior to the preparation of the group accounts.

2   Marchant disposed of an 8% equity interest in Nathan on 30 April 20X4 for a cash consideration of $18 million and had accounted for the gain or loss in other income. The carrying amount of the net assets of Nathan at 30 April 20X4 was $120 million before any adjustments on consolidation. Marchant accounts for investments in subsidiaries using IFRS 9 *Financial Instruments* and has made an election to show gains and losses in other comprehensive income. The carrying amount of the investment in Nathan was $90 million at 30 April 20X3 and $95 million at 30 April 20X4 before the disposal of the equity interest.

3   Marchant acquired 60% of the equity interests of Option, a public limited company, on 30 April 20X2. The purchase consideration was cash of $70 million. Option's identifiable net assets were fair valued at $86 million and the NCI had a fair value of $28 million at that date. On 1 November 20X3, Marchant disposed of a 40% equity interest in Option for a consideration of $50 million. Option's identifiable net assets were $90 million and the value of the NCI was $34 million at the date of disposal. The remaining equity interest was fair valued at $40 million. After the disposal, Marchant exerts significant influence. Any increase in net assets since acquisition has been reported in profit or loss and the carrying amount of the investment in Option had not changed since acquisition. Goodwill had been impairment tested and no impairment was required. No entries had been made in the financial statements of Marchant for this transaction other than for cash received.

4   Marchant sold inventory to Nathan for its fair value of $12 million. Marchant made a loss on the transaction of $2 million. Nathan still holds $8 million of this inventory at the year end.

5   Ignore the taxation effects of the above adjustments. Any expense adjustments should be amended in other expenses.

Required:

(a)   (i)   Prepare a consolidated statement of profit or loss and other comprehensive income for the year ended 30 April 20X4 for the Marchant Group.

Note: Do not adjust your answer for the information presented in part (b)

(18 marks)

(ii)   Explain, with suitable calculations, how the sale of the 8% interest in Nathan should be dealt with in the group statement of financial position at 30 April 20X4.   **(5 marks)**

(b)   Marchant held a portfolio of trade receivables with a carrying amount of $4 million at 30 April 20X4. At that date, the entity entered into a factoring agreement with a bank, whereby it transferred the receivables in exchange for $3.6 million in cash. Marchant has agreed to reimburse the factor for any shortfall between the amount collected and $3.6 million. Once the receivables have been collected, any amounts above $3.6 million, less interest on this amount, will be repaid to Marchant. Marchant has derecognised the receivables and charged $0.4 million as a loss to profit or loss.

Required:

Outline the rules in IFRS 9 *Financial Instruments* **relating to the derecognition of a financial asset and discuss how these rules affect the treatment of the portfolio of trade receivables in Marchant's financial statements.   (7 marks)**

(Total: 30 marks)

12   ANGEL *Walk in the footsteps of a top tutor*

Tutorial note

This question requires the preparation of a consolidated statement of cash flows. The examining team have said that the preparation of full consolidated financial statements is unlikely to appear in the Strategic Business Reporting exam. However this question still provides important revision of a range of consolidation issues.

The following draft group financial statements relate to Angel, a public limited company:

Angel Group: Statement of financial position as at 30 November 20X3

	30 November 20X3 $m	30 November 20X2 $m
Assets		
Non-current assets		
Property, plant and equipment	475	465
Goodwill	105	120
Other intangible assets	150	240
Investment in associate	80	
Financial assets	215	180
	1,025	1,005
Current assets		
Inventories	155	190
Trade receivables	125	180
Cash and cash equivalents	465	355
	745	725
Total assets	1,770	1,730
Equity and liabilities		
Share capital	850	625
Retained earnings	456	359
Other components of equity	29	20
	1,335	1,004
Non-controlling interest	90	65
Total equity	1,425	1,069

	30 November 20X3 $m	30 November 20X2 $m
Non-current liabilities		
Long-term borrowings	26	57
Deferred tax	35	31
Retirement benefit liability	80	74
Total non-current liabilities	141	162
Current liabilities		
Trade payables	155	361
Current tax payable	49	138
Total current liabilities	204	499
Total liabilities	345	661
Total equity and liabilities	1,770	1,730

Angel Group: Statement of profit or loss and other comprehensive income for the year ended 30 November 20X3

	$m
Revenue	1,238
Cost of sales	(986)
Gross profit	252
Other income	30
Administrative expenses	(45)
Other expenses	(50)
Operating profit	187
Finance costs	(11)
Share of profit of associate	12
Profit before tax	188
Income tax expense	(46)
Profit for the year	142
Profit attributable to:	
Owners of parent	111
Non-controlling interest	31
	142

	$m
Other comprehensive income:	
Items that will not be reclassified to profit or loss	
Revaluation of property, plant and equipment	8
Actuarial losses on defined benefit plan	(4)
Tax relating to items not reclassified	(2)
	___
Total items that will not be reclassified to profit or loss	2
	___
Items that may be reclassified to profit or loss	
Financial assets	4
Tax relating to items that may be reclassified	(1)
	___
Total items that may be reclassified to profit or loss	3
	___
Other comprehensive income (net of tax) for the year	5
	___
Total comprehensive income for year	147
	___
Total comprehensive income attributable to:	
Owners of the parent	116
Non-controlling interest	31
	___
	147
	___

Angel Group: Extracts from statement of changes in equity for the year ended 30 November 20X3

	Share capital $m	Retained earnings $m	Other components of equity – financial assets reserve $m	Other components of equity – revaluation reserve $m	Non-controlling interest $m
Balance 1 December 20X2	625	359	15	5	65
Share capital issued	225				
Dividends for year		(10)			(6)
Total comprehensive income for the year		107	3	6	31
	___	___	___	___	___
Balance 30 November 20X3	850	456	18	11	90
	___	___	___	___	___

The following information relates to the financial statements of the Angel Group:

(i)   On 1 December 20X2, Angel acquired all of the share capital of Sweety for $30 million. The carrying amounts of the identifiable net assets in Sweety's individual financial statements and the fair values are set out below, together with their tax base. Goodwill arising on acquisition is not deductible for tax purposes. There were no other acquisitions in the period. The tax rate is 30%.

The fair values in the table below have been reflected in the year-end balances of the Angel Group.

	Carrying amounts $ million	Tax base $ million	Fair values $million (excluding deferred taxation)
Property, plant and equipment	12	10	14
Inventories	5	4	6
Trade receivables	3	3	3
Cash and cash equivalents	2	2	2
Total assets	22	19	25
Trade payables	(4)	(4)	(4)
Retirement benefit obligations	(1)		(1)
Deferred tax liability	(0.6)		
Net assets at acquisition	16.4	15	20

(ii)   The retirement benefit is classified as a non-current liability in the statement of financial position and comprises the following:

	$m
Net obligation at 1 December 20X2	74
Net interest cost	3
Current service cost	8
Contributions to scheme	(9)
Remeasurements – actuarial losses	4
Net obligation at 30 November 20X3	80

The benefits paid in the period by the trustees of the scheme were $6 million. Angel had included the obligation assumed on the purchase of Sweety in current service cost above, although the charge to administrative expenses was correct in the statement of profit and loss and other comprehensive income. There were no tax implications regarding the retirement benefit obligation. Defined benefit costs are included in administrative expenses.

(iii) Property, plant and equipment (PPE) with a carrying amount of $49 million was disposed of for cash proceeds of $63 million. The gain on disposal is included in administrative expenses. Depreciation charged to profit or loss in the year was $29 million.

(iv) Angel purchased a 30% interest in an associate for cash on 1 December 20X2. The net assets of the associate at the date of acquisition were $280 million. The associate made a profit after tax of $40 million and paid a dividend of $10 million out of these profits in the year ended 30 November 20X3. Angel does not hold investments in any other associate entities.

(v) An impairment test carried out at 30 November 20X3 showed that goodwill and other intangible assets were impaired. The impairment of goodwill relates to 100% owned subsidiaries.

(vi) The following schedule relates to the financial assets owned by Angel:

	$m
Balance 1 December 20X2	180
Less carrying amount of financial assets disposed	(26)
Add purchases of financial assets	57
Add gain on revaluation of financial assets	4
Balance at 30 November 20X3	215

The sale proceeds of the financial assets were $40 million. Profit on the sale of the financial assets is included in 'other income' in the financial statements.

(vii) The finance costs were all paid in cash in the period.

Required:

(a) **Prepare a consolidated statement of cash flows using the indirect method for the Angel Group plc for the year ended 30 November 20X3 in accordance with the requirements of IAS 7** *Statement of Cash Flows.*

   Note: The notes to the statement of cash flows are not required. **(25 marks)**

(b) The directors of Angel have deposited funds with a bank in two accounts as follows:

   (i) $3 million into a 12-month term account, earning 3.5% interest. The cash can be withdrawn by giving 14 days' notice but Angel will incur a penalty, being the loss of all interest earned.

   (ii) $7 million into a 12-month term account earning 3% interest. The cash can be withdrawn by giving 21 days' notice. Interest will be paid for the period of the deposit but if money is withdrawn, the interest will be at the rate of 2%, which is equivalent to the bank's stated rate for short-term deposits.

   Angel is confident that it will not need to withdraw the cash from the higher-rate deposit within the term, but wants to keep easy access to the remaining $7 million to cover any working capital shortfalls which might arise.

   Required:

   Advise Angel on whether each of the funds meets the definition of a 'cash equivalent'. **(5 marks)**

   (Total: 30 marks)

13   TRAVELER   *Walk in the footsteps of a top tutor*

Tutorial note

This question requires the preparation of a consolidated statement of financial position. The examining team have said that the preparation of full consolidated financial statements is unlikely to appear in the Strategic Business Reporting exam. However this question still provides important revision of a range of consolidation issues.

Traveler, a public limited company, operates in the manufacturing sector. The draft statements of financial position are as follows at 30 November 20X1:

	Traveler $m	Data $m	Captive $m
Assets:			
Non-current assets			
Property, plant and equipment	439	810	620
Investments in subsidiaries			
Data	820		
Captive	541		
Financial assets	108	10	20
	1,908	820	640
Current assets	1,067	781	350
Total assets	2,975	1,601	990
Equity and liabilities:			
Share capital	1,120	600	390
Retained earnings	1,066	442	169
Other components of equity	60	37	45
Total equity	2,246	1,079	604
Non-current liabilities	455	323	73
Current liabilities	274	199	313
Total equity and liabilities	2,975	1,601	990

The following information is relevant to the preparation of the group financial statements:

1   On 1 December 20X0, Traveler acquired 60% of the equity interests of Data, a public limited company. The purchase consideration comprised cash of $600 million. At acquisition, the fair value of the non-controlling interest in Data was $395 million. Traveler wishes to use the 'full goodwill' method. On 1 December 20X0, the fair value of the identifiable net assets acquired was $935 million and retained earnings of Data were $299 million and other components of equity were $26 million. The excess in fair value is due to non-depreciable land.

On 30 November 20X1, Traveler acquired a further 20% interest in Data for a cash consideration of $220 million.

2   On 1 December 20X0, Traveler acquired 80% of the equity interests of Captive for a consideration of $541 million. The consideration comprised cash of $477 million and the transfer of non-depreciable land with a fair value of $64 million. The carrying amount of the land at the acquisition date was $56 million. At the year end, this asset was still included in the non-current assets of Traveler and the sale proceeds had been credited to profit or loss.

At the date of acquisition, the identifiable net assets of Captive had a fair value of $526 million, retained earnings were $90 million and other components of equity were $24 million. The excess in fair value is due to non-depreciable land. This acquisition was accounted for using the partial goodwill method in accordance with IFRS 3 *Business Combinations*.

3   Goodwill was impairment tested after the additional acquisition in Data on 30 November 20X1. The recoverable amount of Data was $1,099 million and that of Captive was $700 million.

Required:

(a)   Prepare a consolidated statement of financial position for the Traveler Group for the year ended 30 November 20X1.   (23 marks)

Traveler has three distinct business segments. The management has calculated the net assets, turnover and profit before common costs, which are to be allocated to these segments. However, they are unsure as to how they should allocate certain common costs and whether they can exercise judgement in the allocation process. They wish to allocate head office management expenses; pension expense; the cost of managing properties and interest and related interest bearing assets. They also are uncertain as to whether the allocation of costs has to be in conformity with the accounting policies used in the financial statements.

Required:

**(b)   Advise the management of Traveler on the points raised in the above paragraph.
                                                                                (7 marks)**

(Total: 30 marks)

14 ROSE *Walk in the footsteps of a top tutor*

Tutorial note

This question requires the preparation of a consolidated statement of financial position where one of the subsidiaries presents its financial statements in a different currency to the group. The examining team have said that the preparation of full consolidated financial statements is unlikely to appear in the Strategic Business Reporting exam. However this question still provides important revision of a range of consolidation issues.

Rose, a public limited company, operates in the mining sector. The draft statements of financial position are as follows, at 30 April 20X1:

	Rose $m	Petal $m	Stem Dinars m
Assets			
Non-current assets			
Property, plant and equipment	385	117	430
Investments in subsidiaries			
Petal	113		
Stem	46		
	544	117	430
Current assets	118	100	330
Total assets	662	217	760
Equity and liabilities			
Share capital	158	38	200
Retained earnings	256	56	300
Other components of equity	7	4	–
Total equity	421	98	500
Non-current liabilities	56	42	160
Current liabilities	185	77	100
Total liabilities	241	119	260
Total equity and liabilities	662	217	760

The following information is relevant to the preparation of the group financial statements:

1   On 1 May 20X0, Rose acquired 70% of the equity interests of Petal, a public limited company. The purchase consideration comprised cash of $94 million. The fair value of the identifiable net assets recognised by Petal was $120 million excluding the patent below. The identifiable net assets of Petal at 1 May 20X0 included a patent which had a fair value of $4 million. This had not been recognised in the financial statements of Petal. The patent had a remaining term of four years to run at that date and is not renewable. The retained earnings of Petal were $49 million and other components of equity were $3 million at the date of acquisition. The remaining excess of the fair value of the net assets is due to an increase in the value of land.

Rose wishes to use the 'full goodwill' method. The fair value of the non-controlling interest in Petal was $46 million on 1 May 20X0. There have been no issues of ordinary shares since acquisition and goodwill on acquisition is not impaired.

Rose acquired a further 10% interest from the non-controlling interest in Petal on 30 April 20X1 for a cash consideration of $19 million.

2   Rose acquired 52% of the ordinary shares of Stem on 1 May 20X0 when Stem's retained earnings were 220 million dinars. The fair value of the identifiable net assets of Stem on 1 May 20X0 was 495 million dinars. The excess of the fair value over the net assets of Stem is due to an increase in the value of land. Rose wishes to use the 'full goodwill' method. The fair value of the non-controlling interest in Stem at 1 May 20X0 was 250 million dinars. There have been no issues of ordinary shares and no impairment of goodwill since acquisition.

The following exchange rates are relevant to the preparation of the group financial statements:

	Dinars to $
1 May 20X0	6
30 April 20X1	5
Average for year to 30 April 20X1	5.8

Required:

(a)   **Prepare a consolidated statement of financial position of the Rose Group at 30 April 20X1, in accordance with International Financial Reporting Standards, showing the exchange difference arising on the translation of Stem's net assets. Ignore deferred taxation.**   **(22 marks)**

(b)   The directors of Rose are not fully aware of the requirements of IAS 21 *The Effects of Changes in Foreign Exchange Rates* in relation to exchange rate differences. They would like advice on how exchange differences should be recorded on both monetary and non-monetary assets in the financial statements and how these differ from the requirements for the translation of an overseas entity. The directors also wish advice on what would happen to the exchange differences if Rose sold all of its equity shares in Stem.

Required:

Provide a brief memo for the directors of Rose which identifies the correct accounting treatment for the various issues raised.   **(8 marks)**

(Total: 30 marks)

SECTION A QUESTIONS – REPORTING AND ETHICAL IMPLICATIONS

15   FISKERTON (DEC 2018)   *Walk in the footsteps of a top tutor*

Background

The following is an extract from the statement of financial position of Fiskerton, a public limited entity as at 30 September 20X8.

	$000
Non-current assets	160,901
Current assets	110,318
Equity share capital ($1 each)	10,000
Other components of equity	20,151
Retained earnings	70,253
Non-current liabilities (bank loan)	50,000
Current liabilities	120,815

The bank loan has a covenant attached whereby it will become immediately repayable should the gearing ratio (long-term debt to equity) of Fiskerton exceed 50%. Fiskerton has a negative cash balance as at 30 September 20X8.

Halam property

Included within the non-current assets of Fiskerton is a property in Halam which has been leased to Edingley under a 40-year lease. The property was acquired for $20 million on 1 October 20X7 and was immediately leased to Edingley.

The asset was expected to have a useful life of 40 years at the date of acquisition and have a minimal residual value. Fiskerton has classified the building as an investment property and has adopted the fair value model.

The property was initially revalued to $22 million on 31 March 20X8. Interim financial statements had indicated that gearing was 51% prior to this revaluation. The managing director was made aware of this breach of covenant and so instructed that the property should be revalued. The property is now carried at a value of $28 million which was determined by the sale of a similar sized property on 30 September 20X8. This property was located in a much more prosperous area and built with a higher grade of material. An independent professional valuer has estimated the value to be no more than $22 million. The managing director has argued that fair values should be referenced to an active market and is refusing to adjust the financial statements, even though he knows it is contrary to international accounting standards.

Sales contract

Fiskerton has entered into a sales contract for the construction of an asset with a customer whereby the customer pays an initial deposit. The deposit is refundable only if Fiskerton fails to complete the construction of the asset. The remainder is payable on delivery of the asset. If the customer defaults on the contract prior to completion, Fiskerton has the right to retain the deposit. The managing director believes that, as completion of the asset is performed over time, revenue should be recognised accordingly. He has persuaded the accountant to include the deposit and a percentage of the remaining balance for construction work in revenue to date.

Required:

(a)   Discuss how the Halam property should have been accounted for and explain the implications for the financial statements and the debt covenant of Fiskerton.

(7 marks)

(b)   In accordance with IFRS 15 *Revenue from Contracts with Customers*, discuss whether revenue arising from the sales contract should be recognised on a stage of completion basis.

(4 marks)

(c)   Explain any ethical issues which may arise for the managing director and the accountant from each of the scenarios.

(7 marks)

Professional marks will be awarded in part (c) for the quality of the discussion.

(2 marks)

(Total: 20 marks)

16   FARHAM (SEP 2018) *Walk in the footsteps of a top tutor*

Background

Farham manufactures white goods such as washing machines, tumble dryers and dishwashers. The industry is highly competitive with a large number of products on the market. Brand loyalty is consequently an important feature in the industry. Farham operates a profit related bonus scheme for its managers based upon the consolidated financial statements but recent results have been poor and bonus targets have rarely been achieved. As a consequence, the company is looking to restructure and sell its 80% owned subsidiary Newall which has been making substantial losses. The current year end is 30 June 20X8.

Factory subsidence

Farham has a production facility which started to show signs of subsidence since January 20X8. It is probable that Farham will have to undertake a major repair sometime during 20X9 to correct the problem. Farham does have an insurance policy but it is unlikely to cover subsidence. The chief operating officer (COO) refuses to disclose the issue at 30 June 20X8 since no repair costs have yet been undertaken although she is aware that this is contrary to international accounting standards. The COO does not think that the subsidence is an indicator of impairment. She argues that no provision for the repair to the factory should be made because there is no legal or constructive obligation to repair the factory.

Farham has a revaluation policy for property, plant and equipment and there is a balance on the revaluation surplus of $10 million in the financial statements for the year ended 30 June 20X8. None of this balance relates to the production facility but the COO is of the opinion that this surplus can be used for any future loss arising from the subsidence of the production facility.

(5 marks)

Sale of Newall

At 30 June 20X8 Farham had a plan to sell its 80% subsidiary Newall. This plan has been approved by the board and reported in the media. It is expected that Oldcastle, an entity which currently owns the other 20% of Newall, will acquire the 80% equity interest. The sale is expected to be complete by December 20X8. Newall is expected to have substantial trading losses in the period up to the sale. The accountant of Farham wishes to show Newall as held for sale in the consolidated financial statements and to create a restructuring provision to include the expected costs of disposal and future trading losses. The COO does not wish Newall to be disclosed as held for sale nor to provide for the expected losses. The COO is concerned as to how this may affect the sales price and would almost certainly mean bonus targets would not be met. The COO has argued that they have a duty to secure a high sales price to maximise the return for shareholders of Farham. She has also implied that the accountant may lose his job if he were to put such a provision in the financial statements. The expected costs from the sale are as follows:

	$m
Future trading losses	30
Various legal costs of sale	2
Redundancy costs for Newall employees	5
Impairment losses on owned assets	8

Included within the future trading losses is an early termination penalty of $6 million for a leased asset which is deemed surplus to requirements. **(6 marks)**

Required:

(a) **Discuss the accounting treatment which Farham should adopt to address each of the issues above for the consolidated financial statements.**

Note: The mark allocation is shown against each of the two issues above.

(b) **Discuss the ethical issues arising from the scenario, including any actions which Farham and the accountant should undertake.** **(7 marks)**

Professional marks will be awarded in part (b) for the quality of the discussion.

(2 marks)

(Total: 20 marks)

17 JONJON *Walk in the footsteps of a top tutor*

Background

JonJon is a public limited company that prepares financial statements in accordance with International Financial Reporting Standards. JonJon has a number of bank loans, which are repayable if it breaches its covenants. The covenants are based on profit before tax and reported assets. A new accountant has recently started working at JonJon and has discovered some issues relating to the financial statements for the year ended 31 December 20X5.

Intangible asset

JonJon's statement of financial position includes an intangible asset. This asset is a portfolio of customers acquired from a similar business which had gone into liquidation two years ago. The accountant has asked the finance director why the asset has not been amortised in the current period. The finance director replied that he changed the assessment of the useful life of this intangible asset from 'finite' to 'indefinite'. He justified this on the grounds that it is impossible to foresee the length of this intangible asset's useful life due to a number of factors, such as technological evolution and changing consumer behaviour.

Fair value

IAS 40

JonJon owns investment properties that are measured using the fair value method. The accountant has discovered that the fair value is calculated as 'new-build value less obsolescence'. Valuations are conducted by the finance director. In order to determine the obsolescence, the director takes account of the age of the property and the nature of its use. Sales values for similar properties in similar locations are available and are significantly less than the fair value estimated by the director.

Impairment test

IAS 36

JonJon has three main cash generating units (CGUs) which have goodwill attributed to them. The finance director has asked the accountant to perform an impairment test of the CGUs, using the most recent financial forecasts as the basis for value in use calculations. The realised cash flows for the CGUs were negative in 20X5 and far below forecasted cash flows for that period. The directors have significantly raised cash flow forecasts for 20X6 with little justification. The projected cash flows have been calculated by adding back depreciation charges to the budgeted result for the period with expected changes in working capital and capital expenditure not taken into account. The finance director has told the accountant that future promotions and pay rises are dependent on following this instruction.

Required:

Discuss the accounting and ethical implications of the above situations from the perspective of the reporting accountant. **(18 marks)**

Professional marks will be awarded in this question for the application of ethical principles.

(2 marks)

(Total: 20 marks)

18 CLOUD *Walk in the footsteps of a top tutor*

> *Question debrief*

Background

Cloud, a public limited company, is preparing financial statements for the year ended 31 December 20X1. The profit figure reported in the interim financial statements was lower than shareholders expected, and net operating cash flows for the year are below budget. The directors of Cloud receive a bonus if Cloud's operating cash flow and profit before tax exceed a predetermined target for the year. The finance director is perceived to be a dominant personality, and members of the accounts department, many of whom are ACCA members, follow his instructions without question.

Presentation of loan in statement of cash flows

Cloud has entered into a long-term contract with a major customer and negotiated a new bank loan on the strength of this contract. The proceeds of the loan were received in the current period and are to be repaid over four years to 31 December 20X5. Cloud has reported the loan proceeds as an operating cash flow because it relates to a long-term trading contract.

Share sale

During the period Cloud sold 5% of the equity shares of Fog for $2 million. Prior to the sale, Cloud owned 100% of the shares of Fog. This transaction has improved Cloud's cash position while enabling it to retain control over Fog. At the date of the share sale, the goodwill and net assets of Fog were carried in the consolidated statement of financial position at $5 million and $25 million respectively. The non-controlling interest at acquisition was measured at fair value. Cloud has recorded a profit on the disposal of the shares in the consolidated statement of profit or loss.

Revaluation of property, plant and equipment

Cloud purchased an item of property, plant and equipment for $10 million on 1 January 20X0. The useful economic life was estimated to be five years. At 31 December 20X0, the asset was revalued to $12 million. At 31 December 20X1, the asset's value had fallen to $4 million. The downwards revaluation was recorded in other comprehensive income.

Required:

Explain, with suitable calculations, how the above transactions should be dealt with in the financial statements for the year ended 31 December 20X1 and discuss the ethical and professional issues raised. **(18 marks)**

Professional marks will be awarded in this question for the application of ethical principles.

(2 marks)

(Total: 20 marks)

 Calculate your allowed time and allocate the time to the separate parts

19 TILES *Walk in the footsteps of a top tutor*

Background

Tiles is a public limited company that prepares its financial statements in accordance with International Financial Reporting Standards. Results over the past five years have been disappointing and this has caused many of the largest shareholders to become increasingly disgruntled. At the latest shareholder meeting the board of directors was criticised for being slow to react to changing economic circumstances and for being over-paid. The shareholders told the directors that they expect to see substantial improvements in recurring profit for the year ended 30 April 20X5.

Deferred tax asset

Tiles incurred substantial losses in the financial years 30 April 20X2 to 30 April 20X4. In the financial year to 30 April 20X5, it made a small profit before tax due to non-operating gains. In the financial statements for the year ended 30 April 20X5 Tiles has recognised a material deferred tax asset in respect of its unused trading losses. This was based on the budgets for the years 20X6 − 20X9. The finance director instructed the financial controller to include high growth rates in these budgets due to positive indications from customers about future orders, as well as Tiles' plans to expand into new markets and to sell new products currently under development. The tax losses expire in 20X9.

Discontinued operation

On 1 January 20X4, the shareholders had, at a general meeting of the company, authorised the directors of Tiles to sell all of its holding of shares in a subsidiary within the year. Tiles had shown the subsidiary as an asset held for sale and presented it as a discontinued operation in the financial statements for the year ended 30 April 20X4 and 30 April 20X5. Tiles made certain organisational changes during the year to 30 April 20X5, which resulted in additional activities being transferred to the subsidiary. The subsidiary made a significant loss in both 20X4 and 20X5.

Disclosure of bonuses

During the year ended 30 April 20X5, the directors of Tiles accrued large performance related bonuses. These are payable in the year ended 30 April 20X6. All accounting entries relating to these bonuses have been posted correctly but the finance director has omitted the expense from the current year directors' remuneration disclosure note. She believes that disclosure of this information would lead to negative press about Tiles and would cause employee and shareholder dissatisfaction, both of which may depress Tiles' share price. The finance director has therefore justified non-disclosure on the grounds that it will maximise shareholder wealth.

Required:

Explain how the above transactions should be dealt with in the financial statements for the year ended 30 April 20X5 and discuss the ethical issues raised. **(18 marks)**

Professional marks will be awarded in this question for the application of ethical principles.

(2 marks)

(Total: 20 marks)

20 GARDEN *Walk in the footsteps of a top tutor*

Background

Garden is a public listed company with a reporting date of 30 November 20X6. It owns and operates various online businesses. Its customers order goods through Garden's websites, and these goods are delivered by third party couriers. At 30 November 20X6, the finance director owns 15% of Garden's ordinary shares and the operations director owns 10%. The rest of the shares are owned by numerous other shareholders. All ordinary shares carry equal voting rights. At the most recent annual general meeting, some of the shareholders expressed dis-satisfaction with the financial performance of Garden. They also complained that the directors were overpaid and were not demonstrating effective stewardship of the company's assets The accountant of Garden started her employment during the year ended 30 November 20X6 and has encountered a number of issues.

Share-based payment

On 1 December 20X5, a share-based payment scheme was introduced for Garden's six directors. The directors are entitled to 600,000 share options each if they remain employed by the company until 30 November 20X8. The fair value of each share option was $4 at 1 December 20X5 and $5 at 30 November 20X6. At 1 December 20X5 it was estimated that none of the directors would leave before the end of three years but, as at 30 November 20X6, the estimated number of leavers was revised to one. The finance director has told the accountant that no entries or disclosures are required for this scheme in the current year's financial statements because it has not yet vested.

The directors' son

The wife of the finance director is the sales director of Garden. Their son is undertaking an internship with Garden and receives a salary of $30,000 per annum, which is in line with market rates. The finance director has ordered the accountant to omit any reference to his son's salary from the financial statements.

Operating segments

At the start of the current year, Garden purchased the trade and assets of a fashion retail chain that operates a number of shops in large towns and cities. The chain did not sell its products online. The press were critical of Garden's decision, accusing them of over-paying for the chain and of expanding into a sector in which they lack experience and expertise. The performance of the shops, which is monitored internally by Garden's chief operating decision makers, has been poor. When reviewing the operating segment disclosure note prepared by the finance director the accountant noticed that the new retail business has been aggregated with the rest of Garden's trading operations and disclosed as a single reportable segment. The gross profit margins made from the retail outlets are much lower than those made from Garden's online operations. From overhearing conversations, the accountant is aware that Garden's finance director is a good friend of the former owner of the retail chain.

Required:

Discuss the accounting and ethical implications of the above from the perspective of the accountant. **(18 marks)**

Professional marks will be awarded in this question for the application of ethical principles.

(2 marks)

(Total: 20 marks)

21 CHERRY *Walk in the footsteps of a top tutor*

Background

Cherry is a large public limited company. It prepares its financial statements using IFRS Standards and has a reporting date of 30 November 20X6. A bonus is paid to the directors each year which is based upon the operating profit margin of Cherry.

Change in accounting policy for pension scheme

On 1 December 20X5, there was an amendment to Cherry's defined benefit scheme whereby the promised pension entitlement was increased from 10% of final salary to 15%. The directors believe that the pension scheme, which is in deficit, is not an integral part of the operating activities of Cherry. As such they have changed their accounting policy so that, from the current year, all gains and losses on the pension scheme are recognised in other comprehensive income. They believe that this will make the financial statements more consistent, more understandable and can be justified on the grounds of fair presentation.

Trademark

On 1 December 20X2, Cherry acquired a trademark, Golfo, for a line of golf clothing for $3 million. Initially, because of the difficulty in determining its useful life, Cherry decided to amortise the trademark over a 10-year life, using the straight-line method. On 1 December 20X5, a competitor unexpectedly revealed a technological breakthrough which is expected to result in a product which, when launched in May 20X8, will significantly reduce the demand for the Golfo product-line. Cherry now intends to continue manufacturing Golfo products until 31 May 20X8. Amortisation of $300,000 in relation to the Golfo trademark has been charged in the financial statements for the year ended 30 November 20X6.

Sale and leaseback

Cherry sold a building for its fair value of $5 million to a finance company on 30 November 20X6 when its carrying amount was $3.5 million. The building was leased back from the finance company for a period of 5 years. The remaining useful life of the building was deemed to be 25 years so it can be concluded that control of the building has transferred to the finance company. Lease rentals are $440,000 payable annually in arrears. The interest rate implicit in the lease is 7%. The present value of the annual lease payments is $1.8 million. Cherry has recorded the cash proceeds, derecognised the building, and recorded a profit on disposal of $1.5 million in the statement of profit or loss. No other accounting entries have been posted.

The directors have told the financial controller that the accounting treatments outlined above are correct. Any further time that the financial controller spends reviewing these transactions will be looked on unfavourably when deciding her bonus for the year.

Required:

Discuss the accounting and ethical implications of the above situations. **(18 marks)**

Professional marks will be awarded in this question for the application of ethical principles.

(2 marks)

(Total: 20 marks)

22 ANOUK *Online question assistance*

Background

Anouk is a public limited entity with a reporting date of 31 December 20X1. It has covenants attached to some of the bank loan balances included within liabilities on its statement of financial position. The covenants create a legal obligation to repay the loans in full if Anouk's liabilities exceed a specified level. A new financial controller was appointed in January 20X2 and has discovered some financial reporting issues in relation to the year ended 31 December 20X1.

Receivables factoring

On 31 December 20X1 Anouk sold some of its trade receivables to a debt factor. The factor advanced 20% of the $40 million receivables sold. Further amounts become payable to Anouk but are subject to an imputed interest charge so that Anouk receives progressively less of the remaining balance the longer it takes the factor to recover the funds. The factor has full recourse to Anouk for a six-month period after which Anouk has no further obligations and has no rights to receive any further payments from the factor.

The directors are concerned about the negative impact that any potential debt factoring arrangements may have on its loan covenants. As such, they have ordered the financial controller to treat the factoring arrangement in accordance with its legal form.

B-shares

One of Anouk's subsidiaries, Vianne, has two classes of shares: A and B. A-shares carry voting powers and B-shares are issued to meet regulatory requirements. Vianne's shareholder agreement stipulates that the minority B shareholders can exercise a put option every three years which requires Anouk to buy their shares. The exercise price is the original cost paid by the shareholders. In Anouk's consolidated statement of financial position, the B-shares owned by minority shareholders are reported in equity as a non-controlling interest.

Crane

On the 31 December 20X1, Anouk signed a contract to use a crane for the next five years. The supplier of the crane is permitted to substitute the crane for an alternative model during the period of use, and is required to do so if the crane develops a fault. Due to the size of the crane, the supplier would have to incur significant costs to substitute it. The contract states that Anouk can use the crane for any construction activities it wishes. However, the contract also states that the crane cannot be used if wind speed exceeds 14 metres per second. Anouk must pay a fixed monthly rental fee for use of the crane. Anouk has posted no accounting entries in respect of this contract. The financial controller found this contract by accident and suspects that the directors had attempted to conceal it.

Required:

Discuss the accounting and ethical implications of the above. **(18 marks)**

Professional marks will be awarded in this question for the application of ethical principles.

(2 marks)

(Total: 20 marks)

 Online question assistance

SECTION B QUESTIONS

23   FILL (DEC 2018)

(a)   Fill is a coal mining company and sells its coal on the spot and futures markets. On the spot market, the commodity is traded for immediate delivery and, on the forward market, the commodity is traded for future delivery. The inventory is divided into different grades of coal. One of the categories included in inventories at 30 November 20X6 is coal with a low carbon content which is of a low quality. Fill will not process this low quality coal until all of the other coal has been extracted from the mine, which is likely to be in three years' time. Based on market information, Fill has calculated that the three-year forecast price of coal will be 20% lower than the current spot price.

The directors of Fill would like advice on two matters:

(i)   whether the *Conceptual Framework* affects the valuation of inventories;

(ii)   how to calculate the net realisable value of the coal inventory, including the low quality coal.   **(7 marks)**

(b)   At 30 November 20X6, the directors of Fill estimate that a piece of mining equipment needs to be reconditioned every two years. They estimate that these costs will amount to $2 million for parts and $1 million for the labour cost of their own employees. The directors are proposing to create a provision for the next reconditioning which is due in two years' time in 20X8, along with essential maintenance costs. There is no legal obligation to maintain the mining equipment.

As explained above, it is expected that there will be future reductions in the selling prices of coal which will affect the forward contracts being signed over the next two years by Fill.

The directors of Fill require advice on how to treat the reconditioning costs and whether the decline in the price of coal is an impairment indicator.   **(8 marks)**

(c)   Fill jointly controls coal mines with other entities. The Theta mine was purchased by three participants during the year. Fill owns 40%, and the other two participants own 35% and 25% of the mine. The operating agreement requires any major decisions to be approved by parties representing 72% of the interest in the mine.

The directors of Fill wish advice on whether the *Conceptual Framework* will affect the decision as to whether Fill controls the mine.

The directors are also wondering whether the acquisition of the 40% interest would be considered a business combination under IFRS Standards.   **(10 marks)**

Required:

Advise the directors of Fill on how the above transactions should be dealt with in its financial statements with reference to relevant IFRS Standards and the *Conceptual Framework*.

Note: The split of the mark allocation is shown against each of the three issues above.

(Total: 25 marks)

24   HOLLS (DEC 2018) *Walk in the footsteps of a top tutor*

(a)   The IFRS *Practice Statement Management Commentary* provides a broad, non-binding framework for the presentation of management commentary which relates to financial statements which have been prepared in accordance with IFRS Standards. The management commentary is within the scope of the Conceptual Framework and, therefore, the qualitative characteristics will be applied to both the financial statements and the management commentary.

Required:

(i)   **Discuss briefly the arguments for and against issuing the IFRS *Practice Statement Management Commentary* as a non-binding framework or as an IFRS Standard.**   **(4 marks)**

(ii)   **Discuss how the qualitative characteristics of understandability, relevance and comparability should be applied to the preparation of the management commentary.**   **(5 marks)**

(b)   Holls Group is preparing its financial statements for the year ended 30 November 20X7. The directors of Holls have been asked by an investor to explain the accounting for taxation in the financial statements.

The Group operates in several tax jurisdictions and is subject to annual tax audits which can result in amendments to the amount of tax to be paid.

The profit from continuing operations was $300 million in the year to 30 November 20X7 and the reported tax charge was $87 million. The investor was confused as to why the tax charge was not the tax rate multiplied by the profit from continuing operations. The directors have prepared a reconciliation of the notional tax charge on profits as compared with the actual tax charge for the period.

	$ million
Profit from continuing operations before taxation	300
Notional charge at local corporation tax rate of 22%	66
Differences in overseas tax rates	10
Tax relating to non-taxable gains on disposals of businesses	(12)
Tax relating to the impairment of brands	9
Other tax adjustments	14
Tax charge for the year	87

The amount of income taxes paid as shown in the statement of cash flows is $95 million but there is no current explanation of the tax effects of the above items in the financial statements.

The tax rate applicable to Holls for the year ended 30 November 20X7 is 22%. There is a proposal in the local tax legislation that a new tax rate of 25% will apply from 1 January 20X8. In the country where Holls is domiciled, tax laws and rate changes are enacted when the government approves the legislation. The government approved the legislation on 12 November 20X7. The current weighted average tax rate for the Group is 27%. Holls does not currently disclose its opinion of how the tax rate may alter in the future but the government is likely to change with the result that a new government will almost certainly increase the corporate tax rate.

At 30 November 20X7, Holls has deductible temporary differences of $4.5 million which are expected to reverse in the next year. In addition, Holls also has taxable temporary differences of $5 million which relate to the same taxable company and the tax authority. Holls expects $3 million of those taxable temporary differences to reverse in 20X8 and the remaining $2 million to reverse in 20X9. Prior to the current year, Holls had made significant losses.

Required:

With reference to the above information, explain to the investor, the nature of accounting for taxation in financial statements.

Note: Your answer should explain the tax reconciliation, discuss the implications of current and future tax rates, and provide an explanation of accounting for deferred taxation in accordance with relevant IFRS Standards. **(14 marks)**

Professional marks will be awarded in part (b) for clarity and quality of discussion.

(2 marks)

(Total: 25 marks)

25 SKIZER (SEP 2018) *Walk in the footsteps of a top tutor*

(a) Skizer is a pharmaceutical company which develops new products with other pharmaceutical companies that have the appropriate production facilities.

Stakes in development projects

When Skizer acquires a stake in a development project, it makes an initial payment to the other pharmaceutical company. It then makes a series of further stage payments until the product development is complete and it has been approved by the authorities. In the financial statements for the year ended 31 August 20X7, Skizer has treated the different stakes in the development projects as separate intangible assets because of the anticipated future economic benefits related to Skizer's ownership of the product rights. However, in the year to 31 August 20X8, the directors of Skizer decided that all such intangible assets were to be expensed as research and development costs as they were unsure as to whether the payments should have been initially recognised as intangible assets. This write off was to be treated as a change in an accounting estimate.

Sale of development project

On 1 September 20X6, Skizer acquired a development project as part of a business combination and correctly recognised the project as an intangible asset. However, in the financial statements to 31 August 20X7, Skizer recognised an impairment loss for the full amount of the intangible asset because of the uncertainties surrounding the completion of the project. During the year ended 31 August 20X8, the directors of Skizer judged that it could not complete the project on its own and could not find a suitable entity to jointly develop it. Thus, Skizer decided to sell the project, including all rights to future development. Skizer succeeded in selling the project and, as the project had a nil carrying value, it treated the sale proceeds as revenue in the financial statements. The directors of Skizer argued that IFRS 15 *Revenue from Contracts with Customers* states that revenue should be recognised when control is passed at a point in time. The directors of Skizer argued that the sale of the rights was part of their business model and that control of the project had passed to the purchaser.

Required:

(i) Outline the criteria in IAS 38 *Intangible Assets* for the recognition of an intangible asset and discuss whether these are consistent with the *Conceptual Framework*.

(5 marks)

(ii) Discuss the implications for Skizer's financial statements for both the years ended 31 August 20X7 and 20X8 if the recognition criteria in IAS 38 for an intangible asset were met as regards the stakes in the development projects above. Your answer should also briefly consider the implications if the recognition criteria were not met.

(5 marks)

(iii) Discuss whether the proceeds of the sale of the development project above should be treated as revenue in the financial statements for the year ended 31 August 20X8.

(4 marks)

(b) External disclosure of information on intangibles is useful only insofar as it is understood and is relevant to investors. It appears that investors are increasingly interested in and understand disclosures relating to intangibles. A concern is that, due to the nature of IFRS disclosure requirements, investors may feel that the information disclosed has limited usefulness, thereby making comparisons between companies difficult. Many companies spend a huge amount of capital on intangible investment, which is mainly developed within the company and thus may not be reported. Often, it is not obvious that intangibles can be valued or even separately identified for accounting purposes.

The Integrated Reporting Framework may be one way to solve this problem.

Required:

(i) Discuss the potential issues which investors may have with:

– accounting for the different types of intangible asset acquired in a business combination;

– the choice of accounting policy of cost or revaluation models, allowed under IAS 38 *Intangible Assets* for intangible assets;

– the capitalisation of development expenditure. (7 marks)

(ii) Discuss whether integrated reporting can enhance the current reporting requirements for intangible assets. (4 Marks)

(Total: 25 marks)

26   TOOBASCO (SEP 2018) *Walk in the footsteps of a top tutor*

(a)   Toobasco is in the retail industry. In the reporting of financial information, the directors have disclosed several alternative performance measures (APMs), other than those defined or specified under International Financial Reporting Standards. The directors have disclosed the following APMs:

   (i)   'Operating profit before extraordinary items' is often used as the headline measure of the Group's performance, and is based on operating profit before the impact of extraordinary items. Extraordinary items relate to certain costs or incomes which are excluded by virtue of their size and are deemed to be non-recurring. Toobasco has included restructuring costs and impairment losses in extraordinary items. Both items had appeared at similar amounts in the financial statements of the two previous years and were likely to occur in future years.

   (ii)   'Operating free cash flow' is calculated as cash generated from operations less purchase of property, plant and equipment, purchase of own shares, and the purchase of intangible assets. The directors have described this figure as representing the residual cash flow in the business but have given no detail of its calculation. They have emphasised its importance to the success of the business. They have also shown free cash flow per share in bold next to earnings per share in order to emphasise the entity's ability to turn its earnings into cash.

   (iii)   'EBITDAR' is defined as earnings before interest, tax, depreciation, amortisation and rent. EBITDAR uses operating profit as the underlying earnings. In an earnings release, just prior to the financial year end, the directors disclosed that EBITDAR had improved by $180 million because of cost savings associated with the acquisition of an entity six months earlier. The directors discussed EBITDAR at length describing it as 'record performance' but did not disclose any comparable IFRS information and there was no reconciliation to any IFRS measure. In previous years, rent had been deducted from the earnings figure to arrive at this APM.

   (iv)   The directors have not taken any tax effects into account when calculating the remaining APMs.

Required:

Advise the directors whether the above APMs would achieve fair presentation in the financial statements.   **(10 marks)**

(b) Daveed is a car retailer who leases vehicles to customers under operating leases and often sells the cars to third parties when the lease ends. Net cash generated from operating activities for the year ended 31 August 20X8 for the Daveed Group is as follows:

Year ended 31 August 20X8	$m
Cash generated from operating activities	345
Income taxes paid	(21)
Pension deficit payments	(33)
Interest paid	(25)
Associate share of profits	12
	___
Net cash generated from operating activities	278
	___

Cash generated from operating activities was calculated using the indirect method.

Net cash flows generated from investing activities included interest received of $10 million and net capital expenditure of $46 million excluding the business acquisition at (iii) below.

There were also some errors in the presentation of the statement of cash flows which could have an impact on the calculation of net cash generated from operating activities.

The directors have provided the following information as regards any potential errors:

(i) Cars are treated as property, plant and equipment when held under operating leases and when they become available for sale, they are transferred to inventory at their carrying amount. In its statement of cash flows for the year ended 31 August 20X8, cash flows from investing activities included cash inflows relating to the disposal of cars ($30 million).

(ii) On 1 September 20X7, Daveed purchased a 25% interest in an associate for cash. The associate reported a profit after tax of $16 million and paid a dividend of $4 million out of these profits in the year ended 31 August 20X8. As can be seen in the calculation above, the directors included a figure of $12 million when calculating net cash generated from operating activities. The associate was correctly recorded at $23 million in the statement of financial position at 31 August 20X8 and profit for the year of $4 million was included in the statement of profit or loss. No adjustment was made for Daveed's share of the associate's profit when calculating cash generated from operating activities.

(iii) Daveed also acquired a digital mapping business during the year ended 31 August 20X8. The statement of cash flows showed a loss of $28 million in net cash inflow generated from operating activities as the effect of changes in foreign exchange rates arising on the retranslation of this overseas subsidiary. The assets and liabilities of the acquired subsidiary had been correctly included in the calculation of the cash movement during the year.

(iv) During the year to 31 August 20X8, Daveed made exceptional contributions to the pension plan assets of $33 million but the statement of cash flows had not recorded the cash tax benefit of $6 million.

(v)   Additionally, Daveed had capitalised the interest paid of $25 million into property, plant and equipment ($18 million) and inventory ($7 million).

(vi)   Daveed has defined operating free cash flow as net cash generated by operating activities as adjusted for net capital expenditure, purchase of associate and dividends received, interest received and paid. Any exceptional items should also be excluded from the calculation of free cash flow.

Required:

Prepare:

(i)   a schedule that calculates net cash generated from operating activities to correct any errors above   **(4 marks)**

(ii)   a reconciliation from net cash generated by operating activities to operating free cash flow (as described in note (vi) above)   **(4 marks)**

(iii)   an explanation of the adjustments made in parts (i) and (ii) above.   (5 marks)

Professional marks will be awarded in part (b) for clarity and quality of discussion.

(2 marks)

(Total: 25 marks)

27   PLAYER TWO

(a)   Player Two, a public limited company, operates a number of retail stores that sell computer and video games. It prepares financial statements in accordance with International Financial Reporting Standards. In its financial statement disclosure notes for the year ended 31 December 20X1 it has reported an alternative performance measure (APM): adjusted basic EPS (earnings per share). This APM does not feature on the face of its statement of profit or loss and other comprehensive income. The following is an extract from its financial statement disclosures:

	20X1
Profit after tax ($m)	2.5
Adjusting items ($m)	10.3
	————
Adjusted profit after tax ($m)	12.8
	————
Shares outstanding (m)	122.2
Adjusted basic EPS	10.5c

Player Two also discloses similar information for the prior period.

The disclosure note states that 'adjusting items' comprise:

* $6.8 million amortisation charge in relation to acquired brands and intangible assets (20X0: $6.9 million).

* $1.4 million restructuring costs (20X0: $0.9 million)

* $2.1 million impairment charge relating to retail stores.

Required:

Discuss, with reference to Player Two's disclosure of adjusted EPS, the benefits and limitations of additional performance measures for the primary users of financial statements. **(15 marks)**

(b) Wrap is a public limited company that operates in the media industry. This industry is currently experiencing little economic growth. Wrap's market capitalisation (the market price per share multiplied by the number of shares outstanding) is less than its net asset value per the financial statements.

In accordance with IAS 36 *Impairment of Assets*, Wrap has carried out various impairment reviews. Cash generating unit D, a magazine publishing business to which goodwill has been allocated, was tested for impairment and was deemed not to be impaired. Wrap has produced the following disclosure note for inclusion in the financial statements:

'The recoverable amount of cash generating unit D has been determined as its value in use. The calculation of value in use was based on cash flow projections that were approved by management. The average discount rate used by Wrap during the year was 10%. The future cash flows of unit D beyond the budgeted period were extrapolated using an 8 per cent growth rate. Management believes that any reasonably possible change in the key assumptions on which D's recoverable amount is based would not cause D's carrying amount to exceed its recoverable amount.'

Required:

Discuss why the information contained in this disclosure may be of limited use to the users of Wrap's financial statements. **(8 marks)**

Professional marks will be awarded in this question for clarity and quality of presentation. **(2 marks)**

(Total: 25 marks)

28 ZACK *Walk in the footsteps of a top tutor*

(a) In February 20X2, an inter-city train operated by Zack did what appeared to be superficial damage to a storage facility of a local company. The directors of the company expressed an intention to sue Zack but, in the absence of legal proceedings, Zack had not recognised a provision in its financial statements to 31 March 20X2. In July 20X2, Zack received notification for damages of $1.2 million, which was based upon the estimated cost to repair the building. The local company claimed the building was much more than a storage facility as it was a valuable piece of architecture which had been damaged to a greater extent than was originally thought. The head of legal services advised Zack that the company was clearly negligent but the view obtained from an expert was that the value of the building was $800,000. Zack had an insurance policy that would cover the first $200,000 of such claims.

After the financial statements for the year ended 31 March 20X3 were authorised, the case came to court and the judge determined that the storage facility actually was a valuable piece of architecture. The court ruled that Zack was negligent and awarded $300,000 for the damage to the fabric of the facility.

Required:

Advise the directors of Zack as to the correct accounting treatment of the above in the financial statements for the year ended 31 March 20X3. **(7 marks)**

(b) The directors have discovered that some accruals were double-counted within the trade payables balance as at 31 March 20X2. This meant that expenditure for services was overstated in the prior year financial statements by $2 million. Zack has since reviewed its accounting systems and processes and has made appropriate changes. It has introduced additional internal controls to ensure that such estimation problems are unlikely to recur.

The directors of Zack are aware that they should follow the requirements of IAS 8 *Accounting Policies, Changes in Accounting Estimates and Errors* when selecting or changing accounting policies, changing estimation techniques, and correcting errors. They are also aware that the Board has issued an exposure draft (ED/2018/1 *Accounting Policy Changes)* to address growing criticism of IAS 8.

Required:

(i) **Discuss the correct treatment of the Zack's accruals error in its financial statements for the year ended 31 March 20X3.** **(4 marks)**

(ii) **Discuss the role of judgement when selecting an entity's accounting policies.** **(7 marks)**

(iii) **Discuss potential criticisms of IAS 8 and any proposals from the Board to address these criticisms. Your answer should refer to the Board's exposure draft (ED/2018/1).** **(7 marks)**

(Total: 25 marks)

29 MCVEIGH (DEC 18)

(a) McVeigh, a public limited company, has a reporting date of 31 May 20X3.

McVeigh granted interest-free loans of $10 million to its employees on 1 June 20X2. The loans will be repaid by the employees on 31 May 20X4 as a single payment. On 1 June 20X2, the market rate of interest for a two-year loan was 6% per annum.

At the reporting date, the credit risk associated with the loans was low.

The only accounting entry posted by McVeigh in respect of the above transaction was to charge the $10 million cash outflow to the statement of profit or loss as a cost of sale.

Required:

Advise the directors of McVeigh as to the correct accounting treatment of the above transaction in the year ended 31 May 20X3. **(7 marks)**

(b)   **Plan A**

All of McVeigh's new employees are auto-enrolled into its defined contribution pension plan. However, McVeigh has established a voluntary fund (Plan A) in order to provide enhanced benefits to these employees. McVeigh has accounted for Plan A as a defined benefit plan. McVeigh has a history of paying benefits to its former employees, even increasing them to keep pace with inflation since the commencement of Plan A.

The main characteristics of Plan A are as follows:

*   Plan A is totally funded by McVeigh

*   the contributions to the Plan are made periodically

*   the post retirement benefit is calculated based on a percentage of the final salaries of Plan participants dependent on the years of service

According to the underlying contract, McVeigh can terminate Plan A whenever it wishes. If this occurs then McVeigh must fund lifetime annuities for retired scheme members.

McVeigh accounts for Plan A as a defined benefit plan.

Plan B

McVeigh has another defined benefit pension plan (Plan B) for long-standing employees. The net deficit recognised at 1 June 20X2 was $125 million and the interest rate on good quality corporate bonds at this date was 4%. A net interest component of $5 million ($125m × 4%) has been charged to profit or loss. The current service cost for the year was calculated using assumptions as at 1 June 20X2 and expensed to profit or loss as part of the service cost component.

On 1 March 20X3, members of Plan B were offered a settlement. A loss on settlement of $3 million was calculated and accounted for as part of the service cost component. This was determined by measuring the deficit on 1 March 20X3 both before and after the settlement using updated assumptions. On 1 March 20X3, interest rates on good quality bonds had fallen to 3%.

A remeasurement loss has been calculated and is being released to other comprehensive income over the average remaining working life of the scheme's members. The loss is presented as an item that might be reclassified to profit or loss in the future.

Required:

(i)   Discuss why it was appropriate to treat Plan A as a defined benefit plan rather than as a defined contribution plan.   **(7 marks)**

(ii)   Discuss whether the recognition of a net defined benefit liability, in accordance with IAS 19 *Employee Benefits*, is consistent with the recognition criteria in the *Conceptual Framework*.   **(5 marks)**

(iii) Advise the directors of McVeigh as to why the current accounting treatment of Plan B is incorrect.   **(6 marks)**

(Total: 25 marks)

30   MEHRAN (SEP 18) *Walk in the footsteps of a top tutor*

(a)   Mehran is a public limited company. It operates in a number of business sectors, including farming, mining and retail. The directors require advice about how to apply IFRS 13 *Fair Value Measurement.*

(i)   Mehran has just acquired a company, which comprises a farming and mining business. Mehran wishes advice on how to fair value some of the assets acquired.

One such asset is a piece of land, which is currently used for farming. The fair value of the land if used for farming is $5 million. If the land is used for farming purposes, a tax credit of $0.1 million arises.

Mehran has determined that market participants would consider that the land could have an alternative use for residential purposes. The fair value of the land for residential purposes before associated costs is thought to be $7.4 million. In order to transform the land from farming to residential use, there would be legal costs of $200,000, a viability analysis cost of $300,000 and costs of demolition of the farm buildings of $100,000. Additionally, permission for residential use has not been formally given by the legal authority and because of this, market participants have indicated that the fair value of the land, after the above costs, would be discounted by 20% because of the risk of not obtaining planning permission.

In addition, Mehran has acquired the brand name associated with the produce from the farm. Mehran has decided to discontinue the brand on the assumption that it is similar to its existing brands. Mehran has determined that if it ceases to use the brand, then the indirect benefits will be $20 million. If it continues to use the brand, then the direct benefit will be $17 million. Other companies in this market do not have brands that are as strong as Mehran's and so would not see any significant benefit from the discontinuation.

(9 marks)

(ii)   Mehran owns a non-controlling equity interest in Erham, a private company, and wishes to fair value it as at its financial year end of 31 March 20X6. Mehran acquired the ordinary share interest in Erham on 1 April 20X4. During the current financial year, Erham has issued further equity capital through the issue of preferred shares to a venture capital fund. As a result of the preferred share issue, the venture capital fund now holds a controlling interest in Erham. The terms of the preferred shares, including the voting rights, are similar to those of the ordinary shares, except that the preferred shares have a cumulative fixed dividend entitlement for a period of four years and the preferred shares rank ahead of the ordinary shares upon the liquidation of Erham. The transaction price for the preferred shares was $15 per share. Mehran wishes to know the factors which should be taken into account in measuring the fair value of their holding in the ordinary shares of Erham at 31 March 20X6 using a market-based approach.   **(6 marks)**

Required:

Discuss the way in which Mehran should fair value the above assets with reference to the principles of *IFRS 13 Fair Value Measurement.*

Note: The mark allocation is shown against each of the two issues above.

(b) Mehran has recognised provisions in its financial statements for the year ended 31 March 20X6. It has produced the following provisions disclosure note:

	Customer refunds $m	Reorganisations $m	Total $m
1 April 20X5	10.2	8.0	18.2
Charged to profit or loss	13.1	10.2	23.3
Utilised	(9.1)	(9.6)	(18.7)
31 March 20X6	14.2	8.6	22.8
Of which:			
Current	14.2	8.0	22.2
Non-current	–	0.6	0.6

Provisions for customer refunds reflect the company's expected liability for returns of goods sold in retail stores based on experience of rates of return. Provisions for reorganisations reflect restructuring and redundancy costs, principally in relation to our retail operations as well as restructurings in Finance and IT.

The directors of Mehran have been asked by an investor to explain the accounting for provisions in the financial statements and to explain why the information provided in the provisions disclosure note is useful.

Required:

Explain to the investor the nature of accounting for provisions in financial statements. Your answer should explain the benefits and limitations of the information provided in Mehran's disclosure note. **(8 marks)**

Professional marks will be awarded in part (b) for clarity and quality of presentation.

(2 marks)

(Total: 25 marks)

31   CARSOON

Carsoon Co is a public limited. It constructs premises for third parties. It has a year end of 28 February 20X7.

(a)   (i)   On 1 March 20X6, Carsoon invested in a debt instrument with a fair value of $6 million and has assessed that the financial asset is aligned with the fair value through other comprehensive income business model. The instrument has an interest rate of 4% over a period of six years. The effective interest rate is also 4%. On 1 March 20X6, the debt instrument is not impaired in any way. During the year to 28 February 20X7, there was a change in interest rates and the fair value of the instrument seemed to be affected. The instrument was quoted in an active market at $5.3 million but the price based upon an in-house model showed that the fair value of the instrument was $5.5 million. This valuation was based upon the average change in value of a range of instruments across a number of jurisdictions.

The directors of Carsoon felt that the instrument should be valued at $5.5 million and that this should be shown as a Level 1 measurement under IFRS 13 *Fair Value Measurement*. There has not been a significant increase in credit risk since 1 March 20X6, and expected credit losses should be measured at an amount equal to 12-month expected credit losses of $400,000. Carsoon sold the debt instrument on 1 March 20X7 for $5.3 million.

The directors of Carsoon wish to know how to account for the debt instrument until its sale on 1 March 20X7. **(8 marks)**

(ii) Carsoon constructs retail vehicle outlets and enters into contracts with customers to construct buildings on their land. The contracts have standard terms, which include penalties payable by Carsoon if the contract is delayed.

In the year ended 28 February 20X7, Carsoon incurred general and administrative costs of $10 million, and costs relating to wasted materials of $5 million. These have been recognised as contract assets.

Due to poor weather, one of the projects was delayed. As a result, Carsoon faced contractual penalties. Carsoon felt that the penalties should be shown as a contingent liability. Additionally, during the year, Carsoon agreed to construct a storage facility on the same customer's land for $7 million at a cost of $5 million. This was completed during the current financial year.

The directors of Carsoon wish to know how to account for the $15 million costs, the penalties, and the storage facility in accordance with IFRS 15 *Revenue from Contracts with Customers*. **(7 marks)**

Required:

Advise Carsoon on how the above transactions should be dealt with in its financial statements with reference to relevant International Financial Reporting Standards.

Note: The mark allocation is shown against each of the two issues above.

(b) The directors of Carsoon are committed to producing high quality reports that enable its investors to assess the performance and position of the business. They have heard that the International Accounting Standards Board has published a Practice Statement on management commentary. However, they are unsure what is meant by management commentary, and the extent to which it provides useful information.

Required:

Discuss the nature of management commentary and the extent to which it embodies the qualitative characteristics of useful financial information (as outlined in the *Conceptual Framework for Financial Reporting*). **(10 marks)**

(Total: 25 marks)

32 SKYE *Online question assistance*

(a) Skye is a public limited company which has a functional currency of dollars ($). It has entered into a number of transactions in the year ended 31 May 20X7. The directors require advice about how they should be accounted for.

(i) Skye has B shares in issue which allow the holders to request redemption at specified dates and amounts. The legal charter of Skye states that the entity has a choice whether or not to accept the request for repayment of the B shares. There are no other conditions attached to the shares and Skye has never refused to redeem any of the shares up to the current year end of 31 May 20X7. In all other respects the instruments have the characteristics of equity.

Skye also has preference shares in issue which are puttable by the holders at any time after 31 May 20X7. Under the terms of the shares, Skye is only permitted to satisfy the obligation for the preference shares when it has sufficient distributable reserves. Local legislation is quite restrictive in defining the profits available for distribution.

The directors of Skye wish to know if the above financial instruments should be classified as equity items or financial liabilities as at 31 May 20X7. **(6 marks)**

(ii) Skye has a foreign branch which has a functional currency of dollars ($). The branch's taxable profits are determined in dinars. On 1 June 20X6, the branch acquired a property for 6 million dinars. The property had an expected useful life of 12 years with a zero residual value. The asset is written off for tax purposes over eight years. The tax rate in Skye's jurisdiction is 30% and in the branch's jurisdiction is 20%. The foreign branch uses the cost model for valuing its property and measures the tax base at the exchange rate at the reporting date.

Exchange rates	$1 = dinars
1 June 20X6	5
31 May 20X7	6

The directors require advice as to the deferred tax implications of the above.
(7 marks)

Required:

Advise the directors of Skye on how the above transactions should be dealt with in its financial statements with reference to relevant International Financial Reporting Standards.

(b) The 2010 *Conceptual Framework* was criticised for its many notable omissions. One such omission that the 2018 *Conceptual Framework* addressed was the role of prudence. The revised *Conceptual Framework* also details factors that should be considered when selecting a measurement basis. This information should assist the preparers of financial statements when applying an accounting standard that offers a choice of measurement basis (such as IAS 40 *Investment Property).*

Required:

(i) Discuss what is meant by prudence and the extent to which prudence is consistent with the fundamental qualitative characteristic of faithful representation. **(6 marks)**

(ii) With reference to the *Conceptual Framework* discuss the factors that preparers of the financial statements should consider when an accounting standard offers a choice of measurement basis. **(6 marks)**

(Total: 25 marks)

 Online question assistance

33 WHITEBIRK

(a) Whitebirk meets the definition of a small entity in its jurisdiction and complies with the *IFRS for SMEs Standard* (the SMEs Standard). Whitebirk has entered into the following transactions during the year ended 31 May 20X6.

(i) Whitebirk requires a new machine, which will be included as part of its property, plant and equipment. Whitebirk therefore commenced construction of the machine on 1 February 20X6, and this continued until its completion which was after the year end of 31 May 20X6. The direct costs were $2 million in February 2016 and then $1 million in each subsequent month until the year end. Whitebirk has incurred finance costs on its general borrowings during the period, which could have been avoided if the machine had not been constructed. Whitebirk has calculated that the weighted average cost of borrowings for the period 1 February – 31 May 20X6 on an annualised basis amounted to 9% per annum.

(ii) Whitebirk has incurred $1 million of research expenditure to develop a new product in the year to 31 May 20X6. Additionally, it incurred $0.5 million of development expenditure to bring another product to a stage where it is ready to be marketed and sold.

Required:

(i) **In accordance with IAS 23 *Borrowing Cost* and IAS 38 *Intangible Assets*, advise the directors of Whitebirk on how the borrowing costs (note i) and the research and development expenditure (note ii) would be accounted for in the year ended 31 May 20X6.** **(8 marks)**

(ii) **Discuss how the two transactions would be dealt with under the SMEs Standard in the year ended 31 May 20X6.** **(4 marks)**

(b) One of the reasons why Whitebirk prepares its financial statements using the SMEs Standard is because of the difficulties involved every time a new IFRS Standard is issued. The directors believe that the practicalities and financial statement implications of regularly implementing new IFRS Standards are overly onerous to an entity the size of Whitebirk. However, Whitebirk may have to transition to full IFRS Standards if it continues to grow in size.

Required:

(i) Discuss the key practical considerations and financial statement implications that an entity must consider when implementing a new IFRS Standard.

(10 marks)

(ii) Briefly explain the principles outlined in IFRS 1 *First Time Adoption of IFRS* that must be applied when an entity adopts full IFRS Standards for the first time.

(3 marks)

(Total: 25 marks)

34   ASPIRE   *Walk in the footsteps of a top tutor*

(a) Aspire, a public limited company, operates many of its activities overseas. The directors have asked for advice on the correct accounting treatment of several aspects of Aspire's overseas operations. Aspire has a financial statement year end of 30 April 20X4. Aspire's functional currency is the dollar. The average currency exchange rate for the year is not materially different from the actual rate.

Exchange rates	dinars: $1
1 May 20X3	5.0
30 April 20X4	6.0
Average exchange rate for year ended 30 April 20X4	5.6

(i) Aspire has created a new subsidiary, which is incorporated in the same country as Aspire. The subsidiary has issued 2 million dinars of equity capital to Aspire, which paid for these shares in dinars. The subsidiary has also raised 100,000 dinars of equity capital from external sources and has deposited the whole of the capital with a bank in an overseas country whose currency is the dinar. The capital is to be invested in dinar denominated bonds. The subsidiary has a small number of staff and its operating expenses, which are low, are incurred in dollars. The profits are under the control of Aspire. Any income from the investment is either passed on to Aspire in the form of a dividend or reinvested under instruction from Aspire. The subsidiary does not make any decisions as to where to place the investments.

Aspire would like advice on how to determine the functional currency of the subsidiary. **(7 marks)**

(ii) Aspire took out a foreign currency loan of 5 million dinars at a fixed interest rate of 8% on 1 May 20X3. The effective rate of interest on the loan is also 8%. Annual interest payments commenced on 30 April 20X4. The loan will be repaid on 30 April 20X5.

Aspire requires advice on how to account for the loan and interest in the financial statements for the year ended 30 April 20X4. **(7 marks)**

Required:

Advise the directors of Aspire on their various requests above, showing suitable calculations where necessary.

Note: The mark allocation is shown against each of the two issues above.

(b) The directors of Aspire wish to report an additional performance measure (APM) to its stakeholders. The APM will be calculated by taking 'profit before interest and tax' (profit from operations) for the period and then eliminating foreign exchange gains and losses. The APM will be displayed on the face of the statement of profit or loss, below 'profit after tax', and an explanation of how it is derived will be provided in the disclosure notes.

After adjustments for the issues in part (a), Aspire will report a loss before finance costs and tax of $2 million. Total foreign currency losses reported in profit or loss amount to $3 million. The majority of the exchanges losses arise on the settlement and retranslation of receivables arising from sales to overseas customers. Aspire offers most customers credit terms of 60 days.

Required:

Discuss the potential advantages and disadvantages of the additional performance measure proposed by the directors of Aspire. **(9 marks)**

Professional marks will be awarded in part (b) for clarity and quality of presentation.
(2 marks)

(Total: 25 marks)

35 BUSINESS COMBINATIONS *Walk in the footsteps of a top tutor*

(a) You work for an accountancy firm. You have asked to provide advice to clients about the following transactions:

(i) Kayte operates in the shipping industry and owns vessels for transportation. In June 20X4, Kayte acquired Ceemone whose assets were entirely investments in small companies. The small companies each owned and operated one or two shipping vessels. There were no employees in Ceemone or the small companies. At the acquisition date, there were only limited activities related to managing the small companies as most activities were outsourced. All the personnel in Ceemone were employed by a separate management company. The companies owning the vessels had an agreement with the management company concerning assistance with chartering, purchase and sale of vessels and any technical management. The management company used a shipbroker to assist with some of these tasks.

Kayte argued that the vessels were only passive investments and that Ceemone did not own a business consisting of processes, since all activities regarding commercial and technical management were outsourced to the management company. As a result, Kayte proposes to account for the investment in Ceemone as an asset acquisition, with the consideration paid and related transaction costs recognised as the acquisition price of the vessels. The directors of Kayte require advice as to whether this is in accordance with IFRS Standards. **(7 marks)**

(ii) On 1 September 20X4, Bimbi, a listed bank, entered into a business combination with another listed bank, Lental. The business combination has taken place in two stages, which were contingent upon each other. On 1 September 20X4, Bimbi acquired 45% of the share capital and voting rights of Lental for cash. On 1 November 20X4, Lental merged with Bimbi and Bimbi issued new A-shares to Lental's shareholders for their 55% interest.

On 31 August 20X4, Bimbi had a market value of $70 million and Lental a market value of $90 million. Bimbi's business represents 45% and Lental's business 55% of the total value of the combined businesses.

After the transaction, the former shareholders of Bimbi excluding those of Lental owned 51% and the former shareholders of Lental owned 49% of the votes of the combined entity. The Chief Operating Officer (COO) of Lental is the biggest individual owner of the combined entity with a 25% interest. The purchase agreement provides for a board of six directors for the combined entity, five of whom will be former board members of Bimbi with one seat reserved for a former board member of Lental. The board of directors nominates the members of the management team. The management comprised the COO and four other members, two from Bimbi and two from Lental. Under the terms of the purchase agreement, the COO of Lental is the COO of the combined entity.

Bimbi proposes to identify Lental as the acquirer in the business combination but requires advice as to whether this is correct. **(8 marks)**

Required:

Advise how the two transactions should be accounted for.

Note: The mark allocation is shown against each of the two issues above.

(b) On 1 January 20X4, Bolo purchased 45% of the ordinary shares of Kata. Consideration paid was $3 million. The carrying amounts of the net assets of Kata at that date were $2.4 million and approximated their fair values. The statement of financial position for Kata as at 31 December 20X4 was as follows:

	$m
Property, plant & equipment	14
Inventories	1

Total assets	15

Share capital	1
Retained earnings	2
Loans	12

Equity and liabilities	15

The directors of Bolo are unsure whether to treat Kata as an associate or a subsidiary in the consolidated financial statements. When relevant, Bolo measures non-controlling interests using the proportion of net assets method.

Required:

Discuss and compare the impact on the consolidated financial statements of Bolo for the year ended 31 December 20X4 if the investment in Kata is accounted for as:

- **a subsidiary, or**

- **an associate.** **(8 marks)**

Professional marks will be awarded in part (b) for clarity and quality of presentation.

(2 marks)

(Total: 25 marks)

36 MARGIE *Walk in the footsteps of a top tutor*

(a) Margie, a public limited company, has entered into several share related transactions during the period and wishes to obtain advice on how to account for them.

(i) On 1 May 20X2, Margie granted 500 share appreciation rights (SARs) to its 300 managers. All of the rights vested on 30 April 20X4 but they can be exercised from 1 May 20X4 up to 30 April 20X6. At the grant date, the value of each SAR was $10 and it was estimated that 5% of the managers would leave during the vesting period. The fair value of each SAR is as follows:

Date	Fair value ($)
30 April 20X3	9
30 April 20X4	11
30 April 20X5	12

All of the managers who were expected to leave employment did leave the company as expected before 30 April 20X4. On 30 April 20X5, 60 managers exercised their options when the intrinsic value of the right was $10.50 and were paid in cash.

Margie is confused as to whether to account for the SARs under IFRS 2 *Share-based Payment* or IFRS 13 *Fair Value Measurement*, and would like advice as to how the SARs should have been accounted for between the grant date and 30 April 20X5. **(6 marks)**

(ii) Margie issued shares during the financial year. Some of those shares were subscribed for by employees who were existing shareholders, and some were issued to an entity, Grief, which owned 5% of Margie's share capital. Before the shares were issued, Margie offered to buy a building from Grief and agreed that the purchase price would be settled by the issue of shares.

Margie requires advice about how to account for these two transactions. **(5 marks)**

(iii) Margie has entered into a contract with a producer to purchase 350 tonnes of wheat. The purchase price will be settled in cash at an amount equal to the value of 2,500 of Margie's shares. Margie may settle the contract at any time by paying the producer an amount equal to the current market value of 2,500 of Margie shares, less the market value of 350 tonnes of wheat. Margie has no intention of taking physical delivery of the wheat.

The directors of Margie are unsure as to whether this transaction is a share-based payment and require advice as to how it should be accounted for in the financial statements. **(7 marks)**

Required:

Advise the directors of Margie on their various requests above.

Note: The mark allocation is shown against each of the three issues.

(b) Entities are investing more time and money in implementing sustainable development practices. A key sustainable development goal set by many entities is to minimise the impact of business operations on the environment. Margie is considering preparing extensive disclosures about its sustainable development goals, including its environmental impacts.

Required:

Discuss recent developments in the area of sustainability reporting and the potential benefits that might arise when an entity discloses its impact on the environment to its stakeholders. **(7 marks)**

(Total: 25 marks)

37 KAYTE *Online question assistance*

Kayte, a public limited company, operates in a number of industries. It has a reporting date of 30 November 20X3.

(a) One of the industries that Kayte operates in is shipping. Kayte's owns shipping vessels – classified as property, plant and equipment and measured using the cost model– which constitute a material part of its total assets. The economic life of the vessels is estimated to be 30 years, but the useful life of some of the vessels is only 10 years because Kayte's policy is to sell these vessels when they are 10 years old. Kayte estimated the residual value of these vessels at sale to be half of acquisition cost and this value was assumed to be constant during their useful life. Kayte argued that the estimates of residual value used were conservative in view of an immature market with a high degree of uncertainty and presented documentation which indicated some vessels were being sold for a price considerably above carrying value. Broker valuations of the residual value were considerably higher than those used by Kayte. Kayte argued against broker valuations on the grounds that it would result in greater volatility in reporting.

Kayte keeps some of the vessels for the whole 30 years and these vessels are required to undergo an engine overhaul in dry dock every 10 years to restore their service potential, hence the reason why some of the vessels are sold. The residual value of the vessels kept for 30 years is based upon the steel value of the vessel at the end of its economic life. In the current period, one of the vessels had to have its engine totally replaced after only eight years. Normally, engines last for the 30-year economic life if overhauled every 10 years. Additionally, one type of vessel was having its funnels replaced after 15 years but the funnels had not been depreciated separately.

Required:

Advise the directors of Kayte on the accounting issues above. **(11 marks)**

(b) Throughout its other business operations, Kayte is reliant on skilled workers to design and manufacture high-tech products. Because of the importance of Kayte's workforce to its business operations, the directors wish to disclose the following key performance indicators (KPIs) in the annual integrated report <IR>.

	20X3	20X2
Average employee salary ($)	30,325	29,956
Revenue per employee ($)	116,432	102,124
Sick days per employee	4.9	2.1
Employee turnover (%)	18.7	13.9

The national rate of inflation is currently 2%.

Employee turnover has been calculated as the number of employees who left Kayte during the year as a % of the average number of employees throughout the year. The average rate of employee turnover in the industry is 14.1%.

Required:

(i) Briefly discuss some of the factors that management should consider when disclosing KPIs in the reporting entity's <IR>. **(4 marks)**

(ii) Discuss how the KPIs might be interpreted by users of the <IR>. **(8 marks)**

Professional marks will be awarded in part (b) for clarity and quality of presentation.

(2 marks)

(Total: 25 marks)

 Online question assistance

38 VERGE *Walk in the footsteps of a top tutor*

(a) (i) In its annual financial statements for the year ended 31 March 20X3, Verge, a public limited company, had identified the following operating segments:

(i) Segment 1 local train operations

(ii) Segment 2 inter-city train operations

(iii) Segment 3 railway constructions

The company disclosed two reportable segments. Segments 1 and 2 were aggregated into a single reportable operating segment. Operating segments 1 and 2 have been aggregated on the basis of their similar business characteristics, and the nature of their products and services. In the local train market, it is the local transport authority which awards the contract and pays Verge for its services. In the local train market, contracts are awarded following a competitive tender process, and the ticket prices paid by passengers are set by and paid to the transport authority. In the inter-city train market, ticket prices are set by Verge and the passengers pay Verge for the service provided. **(7 marks)**

(ii)   Verge entered into a contract with a government body on 1 April 20X1 to undertake maintenance services on a new railway line. The total revenue from the contract is $5 million over a three-year period. The contract states that $1 million will be paid at the commencement of the contract but although invoices will be subsequently sent at the end of each year, the government authority will only settle the subsequent amounts owing when the contract is completed. The invoices sent by Verge to date (including $1 million above) were as follows:

Year ended 31 March 20X2 $2.8 million

Year ended 31 March 20X3 $1.2 million

The balance will be invoiced on 31 March 20X4. Verge has only accounted for the initial payment in the financial statements to 31 March 20X2 as no subsequent amounts are to be paid until 31 March 20X4. The amounts of the invoices reflect the work undertaken in the period. Verge wishes to know how to account for the revenue on the contract in the financial statements to date.

Market interest rates are currently at 6%.   **(7 marks)**

Required:

Advise Verge on how the above accounting issues should be dealt with in its financial statements for the years ending 31 March 20X2 (where applicable) and 31 March 20X3.

Note: The mark allocation is shown against each of the two issues above.

(b)   The directors of Verge have prepared forecasts for the next five years and they are concerned that the company does not have sufficient liquid assets to fulfil its expansion plans. The directors propose to raise the required funds on 1 April 20X3 in one of the following ways:

(i)   The issue of 5 million ordinary shares.

(ii)   The issue of 10 million convertible bonds in exchange for cash proceeds. Interest is payable annually in arrears. The bond holders will be able to redeem the bonds on 31 March 20X6 in the form of cash or a fixed number of Verge's ordinary shares.

The directors are unsure of the impact of the proposals on the financial statements.

Required:

Discuss the impact of the above proposals on the financial statements of Verge. Your answer should consider the potential impact on basic and diluted earnings per share and on the primary users' perception of Verge's financial performance and position.   **(9 marks)**

Professional marks will be awarded in part (b) for clarity and quality of presentation.
                                    (2 marks)

                                    (Total: 25 marks)

39 ARON

(a) The directors of Aron would like advice with regards some financial instrument transactions that took place during the year ended 31 May 20X7.

(i) Aron issued one million convertible bonds on 1 June 20X6. The bonds had a term of three years and were issued for their fair value of $100 million, which is also the par value. Interest is paid annually in arrears at a rate of 6% per annum. Bonds without the conversion option attracted an interest rate of 9% per annum on 1 June 20X6. The company incurred issue costs of $1 million. The impact of the issue costs is to increase the effective interest rate to 9.38%. At 31 May 20X9 the bondholders can opt to be repaid the par value in cash, or they can opt to receive a fixed number of ordinary shares in Aron. **(6 marks)**

(ii) Aron held 3% holding of the shares in Smart, a public limited company. The investment was designated upon recognition as fair value through other comprehensive income and as at 31 May 20X7 was fair valued at $5 million. The cumulative gain recognised in equity relating to this investment was $400,000. On the same day, the whole of the share capital of Smart was acquired by Given, a public limited company, and as a result, Aron received shares in Given with a fair value of $5.5 million in exchange for its holding in Smart.

The company wishes to know how the exchange of shares in Smart for the shares in Given should be accounted for in its financial records. **(4 marks)**

(iii) On 1 June 20X6, Aron purchased $10 million of bonds at par. These bonds had been issued by Winston, an entity operating in the video games industry. The bonds are due to be redeemed at a premium on 31 May 20X9, with Aron also receiving 5% interest annually in arrears. The effective rate of interest on the bonds is 15%. Aron often holds bonds until the redemption date, but will sell prior to maturity if investments with higher returns become available. Winston's bonds were deemed to have a low credit risk at inception.

On 31 May 20X7, Aron received the interest due on the bonds. However, there were wider concerns about the economic performance and financial stability of the video games industry. As a result, there has been a fall in the fair value of bonds issued by Winston and similar companies. The fair value of the Aron's investment at 31 May 20X7 was $9 million. Nonetheless, based on Winston's strong working capital management and market optimism about the entity's forthcoming products, the bonds were still deemed to have a low credit risk.

The financial controller of Aron calculated the following expected credit losses for the Winston bonds as at 31 May 20X7:

12 month expected credit losses	$0.2m
Lifetime expected credit losses	$0.4m

(7 marks)

Required:

Advise Aron on how to deal with the above transactions in the financial statements for the year ended 31 May 20X7.

Note: The mark allocation is shown against each of the three issues.

(b)   The directors of Aron have observed that IFRS 9 *Financial Instruments* relies very heavily on fair value measurement. They are concerned that fair value measurement is both judgemental and volatile. They believe that the reliance on fair value measurement when accounting for financial instruments makes the financial statements less useful to stakeholders.

Required:

Discuss the validity of the directors' observations.   **(8 marks)**

(Total: 25 marks)

40   ALEXANDRA

(a)   **(i)**   In November 20X0, Alexandra defaulted on an interest payment on an issued bond loan of $100 million repayable in 20X5. The loan agreement stipulates that such default leads to an obligation to repay the whole of the loan immediately, including accrued interest and expenses. The bondholders, however, issued a waiver postponing the interest payment until 31 May 20X1. On 17 May 20X1, Alexandra felt that a further waiver was required, so requested a meeting of the bondholders and agreed a further waiver of the interest payment to 5 July 20X1, when Alexandra was confident it could make the payments. Alexandra classified the loan as long-term debt in its statement of financial position at 30 April 20X1 on the basis that the loan was not in default at the end of the reporting period as the bondholders had issued waivers and had not sought redemption.   **(5 marks)**

(ii)   In the year to 30 April 20X1, Alexandra acquired a major subsidiary. The inventory acquired in this business combination was valued at its fair value at the acquisition date in accordance with IFRS 3 *Business Combinations*. The inventory increased in value as a result of the fair value exercise. A significant part of the acquired inventory was sold in the post-acquisition period but before 30 April 20X1.

In the consolidated statement of profit or loss and other comprehensive income, the cost of inventories acquired in the business combination and sold by the acquirer after the business combination was disclosed on two different lines. The inventory was partly shown as cost of goods sold and partly as a 'non-recurring item' within operating income. The part presented under cost of goods sold corresponded to the inventory's carrying amount in the subsidiary's financial statements. The part presented as a 'non-recurring item' corresponded to the fair value increase recognised on the business combination. The 'non-recurring item' amounted to 25% of Alexandra's earnings before interest and tax (EBIT).

Alexandra disclosed the accounting policy and explained in the notes to the financial statements that showing the inventory at fair value would result in a fall in the gross margin due to the fair value increase. Further, Alexandra argued that isolating this part of the margin in the 'non-recurring items', whose nature is transparently presented in the notes, enabled the user to evaluate the structural evolution of its gross margin.   **(6 marks)**

(iii) Alexandra acquired another subsidiary, Chrissy, on 30 April 20X1. At the time of the acquisition, Chrissy was being sued as there is an alleged mis-selling case potentially implicating the entity. The claimants are suing for damages of $10 million. Alexandra estimates that the fair value of any contingent liability is $4 million and feels that it is more likely than not that no outflow of funds will occur.

Alexandra wishes to know how to account for this potential liability in Chrissy's entity financial statements and whether the treatment would be the same in the consolidated financial statements. **(4 marks)**

Required:

Discuss how the above transactions should be dealt with in the year ended 30 April 20X1.

(b) IAS 1 *Presentation of Financial Statements* says that financial statements should be classified and aggregated in a manner which makes them understandable and comparable. This will help make the financial statements useful to a wide range of users so that they may attempt to assess the future net cash inflows of an entity. However, the International Integrated Reporting Council (IIRC) is calling for a shift in thinking more to the long term, to think beyond what can be measured in quantitative terms and to think about how the entity creates value for its owners. Historical financial statements are essential in corporate reporting, particularly for compliance purposes, but it can be argued that they do not provide meaningful information.

Required:

Discuss the principles and key components of the IIRC's Framework, and any concerns which could question the Framework's suitability for assessing the prospects of an entity. **(8 marks)**

Professional marks will be awarded in part (b) for clarity and quality of presentation.
(2 marks)

(Total: 25 marks)

41 KLANCET *Walk in the footsteps of a top tutor*

Klancet, a public limited company, is a pharmaceutical company and is seeking advice on several financial reporting issues.

(a) **(i)** Klancet produces and sells its range of drugs through three separate divisions. In addition, there are two laboratories which carry out research and development activities.

In the first of these laboratories, the research and development activity is funded internally and centrally for each of the three sales divisions. It does not carry out research and development activities for other entities. Each of the three divisions is given a budget allocation which it uses to purchase research and development activities from the laboratory. The laboratory is directly accountable to the division heads for this expenditure.

The second laboratory performs contract investigation activities for other laboratories and pharmaceutical companies. This laboratory earns 75% of its revenues from external customers and these external revenues represent 18% of the organisation's total revenues.

The performance of the second laboratory's activities and of the three separate divisions is regularly reviewed by the chief operating decision maker (CODM). In addition to the heads of divisions, there is a head of the second laboratory. The head of the second laboratory is directly accountable to the CODM and they discuss the operating activities, allocation of resources and financial results of the laboratory.

Klancet is uncertain as to whether the research and development laboratories should be reported as two separate segments under IFRS 8 *Operating Segments*, and would like advice on this issue. **(8 marks)**

(ii) Klancet has agreed to sell a patent right to another pharmaceutical group, Jancy. Jancy would like to use the patent to develop a more complex drug. Klancet will receive publicly listed shares of the Jancy group in exchange for the right. The value of the listed shares represents the fair value of the patent. If Jancy is successful in developing a drug and bringing it to the market, Klancet will also receive a 5% royalty on all sales.

Additionally, Klancet won a competitive bidding arrangement to acquire a patent. The purchase price was settled by Klancet issuing new publicly listed shares of its own.

Klancet's management would like advice on how to account for the above transactions. **(6 marks)**

Required:

Advise Klancet on how the above transactions should be dealt with in its financial statements with reference to relevant International Financial Reporting Standards.

Note: The mark allocation is shown against each of the two issues above.

(b) On 1 July 20X6, Klancet purchased a debt instrument for its nominal value of $5 million. The transaction was at fair value. Klancet's business model is to hold financial assets to collect the contractual cash flows but also sell financial assets if investments with higher returns become available. Interest is received at a rate of 4% annually in arrears. The effective rate of interest is 10%.

On 30 June 20X7, the fair value of the debt instrument was $4.5 million. There has not been a significant increase in credit risk since inception. Expected credit losses are immaterial.

The directors are unsure how to account for this financial instrument. They also wish to know if the correct accounting treatment is consistent with the *Conceptual Framework*.

Required:

(i) **Discuss, with reference to IFRS 9 *Financial Instruments*, how the above transactions should be dealt with in Klancet's financial statements for the year ended 30 June 20X7.** **(4 marks)**

(ii) **Discuss whether the accounting treatment of this transaction is consistent with the *Conceptual Framework*.** **(7 marks)**

(Total: 25 marks)

42   EMCEE *Walk in the footsteps of a top tutor*

(a)   (i)   Emcee, a public limited company, is a sports organisation which owns several football and basketball teams. It has a financial year end of 31 May 20X6.

Emcee purchases and sells players' registrations on a regular basis. Emcee must purchase registrations for that player to play for the club. Player registrations are contractual obligations between the player and Emcee. The costs of acquiring player registrations include transfer fees, league levy fees, and player agents' fees incurred by the club. Also, players' contracts can be extended and this incurs additional costs for Emcee.

At the end of every season, which also is the financial year end of Emcee, the club reviews its playing staff and makes decisions as to whether they wish to sell any players' registrations. These registrations are actively marketed by circulating other clubs with a list of players' registrations and their estimated selling price. Players' registrations are also sold during the season, often with performance conditions attached. Occasionally, it becomes clear that a player will not play for the club again because of, for example, a player sustaining a career threatening injury or being permanently removed from the playing squad for another reason. The playing registrations of certain players were sold after the year end, for total proceeds, net of associated costs, of $25 million. These registrations had a carrying amount of $7 million.

Emcee would like to know the financial reporting treatment of the acquisition, extension, review and sale of players' registrations in the circumstances outlined above.   **(9 marks)**

(ii)   In the consolidated financial statements for 20X6, Emcee recognised a net deferred tax asset of $16 million. This asset was made up of $3 million relating to taxable temporary differences and $19 million relating to the carry-forward of unused tax losses. The local tax regulation allows unused tax losses to be carried forward indefinitely. Emcee expects that within five years, future taxable profits before tax would be available against which the unused tax losses could be offset. This view was based on the budgets for the years 20X6-20Y1. The budgets were primarily based on general assumptions about economic improvement indicators. Additionally, the entity expected a substantial reduction in the future impairments which the entity had recently suffered and this would result in a substantial increase in future taxable profit.

Emcee had recognised material losses during the previous five years, with an average annual loss of $19 million. A comparison of Emcee's budgeted results for the previous two years to its actual results indicated material differences relating principally to impairment losses. In the interim financial statements for the first half of the year to 31 May 20X6, Emcee recognised impairment losses equal to budgeted impairment losses for the whole year. In its financial statements for the year ended 31 May 20X6, Emcee disclosed a material uncertainty about its ability to continue as a going concern. The current tax rate in the jurisdiction is 30%.   **(8 marks)**

Required:

Discuss how the above matters should be dealt with in Emcee's financial statements.

Note: The mark allocation is shown against each of the two issues above.

(b) Developing a framework for disclosure is at the forefront of current debate and there are many bodies around the world attempting to establish an overarching framework to make financial statement disclosures more effective, coordinated and less redundant. Some argue that disclosure notes are too lengthy and numerous. Others argue that there is no such thing as too much 'useful' information for users.

Required:

Discuss why it is important to ensure the optimal level of disclosure in annual reports, and the role of materiality when preparing financial statement disclosure notes. **(8 marks)**

(Total: 25 marks)

43   GASNATURE *Walk in the footsteps of a top tutor*

 Question debrief

(a) Gasnature is a public limited company involved in the production and trading of natural gas and oil. It prepares its financial statements using International Financial Reporting Standards. The directors require advice about the accounting treatment of some of the transactions that Gasnature has entered into during the year.

(i) Gasnature jointly owns an underground storage facility with another entity, Gogas. Both parties extract gas from offshore gas fields, which they own and operate independently from each other. Gasnature owns 55% of the underground facility and Gogas owns 45%. They have agreed to share services and costs accordingly, with decisions regarding the storage facility requiring unanimous agreement of the parties. Local legislation requires the decommissioning of the storage facility at the end of its useful life.

Gasnature wishes to know how to treat the agreement with Gogas including any obligation or possible obligation arising on the underground storage facility.

(7 marks)

(ii) Gasnature has entered into a 10-year contract with Agas for the purchase of natural gas. Gasnature has made an advance payment to Agas for an amount equal to the total quantity of gas contracted for 10 years which has been calculated using the forecasted price of gas. The advance carries interest of 6% per annum, which is settled by way of the supply of extra gas. Fixed quantities of gas have to be supplied each month and there is a price adjustment mechanism in the contract whereby the difference between the forecasted price of gas and the prevailing market price is settled in cash monthly. If Agas does not deliver gas as agreed, Gasnature has the right to claim compensation at the current market price of gas.

Gasnature wishes to know whether the contract with Agas should be accounted for under IFRS 9 *Financial Instruments*. **(6 marks)**

Required:

Discuss, with reference to International Financial Reporting Standards, how Gasnature should account for the above agreement and contract

(b) Gasnature's institutional shareholders invest in a wide-range of entities. Gasnature's directors are concerned that certain IFRS and IAS Standards permit entities to choose between different measurement bases and presentation methods. They believe that these choices hinder its shareholders from comparing Gasnature to other entities on a like-for-like basis.

Required:

Outline the main accounting choices permitted by IAS 16 *Property, Plant and Equipment* and IAS 20 *Accounting for Government Grants and Disclosure of Government Assistance* and discuss the potential impact of these on investors' analysis of financial statements. **(10 marks)**

Professional marks will be awarded in part (b) for clarity and quality of presentation.
(2 marks)

(Total: 25 marks)

 Calculate your allowed time and allocate the time to the separate parts

---

44 JANNE *Walk in the footsteps of a top tutor*

(a) **(i)** Janne is considering leasing land to Maret for a term of 30 years. The title will remain with Janne at the end of the initial lease term. Maret can lease the land indefinitely at a small immaterial rent at the end of the lease or may purchase the land at a 90% discount to the market value after the initial lease term. Maret is to pay Janne a premium of $3 million at the commencement of the lease, which equates to 70% of the value of the land. Additionally, Janne will receive an annual rental payment of 4% of the market value of the land as at the commencement of the lease.

The directors of Janne are unsure as to whether the lease should be classified as a finance lease or an operating lease. **(7 marks)**

(ii) Janne's trade receivables are short-term and do not contain a significant financing component. Using historical observed default rates, updated for changes in forward-looking estimates, Janne estimates the following default rates for its trade receivables that are outstanding as at 31 May 20X3:

	Not overdue	1–30 days overdue	31–60 days overdue	61+ days overdue
Default rate	0.5%	1.5%	6.1%	16.5%

The trade receivables of Janne as at 31 May 20X3, the reporting date, are as follows:

	Gross carrying amount ($m)
Not overdue	10.1
1 – 30 days overdue	4.3
31 – 60 days overdue	1.6
61 + days overdue	1.0

There is a loss allowance brought forward from the previous financial year of $0.2 million in respect of trade receivables.

The directors of Janne require advice on how to calculate and account for the current year loss allowance. **(6 marks)**

(iii) Janne purchases investment properties and funds this by issuing bonds in the market. The liability in respect of the bonds is designated to be measured at fair value through profit or loss. The bonds had an overall fair value decline of $50 million in the year to 31 May 20X3 of which $5 million related to a decrease in Janne's creditworthiness.

The directors of Janne would like advice on how to account for this movement in the fair value of the bonds. **(4 marks)**

Required:

Respond to the directors' requests.

Note: The mark allocation is shown against each of the three issues above.

(b) The directors of Janne believe that some International Financial Reporting Standards are inconsistent with the *Conceptual Framework*. They have made the following comments:

- The recognition of an expense in respect of an equity-settled share-based payment scheme with employees is not in line with the *Conceptual Framework's* definition of an expense.

- The recognition of a liability, rather than income, in respect of non-refundable deposits received from customers is not in line with the *Conceptual Framework's* definition of a liability.

- Internally generated brands meet the definition of an asset, and so the fact that IAS 38 *Intangible Assets* prohibits their recognition in the financial statements contradicts the *Conceptual Framework*.

Required:

Discuss the extent to which each of the directors' comments is valid. **(8 marks)**

(Total: 25 marks)

45 EVOLVE *Walk in the footsteps of a top tutor*

 Question debrief

(a) Evolve is a real estate company, which is listed on the stock exchange and has a year end of 31 August.

(i) At 31 August 20X6, Evolve controlled a wholly owned subsidiary, Resource, whose only assets were land and buildings, which were all measured in accordance with International Financial Reporting Standards. On 1 August 20X6, Evolve published a statement stating that a binding offer for the sale of Resource had been made and accepted and, at that date, the sale was expected to be completed by 31 August 20X6. The non-current assets of Resource were measured at the lower of their carrying amount or fair value less costs to sell at 31 August 20X6, based on the selling price in the binding offer. This measurement was in accordance with IFRS 5 *Non-current Assets Held for Sale and Discontinued Operations*. However, Evolve did not classify the non-current assets of Resource as held for sale in the financial statements at 31 August 20X6 because there were uncertainties regarding the negotiations with the buyer and a risk that the agreement would not be finalised. There was no disclosure of these uncertainties and the original agreement was finalised on 20 September 20X6. **(7 marks)**

(ii)   Evolve operates in a jurisdiction with a specific tax regime for listed real estate companies. Upon adoption of this tax regime, the entity has to pay a single tax payment based on the unrealised gains of its investment properties. Evolve purchased Monk whose only asset was an investment property for $10 million. The purchase price of Monk was below the market value of the investment property, which was $14 million, and Evolve chose to account for the investment property under the cost model. However, Evolve considered that the transaction constituted a 'bargain purchase' under IFRS 3 *Business Combinations*. As a result, Evolve accounted for the potential gain of $4 million in profit or loss and increased the 'cost' of the investment property to $14 million. At the same time, Evolve opted for the specific tax regime for the newly acquired investment property and agreed to pay the corresponding tax of $1 million. Evolve considered that the tax payment qualifies as an expenditure necessary to bring the property to the condition necessary for its operations, and therefore was directly attributable to the acquisition of the property. Hence, the tax payment was capitalised and the value of the investment property was stated at $15 million. **(6 marks)**

Required:

Advise Evolve on how the above transactions should be correctly dealt with in its financial statements with reference to relevant International Financial Reporting Standards.

Note: The mark allocation is shown against each of the two issues above.

(b)   The International Accounting Standards Board (the Board) is undertaking a broad-based initiative to explore how disclosures in financial reporting can be improved. The Disclosure Initiative is made up of a number of implementation and research projects, one of which is concerned with materiality. The Board have now issued a Practice Statement in which it provides further guidance on the application of materiality to financial statements.

Required:

Discuss why the concept of materiality is so important to preparers and users of financial statements.

Your answer should include reference to the Board's materiality Practice Statement. (10 marks)

Professional marks will be awarded in part (b) for clarity and quality of presentation.

(2 marks)

(Total: 25 marks)

 Calculate your allowed time and allocate the time to the separate parts

46   ARTWRIGHT

(a)   (i)   Artwright trades in the chemical industry. The entity has development and production operations in various countries. It has entered into an agreement with Jomaster under which Artwright will licence Jomaster's know-how and technology to manufacture a chemical compound, Volut. The know-how and technology has a fair value of $4 million. Artwright cannot use the know-how and technology for manufacturing any other compound than Volut. Artwright has not concluded that economic benefits are likely to flow from this compound but will use Jomaster's technology for a period of three years. Artwright will have to keep updating the technology in accordance with Jomaster's requirements. The agreement stipulates that Artwright will make a non-refundable payment of $4 million to Jomaster for access to the technology. Additionally, Jomaster will also receive a 10% royalty from sales of the chemical compound.

Additionally, Artwright is interested in another compound, Yacton, which is being developed by Jomaster. The compound is in the second phase of development. The intellectual property of compound Yacton has been put into a newly formed shell company, Conew, which has no employees. The compound is the only asset of Conew. Artwright is intending to acquire a 65% interest in Conew, which will give it control over the entity and the compound. Artwright will provide the necessary resources to develop the compound.

The directors of Artwright require advice about how the above events are accounted for in accordance with International Financial Reporting Standards.

(8 marks)

(ii)   Artwright has entered into three derivative contracts during the year ended 30 November 20X4, details of which are as follows:

	Initial recognition at fair value	Fair value at the year-end	Reason
A	Nil	$20m (liability)	Artwright believes that oil prices are due to rise in the future so during the year has entered into futures contracts to buy oil at a fixed price. Artwright has no exposure to oil prices in the course of its business. In fact, oil prices have fallen resulting in the loss at the year-end.
B	$1m	$9m (liability)	Artwright has an investment in equity designated to be measured at fair value through other comprehensive income. Artwright is concerned the investment will fall in value and it wishes to cover this risk. Thus during the year it entered into derivative B to cover any fall in value and designated this as a hedging instrument as part of a fair value hedge. In fact, by the reporting date, the asset increased in value by $8.5 million.

	Initial recognition at fair value	Fair value at the year-end	Reason
C	Nil	$25m (asset)	Artwright is concerned about the potential for raw material prices to rise. It managed this risk by entering into derivative C – a futures contract. This arrangement has been designated as a cash flow hedge. At the year-end the raw material prices have risen, potentially giving the company an increased future cost of $24 million.

Assume that all designated hedges meet the effectiveness criteria outlined in IFRS 9 *Financial Instruments*.

The directors of Artwright would like an outline of the hedge effectiveness criteria and also require advice on how the three derivatives should be accounted for in the financial statements for the year ended 30 November 20X4. **(9 marks)**

Required:

With reference to relevant International Financial Reporting Standards, respond to the directors requests.

Note: The mark allocation is shown against each of the two issues above.

(b) The difference between debt and equity in an entity's statement of financial position is not easily distinguishable for preparers of financial statements. The classification of a financial instrument as debt or equity can have a large impact on the financial statements of an entity.

Required:

Explain the likely impact on the financial statements if a financial liability was misclassified as an equity item. **(6 marks)**

Professional marks will be awarded in part (b) for clarity and quality of presentation.

(2 marks)

(Total: 25 marks)

47 LUCKY DAIRY

(a) **(i)** The Lucky Dairy, a public limited company, produces milk for supply to various customers. It is responsible for producing twenty five per cent of the country's milk consumption. The company owns cows and heifers (young female cows).

The herd as at 31 May 20X2 is comprised as follows:

70,000 – 3 year old cows (all purchased before 1 June 20X1)

25,000 – 2 year old heifers purchased for $46 each on 1 December 20X1

There were no animals born or sold in the year. The per unit values less estimated costs to sell were as follows:

	$
2 year old animal at 31 May 20X1	50
2 year old animal at 31 May 20X2	55
3 year old animal at 31 May 20X2	60

The directors would like advice on how the herd should be accounted for in its primary financial statements for the year ended 31 May 20X2. Advice about disclosure notes is not required. **(6 marks)**

(ii) On 1 December 20X1 Lucky Dairy purchased interest-bearing bonds in Jags, another listed company, for $10 million and classified these assets to be measured at amortised cost. Just prior to the date of the bond purchase, Jags had released an interim financial report that demonstrated encouraging year-on-year growth and a strong financial position. As such, external agencies had graded the bonds as having a low credit risk. In May 20X2, Jags released its annual financial statements and these showed a weak trading performance in the final six months of its reporting period as well as a large decline in the cash generated from its operations compared to the prior year. These financial statements show that, at the period end, Jags was relatively close to breaching its loan covenants. The listed bond price of Jags has fallen by 20% since December 20X1 despite an overall increase in bond prices for other listed entities in the same sector. It has been reported that external agencies are reviewing and re-assessing the credit rating of Jags. Despite encountering financial difficulties, Jags has met all of its obligations to its lenders and bond holders.

The directors of Lucky Dairy would like advice on how the above information will impact the carrying amount of its financial assets. **(8 marks)**

Required:

Advise Lucky Dairy on how the above transactions should be correctly dealt with in its financial statements with reference to relevant International Financial Reporting Standards.

Note: The mark allocation is shown against each of the two issues above.

(b) Lucky Dairy's directors have been reviewing the International Integrated Reporting Council's *Framework for Integrated Reporting*. The directors believe that International Financial Reporting Standards are already extensive and provide stakeholders with a comprehensive understanding of an entity's financial position and performance for the year. In particular, statements of cash flow enable stakeholders to assess the liquidity, solvency and financial adaptability of a business. They are concerned that any additional disclosures could be excessive and obscure the most useful information within a set of financial statements. They are therefore unsure as to the rationale for the implementation of a separate, or combined, integrated report.

Required:

Discuss the extent to which statements of cash flow provide stakeholders with useful information about an entity and whether this information would be improved by the entity introducing an Integrated Report. **(9 marks)**

Professional marks will be awarded in part (b) for clarity and quality of presentation.
(2 marks)

(Total: 25 marks)

UK GAAP FOCUS

48   FILL (DEC 2018)

(a)   On 1 December 20X6, Fill purchased an open cast coal mine in the UK. The negotiation and purchase of a coal mining licence took a substantial amount of time to complete, and resulted in Fill incurring significant borrowing costs. Fill also acquired equipment which will be used for the construction of various mines throughout the UK. Fill wishes to capitalise the borrowing costs on the acquisition of the licence and the equipment.

However, during the last six months of the year ended 30 November 20X8, there has been a significant decline in the spot price of coal and it is expected that future reductions in selling prices may occur. Currently, the forward contracts being signed over the next two years by Fill indicate a reduction in the price of coal. At 30 November 20X8, the mine has a useful remaining life of four years. As a result of the decline in the price of coal, Fill has decided to sell the mine and has approached several potential buyers.

Required:

Advise the directors of Fill on how to treat the above events under FRS 102 *The Financial Reporting Standard applicable in the UK and Republic of Ireland.* **(8 marks)**

(b)   Several years ago, Fill had purchased an interest of 10% in another mining company. However, over the last two years, Fill has made several other purchases of shares with the result that, at 30 November 20X8, it owned 51% of the equity of the mining company. Fill had incurred significant legal and advisory costs in acquiring control. The mining company has reserves which contain different grades of coal. As the entity cannot process some high quality coal for several years, contingent consideration for the purchase of the entity has been agreed. On the date that Fill gained control of the mining company, the fair value of the contingent consideration was estimated at $10 million.

Required:

Advise the directors of Fill on the differences in treatment of the above purchase of the mining company between IFRS 3 *Business Combinations* **and FRS 102** *The Financial Reporting Standard applicable in the UK and Republic of Ireland.* **(7 marks)**

(Total: 15 marks)

49 SKIZER (SEP 2018)

Skizer is a pharmaceutical company which develops new products with other pharmaceutical companies that have the appropriate production facilities. Stakes in development projects When Skizer acquires a stake in a development project, it makes an initial payment to the other pharmaceutical company. It then makes a series of further stage payments until the product development is complete and it has been approved by the authorities. In the financial statements for the year ended 31 August 20X7, Skizer has treated the different stakes in the development projects as separate intangible assets because of the anticipated future economic benefits related to Skizer's ownership of the product rights. However, in the year to 31 August 20X8, the directors of Skizer decided that all such intangible assets were to be expensed as research and development costs as they were unsure as to whether the payments should have been initially recognised as intangible assets. This write off was to be treated as a change in an accounting estimate.

Required:

(a) Outline the criteria in FRS 102 *The Financial Reporting Standard applicable in the UK and Republic of Ireland* for the recognition of an intangible asset and discuss whether these are consistent with the *Conceptual Framework*. **(6 marks)**

(b) Discuss the required treatment under FRS 102 for the stakes in the development projects for both the years ended 31 August 20X7 and 20X8 assuming that the recognition criteria for an intangible asset were met. Your answer should also briefly consider the implications if the recognition criteria were not met. **(5 marks)**

(c) Discuss the key differences between International Financial Reporting Standards and FRS 102 with regards to the recognition of intangible assets. **(4 marks)**

(Total: 15 marks)

50 BOBARRA

(a) Shortly before the financial year-end, Bobarra signed a letter of intent to buy a group of companies in the United Kingdom (UK). The UK group was diverse in nature and included subsidiaries, which the entity was prepared to sell. One subsidiary was operating in a country that was engaged in civil war and so the group had lost managerial control over the entity. Another subsidiary was being held by the group specifically to make a profit on its resale. Bobarra has little experience of UK company legislation and UK Generally Accepted Accounting Practice (UK GAAP).

The directors require advice on the requirements to prepare group financial statements in the UK and any relevant exemptions and exclusions from consolidation available in the UK. **(9 marks)**

(b) At 30 November 20X6, three people own the shares of Bobarra. The finance director owns 60%, and the operations director owns 30%. The third owner is a passive investor who does not help manage the entity. All ordinary shares carry equal voting rights. The wife of the finance director is the sales director of Bobarra. Their son is currently undertaking an apprenticeship with Bobarra and receives a salary of $30,000 per annum, which is normal compensation. The finance director and sales director have set up a trust for the sole benefit of their son. The trust owns 60% of the ordinary shares of Santarem which carry voting rights. The finance director and sales director are trustees of the trust.

Finally, Bobarra owns 100% of the shares in Alucant, which in turn owns 100% of the shares in Cantor. Alucant also has a 80% holding of the shares of Drumby. There have been transactions in the year between Bobarra and Drumby.

The directors of Bobarra require advice on the identification of related parties and the preparation of related party disclosure in respect of its separate financial statements for the year ending 30 November 20X6 in accordance with IAS 24 *Related Party Disclosures* and FRS 102 *The Financial Reporting Standard applicable in the UK and Republic of Ireland* **(7 marks)**

Required:

Advise Bobarra on the matters set out above. **(Total: 16 marks)**

51 HARRIS

The directors of Harris are looking at the requirements of IFRS 3 *Business Combinations* and FRS 102 *The Financial Reporting Standard applicable in the UK and Republic of Ireland*. The directors would like advice on the accounting treatment of goodwill because the entity is preparing to purchase a UK subsidiary at a competitive price.

The directors are also concerned about the differences between IAS 12 *Income Taxes* and FRS 102 with regards to the recognition of deferred tax assets and liabilities.

Required:

(a) **Discuss the key differences with regards to accounting for goodwill under IFRS 3 and FRS 102.** **(9 marks)**

(b) **Discuss the differences in the general recognition principles between IAS 12 and FRS 102 in accounting for deferred tax.** **(6 marks)**

(Total: 15 marks)

52 ROWLING

Rowling, a public limited company, purchases and develops numerous intangible assets. Two of the directors of Rowling are qualified accountants who were trained in International Financial Reporting Standards. The directors of Rowling are aware that the UK Financial Reporting Council in the UK has published a range of Financial Reporting Standards (FRSs) – FRS 100, 101, 102 and 105 – but do not understand the scope of these or what entities they apply to. Moreover they require an explanation of how International Financial Reporting Standards and FRS 102 differ with regards to the recognition of intangible assets.

Required:

Prepare a draft memorandum to the directors setting out:

- **the scope of FRS 100, FRS 101, FRS 102 and FRS 105** **(9 marks)**

- **the differences between International Financial Reporting Standards and FRS 102 with regards to the recognition of intangible assets.** **(6 marks)**

(Total: 15 marks)

53 TOTO

On 1 January 20X1, Toto enters into a lease. The lease term is three years and the asset, which is not specialised, has a useful economic life of ten years. Ownership of the asset does not transfer to Toto at the end of the lease term. Toto must make lease payments annually in arrears. No other fees or costs are required. The lease payments are material to Toto's financial statements.

Required:

Compare the impact of the above on the financial statements of Toto for the year ended 31 December 20X1 If the lease is accounted for in accordance with:

- **IFRS 16 *Leases*, or**

- **FRS 102 *The Financial Reporting Standard applicable in the UK and Republic of Ireland.***

Your answer should make reference to key financial statement ratios. (15 marks)

54 HOWEY

Howey, a public limited company, intends to dispose of part of its business. This meets the criteria in IFRS 5 *Non-current Assets Held for Sale and Discontinued Operations* to be classified as a discontinued operation. They are also considering acquiring a subsidiary exclusively with a view to resale.

Required:

(a) **Discuss the differences between the treatment of non-current assets held for sale and discontinued operations under FRS 102 *The Financial Reporting Standard applicable in the UK and Republic of Ireland* and International Financial Reporting Standards.** (9 marks)

(b) **Discuss why a UK entity might choose to adopt FRS 102 instead of applying International Financial Reporting Standards.** (6 marks)

(Total: 15 marks)

55 LOKI

On 1 January 20X1, Loki purchased 70% of the ordinary shares of Odin for cash consideration of $300 million. The identifiable net assets of Odin at this date had a carrying amount of $200 million and a fair value of $280 million. If accounting standards permit, Loki measures non-controlling interests (NCI) at acquisition at fair value. The fair value of the NCI at acquisition was $120 million.

On 31 December 20X2, Loki performed an impairment review. Odin was deemed to be a cash generating unit. The net assets of Odin (excluding goodwill) were carried in the consolidated financial statements of the Loki group at $260 million. The recoverable amount of Odin was calculated as $350 million.

If required, you should assume that the goodwill arising on the acquisition of Odin was attributed a useful economic life of ten years as at the acquisition date.

Required:

(a)   Discuss, with calculations, how the impairment review should be accounted for in accordance with International Financial Reporting Standards.   **(6 marks)**

(b)   Discuss, with calculations, how the impairment review should be accounted for if Loki prepared its financial statements in accordance with FRS 102.   **(9 marks)**

(Total: 15 marks)

Section 2

ANSWERS TO PRACTICE QUESTIONS

SECTION A QUESTIONS – GROUP FINANCIAL STATEMENTS

1   **MOYES (DEC 2018)** *Walk in the footsteps of a top tutor*

Key answer tips

This question examines consolidated statements of cash flow. However, note that the calculation of cash generated from operations was only worth six marks. In contrast, discussion of the adjustments made to profit before tax (part (a) (ii)) and discussion of the impact of a change in group structure (part (b)) were worth twelve marks. To succeed in SBR, you must feel confident with the discursive requirements.

When preparing a statement of cash flows (or extracts from the statement), pay careful attention to whether the figures need brackets.

(a)   **Explanatory note to: The directors of Moyes**

Subject: Cash flows generated from operations

(i)   **Cash generated from operations**

Tutorial note

Make sure that your reconciliation is clearly labelled. This will help the markers to award you credit if you have made mistakes.

	$m
Profit before tax	209
Share of profit of associate	(67)
Service cost component	24
Contributions into the pension scheme	(15)
Impairment of goodwill	10
Depreciation	99
Impairment of property, plant and equipment ($43m – $20m)	23
Reduction in inventories ($126m – $165m + $6m)	33
Loss on inventory	6
Increase in receivables	(7)
Increase in current liabilities	18
Cash generated from operations	333

Tutorial note

Note that the same answer would have been obtained if no separate adjustment was made for the $6 million loss on inventories and if the reduction in inventories was presented as $39 million ($126m – $165m).

(ii) Explanation of adjustments

Tutorial note

Work through your calculation of cash generated from operations and discuss the rationale behind each adjustment you have made to profit before tax.

Indirect method

Cash flows from operating activities are principally derived from the key trading activities of the entity. This would include cash receipts from the sale of goods, cash payments to suppliers and cash payments on behalf of employees. The indirect method adjusts profit or loss for the effects of transactions of a non-cash nature, any deferrals or accruals from past or future operating cash receipts or payments and any items of income or expense associated with investing or financing cash flows.

Associate

The share of profit of associate is an item of income associated with investing activities and so has been deducted.

Non-cash flows

Non-cash flows which have reduced profit and must subsequently be added back include the service cost component, depreciation, exchange losses and impairments. With the impairment of property, plant and equipment, the first $20 million of impairment will be allocated to the revaluation surplus so only $23 million would have reduced operating profits and should be added back.

Pension

In relation to the pension scheme, the remeasurement component can be ignored as it is neither a cash flow nor an expense to operating profits. Cash contributions should be deducted, though, as these represent an operating cash payment ultimately to be received by Moyes' employees. Benefits paid to retired employees are a cash outflow for the pension scheme rather than for Moyes and so should be ignored.

Working capital

The movements on receivables, payables and inventory are adjusted so that the timing differences between when cash is paid or received and when the items are accrued in the financial statements are accounted for.

Inventory is measured at the lower of cost and net realisable value. The inventory has suffered an overall loss of $6 million (Dinar 80 million/5 – Dinar 60 million/6). This is not a cash flow and would be added back to profits in the reconciliation. However, the loss of $6 million should also be adjusted in the year-on-year inventory movements. The net effect of this on the statement of cash flows will be nil.

(b)   Change in structure

Tutorial note

Students are generally good at dealing with changes in group structures in numerical questions. Make sure that you understand the principles behind the numerical treatment so that you are able to address discursive questions as well.

When the parent company acquires or sells a subsidiary during the financial year, cash flows arising from the acquisition or disposal are presented as investing activities.

In relation to Davenport, no cash consideration has been paid during the current year because the consideration consisted of a share for share exchange and deferred cash. The deferred cash would be presented as a negative cash flow within investing activities when paid in two years' time.

This does not mean that there would be no impact on the current year's statement of cash flows. On gaining control, Moyes would consolidate 100% of the assets and liabilities of Davenport which would presumably include some cash or cash equivalents at the date of acquisition. These would be presented as a cash inflow at the date of acquisition net of any overdrafts held at acquisition.

Adjustments would also need to be made to the opening balances of assets and liabilities by adding the fair values of the identifiable net assets at acquisition to the respective balances. This would be necessary to ensure that only the cash flow effects are reported in the consolidated statement of cash flows.

On the disposal of Barham, the net assets at disposal, including goodwill, are removed from the consolidated financial statements. Since Barham is overdrawn, this will have a positive cash flow effect for the group. The overdraft will be added to the proceeds (less any cash and cash equivalents at disposal) to give an overall inflow presented in investing activities. Care would once again be necessary to ensure that all balances at the disposal date are removed from the corresponding assets and liabilities so that only cash flows are recorded within the consolidated statement of cash flows.

Dividends

Tutorial note

The question asked about changes in group structure and dividends. Make sure that you address both aspects. The examining team regularly comment that students fail to address all parts of the exam questions.

Dividends received by Moyes from Davenport are not included in the consolidated statement of cash flows since cash has in effect been transferred from one group member to another.

The non-controlling interest's share of the dividend would be presented as a cash outflow in financing activities.

(c)   Assets held for sale

Tutorial note

Start with the definition of an asset held for sale and then apply it to the scenario.

IFRS 5 *Non-current Assets Held for Sale and Discontinued Operations* defines an asset held for sale as one where the carrying amount will be recovered principally through a sales transaction. To be classified as held for sale, a sale has to be highly probable and the asset should be available for sale in its present condition.

At face value, Watson would not appear to meet this definition as no sales transaction is to take place.

IFRS 5 does not explicitly extend the requirements for held for sale to situations where control is lost. However, the Board have confirmed that in instances where control is lost, the subsidiary's assets and liabilities should be derecognised. Loss of control is a significant economic event and fundamentally changes the investor–investee relationship. Therefore situations where the parent is committed to lose control should trigger a reclassification as held for sale. Whether this should be extended to situations where control is lost to other causes would be judgemental. It is possible therefore that Watson should be classified as held for sale.

Discontinued operations

Tutorial note

Start with the definition of an asset held for sale and then apply it to the scenario. Remember you were asked to discuss both Barham and Watson.

IFRS 5 defines a discontinued operation as a component of an entity which either has been disposed of or is classified as held for sale, and

(i) represents a separate major line of business or geographical area of operations

(ii) is a single co-ordinated plan to dispose of a separate major line or area of operations

(iii) is a subsidiary acquired exclusively for resale.

Barham has been sold during the year but there appears to be other subsidiaries which operate in similar geographical regions and produce similar products. Little guidance is given as to what would constitute a separate major line of business or geographical area of operations. The definition is subjective and the directors should consider factors such as materiality and relevance before determining whether Barham should be presented as discontinued or not.

The same is true for Watson. Assuming it can be classified as held for sale, it would need to be a separate major line of business or geographical area of operation to be presented as a discontinued operation.

(d) **Probability**

Tutorial note

This question requires knowledge of the recognition criteria in a range of IFRS and IAS Standards, as well as in the Conceptual Framework. This content is core. If your knowledge here is lacking then you should revisit the Study Text.

Different accounting standards use different levels of probabilities to discuss when assets and liabilities should be recognised in the financial statements. For example, economic benefits from property, plant and equipment and intangible assets need to be probable to be recognised; to be classified as held for sale, the sale has to be highly probable.

Under IAS 37 *Provisions, Contingent Liabilities and Contingent Assets*, a provision should only be recognised if an outflow of economic resources is probable. Contingent assets, on the other hand, can only be recognised if the inflow is economic benefits is virtually certain. This could lead to a situation where two sides of the same court case have two different accounting treatments despite the likelihood of pay-out being identical for both parties.

Contingent consideration transferred on a business combination is recognised in the financial statements regardless of the level of probability. Instead the fair value is adjusted to reflect the level of uncertainty of the contingent consideration.

Tutorial note

The Conceptual Framework has been recently revised. Ensure your knowledge is up-to-date.

In the 2018 *Conceptual Framework*, the Board confirmed a new approach to recognition which requires decisions to be made with reference to the qualitative characteristics of financial information. The *Conceptual Framework* says than an item is recognised if it meets the definition of an element and if recognition provides users of financial statements with:

– relevant information

– a faithful representation of the asset or liability.

The key change in the 2018 *Conceptual Framework* was therefore to remove the probability criterion. The *Conceptual Framework* will inform the revision of current IFRS and IAS Standards as well as the development of new standards, and this may mean that more assets and liabilities with a low probability of inflow or outflow of economic resources will be recognised in the future. The Board accepts that prudence could still mean there will be inconsistencies in the recognition of assets and liabilities within financial reporting standards but may be a necessary consequence of providing investors and lenders with the most useful information.

		Marks
Marking guide		
		Marks
(a)	– calculation of cash flow generated from operations	6
	– explanation of the adjustments and use of the scenario	6
		12
(b)	– application of the following discussion to the scenario:	
	purchase consideration (shares and deferred cash)	1
	impact on consolidated statement of cash flows of:	
	subsidiary acquisition (including dividend)	3
	subsidiary disposal	2
		6
(c)	– IFRS 5 definition of discontinued operation and application to the scenario	3
	– consideration of held for sale and application to the scenario	1
	– consideration of loss of control and application to the scenario	2
		6
(d)	– inconsistent application of the probability criterion (including examples)	3
	– Conceptual Framework	3
		6
Total		**30**

Examiner's comments

Statements of cash flow will be examined regularly in the SBR exam as they form part of the group accounting aspect of the syllabus. Many candidates ignored the fact that they had to draft an explanatory note and simply showed the calculation of cash generated from operations. Some candidates showed the accounting entries for the various elements set out in the question even though this was not required. The maximum marks available for simply showing the calculation was 6 marks which represented only half of the marks for this part of the question. To gain these marks, candidates had to ensure that the cash flow adjustments were in the right direction. For example, depreciation had to be added back to profit before tax and not deducted in order to gain credit. Candidates performed well on this part of the question, gaining full marks in many cases.

The second part of the question required an explanation of how the changes to the group structure and dividend would impact upon the consolidated statement of cash flows. This aspect of the syllabus has historically been examined as a calculation but in this exam, candidates were required to explain the principles behind the adjustments to the statement of cash flows. Where attempts were made at explanations in this question then candidates performed quite well.

The third part of the question required candidates to advise the directors as to the held for sale and discontinued operation classifications. It is important for candidates to realise that there is only a small number of marks available for simply setting out the rules in IFRS 5 and that the majority of the marks are awarded for the application of the principles in the standard. Also, the question asked for a discussion of both held for sale and discontinued operation criteria and thus it is important for candidates to deal with both issues. However, several candidates focussed on held for sale with little discussion of discontinued operations.

2   **BANANA (SEP 2018)**   *Walk in the footsteps of a top tutor*

Key answer tips

This question examines core issues in group accounting, such as the calculation of goodwill and the accounting treatment of associates.

In SBR you will be asked to 'discuss' the correct accounting treatment of transactions. Calculations are not enough to pass the exam.

Part (c) tests financial instrument derecognition issues. This is a common exam topic. Make sure that you know the key principles that govern the classification, recognition, measurement, derecognition and impairment of financial instruments.

(a) (i) **Goodwill**

Tutorial note

This answer involves some calculations but the majority of it is discursive. If you neglect the discussion element then you will not pass.

According to IFRS 3 *Business Combinations*, goodwill should be calculated by comparing the fair value of the consideration with the fair value of the identifiable net assets at acquisition.

The shares have been correctly valued using the market price of Banana at acquisition.

Contingent consideration should be included at its fair value which should be assessed taking into account the probability of the targets being achieved as well as being discounted to present value. It would appear reasonable to measure the consideration at a value of $4 million ($16 million × 25%). A corresponding liability should be included within the consolidated financial statements with subsequent remeasurement. This would be adjusted prospectively to profit or loss rather than adjusting the consideration and goodwill.

The finance director has measured the non-controlling interest using the proportional method rather than at fair value. Although either method is permitted on an acquisition by acquisition basis, the accounting policy of the Banana group is to measure non-controlling interest at fair value. The fair value of the non-controlling interest at acquisition is $17 million (20% × 20 million × $4.25).

Net assets at acquisition were incorrectly included at their carrying amount of $70 million. This should be adjusted to fair value of $75 million with a corresponding $5 million increase to land in the consolidated statement of financial position.

Tutorial note

Goodwill calculations are a common exam topic. Learn the proforma.

Goodwill should have been calculated as follows:

	$m
Fair value of share exchange	68
Contingent consideration	4
Add NCI at acquisition	17
Less net assets at acquisition	(75)
Goodwill at acquisition	14

The correcting entry required to the consolidated financial statements is:

Dr Goodwill	$2 million
Dr Land	$5 million
Cr Non-controlling interest	$3 million
Cr Liabilities	$4 million

Tutorial note

Make sure that your debits and credits balance.

If you don't feel comfortable with debits and credits then you could refer to increases or decreases instead.

(ii) **Equity accounting**

Tutorial note

There is only one mark available for the correct calculation of the associate's carrying amount. The discussion element is crucial.

If an entity holds 20% or more of the voting power of the investee, it is presumed that the entity has significant influence unless it can be clearly demonstrated that this is not the case. The existence of significant influence by an entity is usually evidenced by representation on the board of directors or participation in key policy making processes. Banana has 40% of the equity of Strawberry and can appoint one director to the board. It would appear that Banana has significant influence but not control. Strawberry should be classified as an associate and be equity accounted for within the consolidated financial statements.

The equity method is a method of accounting whereby the investment is initially recognised at cost and adjusted thereafter for the post-acquisition change in the investor's share of the investee's net assets. The investor's profit or loss includes its share of the investee's profit or loss and the investor's other comprehensive income includes its share of the investee's other comprehensive income. At 1 October 20X7, Strawberry should have been included in the consolidated financial statements at a carrying amount of $20.4 million ($18 million + (40% × ($50 million – $44 million))).

(iii) **Disposal**

Tutorial note

Show all of your workings. Make sure they are clearly labelled.

On disposal of 75% of the shares, Banana no longer exercises significant influence over Strawberry and a profit on disposal of $3.1 million should have been calculated.

Tutorial note

You can still score full marks if you answer to part (ii) was incorrect. Markers apply the 'own figure rule'.

	$m
Proceeds	19.0
Fair value retained	4.5
Carrying amount of associate (part (ii))	(20.4)
	———
Profit on disposal	3.1
	———

Banana is incorrect to have recorded a loss in reserves of $14 million and this should be reversed. Instead, a gain of $3.1 million should have been included within the consolidated statement of profit or loss.

Tutorial note

The definition of a financial asset includes an investment in the equity shares of another entity. Lots of students forget this.

If no designation was made to measure the shares at fair value through other comprehensive income then Banana would measure them at fair value through profit or loss.

The retained 10% investment is a financial asset. Per IFRS 9 *Financial Instruments* it is initially recognised at fair value of $4.5 million. Banana does not intend to sell their remaining interest so, as long as they make an irrecoverable election, they can treat the remaining interest at fair value through other comprehensive income. The investment will be restated to its fair value of $4 million at the reporting date with a corresponding loss of $0.5 million reported in other comprehensive income.

(b)   Melon – current treatment

Tutorial note

If your conclusion differs from the one below then you can still score well. Make sure that you state the relevant rules from the accounting standard and then apply them to the scenario.

Melon should only be treated as an asset acquisition if the acquisition does not meet the definition of a business combination. In accordance with IFRS 3 *Business Combinations*, an entity should determine whether a transaction is a business combination by applying the definition of a business in IFRS 3.

Tutorial note

State the definition of a business and then apply it to the scenario.

IFRS 3 defines a business as an integrated set of activities and assets which are capable of being conducted and managed for the purpose of providing a return in the form of dividends, lower costs or other economic benefits directly to investors or other owners, members or participants. A business will typically have inputs and processes applied to the ability to create outputs. Outputs are the result of inputs and processes and are usually present within a business but are not a necessary requirement for a set of integrated activities and assets to be defined as a business at acquisition.

Melon has both inputs and processes. The licence is an input as it is an economic resource within the control of Melon which is capable of providing outputs once one or more processes are applied to it. Additionally, the seller does not have to be operating the activities as a business for the acquisition to be classified as a business. It is not relevant therefore that Melon does not have staff and instead outsources its activities. The definition of a business requires just that the activities could have been operated as a business. Processes are in place through the research activities, integration with the management company and supervisory and administrative functions performed. The research activities are still at an early stage, so no output is yet obtainable but, as identified, this is not a necessary prerequisite for the acquisition to be treated as a business. It can be concluded that Melon is a business and it is incorrect to treat Melon as an asset acquisition.

Exposure draft

Tutorial note

Exposure drafts are regularly examined in the SBR exam. Study all of the examinable documents.

The Board has sought to give greater clarity to the definition of a business since the definition has proven difficult to apply in practice. Consequently, an exposure draft has been issued. This proposes that no business acquisition has occurred if substantially all of the fair value of the gross assets acquired is concentrated in a single asset or group of similar assets.

Research activities appear to be at a very early stage and, whilst in substance are very different in nature to the licence itself, are likely to be of relatively low value. It is therefore plausible that substantially all of the fair value is concentrated in the licence itself. If so, the acquisition would not be treated as a business combination.

Should it be determined that the research activities are of sufficient value then this means that not all the fair value is concentrated in a single asset. This would mean that the acquisition would be treated as a business combination. Further information is therefore required.

(c)   **Bonds**

Tutorial note

The bonds have been 'sold' so a key issue in this question concerns derecognition. In other words, should the financial asset be removed from the statement of financial position? Begin your answer with the rules governing derecognition from IFRS 9 Financial Instruments. Then apply these rules to the bond sale.

IFRS 9 *Financial Instruments* requires that a financial asset only qualifies for derecognition once the entity has transferred the contractual rights to receive the cash flows from the asset or where the entity has retained the contractual rights but has an unavoidable obligation to pass on the cash flows to a third party. The substance of the disposal of the bonds needs to be assessed by a consideration of the risks and rewards of ownership.

Banana has not transferred the contractual rights to receive the cash flows from the bonds. The third party is obliged to return the coupon interest to Banana and to pay additional amounts should the fair values of the bonds increase. Consequently, Banana still has the rights associated with the interest and will also benefit from any appreciation in the value of the bonds. Banana still retains the risks of ownership as it has to compensate the third party should the fair value of the bonds depreciate in value.

If the sale were a genuine transfer of risks and rewards of ownership, then the sales price would be approximate to the fair value of the bonds. It would only be in unusual circumstances, such as a forced sale of Banana's assets arising from severe financial difficulties, that this would not be the case. The sales price of $8 million is well below the current fair value of the bonds of $10.5 million. Additionally, Banana is likely to exercise their option to repurchase the bonds.

It can be concluded that no transfer of rights has taken place and therefore the asset should not be derecognised.

Tutorial note

Once you have reached a conclusion about derecognition then you need to think in more detail about the specific financial statement impact of the transaction in the year ended 30 June 20X7.

To measure the asset at amortised cost, the entity must have a business model where they intend to collect the contractual cash flows over the life of the asset. Banana maintains these rights and therefore the sale does not contradict its business model. The bonds should continue to be measured at amortised cost in the consolidated financial statements of Banana.

The carrying amount of the bonds at 1 June 20X7 would have been $10.2 million ($10 million + (7% × $10m) − (5% × $10m)). Amortised cost prohibits restatement to fair value. The carrying amount of the bonds at 30 June 20X8 should be $10.4 million ($10.2m + (7% × $10.2m) − (5% × $10m)).

The proceeds received of $8 million should be recognised as a financial liability measured at amortised cost. An interest charge of $0.8 million would accrue between 1 July 20X6 and 1 July 20X8, being the difference between the sale and repurchase price of the bonds.

Marking scheme			
			Marks
(a)	(i)	Goodwill and contingent consideration	3
		Why existing goodwill calculation is incorrect	3
		Correct calculation and entry	2
			8
	(ii)	Significant influence	2
		Equity accounting	1
		Carrying amount	1
			4
	(iii)	Calculation of gain	1
		Rationale for gain	1
		Correct treatment after disposal	2
			4
(b)		Rationale for inclusion as a business combination	**7**
(c)		Consideration of IFRS 9 principles	4
		Transfer of rights/conclusions	1
		Carrying amount of bonds	2
			7
Total			**30**

Examiner's comments

The first part required the candidate to prepare an explanatory note discussing three separate issues. Many candidates gained high marks in this section, provided they separated the complex calculations from their explanations. Techniques such as producing the calculations on one page whilst simultaneously explaining them on a second page proved an efficient exam technique. Whilst most candidates are naturally drawn to the numbers, most of the marks in this section were allocated to the explanation and the application of IFRS 3 *Business Combinations*. Weak answers to (i) provided insufficient explanation of the accounting treatment relating to each aspect of the goodwill calculation, for which marks were available if explained.

Part (ii) was generally well-answered although in some cases the carrying amount of the associate was overlooked or incorrect. In part (iii) explanations were generally good, although the disposal calculation was often incorrect (for example, omitting the fair value of the retained investment).

Part (b) was generally weak. Most candidates provided limited or no discussion of the exposure draft. Many answers focused on defining an asset, with minimal reference to the requirements of a business combination under IFRS 3. Within the question that examines current issues, it is likely that exposure drafts may be examined in terms of the key areas of change. It is important that candidates read around the subject.

In part (c), providing that candidates identified the key aspect of substance, marks were awarded accordingly.

3   BUBBLE *Walk in the footsteps of a top tutor*

Key answer tips

It is important to be able to calculate the exchange differences that arise when an overseas subsidiary is translated into the presentation currency of the group. Memorise the necessary proformas before attempting this question.

The consolidation question in the Strategic Business Reporting exam is likely to require both discussion and calculations. Easy marks can be obtained on the former, but students tend to prioritise the latter.

(a)   (i)   Goodwill

Tutorial note

The question asks you to 'advise'. Calculations alone are not sufficient to score full marks.

IFRS 3 *Business Combinations* says that goodwill is recognised at the acquisition date. It is calculated as the difference between:

- the total of the fair value of the consideration transferred to acquire control and the non-controlling interest, and

- the fair value of the subsidiary's identifiable net assets.

According to IAS 21 *The Effects of Changes in Foreign Exchange Rates*, goodwill arising on acquisition of foreign operations is treated as the foreign operation's asset. At each reporting date, it is translated at the closing rate of exchange. Goodwill should be reviewed for impairment annually.

Goodwill is calculated initially in foreign currency as follows:

	Dm
Fair value of consideration ($46m × 8)	368
NCI at acquisition (210m shares × 40% × 2.62 dinars)	220
Fair value of identifiable net assets (W1)	(488)
Goodwill at acquisition	100
Impairment (20%)	(20)
Goodwill at reporting date	80

The goodwill of Tyslar as at 31 October 20X5 is therefore $8.4 million (D80m/9.5).

(W1) Net assets at acquisition

	Dinars m
Share capital	210
Retained earnings	258
Fair value adjustment	20
(70m – 50m)	
	488

The subsidiary's net assets should be measured in the consolidated financial statements at fair value at the acquisition date. As such, the land carried at 50m dinars in the separate financial statements should be remeasured to 70m dinars (and then translated into dollars at the appropriate rate).

(ii)   Translation reserve

Foreign exchange differences arise when translating Tyslar into the presentation currency of the group. This is because:

- goodwill is retranslated every year at the closing rate

- the opening net assets are retranslated every year at the closing rate

- profit for the year is translated in the statement of profit or loss at the average rate but net assets in the statement of financial position are translated at the closing rate.

Exchange differences arising on the retranslation of an overseas subsidiary are recorded in other comprehensive income. They are presented as an item that may be reclassified to profit or loss in the future.

Exchange differences arising on the translation of the subsidiary's opening net assets and profit are attributable to the owners of the group and the non-controlling interest (NCI). Exchange differences arising on the translation of goodwill are attributable to the owners of the group and the NCI if the NCI at acquisition was valued at its fair value.

The exchange differences attributable to the owners of the group are held in a translation reserve in equity. This is calculated as follows:

	$m
Group share of goodwill forex loss (W2)	(1.0)
Group share of net asset and profit forex loss (W3)	(6.1)
	(7.1)

(W2) Exchange loss on Tyslar's goodwill

Tutorial note

If goodwill is calculated using the fair value method, the exchange gain or loss and any impairment must be apportioned between the group and the NCI.

	Dm	Exchange rate	$m
Opening (acquisition) goodwill (part (a) (i))	100	8.0	12.5
Impairment (part (a) (i))	(20)	8.5	(2.4)
Exchange loss (bal. fig)			(1.7)
Closing goodwill	80	9.5	8.4

Goodwill has been calculated using the fair value method. Therefore, the exchange loss must be allocated between the group and the NCI based on their respective shareholdings.

Group: $1.7m × 60% = $1.0m

NCI: $1.7m × 40% = $0.7m

(W3) Exchange loss on Tyslar's opening net assets and profit

Tutorial note

Make sure that you learn this proforma.

	Dm	Exchange rate	$m
	488	8.0	61.0
	34	8.5	4.0
			(10.1)
	522	9.5	54.9

The exchange loss on the opening net assets and profit must be allocated between the group and the NCI based on their respective shareholdings:

Group: $10.1m × 60% = $6.1m

NCI: $10.1m × 40% = $4.0m

(W4) Net assets at reporting date

	Dm
Share capital	210
Retained earnings	292
Fair value adjustment	20
	522

(iii) Overseas property

The property should have been recognised at $7 million, which is the fair value of the consideration transferred to acquire it. A profit on the disposal of the land of $2 million ($7m – $5m) should also have been recorded. The correcting entry is:

Dr PPE $2m

Cr P/L $2m

The staff relocation costs should not have been capitalised. The correcting entry is:

Dr P/L $0.5m

Cr PPE $0.5m

The building should be depreciated over its useful life, giving a current year charge of $0.1 million ($7m/35 × 6/12):

Dr P/L $0.1m

Cr PPE $0.1m

At the reporting date, the building should be revalued from its carrying amount of $6.9 million ($7m − $0.1m) to its fair value of $7.9 million (D75m/9.5). The gain is recorded in other comprehensive income. The entry to record it is:

Dr PPE $1.0m

Cr OCI $1.0m

The total property, plant and equipment balance is calculated as follows:

	$m
Bubble	280.0
Tyslar (D390/9.5)	41.1
Tyslar fair value adjustment (D20m/9.5)	2.1
PPE cost adjustment	2.0
Removal of incorrect costs	(0.5)
Depreciation	(0.1)
Revaluation	1.0
	———
	325.6
	———

(b)   Functional currency

Tutorial note

Remember to state the rules (how is a functional currency determined) and then apply those rules to the scenario.

IAS 21 *The Effects of Changes in Foreign Exchange Rates* says that the functional currency is the currency of the primary economic environment in which the entity operates. The primary economic environment in which an entity operates is normally the one in which it primarily generates and expends cash.

The following factors should be considered in determining Tyslar's functional currency:

•   The currency that mainly influences the determination of the sales prices

•   The currency of the country whose competitive forces and regulations mainly influences operating costs.

The currency that dominates the determination of sales prices will normally be the currency in which the sales prices for goods and services are denominated and settled. In Tyslar's case, sale prices are influenced by local demand and supply, and are traded in dinars. Analysis of the revenue stream points to the dinar as being the functional currency. The cost analysis is indeterminate because the expenses are influenced by the dinar and the dollar.

IAS 21 also requires entities to consider secondary factors when determining the functional currency. These factors include the degree of autonomy and the independence of financing. Tyslar operates with a considerable degree of autonomy both financially and in terms of its management. Tyslar does not depend on the group for finance.

In conclusion, Tyslar's functional currency will be the dinar because its revenue is clearly influenced by the dinar.

Marking scheme		
		Marks
(a)	Goodwill calculation and discussion	7
	Group translation reserve	10
	Property, plant and equipment	7
(b)	Functional currency discussion – 1 mark per point	6
		———
Total		**30**
		———

4   JOCATT *Walk in the footsteps of a top tutor*

Key answer tips

There are always easy marks in cash flow questions – read the question very carefully and you should find lots of figures that can be put straight into your proforma. Make sure that you get your brackets the right way around or you will lose marks.

(a)   (i)   Acquisition of Tigret

Jocatt obtained control over Tigret in stages (also known as a 'step acquisition'). On 30 June 20X2, Jocatt should have revalued the previous 8% investment to its fair value of $5 million and it in the goodwill calculation. This adjustment will increase goodwill by $5 million. A gain of $1 million ($5m – $4m) should have been recorded in the consolidated statement of profit or loss. The adjusting entry is:

Dr Goodwill $5m

Cr Financial assets $4m

Cr Profit or loss $1m

The identifiable net assets of TIgret at acquisition are consolidated at their fair value of $45 million. This creates a taxable temporary difference of $10 million because the carrying amount of the net assets in the consolidated financial statements exceeds the tax base of $35 million. A deferred tax liability arises for $3 million ($10m × 30%) in the consolidated statement of financial position. This is treated as part of the subsidiary's acquisition net assets and therefore goodwill at acquisition will also increase by $3 million:

Dr Goodwill $3m

Cr Deferred tax liabilities $3m

Goodwill at the acquisition date is calculated as follows:

	$m
Fair value of consideration ($15m + $15m)	30
Fair value of previous equity interest	5
Fair value of non-controlling interest	20
Fair value of net assets at acquisition (excl. deferred tax)	(45)
Deferred tax	3
Goodwill on acquisition	13

Tutorial note

An alternative calculation for goodwill would be:

$5m draft + $5m step acquisition adjustment + $3m deferred tax adjustment = $13 million

(ii) **Extracts from Jocatt Group: Statement of Cash flows for the year ended 30 November 20X2**

	$m	$m
Cash flows from operating activities:		
Profit before tax ($44m + $1m gain on Tigret)	45	
Finance costs	8	
Retirement benefit service cost	16	
Depreciation	27	
Gain on investment property (W2)	(2)	
Profit on sale of land ($19m – $10m)	(9)	
Impairment of goodwill (W1)	33	
Gain on Tigret	(1)	
Cash paid to retirement benefit scheme (W4)	(7)	
Decrease in trade receivables ($62m – $113m – $5m)	56	
Decrease in inventories ($105m – $128m)	23	
Increase in trade payables ($144m – $55m – $6m)	83	
Cash generated from operations		272
Interest paid		
($8m – $2m interest on defined benefit plan)		(6)
Income taxes paid (W3)		(18)
		248

	$m	$m
Cash flows from financing activities:		
Repayment of long-term borrowings ($71m – $67m)		(4)
Non-controlling interest dividend (per SOCIE)		(11)
Dividends paid by Jocatt (per SOCIE)		(5)
		(20)

Workings

(W1) Goodwill

Tutorial note

Reconcile the movement in the carrying amount of goodwill between the two reporting dates to calculate the impairment. This should be added back in the reconciliation between profit before tax and cash generated from operations.

	$m
Opening balance at 1 December 20X1	68
Acquisition of Tigret (part (i))	13
Impairment (bal. fig.)	(33)
Closing balance at 30 November 20X2	48.0
($40m + $8m (part (i)))	

(W2) Investment property

Tutorial note

Fair value gains and losses on investment properties are recorded in the statement of profit or loss.

	$m
Opening balance at 1 December 20X1	6
Gain (bal. fig.)	2
Closing balance at 30 November 20X2	8

(W3) Taxation

Tutorial note

Reconcile the opening and closing balances for both the income tax liability and the deferred tax liability in a single working. Remember to include any charge for the year included in profit or loss and also in other comprehensive income. You should also ensure that you correctly deal with any tax-related balances on a subsidiary acquired or disposed of during the year.

	$m
Opening tax balances at 1 December 20X1 ($41m + $30m)	71
Deferred tax on acquisition (part (i))	3
Charge for year per profit or loss	11
Charge for year in OCI	1
Tax paid (bal. fig.)	(18)
	——
Closing tax balances at 30 November 20X2	68
($32m + $3m (part (i)) + $33m)	——

(W4) Defined benefit scheme

Tutorial note

The movement on the defined benefit plan during the year comprises the service cost component, the net interest component, and the remeasurement component. Remember that the remeasurement component is taken to other comprehensive income for the year – it is therefore not an item that should be adjusted for within operating activities. The cash contributions paid into the plan are presented in operating activities.

	$m
Opening balance at 1 December 20X1	22
Service cost component	16
Net interest component	2
Net remeasurement component gain for year (per OCI)	(8)
Contributions paid (bal. fig.)	(7)
	——
Closing balance at 30 November 20X2	25
	——

(b)   Indirect and direct method

The direct method presents separate categories of cash inflows and outflows whereas the indirect method is a reconciliation of profit before tax reported in the statement of profit or loss to the cash flow from operations. The adjustments include non-cash items in the statement of profit or loss plus operating cash flows that were not included in profit or loss.

A problem for users is the fact that entities can choose the method used. This limits comparability.

The majority of companies use the indirect method for the preparation of statements of cash flow. Most companies justify this on the grounds that the direct method is too costly.

Users often prefer the direct method because it reports operating cash flows in understandable categories, such as cash collected from customers, cash paid to suppliers, cash paid to employees and cash paid for other operating expenses. When presented in this way, users can assess the major trends in cash flows and can compare these to the entity's competitors.

The complicated adjustments required by the indirect method are difficult to understand and can be confusing to users. In many cases these adjustments cannot be reconciled to observed changes in the statement of financial position.

		Marking scheme	
			Marks
(a)	(i)	Acquisition of Tlgret – 1 mark per point	**7**
	(ii)	Profit before tax	1
		Finance costs	1
		Retirement benefit expense	1
		Depreciation on PPE	1
		Revaluation gain on investment property	1
		Profit on sale of land	1
		Impairment of goodwill	1
		Gain on Tigret	1
		Decrease in trade receivables	1
		Decrease in inventories	1
		Increase in trade payables	1
		Cash paid to defined benefit scheme	1
		Finance costs paid	1
		Income taxes paid	2
		Repayment of long-term borrowings	1
		Non-controlling interest dividend	1
		Dividends paid	1
			──
			27 max
			──
(b)		1 mark per point	**6**
Total			──
			30
			──

5   ZIPPY *Walk in the footsteps of a top tutor*

Key answer tips

In the Strategic Business Reporting exam, it is unlikely that you will be asked to produce full consolidated statements. The questions are more likely to involve explanation and/or the preparation of extracts. Students tend to find this harder, and often say that they are unsure what they need to write. It is therefore crucial to carefully debrief the answer to this question, and learn from the things that you missed. Remember, practice makes perfect.

(a)   (i)   Ginny

First nine months

Tutorial note

Don't jump straight to the disposal calculation. After all, Zippy did not dispose of the shares until nine months into the reporting period.

For the first nine months' of the year Zippy had control over Ginny and so Ginny was a subsidiary during this time. Zippy must consolidate Ginny's incomes and expenses and other comprehensive income (OCI) on a line-by-line basis for the first nine months' of the year.

Ginny made a profit of $32 million for the 12 month period so $24 million (9/12 × $32 million) of this must be consolidated. Of this $9.6 million ($24m × 40%) is attributable to the non-controlling interest.

Ginny recorded OCI of $16 million for the 12 month period so $12 million (9/12 × $16m) must be consolidated. Of this $4.8 million ($12m × 40%) is attributable to the non-controlling interest.

Loss of control

Tutorial note

Remember that not all share sales lead to a loss of control. If control is retained then no profit or loss arises and the transaction is instead accounted for in equity.

The share sale results in Zippy's holding in Ginny falling from 60% to 40% of the equity shares. Zippy has therefore lost control of Ginny. The difference between the proceeds from the disposal (including the fair value of the shares retained) and the goodwill, net assets and NCI of Ginny at the disposal date will give rise to profit or loss on disposal.

This is calculated as follows:

Tutorial note

It is important to remember the following proforma. It is worth a lot of marks.

	$m	$m
Proceeds		44
Fair value of remaining interest		62
		–––
		106
Goodwill at disposal (W1)	26	
Net assets at disposal (W2)	154	
Non-controlling interest at disposal (W3)	(66)	
	–––	
Carrying amount of sub at disposal		(114)
		–––
Loss on disposal		(8)
		–––

When preparing the consolidated statement of profit or loss, the gain of $14 million reported in Ginny's individual financial statements must be removed from investment income. The group will instead report an $8 million loss on disposal.

The remaining investment

Tutorial note

After a subsidiary disposal, students commonly forget to account for the remaining investment. Very easy marks can be scored here.

The remaining 40% investment in Ginny gives Zippy significant influence. As such, Ginny is an associate of Zippy and should be accounted for using the equity method. This means that the group recognises its share of the associate's profit after tax, and its share of the associate's OCI.

Tutorial note

Don't forget to account for the group's share of the associate's other comprehensive income.

The consolidated statement of profit or loss and OCI will show the following amounts:

	$m
Share of profits of associate (40% × 3/12 × $32m)	3.2
Share of other comprehensive income of associate (40% × 3/12 × $16m)	1.6

Workings

Tutorial note

Set out your workings clearly.

(W1) Goodwill at disposal

	$m
Fair value of consideration	90
Fair value of non-controlling interest	50
Fair value of identifiable net assets acquired	(114)
Goodwill	26

(W2) Net assets at disposal

Tutorial note

The question tells you the net assets of Ginny at the start of the year. You need to add on nine months' of total comprehensive income in order to work out the net assets at the disposal date.

	$m
Net assets at 1 July 20X5 –– per question	118
Profit to 31 March 20X6 (9/12 × $32m)	24
OCI to 31 March 20X6 (9/12 × $16m)	12
	154

(W3) NCI at disposal

Tutorial note

When working out the group profit or loss on disposal it is normally wise to leave the NCI at disposal until last. This is because the calculation requires the subsidiary's net assets at the disposal date.

	$m
Non-controlling interest at acquisition	50
NCI share of post-acquisition net asset movement (40% × ($154m (W2) – $114m))	16
	66

(ii)   Ten floor office block

Tutorial note

In this part of the question, there are more marks available for the discussion than for calculations.

IAS 40 *Investment Property* says that portions of a property can be classified as investment property if they can be sold or leased out separately from the rest of the building.

Property occupied by a subsidiary does not qualify as investment property in the consolidated financial statements, because it is being used by the group. The first two floors of Zippy's office block should therefore be classified as property, plant and equipment in the consolidated financial statements.

Depreciation of $1.2 million (($90m × 0.2)/15 years) should therefore be charged to administrative costs.

The first two floors should be revalued to $19.2 million ($96m × 0.2) in the statement of financial position. A revaluation gain should be recorded within other comprehensive income of $2.4 million ($19.2m – (($90m × 0.2) – $1.2m)).

The remaining eight floors qualify as investment property. Investment property measured at fair value is not depreciated. Fair value gains relating to investment properties are recorded in profit or loss.

These eight floors should be revalued to $76.8 million ($96m × 0.8) in the statement of financial position. A revaluation gain of $4.8 million will be recorded in investment income in the statement of profit or loss ($76.8m – ($90m × 0.8)).

Explosion

IAS 36 *Impairment of Assets* does not apply to investment property that is measured at fair value. Investment properties under the fair value model are simply restated to fair value with the gains and losses recorded in profit or loss.

The building should be revalued to $14 million and a $6 million loss ($20m − $14m) should be charged to investment income.

IAS 37 *Provisions, Contingent Liabilities and Contingent Assets* says that a provision should be recognised if there is an obligation from a past event that will lead to a probable outflow of economic benefits that can be measured reliably. The provision of $3 million should be reversed through other expenses as there is no obligation to carry out the repairs.

(iii) **Individual financial statements**

According to IFRS 10 *Consolidated Financial Statements,* consolidated financial statements present the parent and its subsidiaries as a single economic entity.

The second floor of the ten floor office block is being used by another group member. This means that it is being used within the single economic entity for administrative purposes. The second floor must therefore be classified as property, plant and equipment in the consolidated financial statements.

In the individual financial statements of Zippy, the second floor qualifies as an investment property because it is part of a building held to earn rental income (even though no rent is currently charged on the second floor).

As a result of this classification difference, the depreciation charge in the individual financial statements will be lower than in the consolidated financial statements. The carrying amount of investment properties will be higher than in the consolidated financial statements. The revaluation gain in OCI will be lower and the gain in profit or loss will be higher than in the consolidated financial statements.

(b) **Other comprehensive income**

Tutorial note

Other comprehensive income is a popular exam topic. Make sure that you are aware of current debates around its nature and use.

Profit or loss includes all items of income and expense except those which are recognised in other comprehensive income (OCI) as required or permitted by IFRS Standards.

The *Conceptual Framework* states that profit or loss in the primary source of information about the financial performance of an entity and so income and expenses are normally recognised in that statement. According to the *Conceptual Framework*, an income or expense is presented in other comprehensive if it results from remeasuring an item to current value and if it means that:

• profit or loss provides more relevant information, or

• a more faithful representation is provided of an entity's performance.

The Board makes decisions about OCI on a standard-by-standard basis, as these are revised or issued.

Income and expenditure included in other comprehensive income should be reclassified to profit or loss when doing so results in profit or loss providing more relevant information. Again these decisions are made on a standard-by-standard basis. The Board may decide that reclassification is not appropriate if there is no clear basis for identifying the amount or timing of the reclassification.

With regards to defined benefit pension schemes, the service cost is immediately recognised in profit or loss. The remeasurement component is recognised as other comprehensive income and presented as an item not to be reclassified to the profit or loss in the future. The remeasurement component comprises errors within actuarial assumptions about life expectancy, wage inflation, service lives as well as differences between actual and expected returns. It can be argued that there is no correlation between such items and the underlying performance of an entity, thus justifying the decision that this should never be reclassified to profit or loss.

That said, reclassification is criticised for adding unnecessary complexity to financial reporting and potentially enabling earnings management. Reclassification could be easily misunderstood as essentially the same gain gets reported twice, once within OCI and once within profit or loss. Additionally it is likely that there will be a mismatch on reclassification as the gains or losses may be reported in a different period to when the underlying change in value of the asset or liability took place.

Pensions and immediate recognition

Actuarial gains and losses vary significantly from one year to the next. Immediate recognition may create volatility within the statement of financial position and other comprehensive income. It is, however, important that users are fully aware as to the extent of an entity's pension scheme obligations. This may not be evident if there is a deferral of the remeasurement component. It can be argued therefore that the immediate recognition leads to greater transparency of the financial statements.

Marking scheme			
			Marks
(a)	(i)	Discussion – 1 mark per point	5
		Calculations	6
			11
	(ii)	Property discussion and calcs – 1 mark per point	8
	(iii)	Individual financial statements – 1 mark per point	4
(b)		OCI – 1 mark per point	7
Total			30

6 ASHANTI *Online question assistance*

Key answer tips

Parts (a) (i) and (ii) require you to explain the treatment of the share sales. Easy marks are available for your discussion – do not jump straight into calculations or you will miss these.

Present workings clearly. You can still score highly even if you get the wrong answer.

If you don't know how to deal with a specific number or a transaction then leave it out (or guess!). There is no negative marking.

(a) (i) Sale of shares in Bochem

Tutorial note

When dealing with the sale of shares in a subsidiary company, it is vital to establish whether or not the parent has lost control.

Ashanti's sale of shares in Bochem does not lead to a loss of control. Consequently there is no gain or loss to the group arising on this transaction and goodwill is not recalculated. Instead, the transaction is accounted for within equity, as an increase in the non-controlling interest (from 30% to 40%).

The non-controlling interest (NCI) in equity will be increased by $25.1 million (W1). The proceeds received from the sale exceed the increase in the NCI by $8.9 million (W1), and so other components of equity will be increased by this amount.

(W1) Control-to-control calculation

		$m
Proceeds of share disposal		34.0
Carrying amount of Bochem at sale date:		
Net assets (W2)	216.0	
Goodwill (80% × $44m)	35.2	
	–––––	
	251.2	
Change in NCI (10% × 251.2)		25.1
		–––––
Increase in OCE		8.9
		–––––

(W2) Net assets

	Acquisition date	Reporting date
	$m	$m
Equity shares	55	
Retained earnings	85	210
Other equity components	10	
FVA – plant (bal fig)	10	10
Dep'n ($10m/5 × 2 years)		(4)
	160	216

(ii)   Sale of shares in Ceram

Tutorial note

If control over a company is lost then a profit or loss on disposal must be calculated. Take time to memorise the proforma for calculating this profit or loss.

Ashanti controlled Ceram for the first 6 months of the year, and so will consolidate 6/12 of its revenues and costs.

Mid-way through the year, Ashanti has lost control over Ceram. At this point Ceram is derecognised from the consolidated statement of financial position and a gain or loss on disposal arises in the consolidated statement of profit or loss.

This is calculated as follows:

	$m	$m
Proceeds		90.0
Fair value of residual holding at disposal date		45.0
		135.0
Carrying amount of Ceram at disposal:		
Net assets at disposal	160.0	
Goodwill at disposal (W3)	6.2	
NCI at disposal	(35.0)	
		(131.2)
Profit on disposal		3.8

Tutorial note

Don't forget to discuss the treatment of the remaining shares.

The remaining 30% interest in Ceram gives Ashanti significant influence. Therefore, from this date, Ceram is an associate and is accounted for using the equity method. The consolidated statement of profit or loss will report profits from associates of $2.1 million (6/12 × $14m × 30%).

(W3) Goodwill calculation

	$m
Consideration	95.2
Fair value of NCI at acquisition	26.0
	121.2
Fair value of net assets at acquisition	(115.0)
Goodwill at acquisition/reporting date	6.2

(iii) Revenue and cost of sales

Tutorial note

Set out your workings clearly.

Revenue and cost of sales are calculated as follows:

Revenue

	$m
Ashanti	810
Bochem	235
Ceram ($142m × 6/12)	71
Intra-group (W5)	(15)
Sale to Spice (W6)	(5)
	1,096

Cost of sales

	$m
Ashanti	686
Bochem	137
Ceram ($84m × 6/12)	42
Depreciation (W4)	2
Intra-group (W5)	(15)
Unrealised profits (W5)	1
	———
	853

(W4) Depreciation

The fair value adjustment relating to Bochem's plant is $10 million (W2).

One year's worth of depreciation must be charged in the consolidated statement of profit or loss. This amounts to $2 million ($10m / 5 years).

Dr Cost of sales $2m

Cr Property, plant and equipment $2m

(W5) Intra-group trading

Tutorial note

Most consolidated profit or loss questions involve intra-group trading. Make sure that you are happy with the required adjustments because they are a source of easy marks.

Ashanti has sold goods to both Bochem and Ceram. Group revenue and cost of sales will need to be reduced by $15 million ($10m + $5m).

Dr Revenue $15m

Cr Cost of sales $15m

An adjustment is required to remove the unrealised profits within group inventory as a result of the sale to Bochem. The unrealised profits amount to $1 million ($10m × 20% × ½).

Dr Cost of sales $1m

Cr Inventory $1m

(W6) **Sale to Spice**

IFRS 15 *Revenue from Contracts with Customers* says that a contract with a customer should only be accounted for if:

- The parties have approved the contract

- Rights and obligations can be identified from the contract

- Payment terms can be identified

- The contract has commercial substance

- It is probable that the seller will collect the consideration they are entitled to

Based on the information available, it would seem that the final criterion was not met. Therefore, the contract cannot be accounted for and no revenue should have been recognised.

The revenue recognised by Ashanti on this date must be reversed:

Dr Revenue $5m

Cr Receivables $5m

(b) **Control**

Tutorial note

Start by stating the definition of control, as found in IFRS 10 Consolidated Financial Statements. Apply this definition to the scenario and reach an explicit conclusion about whether Ashanti will assume control over Night.

According to IFRS 10 *Consolidated Financial Statements*, an investor controls an investee if the investor has:

- power over the investee

- exposure, or rights, to variable returns from its involvement with the investee

- the ability to use its power over the investee to affect the amount of the investor's returns

When assessing whether control exists, the following should be considered:

- The size of the entity's holding compared to the size of the holding of other investors

- Whether the entity can direct the relevant activities of the investee (such as decisions about operations, capital expenditure, and the appointment and remuneration of key personnel)

- How dispersed the other shareholdings are

- Any potential voting rights (such as those arising from convertible instruments or options) held by the entity or by other entities

- Whether investors are related parties of one another, or if they have close business relationships.

A 49.9% holding is less than 50%, meaning that Ashanti will not have a controlling holding in the voting shares of Night. However, a 49.9% holding is very close to a majority shareholding.

One of the investors will have a holding of greater than 20%, which suggests significant influence. This might place doubt on the ability of Ashanti to control Night. However, IFRS 10 states that it is possible to control an entity when another investor has significant influence. Whilst the other shareholders could vote together as a block and therefore have the controlling vote, this is unlikely. This is because:

- The shareholdings are relatively dispersed

- The other investors do not have a close relationship with one another

- Based on past practice, it is likely that at least one of the other investors will not attend the Annual General Meeting, thus giving Ashanti the majority of the voting rights.

Ashanti controls the board of directors, thus enabling it to make key operating decisions that will affect the profits and returns of Night.

All things considered, it would seem that Ashanti will control Night. Night should therefore be accounted for as a subsidiary from the acquisition date.

Marking scheme			
			Marks
(a)	(i)	Discussion – 1 mark per point	3
		Calculations	3
			6
	(ii)	Discussion – 1 mark per point	4
		Calculations	4
			8
	(iii)	Pro-rating	1
		Intra-group	2
		PURP	1
		Depreciation	2
		Sale to Spice – narrative	2
		Sale to Spice – adjustment	1
			9
(b)		Control – 1 mark per point	7
Total			30

7   TRAILER *Walk in the footsteps of a top tutor*

Key answer tips

Parts (a) (i) and (ii) require you to discuss the treatment of financial reporting issues. Keep an eye on the clock, otherwise you will not have enough time to make a decent attempt at the rest of the question.

Part (a) (iii) asks you to prepare the equity section of the statement of financial position. The easiest way to do this would be to use the standard workings for a consolidated statement of financial position (W1 – W5). Don't forget about the adjustments you have proposed in your answer to the earlier parts of the question. Show all your workings – this will enable you to score highly even if you make a few mistakes.

In part (b), you need to talk about the impact of NCI measurement on the calculation of goodwill arising on the acquisition date as well as the impact on the goodwill impairment review.

(a)   (i)   Loan to charity

Tutorial note

The loan is a financial instrument because Trailer has a contractual right to receive cash.

IFRS 9 *Financial Instruments* says that financial assets should be recognised initially at fair value. According to IFRS 13 *Fair Value Measurement,* this is the selling price of an asset in an orderly transaction between market participants.

Market rate loans attract interest of 6%, whereas the loan advanced to the charity only attracts interest at 3%. As such, the price paid by Trailer of $50 million is not indicative of the asset's fair value. The fair value of the financial asset must therefore be determined. This can be achieved by calculating the present value of all future cash receipts using the prevailing market interest rate for a similar instrument.

Fair value of the financial asset

	Cash flows $m	Discount factor	Present value $m
20X3	1.5	$1/1.06$	1.4
20X4	1.5	$1/1.06^2$	1.3
20X5	51.5	$1/1.06^3$	43.3
			————
			46.0
			————

The financial asset should have been recognised at $46 million rather than $50 million. The $4 million difference between the fair value of the asset and the amount of cash advanced should have been recognised as an expense in profit or loss.

The correcting entry is:

Dr Profit or loss $4.0m

Cr Financial assets $4.0m

The financial asset is then measured at amortised cost because, as per IFRS 9, Trailer intends to hold it the asset to maturity to collect the contractual cash flows. Interest is credited to profit or loss using the effective rate. Cash receipts reduce the carrying amount of the asset.

1 June 20X2	Interest credit (6%)	Cash received	31 May 20X3
$m	$m	$m	$m
46.0	2.8	(1.5)	47.3

The cash receipt has been correctly accounted for. The correcting entry should therefore be:

Dr Financial assets $2.8m

Cr Profit or loss $2.8m

(ii) **Provision for restructuring**

Tutorial note

Remember the criteria for recognising a provision. All three of the criteria must be met before a provision can be recognised.

According to IAS 37 *Provisions, Contingent Liabilities and Contingent Assets*, a provision is recognised if:

- there is an obligation from a past event

- an outflow of economic benefits is probable

- the outflow can be measured reliably.

The first plan has been communicated to those directly affected, creating a constructive obligation to incur expenditure on the restructuring.

IAS 37 says that costs can only be included in a restructuring provision if they result directly from, and are necessarily entailed by, a restructuring. This includes costs such as employee redundancy costs. Expenses that relate to ongoing activities, such as relocation and retraining, are excluded. With regard to the first plan, a provision should be recognised for the redundancy costs of $14 million.

The adjustment required is:

Dr Profit or loss $14m

Cr Provisions $14m

In contrast, Trailer should not recognise a provision for the finance and IT department's re-organisation. The re-organisation is not due to start for two years. External parties are unlikely to have a valid expectation that management is committed to the re-organisation as the time frame allows significant opportunities for management to change the details of the plan or even to decide not to proceed with it. Additionally, identification of the staff that will lose their jobs is not sufficiently detailed to support the recognising of a redundancy provision.

(iii)   **Extract from consolidated Statement of Financial Position at 31 May 20X3**

	$m
Equity attributable to owners of parent	
Share capital	1,750.0
Retained earnings (W5)	1,209.6
Other components of equity (W5)	140.0
	————
	3,099.6
Non-controlling interest (W4)	833.2
	————
Total equity	3,932.8
	————

Workings

(W1) Group structure

Trailer

60%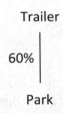

Park

(W2) Net assets

Tutorial note

If you are told the fair value of the net assets of the subsidiary at acquisition then you can calculate the fair value adjustments using a balancing figure approach.

	Acq'n date $m	Rep date $m
Share capital	1,210	1,210
Other components	55	80
Retained earnings	650	930
Fair value adjustment – plant (bal. fig)	35	35
Depreciation ($35m/7)		(5)
	1,950	2,250

Of the $300 million ($2,250m – $1,950m) post-acquisition net asset movement, $25 million ($80m – $55m) relates to other components of equity and $275 million ($300m – $25m) relates to retained earnings.

(W3) Goodwill

Tutorial note

Goodwill needs to be calculated so that an impairment review can be performed.

	$m
Fair value of consideration	1,250
NCI at acquisition (40% × $1,950m)	780
Fair value of identifiable net assets acquired (W2)	(1,950)
Goodwill at acquisition	80

(W4) Non-controlling interest

Tutorial note

There are easy marks available here as long as you know your standard workings.

	$m
NCI in Park at acquisition (W3)	780
NCI % of post-acquisition net assets (40% × $300m (W2))	120
Impairment of other assets (40% × $167m (W6))	(66.8)
	833.2

(W5) Reserves

Retained earnings

Tutorial note

Any adjustments to the statement of profit or loss will impact retained earnings.

	$m
Trailer	1,240
Park: 60% × $275m (W2)	165
Impairment of goodwill (W6)	(80)
Impairment of other assets (60% × $167m (W6))	(100.2)
Financial asset write down (part a (i))	(4.0)
Interest credit (part a (i))	2.8
Restructuring provision (part a (ii)	(14)
	1,209.6

Other components of equity

	$m
Trailer	125
Park: 60% × $25m (W2)	15
	140

(W6) Impairment of Park

Tutorial note

In note 2 of the question, we are told the recoverable amount of the net assets of Park. We therefore need to compare this to the carrying amount of Park's net assets.

Remember that goodwill has been calculated using the proportionate basis. This means that, when performing an impairment review, the goodwill must be grossed up to include the NCI's interest.

	$m	$m
Goodwill (W3)	80	
Notional NCI ($80m × 40/60)	53.3	
	———	
Total notional goodwill		133.3
Net assets at reporting date (W2)		2,250
		———
Total carrying amount of assets		2,383.3
Recoverable amount		(2,083.0)
		———
Impairment		300.3
		———

The impairment is firstly allocated to the total notional goodwill of $133.3m. However, only 60% of the total notional goodwill has been recognised in the statements and therefore only 60% ($80m) of the impairment is accounted for. This expense is all attributable to the owners of Trailer.

The remaining impairment of $167m ($300.3m – $133.3m) is allocated against the other assets of Park in proportion to their carrying amounts. This impairment loss is attributable to the owners of the Trailer and the NCI based on their respective shareholdings.

(b)   **Impact of measuring the NCI at air value**

Tutorial note

When calculating goodwill in this part of the question, you will not be penalised for any mistakes that you made in part (a).

*Remember that goodwill calculated under the fair value method **does not** need grossing up when performing an impairment review.*

Goodwill calculation

	$m
Fair value of consideration	1,250
Fair value of NCI	800
Fair value of identifiable net assets acquired (W2)	(1,950)
Goodwill at acquisition	100

Goodwill impairment review

	$m
Goodwill	100
Net assets at reporting date (W2)	2,250
Total carrying amount	2,350
Recoverable amount	(2,083)
Impairment	267

Allocated to:	
Goodwill	100
Other assets	167
Total	267

Under the previous method used by Trailer, the NCI was recognised at its share of the subsidiary's net assets and so did not include any goodwill. The full goodwill method means that non-controlling interest and goodwill are both increased by the goodwill that relates to the non-controlling interest.

In the case of Park, measuring the NCI at its fair value increases the goodwill arising at acquisition from $80 million to $100 million. The figure used for NCI under the proportionate method of $780m has also increased by $20 million, to $800m at 1 June 20X2.

KAPLAN PUBLISHING

The full goodwill method increases reported net assets, and so any impairment of goodwill will be greater. Thus in the case of Park, the impairment of goodwill will be $100m. This will be charged $60 million to retained earnings and $40 million to the NCI. Under both methods, the impairment of the other assets is $167 million, which is split between retained earnings and the NCI.

Although measuring non-controlling interest at fair value may prove difficult, goodwill impairment testing is easier under full goodwill. This is because there is no need to gross up goodwill.

Marking scheme				Marks
(a)	(i)	Discussion – 1 mark per point		3
		Calculations		3
				———
				6
				———
	(ii)	Discussion – 1 mark per point		**5**
				———
	(iii)	Share capital		1
		NCI		2
		Retained earnings		4
		Fair value adjustment		1
		Goodwill calculation		1
		Goodwill impairment		2
		Other components of equity		1
				———
				12
				———
(b)		NCI discussion – 1 mark per point		4
		Goodwill calculation		1
		Impairment calculation		2
				———
				7
				———
Total				**30**
				———

8   WESTON *Walk in the footsteps of a top tutor*

Key answer tips

Read the question carefully and you should be able to find several figures that you can put straight into your cash flow extracts (e.g. the associate's profits, the service cost component, and depreciation). Prioritise these quick, easy marks – they are essential to pass the exam.

(a) (i) **Weston Group Statement of cash flows for year ended 31 January 20X6**

	$m
Cash flow from operating activities	
Profit before tax (W1)	189
Associate's profits	(16)
Service cost component	11
Depreciation	20
Impairment of goodwill (W5)	6
Cash contributions to pension scheme	(19)
Movements in working capital	
Increase in trade and other payables ($36m – $41m + $10m)	5
Increase in trade and other receivables ($106m – $104m + $23m)	(25)
Decrease in inventories ($108m – $165m + $38m)	19
Cash generated from operations	190
Income taxes paid (W7)	(81)
	109
Cash flows from investing activities	
Purchase of property, plant and equipment (W8)	(84)
Dividends received from associate (W6)	4
Purchase of associate (W6)	(90)
Net proceeds on disposal of Northern (W2)	87.4
	(82.6)

Workings

(W1) Profit

Tutorial note

You need to use the profit before tax from both continuing and discontinued operations.

Total profit before tax is:

	$m
Profit before tax – continuing operations	183
Profit before tax – discontinued operations	6
	189

(W2) Proceeds on disposal of Northern

Tutorial note

The question tells you the loss on the disposal of the subsidiary and gives you enough information to calculate the goodwill, net assets and non-controlling interest at the disposal date. You then need to work backwards, to deduce the cash proceeds received from the subsidiary disposal.

	$m
Cash proceeds from sale (bal. fig.)	85.4
Goodwill at disposal (W3)	(9)
Fair value of net assets at disposal (W4)	(129)
Non-controlling interest at disposal (W4)	23.6
Loss on disposal (per question)	(29)

The net cash impact of the disposal is therefore $87.4 million ($85.4m proceeds + $2m overdraft disposed).

(W3) Goodwill – Northern

Tutorial note

Goodwill calculations are a source of easy marks.

	$m
Consideration	132
Fair value of non-controlling interest	28
	160
Identifiable net assets at acquisition	(124)
Goodwill on acquisition	36
Impairment of goodwill (75%)	(27)
Carrying amount of goodwill at disposal	9

(W4) Net assets and NCI at disposal

Tutorial note

The question gives you the carrying amount of the net assets in Northern's individual financial statements. However, this will not include the fair value uplift that arises on consolidation, or the deferred tax on this uplift.

The carrying amount of the property, plant and equipment at disposal will be $80m, as per the question, plus $16 million fair value uplift less 4/8 depreciation. This amounts to $88 million.

The deferred tax liability recorded on the fair value uplift would have been $4 million (25% × $16m). This will have been released in line with the extra depreciation, so the carrying amount at disposal will be only $2 million ($4m − ($4m × 4/8)). The carrying amount of the entire deferred tax liability at disposal is therefore $8m ($6m per question + $2m above).

The revised carrying amounts at disposal are:

	$m
Property, plant and equipment	88
Inventory	38
Trade receivables	23
Trade and other payables	(10)
Deferred tax	(8)
Bank overdraft	(2)
	–––
	129
	–––

The non-controlling interest in Northern at disposal will be:

	$m
Non-controlling interest at acquisition	28
NCI share of post-acquisition net assets (20% × ($129m − $124m))	1
NCI share of goodwill impairment (20% × $27m) (W3)	(5.4)
	–––
	23.6
	–––

(W5) Goodwill

Tutorial note

Reconcile goodwill year-on-year to identify the impairment charge. This needs to be added back to profit when calculating cash generated from operations.

	$m
Balance at 1 February 20X5	19
Disposal of subsidiary (W3)	(9)
Impairment (bal. fig.)	(6)
Balance at 31 January 20X6	4

(W6) Associate

Tutorial note

Lots of students forget that dividends received from an associate reduce the carrying amount of the group's investment.

	$m
Balance at 1 February 20X5	–
Share of associate profit	16
Dividend received ($10m × 40%)	(4)
Cost of acquisition (bal.fig.)	90
Balance at 31 January 20X6	102

(W7) Taxation

Tutorial note

Deferred tax can be charged to profit or loss, or to other comprehensive income. Don't forget the tax charge relating to the discontinued operation (note (ii) in the question).

	$m
Balance at 1 February 20X5 ($15m + $92m)	107
Charge for year – continuing	40
Charge for year – discontinued	2
Deferred tax at disposal (W4)	(8)
Deferred tax on remeasurement gain (25% × $4m)	1
Cash paid (bal. fig.)	(81)
Balance at 31 January 20X6 ($14m + $47m)	61

Tutorial note

Since the actuarial gain of $4m would be recorded in other comprehensive income, the deferred tax on the actuarial gain of $1m (25% × $4m) will also be in other comprehensive income. Any remaining movement in the deferred tax on the pension will be included within the charge to profit or loss for the year.

(W8) Property, plant and equipment

	$m
Balance at 1 February 20X5	413
Disposal of subsidiary (W4)	(88)
Depreciation charge	(20)
Cash additions (bal. fig.)	84
Balance at 31 January 20X6	389

(ii)   The indirect method

IAS 7 *Statement of Cash Flows* states that the indirect method of calculating cash generated from operations involves adjusting the profit (or loss) for the period for the effects of:

- changes in inventories, payables and receivables

- non-cash items

- items which relate to investing or financing.

With regards to Weston:

- Associate's profits – undistributed profits of an associate are not a cash flow and so must be deducted from the group's profit before tax. Moreover, an associate is a type of investment rather than a part of the entity's operating activities and so any cash flows with associate entities are reported within 'cash flows from investing activities'.

- Service cost, depreciation and impairment – these are non-cash expenses and so are eliminated by adding them back to profit.

- Movements in working capital – businesses buy and sell goods on credit, but only cash receipts and cash payments should be reported in the statement of cash flows. Adjusting for the movement in working capital items eliminates the impact of accruals accounting. In the current year. Some of the year-on-year movement in working capital relates to the disposal of Northern, rather than because of cash flows with customers and suppliers, and so the effect of this disposal has been eliminated.

(b)   Associates

Tutorial note

This part of the question deals with application of knowledge relating to circumstances when significant influence or control may be exercised. You should state and apply relevant definitions within your answer. As the question requirement is for a discussion, you should try to consider all relevant circumstances, and try to avoid writing a 'one-sided' justification of your conclusion.

According IAS 28 *Investments in Associates and Joint Ventures,* significant influence is the power to participate in the financial and operating decisions of the investee but is not control or joint control over the policies.

Where an investor holds 20% or more of the voting power of the investee, it is presumed that the investor has significant influence unless it can be clearly demonstrated that this is not the case. If the investor holds less than 20% of the voting power of the investee, it is presumed that the investor does not have significant influence, unless such influence can be clearly demonstrated.

One investor holding a majority share of the voting power can indicate that other investors do not have significant influence. However, a substantial or majority ownership by an investor does not, however, necessarily preclude other investors from having significant influence.

IAS 28 states that the existence of significant influence by an investor is usually evidenced in one or more of the following ways:

- representation on the board of directors or equivalent governing body of the investee
- participation in the policy-making process
- material transactions between the investor and the investee
- interchange of managerial personnel; or
- provision of essential technical information.

Application to Weston

Weston will hold less than 20% of the voting power so it might be concluded that significant influence does not exist. However, its holding of 19.9% is only just below this threshold. Moreover there are other circumstances that suggest Weston will be able to exercise significant influence.

The shareholders' agreement will allow Weston to participate in some decisions. It needs to be determined whether these include financial and operating policy decisions of Manair, although this is very likely. The representation on the board of directors combined with the additional rights Weston will have under the shareholders' agreement, will give Weston the power to participate in some policy decisions. Additionally, Weston will send a team of management experts to give business advice to the board of Manair.

There are likely to be material transactions between the investor and the investee as Weston will provide Manair with maintenance and technical services. This is another way in which significant influence can be evidenced.

Based on an assessment of all the facts, it appears that Weston will have significant influence over Manair. This means that Manair will most likely constitute an associate and so should be accounted for using the equity method.

Marking scheme		
		Marks
(a)(i)	Cash flows from operating activities	
	Profit	1
	Associate's profit	1
	Pension scheme service cost	1
	Depreciation	1
	Goodwill impairment	1
	Working capital movements	3
	Tax paid	2
	Pension contributions	1
	Cash flows from investing activities	
	Property, plant and equipment	1
	Associate dividend	1
	Purchase of associate	1
	Disposal of Northern	4
		18
(ii)	Indirect method	**5**
(b)	Significant influence discussion – 1 mark per point	**7**
Total		**30**

9   JOEY *Walk in the footsteps of a top tutor*

Key answer tips

Remember to allocate your time carefully when attempting question 1. It would be very easy to get bogged down in a particular issue or adjustment and to then run out of time. Spend your time on the areas of the question that you are most confident with.

(a)   (i)   **Hulty**

Tutorial note

Consideration transferred in a business combination and the identifiable net assets of the subsidiary at the acquisition date should both be measured at fair value. If you struggle to think about the double entries required for these adjustments then think about how you would process them through the standard consolidation workings and what impact this would have on the SFP balances.

Deferred consideration

IFRS 3 *Business Combinations* says that the consideration transferred to achieve control over another business must be measured at fair value. Deferred consideration should be measured at its present value.

The present value of the deferred consideration as at 1 December 20X3 was $41.3 million ($50m × 1/1.10^2$). Goodwill should be increased by this amount and a corresponding liability recognised. The correcting entry is:

Dr Goodwill $41.3m

Cr Liabilities $41.3m

Tutorial note

Don't forget to unwind the discount on the liability.

Interest on the liability should be charged to profit or loss in the year. This amounts to $4.1 million ($41.3m × 10%$). The entry to record this in the consolidated statement of financial position is:

Dr Retained earnings $4.1m

Cr Liabilities $4.1m

Franchise right

IFRS 3 *Business Combinations* says that the identifiable net assets of a subsidiary should be measured at fair value at the acquisition date.

The fair value of the identifiable net assets exceeds their carrying amounts by $20 million ($980m − $960m). This relates to an unrecognised intangible franchise right that must be recognised in the consolidated financial statements as at the acquisition date. This adjustment reduces the amount of goodwill recognised. The correcting adjustment is:

Dr Intangible asset – franchise right	$20m
Cr Goodwill	$20m

The intangible asset should be amortised over its remaining useful life. The current year charge that needs to be recorded in consolidated profit or loss is $5 million ($20m/4 years). The franchise right is an asset held by the subsidiary, so the charge in profit or loss should be allocated between the owners of the parent company and the non-controlling interest based on their respective shareholdings. The entry required to record this in the consolidated statement of financial position is:

Dr Retained earnings ($5m × 80%)	$4m
Dr NCI ($5m × 20%)	$1m
Cr Intangible asset – franchise right	$5m

Total goodwill arising on Hulty

Total goodwill arising on the acquisition of Hulty is therefore $61.3 million ($40m draft + $41.3m − $20m).

(ii) **Margy**

Step acquisition

Joey has achieved control over Margy in stages. On the date that control was achieved the previous shareholding should been included in the goodwill calculation at its fair value. Any gain or loss on revaluing this shareholding to fair value is recorded in the consolidated statement of profit or loss.

The equity accounted investment in Margy of $700 million should therefore have been eliminated and included in the goodwill calculation at its fair value of $705 million. A $5 million gain would arise in consolidated profit or loss.

This adjustment means that the gain on bargain purchase of $655 million is eliminated. The adjusting entry required in the statement of financial position is:

Dr Retained earnings (to remove gain on bargain purchase)	$655m
Dr Goodwill ($705m − $655m)	$50m
Cr Investment in associate	$700m
Cr Retained earnings (gain on step acquisition)	$5m

Building adjustment

During the measurement period, the acquirer must retrospectively adjust the amounts recognised at the acquisition date if further facts and information are obtained. The measurement period ends 12 months after the acquisition date.

The revision of the building's fair value at the acquisition date was determined within 12 months of the business combination so it must therefore be adjusted for as at the acquisition date. This will reduce the amount of property, plant and equipment (PPE) in the consolidated statement of financial position and will increase the goodwill arising on the acquisition of Margy. The adjustment required is:

Dr Goodwill	$40m
Cr PPE	$40m

If the building is worth less than originally estimated then it increases the risk that Joey overpaid for Margy and therefore that goodwill might be impaired. However, no information is provided about this.

Tutorial note

It is common in exams to have to charge depreciation on a fair value uplift. However, if a building was over-valued as at the acquisition date then it is likely that the depreciation subsequently charged is also too high.

The property, plant and equipment has been included in the consolidated financial statements at $200 million, rather than $160 million, and so too much depreciation will have been charged. Depreciation of $2 million ($40m/20 years) must be removed from consolidated profit or loss. The PPE is held by a subsidiary and so this adjustment must be allocated to the owners of the parent and the non-controlling interest based on their respective shareholdings. The adjustment required in the consolidated statement of financial position is:

Dr PPE	$2m
Cr Retained earnings ($2m × 70%)	$1.4m
Cr NCI ($2m × 30%)	$0.6m

Total goodwill arising on Margy

Total goodwill arising on the acquisition of Margy is therefore $90 million ($50m + $40m).

(iii) **Joint arrangement**

Tutorial note

A joint arrangement is an arrangement over which two or more parties have joint control. Remember that joint arrangements may take the form of joint operations or joint ventures. A joint venture, which normally involves the establishment of a separate entity, is accounted for using the equity method.

For the period to 31 May 20X4, the requirement for unanimous key strategic decisions means this is a joint arrangement. Since there is no legal entity, it would be classified as a joint operation. Joey should therefore account for its direct rights to the underlying results and assets.

Up until 31 May 20X4, the joint operation had the following results:

	$m
Revenue (5m × 6/12)	2.5
Cost of sales (2m × 6/12)	(1.0)
Gross profit	1.5

The amount that belongs to CP is therefore:

	$m
10% × Sales (10% × 2.5m)	0.25
30% of gross profit 30% × $1.5m)	0.45
Amount due to CP	0.7

Joey has recorded all of the sales proceeds and costs for the six month period, hence recording a profit of $1.5 million. Joey's profits must therefore be reduced by $0.7 million, and a payable to CP recorded for the same amount. The adjustment required is:

Dr Profit or loss	$0.7m
Cr Accounts payable CP	$0.7m

Tutorial note

The question requires you to 'discuss'. Easier marks are available for the narrative part of your answer.

From 1 June 20X4, Joey has a share of the net assets of the joint arrangement rather than direct rights. This means that the joint arrangement would be classified as a joint venture and must be accounted for in the consolidated financial statements using the equity method.

Joey has accounted for all proceeds and costs of the joint venture. This should be removed from its statement of profit or loss and a payable recorded to transfer this back to JCP

Dr Profit or loss	$1.5 m
Cr Payable to JCP	$1.5 m

Joey should then equity-for its share of JCP's profit of $0.75 million ($1.5m × 50%). This will be recorded in profit or loss and recognised as an investment in the statement of financial position.

Dr Investment in joint venture	$0.75 m
Cr Profit or loss	$0.75 m

(b) (i) Debt and equity

Tutorial note

This is a very common exam requirement. You must memorise the definition of a financial liability.

IAS 32 *Financial Instruments: Presentation* says that a financial liability is a contractual obligation to deliver either cash or another financial asset to the holder. Equity is any contract which evidences a residual interest in the entity's assets after deducting all of its liabilities.

However, a contract may involve the delivery of the entity's own equity instruments. A contract which will be settled by the entity delivering a fixed number of its own equity instruments in exchange for cash or another financial asset is an equity instrument. If there is any variability in the number of own equity instruments to be delivered then the contract is a financial liability.

B shares

The B shares should be classified as equity because there is no contractual obligation to pay the dividends or to redeem the instrument. Dividends can only be paid on the B shares if dividends have been declared on the A shares. However, there is no contractual obligation to declare A share dividends.

Share options

The classification of the share options is dependent on whether there is variability in the number of equity shares delivered. Joey will settle the contract by issuing a fixed number of its own equity instruments in exchange for cash, so the share options would be classified as an equity instrument.

(ii)   Discussion paper

In the discussion paper, the Board propose to classify a financial instrument as a liability if it exhibits one of the following characteristics:

- 'An unavoidable contractual obligation to transfer cash or another financial asset at a specified time other than liquidation, and/or

- An unavoidable contractual obligation for an amount independent of the entity's available economic resources' (DP/2018/1: IN10).

B shares

Under the terms of the B shares, all cash payments are avoidable. This is because the shares are not mandatorily redeemable, and dividends are not payable unless they are paid on A shares. As such, under the proposals, the B shares will still be classified as equity.

Share options

Joey will be issuing a fixed number of its own shares. As such, it is not transferring a financial asset, but equity. Moreover, the obligation to transfer a fixed number of shares means that Joey is promising the option holders a pro-rata share of its net assets on liquidation. The amount that this is worth is dependent on Joey's available economic resources after all economic claims have been settled. As such, under the proposals, the share options would still be classified as equity.

Marking scheme			Marks
(a)	(i)	Hulty – 1 mark per point	8
	(ii)	Margy – 1 mark per point	8
	(iii)	CP – 1 mark per point	6
(a)	(i)	IAS 32 classifications	4
	(ii)	Discussion paper classifications	4
Total			30

10   PARSLEY *Walk in the footsteps of a top tutor*

Key answer tips

Part (a) focusses on group accounting issues. Parsley lost control of Sage during the year. Sage is therefore consolidated until the disposal date and a profit or loss on disposal must be calculated. Saffron is an overseas subsidiary, which must be translated into the group's presentation currency. Exchange differences on the retranslation of Saffron's opening net assets, profit and goodwill are recorded in other comprehensive income.

(a) **Group structure**

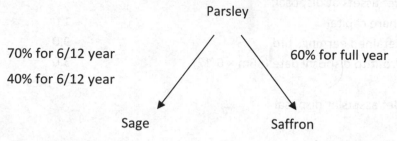

Parsley

70% for 6/12 year

40% for 6/12 year

60% for full year

Sage   Saffron

(i) **Sage**

Tutorial note

Memorise the proforma for calculating the profit or loss arising on the disposal of a subsidiary. This can be worth a lot of marks in the exam.

Parsley lost control over Sage halfway through the year. This means that Parsley must consolidate the line-by-line results of Sage for the first 6 months of the year.

Sage made a profit for the year of $6 million, of which Parsley will consolidate $3 million ($6 million × 6/12). Of this, $2.1 million ($3 million × 70%) is attributable to the equity owners of the Parsley group and the remaining $0.9 million is attributable to the non-controlling interest.

A profit or loss on the disposal of Sage must be reported in the consolidated statement of profit or loss.

This is calculated as follows:

	$m	$m
Proceeds from disposal	6.5	
Fair value of interest retained	9.5	
		16.0
Goodwill disposed:		
Consideration	6.0	
NCI at acquisition ($5m × 30%)	1.5	
Net assets at acquisition	(5.0)	
Goodwill at disposal		(2.5)

	$m	$m
Net assets at disposal:		
Share capital	1.0	
Retained earnings bfd	9.0	
Profit to disposal date ($6m × 6/12)	3.0	
Net assets at disposal		(13.0)
NCI at disposal:		
NCI at acquisition	1.5	
NCI % of post-acquisition net assets ($30\% \times (\$13m - \$5m)$)	2.4	
		3.9
Profit on disposal		4.4

After the share sale, Parsley retains significant influence over Sage. This means that Sage is an associate for the final six months of the year and must be accounted for using the equity method. The group will show its share of the associate's profit as a single line in the consolidated statement of profit or loss. This amounts to $1.2 million ($6m × 6/12 × 40%).

(ii) **Saffron**

Profit or loss

IFRS 3 *Business Combinations* says that the identifiable net assets of a subsidiary should be consolidated at fair value. It would seem that Saffron has a brand that is unrecognised in its individual financial statements but which must be consolidated at its fair value.

The fair value of this brand is calculated as follows:

	FRm
Fair value of net assets	70
Carrying amount of net assets	(60)
Fair value of brand	10

Amortisation must be charged on the brand. In the current period, this will be FR2 million (FR10m/5 years).

Saffron is an overseas subsidiary. Its results, including the above amortisation adjustment, must be translated for inclusion in the consolidated statement of profit or loss and other comprehensive income at the average rate. The results of Saffron will then be consolidated line-by-line. The net impact on consolidated profit will be $6.1 million ((FR30 per P/L − FR2 amortisation)/4.6)). Of this $3.7 million ($6.1m × 60%) is attributable to the equity owners of the parent. The remaining $2.4 million is attributable to the non-controlling interest.

Goodwill impairment and foreign exchange

Tutorial note

Calculate goodwill in the subsidiary's currency and then translate it at the closing rate. The foreign exchange gain or loss is recorded in other comprehensive income, as an item that may be reclassified to profit or loss in the future.

The goodwill of Saffron is calculated as follows:

	FRm
Cost of acquisition	71
FV of NCI at acquisition	29
	100
Less FV net assets at acquisition	(70)
Goodwill at acquisition	30
Impairment	(4)
Goodwill at reporting date	26

Goodwill is translated at the reporting date at the closing rate. This gives rise to a foreign exchange gain, calculated below:

FX gain on retranslation	FRm	Rate	$m
Acquisition	30	5.0	6.0
Impairment	(4)	4.6	(0.9)
FX gain on retranslation		**Bal fig**	**1.4**
Rep date	26	4.0	6.5

The impairment of $0.9 million is recorded in profit or loss. Of this, $0.5 million ($0.9m × 60%) is attributable to the equity owners of the parent. The remaining $0.4 million is attributable to the non-controlling interest.

The gain of $1.4 million is recorded in other comprehensive income. The forex gain attributable to the equity owners of the parent is $0.8 million ($1.4m × 60%) and the remaining $0.6 million is attributable to the non-controlling interest.

Foreign exchange gain on opening net assets and profit

A foreign exchange gain arises on the translation of Saffron's opening net assets and profit:

	FRm	Rate	$m
Opening net assets	70	5.0	14.0
Profit (FR30m – FR2m (W1))	28	4.6	6.1
FX gain on retranslation		**Bal fig**	**4.4**
	——		——
Rep date	98	4.0	24.5
	——		——

The gain of $4.4 million is recorded in other comprehensive income. The forex gain attributable to the equity owners of the parent is $2.6 million ($4.4m × 60%) and the remaining $1.8 million is attributable to the non-controlling interest.

(iii) **Lease**

Tutorial note

To determine the accounting entries in the second year of the lease you will need to determine the carrying amounts of the lease liability and right-of-use asset at the end of the first year.

The year ended 30 April 20X3

IFRS 16 *Leases* says that lease liabilities are recognised at the present value of payments yet to be made. This includes fixed lease payments, as well as variable payments based on the relevant index or rate at the start of the lease. The liability is reduced by cash payments. Interest on the liability increases its carrying amount and is charged to profit or loss.

A right-of-use asset is recognised at the value of the initial lease liability plus payments made before or at commencement and initial direct costs. Assuming the cost model is chosen, the asset is depreciated over the lower of the lease term and its remaining useful economic life.

In the prior year, the right of use asset would have been recognised at $5 million ($3.8m + $1.2m). The depreciation charge in the prior year would have been $1 million ($5m/5 years), and the carrying amount of the asset at the end of the prior year was, therefore, $4 million.

The lease liability would have been recorded at $3.8 million. Interest of $0.38 million ($3.8m × 10%) would have been charged to profit or loss. As such, the liability at 30 April 20X3 was $4.18 million ($3.8m + $0.38m).

The year ended 30 April 20X4

Tutorial note

Remember that you are asked to provide an 'explanation'. Calculations and double entries are not enough to score a high mark.

If changes to lease payments occur then the liability must be recalculated and adjusted. A corresponding entry is made against the carrying amount of the right-of-use asset.

Based on inflation for the last 12 months, the lease payments now due each year are $1.3 million ($1.2m × 108%).

The revised liability is calculated as follows:

	Cash ($m)	Disc.	PV ($m)
1/5/20X3	1.3	1	1.30
1/5/20X4	1.3	$1/1.10^1$	1.18
1/5/20X5	1.3	$1/1.10^2$	1.07
1/5/20X6	1.3	$1/1.10^3$	0.98
Revised liability			4.53

The lease liability must be increased from $4.18 million to $4.53 million. The entry required is:

Dr Right-of-use asset	$0.35m
Cr Lease liability	$0.35m

After this adjustment, the right-of use asset is held at $4.35 million ($4m + $0.35m). Depreciation for the year ended 30 April 20X4 is $1.09 million ($4.35m/4 years).

Dr Depreciation expense	$1.09m
Cr Right-of-use asset	$1.09m

The carrying amount of the right-of use asset at the year-end is $3.26 million ($4.35m – $1.09m).

The current year cash repayment has been incorrectly charged to profit or loss.

Dr Lease liability	$1.3m
Cr Cost of sales	$1.3m

Interest on the outstanding lease liability is $0.32 million (($4.53m – $1.3m) × 10%).

Dr Finance costs	$0.32m
Cr Lease liability	$0.32m

The carrying amount of the lease liability at the year-end is $3.55 million ($4.53m – $1.3m + $0.32m).

(b) IAS 24 *Related Party Disclosures* states that a person or a close member of their family is related to the reporting entity if that person:

- has control, joint control or significant influence over the reporting entity

- is a member of key management personnel of the reporting entity or its parent.

The main circumstances that lead to an entity being related to the reporting entity are as follows:

- the entity and the reporting entity are members of the same group

- one entity is an associate or joint venture of the other

- both entities are joint ventures of the same third party

- the entity is controlled or jointly controlled by a person who is a related party of the reporting entity.

In the absence of related party disclosures, users of financial statements would assume that an entity has acted independently and in its own best interests. Most importantly, they would assume that all transactions have been entered into willingly and at arm's length (i.e. on normal commercial terms at fair value). Where related party relationships and transactions exist, this assumption may not be justified.

Related party relationships and transactions may distort financial position and performance, both favourably and unfavourably. The most obvious example of this type of transaction would be the sale of goods from one party to another on non-commercial terms.

It is a common misapprehension that related party transactions need only be disclosed if they are not on market terms. This is not the case. For example, a parent may instruct all members of its group to buy certain products or services (on commercial terms) from one of its subsidiaries. If the parent were to sell the subsidiary, it would be important for the prospective buyer to be aware that the related party transactions would probably not occur in the future.

Even where there have been no related party transactions, it is still important for some related party relationships to be disclosed. A subsidiary may obtain custom, receive favourable credit ratings, and benefit from a superior management team simply by being a part of a well-respected group. As such, an entity must always disclose information about its parent.

Marking scheme			
			Marks
(a)	(i)	Sage – 1 mark per point	8
	(ii)	Saffron – 1 mark per point	8
	(iii)	Lease – 1 mark per point	8
(b)		Related parties – 1 mark per point	6
Total			**30**

11   MARCHANT   *Walk in the footsteps of a top tutor*

Key answer tips

When producing a consolidated statement of profit or loss and other comprehensive income it is important to understand the group structure. Marchant disposed of shares in Nathan but did not lose control. Therefore, Nathan's incomes and expenses must be consolidated for the full year and no profit or loss on disposal is recorded in the group's financial statements. However, Marchant lost control over Option half way through the year. This means that Option's incomes and expenses must be consolidated for the first 6 months and then a profit on disposal calculated. Marchant retained significant influence over Option, so must account for the remaining holding using the equity method for the second half of the year.

(a)   (i)   Marchant Group: Statement of profit or loss and other comprehensive income for the year ended 30 April 20X4

Tutorial note

If a subsidiary has been disposed of during the year, remember to consolidate its income and expenses up to the disposal.

When producing a statement of profit or loss, you need to split profit and total comprehensive income for the period between the owners of the parent and the non-controlling interest.

	$m
Revenue ($400 + $115 + (6/12 × $70) − $12 (W6))	538.0
Cost of sales ($312 + $65 + (6/12 × $36) − $12 (W6))	(383.0)
Gross profit	155.0
Other income ($21 + $7 + (6/12 × $2) − $5.3 (W3))	23.7
Administrative costs ($15 + $9 + (6/12 × $12)	(30.0)
Other expenses ($35 + $19 + (6/12 × $8) + $5 (W2))	(63.0)
Operating profit	85.7
Share of profits of associates (20% × (6/12 × $15))	1.5
Profit on disposal of subsidiary (W4)	22.0
Finance costs ($5 + $6 + (6/12 × $4))	(13.0)
Finance income ($6 + $5 + (6/12 × $8))	15.0
Profit before tax	111.2
Income tax expense ($19 + $9 + (6/12 × $5)	(30.5)
Profit for the year	80.7

	$m
Other comprehensive income:	
Items which will not be reclassified to profit or loss	
Changes in revaluation surplus ($10 + $2 –$5 (W3))	7.0
Total comprehensive income for the year	87.7
Profit attributable to:	
Owners of the parent (bal. fig.)	70.1
Non-controlling interest (W7)	10.6
	80.7
Total comprehensive income attributable to:	
Owners of the parent (bal. fig.)	76.3
Non-controlling interest (W7)	11.4
	87.7

Workings

(W1) Group structure

Marchant

60% for full year   60% for 6/12 of year
8% disposal on last day   20% for 6/12 of year

Nathan   Option

(W2) Nathan's goodwill

Tutorial note

Remember, impairments recorded against goodwill can never be reversed.

	$m
Fair value of consideration	80
Fair value of non-controlling interest	45
	125
Fair value of identifiable net assets acquired	(110)
Goodwill at acquisition	15
Impairment (20%)	(3)
Goodwill	12

Goodwill has been increased to $17 million ($15m + $2m). However, impairments recorded against goodwill are not allowed to be reversed. Therefore, $5 million ($17m – $12m) must be charged to profit or loss to reduce goodwill to the correct amount of $12 million.

(W3) Disposal of shares in Nathan

Tutorial note

Control over Nathan has not been lost. Therefore, no profit or loss on disposal should be recorded in the consolidated financial statements.

A profit on disposal will have been recorded in the individual accounts of Marchant, calculated as follows:

	$m
Proceeds	18.0
Carrying amount of investment disposed (8/60 × $95m)	(12.7)
	———
Profit	5.3
	———

This profit on disposal must be removed from other income. There will be no profit or loss on disposal in the consolidated financial statements because control over the subsidiary has not been lost.

The current year gain on the investment in Nathan of $5 million ($95m – $90m) must also be removed from other comprehensive income.

(W4) Disposal of Option

Tutorial note

If control over an investment has been lost, a profit or loss on disposal must be calculated and included in the consolidated statement of profit or loss. This calculation is normally worth a lot of marks so it is important to learn the proforma.

As Marchant has sold a controlling interest in Option, a gain or loss on disposal should be calculated. Additionally, the results of Option should only be consolidated in the statement of profit or loss and other comprehensive income for the six months to 1 November 20X3. Thereafter Option should be accounted for using the equity method.

The gain recognised in profit or loss would be as follows:

	$m	$m
Fair value of consideration		50
Fair value of residual interest		40
		90
Less carrying amount of subsidiary:		
Net assets at disposal	90	
Goodwill at disposal (W5)	12	
Non-controlling interest at disposal	(34)	
		(68)
Gain on disposal to profit or loss		22

(W5) Goodwill of Option

Tutorial note

Goodwill calculations are a source of easy marks. Make sure that you know the proforma.

	$m
Fair value of consideration	70
Fair value of non-controlling interest	28
Fair value of identifiable net assets acquired	(86)
Goodwill	12

(W6) Intra-group sale

Tutorial note

Intra-group trading must be eliminated from consolidated revenue and costs of sales. Any unrealised profits should also be eliminated by increasing cost of sales. However, if a loss is made on intra-group trading, it may suggest that the value of the goods have fallen and therefore that the loss is actually realised.

The loss on the sale of the inventory is not eliminated from group profit or loss. Because the sale is at fair value, the inventory value must have been impaired and therefore the loss on sale must remain realised. However, the revenue and cost of sales of $12 million will be eliminated.

(W7) Profit and TCI attributable to the NCI

Tutorial note

When calculating the NCI's share of Nathan's profit and TCI, it is important to think about the date of the share disposal. The 8% holding of Nathan was not sold to the NCI until the very last day of the year. Therefore, when the profits and OCI of Nathan were earned, the NCI share was 40% rather than 48%.

	Nathan	Option
	$m	$m
Profit (6/12 Option)	19.0	7.5
× NCI % (40%)	7.6	3.0

The total profit attributable to the NCI is therefore $10.6 million ($7.6m + $3.0m).

	Nathan	Option
	$m	$m
TCI (6/12 Option)	21.0	7.5
× NCI % (40%)	8.4	3.0

The TCI attributable to the NCI is therefore $11.4 million ($8.4m + $3.0m).

(ii)   Sale of shares in Nathan

Tutorial note

If control over an investment is retained, then a profit or loss on disposal is not included in the consolidated financial statements. Instead, equity is adjusted.

*Note that part (ii) asks you to **explain** how the sale of the shares will be treated. Calculations are not enough to score full marks.*

Once control has been achieved, transactions whereby the parent entity acquires further equity interests from non-controlling interests, or disposes of equity interests without losing control, are accounted for as equity transactions.

Therefore:

- the carrying amount of the non-controlling interests is adjusted to reflect the changes in its interest in the subsidiary

- any difference between the amount by which the non-controlling interests is adjusted and the fair value of the consideration paid or received is recognised directly in equity attributed to the owners of the parent; and

- there is no consequential adjustment to the carrying amount of goodwill, and no gain or loss is recognised in profit or loss or in other comprehensive income.

Sale of equity interest in Nathan

	$m
Fair value of consideration received	18
Increase in non-controlling interest	
($120m net assets + fair value adjustment of $14m (see below) + $12m goodwill) × 8%)	
	(11.7)
Positive movement in parent equity	6.3

The fair value adjustment at acquisition is calculated as follows:

	$m
Share capital	25
Retained earnings	65
Other components of equity	6
Fair value adjustment (bal. fig.)	14
Fair value of net assets	110

(b)   Derecognition

Tutorial note

Start your answer by stating the de-recognition rules from IFRS 9. You would not be expected to know the same level as detail as is provided below.

Derecognition is required if either:

- the contractual rights to the cash flows from the financial asset have expired, or

- the financial asset has been transferred, and the transfer of that asset is eligible for derecognition.

An asset is transferred if the entity has transferred the contractual rights to receive the cash flows.

Once an entity has determined that the asset has been transferred, it then determines whether or not it has transferred substantially all of the risks and rewards of ownership of the asset. If substantially all the risks and rewards have been transferred, the asset is derecognised. If substantially all the risks and rewards have been retained, derecognition of the asset is precluded.

Tutorial note

Now apply the rules that you have stated to the information in the scenario.

Marchant has transferred its rights to receive cash flows. However, it has guaranteed that it will compensate the bank up to $3.6 million. As such, it has retained credit risk associated with the asset.

Additionally, Marchant would seem to have some late payment risk as it will be charged interest on amounts received over $3.6 million.

It would seem that Marchant has not transferred substantially the risks associated with the receivable. Therefore the receivables of $4 million should still be re-instated in the financial statements. Marchant should recognise a liability of $3.6 million for the cash proceeds received and remove the charge of $0.4 million from profit or loss.

Marking scheme		Marks
(a)	Consolidation	1
	Pro-rating of Option	1
	Intra-group trade	2
	Goodwill impairment adjustment	3
	Removal of gain on Nathan	2
	Removal of OCI gain	1
	Gain on disposal of Option	3
	Goodwill calculation for Option	1
	Associate	2
	NCI	2
	Sale of equity interest in Nathan	5
		23
(b)	IFRS 9 *Financial Instruments* derecognition – 1 mark per point	7
Total		30

12 ANGEL *Walk in the footsteps of a top tutor*

Key answer tips

Students generally dislike statements of cash flows. However, there are lots of easy marks available because many of the cash flows do not require any workings – find these in the question and slot them straight into your proforma. Think about whether the figures need brackets – you will lose marks if you get this wrong.

To answer part (b) it is essential to know the definition of a 'cash equivalent'. State this definition and then apply it to each of the two deposits in the question.

(a) Statement of cash flows for the year ended 30 November 20X3

	$m
Profit before tax	188
Adjustments to operating activities	
Finance costs	11
Associate's profit	(12)
Depreciation	29
Financial assets – profit on sale ($40m – $26m)	(14)
Profit on sale of PPE ($63m – $49m)	(14)
Impairment of goodwill and intangible assets (W2)	116.5
Retirement benefit expense (W6)	10
	———
	314.5
Movements in working capital	
Decrease in trade receivables ($125m – $180m – $3m)	58
Decrease in inventories ($155m – $190m – $6m)	41
Decrease in trade payables ($155m – $361m – $4m)	(210)
	———
Cash generated from operations	203.5
Cash paid to retirement benefit scheme (W6)	(9)
Interest paid	(11)
Income taxes paid (W5)	(135.5)
	———
Net cash generated by operating activities	48
	———

	$m
Cash flows from investing activities	
Sale of financial assets	40
Purchase of financial assets	(57)
Purchase of property, plant and equipment (W1)	(66)
Purchase of subsidiary ($30m – $2m)	(28)
Proceeds from sale of property, plant and equipment	63
Dividend received from associate (W4)	3
Purchase of associate (W4)	(71)
Net cash flows used by investing activities	(116)
Cash flows from financing activities	
Proceeds from issue of shares (SOCIE)	225
Repayment of long-term borrowings ($26m – $57m)	(31)
Dividends paid (SOCIE)	(10)
Dividend paid to non-controlling interests (SOCIE)	(6)
Net cash generated by financing activities	178
Net increase in cash and cash equivalents	110
Cash and cash equivalents at beginning of period	355
Cash and cash equivalents at end of period	465

Workings

(W1) Property, plant and equipment

	$m
Balance at 1 December 20X2	465
Disposals	(49)
Depreciation	(29)
Revaluation	8
Acquisition of sub	14
Purchase of PPE (bal. fig.)	66
Balance at 30 November 20X3	475

(W2) Impairments

Tutorial note

Reconcile the goodwill balance year-on-year to find the impairment charge. This is a non-cash expense so must be added back in the reconciliation between profit before tax and cash generated from operations.

	$m
Opening balance at 1 December 20X2	120.0
Current year amount on subsidiary (W3)	11.5
Impairment (bal. fig.)	(26.5)
Closing balance at 30 November 20X3	105.0

Impairments of other intangibles amount to $90m ($240m – 150m).

Total impairments are therefore $116.5m ($90m + $26.5m).

(W3) Purchase of subsidiary

Tutorial note

The subsidiary's identifiable net assets are consolidated at fair value. This means that their carrying amount in the consolidated financial statements differs from their tax base, normally giving rise to a deferred tax liability.

Calculation of deferred tax arising on acquisition:

	$m
Fair values of Sweety's identifiable net assets excluding deferred tax	20.0
Less tax base	(15.0)
Temporary difference arising on acquisition	5.0
Net deferred tax liability arising on acquisition (30% × $5m)	1.5

Calculation of goodwill:	
Purchase consideration	30.0
Fair value of net assets (net of deferred tax)	(20.0)
Deferred taxation	1.5
Goodwill arising on acquisition	11.5

(W4) Associate

Tutorial note

Associates are accounted for using the equity method.

	$m
Balance at 1 December 20X2	nil
Profit for period	12
Dividend received ($10m × 30%)	(3)
Cost of acquisition (bal. fig.)	71
Balance at 30 November 20X3	80

Therefore, cash paid for the investment is $71 million, and the cash dividend received is $3 million.

(W5) Taxation

Tutorial note

When calculating the tax paid during the year, include the opening and closing deferred tax balances in your workings. Also, remember that deferred tax charges may have been recorded in other comprehensive income.

	$m
Balance at 1 December 20X2 ($31m + $138m)	169
Charge for year (P/L)	46
Deferred tax on acquisition (W3)	1.5
Tax on revaluation PPE	2
Tax on financial assets	1
Cash paid (bal. fig.)	(135.5)
Balance at 30 November 20X3 ($35m + $49m)	84

(W6) Retirement benefit

Tutorial note

The service cost component and net interest component are non-cash expenses. These must be added back to profit in the reconciliation between profit before tax and cash generated from operations.

	$m
Opening balance at 1 December 20X2	74
Remeasurement component	4
Current year service cost plus interest	11
Contributions paid	(9)
Closing balance at 30 November 20X3	80

The $11 million service cost and interest figure above includes the carrying amount of the subsidiary's defined benefit obligation at the acquisition date. Therefore, the actual expense is $10m ($11m – $1m). This is added back in the reconciliation between profit before tax and cash generated from operations.

(b) Cash and cash equivalents comprise cash in hand and demand deposits, together with short-term, liquid investments which are readily convertible to a known amount of cash and which are subject to an insignificant risk of changes in value. IAS 7 *Statement of Cash Flow* does not define 'short term' but does state 'an investment normally qualifies as a cash equivalent only when it has a short maturity of, say, three months or less from the date of acquisition'.

Consequently, equity or other investments which do not have a maturity date are normally excluded from cash equivalents.

Tutorial note

Remember to apply the definition of 'cash equivalents' to the scenario.

As regards the deposits, the following is the case:

(i) Although the principal ($3 million) will be recoverable with early withdrawal, the entity will lose all accumulated interest over the term, which seems to be a significant penalty. The cash is not needed to meet short-term cash commitments and so would not qualify as a cash equivalent.

(ii) Although the deposit is stated to have a 12-month maturity period, it can be withdrawn with 21 days' notice. Although this incurs a penalty, the reduction in the rate of interest from 3% to 2% is unlikely to be considered significant and is in line with the bank's short-term deposit rate. The intention of management is to keep these funds available for short-term cash needs and so this deposit is likely to qualify as a cash equivalent.

	Marking scheme		
			Marks
(a)	Finance costs		1
	Associate's profit		1
	Depreciation		1
	Profit on disposal of PPE/financial assets		1
	Impairment of intangibles		2
	Pension expense		1
	Working capital movements		3
	Cash paid to pension		1
	Interest paid		1
	Tax paid		2
	Sale and purchase of financial asset		1
	Purchase of PPE		2
	Purchase of subsidiary		1
	Proceeds from PPE disposal		1
	Dividend from associate		1
	Purchase of associate		1
	Proceeds from shares		1
	Borrowings		1
	Dividends paid		1
	Dividends paid to NCI		1
	Net movement in cash		1
			⎯⎯
			26
		Maximum	25
			⎯⎯
(b)	Cash and cash equivalents – 1 mark per point		5
			⎯⎯
Total			**30**
			⎯⎯

13 TRAVELER *Walk in the footsteps of a top tutor*

Key answer tips

This is a good question for testing your knowledge of a number of consolidation issues. In particular, this group uses both the share of net assets method and the fair value method to value the non-controlling interest at acquisition. This has important implications for subsequent goodwill impairments – goodwill calculated under the share of net asset method must be grossed up to include the non-controlling interest's share when performing an impairment review.

This question also involves the parent company increasing its shareholding in a subsidiary from 60% to 80%. Goodwill is calculated on the date that control is achieved and is not re-calculated. Instead, this increase in the group's shareholding is accounted for in equity.

(a) **Consolidated Statement of Financial Position at 30 November 20X1**

	$m
Assets:	
Non-current assets:	
Property, plant and equipment (W8)	1,845
Goodwill (W3)	69.2
Financial assets ($108m + $10m + $20m)	138
Current assets ($1,067m + $781m + $350m)	2,198
Total assets	**4,250.2**
Equity and liabilities	
Equity attributable to owners of parent	
Share capital	1,120
Retained earnings (W5)	1,058
Other components of equity (W5)	91.7
	2,269.7
Non-controlling interest (W4)	343.5
	2,613.2
Total non-current liabilities ($455m + $323m + $73m)	851.0
Current liabilities ($274m + $199m + $313m)	786.0
Total liabilities	**1,637.0**
Total equity and liabilities	**4,250.2**

Workings

(W1) Group structure

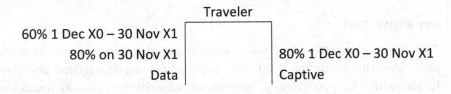

(W2) Net assets

Tutorial note

The identifiable net assets of a subsidiary are consolidated at fair value. Make sure that fair value adjustments are processed through your net asset workings.

Data

	Acq'n date	Rep date
	$m	$m
Share capital	600	600
Retained earnings	299	442
Other Equity	26	37
Fair value adjustment – Land (bal. fig)	10	10
	935	1,089

Of the net asset movement of $154 million ($1,089m – $935m), $11 million ($37m – $26m) relates to other components of equity and the remaining $143 million relates to retained earnings.

Captive

	Acq'n date	Rep date
	$m	$m
Share capital	390	390
Retained earnings	90	169
Other Equity	24	45
Fair value adjustment – Land (bal. fig)	22	22
	526	626

Of the net asset movement of $100 million ($626m – $526m), $21 million ($45m – $24m) relates to other components of equity and the remaining $79 million relates to retained earnings.

(W3) Goodwill

Tutorial note

Pay attention to whether the NCI at acquisition is being measured at its share of the subsidiary's identifiable net assets or at fair value.

Remember that goodwill is calculated at the date control is achieved over another company. It is not recalculated for any further share purchases.

Data

	$m
Fair value of consideration for 60% interest	600
Fair value of non-controlling interest	395
Fair value of identifiable net assets acquired (W2)	(935)
Goodwill at acquisition	60
Impairment (W6)	(50)
Goodwill at reporting date	10

Captive

	$m
Fair value of consideration	541
NCI at acquisition ($526 × 20%)	105.2
Less fair value of identifiable net assets (W2):	(526)
Goodwill	120.2
Impairment (W6)	(61)
	59.2

Total goodwill at the reporting date is $69.2m ($10 + $59.2).

The assets transferred as part of the consideration need to be removed from non-current assets, and the gain on disposal needs to be calculated. The sale consideration of $64 million has been recorded in profit. The carrying amount of the asset is $56 million, giving a gain on disposal of $8 million. The adjustment required to arrive at the gain is:

Dr Retained earnings (W5) $56m

Cr PPE (W8) $56m

(W4) Non-controlling interest

	$m
NCI in Data at acquisition (W3)	395
NCI % of Data's post acquisition net assets (40% × $154m (W2))	61.6
Reduction in NCI (W7)	(228.3)
Impairment of Data goodwill (W6)	(10)
NCI in Captive:	
NCI in Captive at acquisition (W3)	105.2
NCI % of Captive's post-acquisition net assets (20% × $100m (W2))	20.0
	343.5

(W5) Reserves

Retained earnings

	$m
Traveler	1,066.0
Sale of non-current asset (W3)	(56.0)
Impairment of Data goodwill (W6)	(40)
Impairment of Captive goodwill (W6)	(61)
Post-acquisition retained earnings:	
Data (60% × $143m (W2))	85.8
Captive (80% × $79m (W2))	63.2
	1,058

Other components of equity

	$m
Traveler	60.0
Data (60% × $11m (W2))	6.6
Captive (80% × $21m (W2))	16.8
Positive movement in equity (W7)	8.3
	91.7

(W6) Impairment of goodwill

Tutorial note

Pay close attention to whether the non-controlling interest has been valued using the share of net assets method or the fair value method.

If the share of net assets method has been used, then only the goodwill attributable to the parent has been calculated. When performing an impairment review, this goodwill must be notionally grossed up to include the NCI's share.

Data

	$m
Goodwill (W3)	60
Identifiable net assets (W2)	1,089
Total	1,149
Recoverable amount	(1,099)
Goodwill impairment	50

The goodwill impairment relating to Data will be split 80%/20% between the group and the NCI. Thus retained earnings will be debited with $40 million (W5) and NCI with $10 million (W4).

Tutorial note

It could be argued that a 60:40 allocation between group and NCI is also appropriate as this was how profits that arose in the year have been apportioned and the impairment is a loss that arose in the year, albeit calculated at the year end.

Captive

	$m	$m
Goodwill (W3)	120.2	
Notional NCI ($120.2 × 20/80)	30.1	
Total notional goodwill		150.3
Identifiable net assets (W2)		626.0
Total		776.3
Recoverable amount		(700.0)
Impairment		76.3

The impairment is allocated to the notional goodwill. However, only 80% of the notional goodwill has been recognised in the consolidated statements and so only 80% of the impairment is accounted for. This means that the goodwill impairment recognised is $61m ($76.3 × 80%). This expense is all attributable to the group and therefore retained earnings (W5) must be debited with $61m.

(W7) Increase in shareholding

Tutorial note

If the group increases its shareholding in a subsidiary, goodwill is not recalculated. Instead, this transaction is accounted for in equity. The difference between the cash paid and the decrease in the NCI is recorded in other components of equity.

	$m	$m
Fair value of consideration		220
NCI in Data at acquisition (W4)	395	
NCI % of Data's net assets movement (W4)	61.6	
	─────	
NCI per share purchase	456.6	
	─────	
Reduction in NCI (20/40 × $456.6m)		228.3
		─────
Positive movement in equity (W5)		8.3
		─────

(W8) Property, plant and equipment

	$m
Traveler	439
Data	810
Captive	620
Increase in value of land – Data (W2)	10
Increase in value of land – Captive (W2)	22
Less disposal of asset (W3)	(56)
	─────
	1,845
	─────

(b) IFRS 8 *Operating Segments* does not prescribe how centrally incurred expenses and central assets should be allocated to segments. The standard does, however, require that amounts be allocated on a reasonable basis.

Different bases can be appropriate for each type of cost. For example

- The head office management costs could be allocated on the basis of turnover or net assets.

- The pension expense could be allocated on the number of employees or salary expense of each segment.

- The costs of managing properties could be allocated on the basis of the type, value and age of the properties used by each segment.

The standard does not require allocation of costs to be on a consistent basis. An entity may allocate interest to a segment profit or loss but does not have to allocate the related interest-bearing asset to the segment assets or liabilities.

IFRS 8 requires the information presented to be the same basis as it is reported internally, even if the segment information does not comply with IFRS Standards or the accounting policies used in the consolidated financial statements. Examples of such situations include segment information reported on a cash basis (as opposed to an accruals basis), and reporting on a local GAAP basis for segments that are comprised of foreign subsidiaries. Although the basis of measurement is flexible, IFRS 8 requires entities to provide an explanation of:

- the basis of accounting for transactions between reportable segments

- the nature of any differences between the segments' reported amounts and the consolidated totals.

In addition, IFRS 8 requires reconciliations between the segments' reported amounts and the consolidated financial statements.

Marking scheme		Marks
(a)	Property, plant and equipment	2
	Goodwill	3
	Other assets/liabilities	2
	Share capital	1
	Retained earnings	5
	Other components of equity	3
	Non-controlling interest	4
		23
(b)	Operating segment costs – 1 mark per point	7
Total		30

14   ROSE *Walk in the footsteps of a top tutor*

Key answer tips

This question involves consolidating an overseas subsidiary.

When consolidating a subsidiary with a different functional currency to that of the group, its assets and liabilities are translated at the closing exchange rate. Translation differences arise on goodwill and the opening net assets and profit of the subsidiary. Current year exchange differences are recorded in other comprehensive income. The cumulative exchange gains and losses are held in equity.

This question also involves the parent company increasing its shareholding in a subsidiary from 70% to 80%. This results in a decrease in the NCI holding from 30% to 20%, a decline of one third. Such transactions are accounted for within equity and no adjustments are made to goodwill.

(a)   **Rose plc**

Consolidated Statement of Financial Position at 30 April 20X1

Assets	
Non-current assets	$m
Property, plant and equipment (W11)	633
Goodwill ($16m + $6.2m) (W3)	22.2
Intangible assets ($4m – $1m) (W2)	3
Current assets ($118m + $100m + D330m/5)	284
Total assets	942.2
Equity and liabilities:	
Share capital	158
Retained earnings (W5)	267.37
Translation reserve (W7)	10.27
Other components of equity (W6)	4.73
Non-controlling interest (W4)	89.83
Total equity	530.2
Non-current liabilities	130
($56m + $42m + D160m/5)	
Current liabilities ($185m + $77m + D100m/5)	282
Total equity and liabilities	942.2

Workings

(W1) Group structure

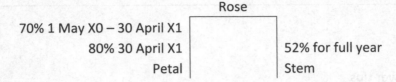

	Rose	
70% 1 May X0 – 30 April X1		
80% 30 April X1		52% for full year
Petal		Stem

(W2) Net assets

Tutorial note

The identifiable net assets of a subsidiary at acquisition are recognised at fair value. Make sure that fair value adjustments are processed through your net asset workings.

Petal

	Acq'n date	Rep date
	$m	$m
Share capital	38	38
Other equity	3	4
Retained earnings	49	56
FV adjustment – land (bal. fig)	30	30
	———	———
FV of recognised net assets	120	128
FV adjustment – patent	4	4
Amortisation ($4m/4 years)	–	(1)
	———	———
FV of identifiable net assets	124	131
	———	———

Of the net asset increase of $7 million ($131m – $124m), $1 million ($4m – $3m) relates to other components of equity and the remaining $6 million relates to retained earnings.

Stem

	Acq'n date	Rep date
	Dinars m	Dinars m
Share capital	200	200
Other equity	–	–
Retained earnings	220	300
FV adjustment – land (bal. fig)	75	75
	———	———
	495	575
	———	———

The net asset increase of D80 million (D575m – D495m) all relates to retained earnings because Stem has no other components of equity.

(W3) Goodwill

> **Tutorial note**
>
> *Goodwill is calculated on the date control is achieved. It is not recalculated when further share purchases are made.*
>
> *Goodwill in an overseas subsidiary should be translated each year at the closing exchange rate.*

Petal

	$m
Fair value of consideration	94
Fair value of NCI at acquisition	46
Fair value of identifiable net assets acquired (W2)	(124)
Goodwill	16

Stem

	Dinars m
Fair value of consideration ($46m × 6 (acquisition rate))	276
Fair value of NCI at acquisition	250
Fair value of identifiable net assets acquired (W2)	(495)
Goodwill	31

Goodwill is deemed to be an asset of the subsidiary and is translated at the closing rate at each reporting date.

Goodwill in Stem is therefore $6.2m (D31m/5).

(W4) Non-controlling Interest

	$m
Petal at acquisition (W3)	46
NCI % of post-acquisition net assets (30% × ($131m – $124m)) (W2)	2.1
Reduction in NCI due to share purchase (W10)	(16.03)
Stem at acquisition (D250m/6) (W3)	41.67
NCI % of post-acquisition net assets (48% × D80m/5.8) (W2)	6.62
Exchange gain – goodwill (W8)	0.49
Exchange gain on net assets (W9)	8.98
	89.83

(W5) Retained earnings

	$m
Rose	256
Rose's share of post-acquisition retained earnings:	
Petal (70% × $6m) (W2)	4.2
Stem (52% × D80m/5.8) (W2)	7.17
	————
	267.37
	————

(W6) Other components of equity

	$m
Rose	7
Petal – negative movement in equity (W10)	(2.97)
Share of Petal's post-acquisition other components	0.7
(70% × $1m) (W2)	
	————
	4.73
	————

(W7) Translation reserve

	$m
Exchange gain on goodwill (W8)	0.54
Exchange gain on net assets (W9)	9.73
	————
	10.27
	————

(W8) Exchange gain on Stem's goodwill

Tutorial note

If goodwill is calculated using the fair value method, the exchange gain or loss (and any impairment) must be apportioned between the group and the NCI.

	Dinars m	Exchange rate	$m
Goodwill at 1 May 20X0 (W3)	31	6.0	5.17
Impairment	–	5.8	–
Exchange gain (bal. fig)	–		1.03
	———		———
Goodwill at 30 April 20X1	31	5.0	6.2
	———		———

The exchange gain is allocated between the group and the NCI as follows:

Group: $1.03m × 52% = $0.54m (W7)

NCI: $1.03m × 48% = $0.49m (W4)

(W9) Exchange gain on Stem's opening net assets and profit

Tutorial note

Exchange gains or losses arising on the opening net assets and profit of an overseas subsidiary must be apportioned between the group and the NCI.

	Dinars m	Exchange rate	$m
Net assets at 1 May 20X0 (W2)	495	6.0	82.5
Profit for the year (W2)	80	5.8	13.79
Exchange gain (bal. fig)	–		18.71
Net assets at 30 April 20X1 (W2)	575	5.0	115.0

The exchange gain on the opening net assets and profit is allocated between the group and the NCI as follows:

Group: $18.71m × 52% = $9.73m (W7)

NCI: $18.71m × 48% = $8.98m (W4)

(W10) Increase in ownership

Tutorial note

Goodwill is not recalculated when the group increases its shareholding in a subsidiary. Instead, the difference between the consideration for the additional shares and the reduction in the NCI is accounted for in other components of equity.

	$m
Fair value of consideration	19
Reduction in NCI in Petal (10/30 × ($46m + $2.1m) (W4))	(16.03)
Negative movement (debit) in equity	2.97

(W11) Property, plant and equipment

	$m
Rose	385
Petal	117
Stem (D430m/5)	86
Petal fair value adjustment (W2)	30
Stem fair value adjustment (D75m/5) (W2)	15
	633

(b)   Foreign exchange

Tutorial note

To score highly, this question requires a detailed knowledge of IAS 21. However, solid marks can still be obtained for demonstrating a basic understanding of the standard.

Monetary items

Monetary items are units of currency held and assets and liabilities to be received or paid in a fixed or determinable number of units of currency. This would include foreign bank accounts, receivables, payables and loans. Non-monetary items are other items which are in the statement of financial position, such as non-current assets, inventories and investments in equity.

Monetary items are retranslated using the closing exchange rate (the year-end rate). The exchange differences on retranslation of monetary assets must be recorded in profit or loss. IAS 21 *The Effects of Changes in Foreign Exchange Rates* is not specific under which heading the exchange gains and losses should be classified.

Non-monetary items

Non-monetary items which are measured in terms of historical cost in a foreign currency are translated using the exchange rate at the date of the transaction. If non-monetary items are measured at fair value in a foreign currency then this amount must be translated using exchange rates at the date when the fair value was measured. Exchange differences on such items are recorded consistently with the recognition of the movement in fair values. For example, exchange differences on an investment property, a fair value through profit and loss financial asset, or arising on impairment will be recorded in profit or loss. Exchange differences on the upwards revaluation of property, plant and equipment would be recorded in other comprehensive income.

Overseas subsidiaries

When translating a foreign subsidiary, the exchange differences on all the net assets, including goodwill, are recorded in other comprehensive income and are held in equity. The proportion belonging to the shareholders of the parent will usually be held in a separate translation reserve. The proportion belonging to the non-controlling interest is not shown separately but subsumed in the non-controlling interest figure in the consolidated financial statements.

If Rose were to sell all of its equity shares in Stem, the cumulative exchange differences belonging to the equity holders of Rose will be reclassified from equity to profit or loss. In addition, the cumulative exchange differences attributable to the non-controlling interest would be derecognised but would not be reclassified to profit or loss.

Marking scheme		Marks
(a)	Amortisation of patent	1
	Acquisition of further interest	5
	Stem – translation and calculation of goodwill	6
	Retained earnings and other equity	4
	Non-controlling interest	3
	Property, plant and equipment	2
	Other assets/liabilities	1
		───
		22
		───
(b)	Currency issues – 1 mark per point	8
Total		30
		───

SECTION A QUESTIONS – REPORTING AND ETHICAL IMPLICATIONS

15 FISKERTON (DEC 2018) *Walk in the footsteps of a top tutor*

Key answer tips

Read the question properly. Part (a) has three requirements: discuss the accounting treatment of the building, explain the impact on the financial statements, and explain the impact on debt covenants. You will miss out on valuable marks if you only discuss the correct accounting treatment.

Part (b) tests revenue recognition. To answer this you need to know the criteria for when revenue is recognised over time.

Nearly half of the available marks in this question are allocated tor ethics (part (c)). Do not neglect this. Make sure that your answer details with the specific accounting issues in the question, and the specific ethical principles that have been breached.

(a) Accounting treatment

According to IFRS 16 *Leases*, the lease is a finance lease. This is because the lease term is equal to the useful life and its residual value is deemed to be minimal. As such, the property should not be held as an investment property but instead derecognised. The fair value gain of $8 million must be reversed. Fiskerton should record a lease receivable equal to the net investment in the lease.

Tutorial note

If the lease was an operating lease then the property should have been presented as an investment property. Rental income would be recognised in profit or loss on a straight line basis.

Note that the fair value gains were incorrectly calculated since adjustments should have been made for the differences between the Halam building and the one sold due to the different location and quality of the materials between the two buildings.

Tutorial note

IFRS 13 Fair Value Measurement states that fair value is the price received when an asset is sold in an orderly transaction between market participants at the measurement date. When deciding on a sale/purchase price, participants would factor in the condition and location of an asset and any restrictions on its use.

A more accurate reflection of fair value would have $22 million.

Impact on financial statements

Tutorial note

Easy marks are available for recalculating the gearing ratio.

The incorrect treatment has enabled Fiskerton to remain within its debt covenant limits. Gearing per the financial extracts is currently around 49.8% (50/(10 + 20.151 + 70.253)). Fair value gains on investment properties are reported within profit or loss. Retained earnings would consequently be restated to $62.253 million ($70.253m − $8m). Gearing would subsequently become 54.1% (50/10 + 20.151 + 62.253). Furthermore, retained earnings would be further reduced by correcting for rental receipts. These presumably have been included in profit or loss rather than deducted from the net investment in the lease. This would in part be offset by interest income which should be recorded in profit or loss at the effective rate of interest.

After correcting for these errors, Fiskerton would be in breach of its debt covenants. They have a negative cash balance and would appear unlikely to be able to repay the loan. Serious consideration should therefore be given as to whether Fiskerton is a going concern. If it is determined that Fiskerton is not a going concern then non-current assets and non-current liabilities should be reclassified to current and recorded at their realisable values.

Tutorial note

According to IAS 1 Presentation of Financial Statements, going concern uncertainties must be disclosed in the financial statements.

If Fiskerton can renegotiate with the bank then the uncertainties surrounding their ability to continue to trade must be disclosed.

(b) **Revenue**

Tutorial note

Do not simply recite the five steps of the revenue recognition model. A lot of this is irrelevant to answering the question. The requirement asks you about the timing of revenue recognition – so only the fifth step is relevant.

Make sure that you know the criteria for recognising revenue over time.

According to IFRS 15 *Revenue from Contracts with Customers*, at the inception of the contract, Fiskerton must determine whether its promise to construct the asset is a performance obligation satisfied over time.

During the production of the asset Fiskerton only has rights to the initial deposit and has no enforceable rights to the remaining balance as construction takes place. Therefore Fiskerton would not be able to receive payment for work performed to date. As such, revenue should not be recognised over time but at the point in time when control passes to the customer (most likely on delivery of the asset to the customer).

(c) **Ethics**

It is concerning that the property has been incorrectly classified as an investment property. Accountants have an ethical duty to be professionally competent and act with due care and attention. It is fundamental that the financial statements comply with the accounting standards and principles which underpin them. This may be a genuine mistake but even so would not be one expected from a professionally qualified accountant. The financial statements must comply with the fair presentation principles embedded within IAS 1 *Presentation of Financial Statements*.

Tutorial note

*Outline the **specific** ethical principles that have been breached.*

The managing director appears to be happy to manipulate the financial statements. A self-interest threat to objectivity arises from the issue over the debt covenants. It is likely that the managing director is concerned about his job security should the bank recall the debt and deem Fiskerton to no longer be a going concern. It appears highly likely that the revaluation was implemented in the interim financial statements to try to maintain a satisfactory gearing ratio. Even more concerning is that the managing director has deliberately overstated the valuation for the year-end financial statements, even though he is aware that it breaches accounting standards. Such deliberate manipulation is contrary to the ethical principles of integrity, professional behaviour and objectivity. It appears that the managing director is trying to defraud the bank by misrepresenting the liquidity of the business to avoid repayment of the loan.

Tutorial note

Make explicit reference to the impact of the revenue error on the financial statements.

The sales contract is further evidence that the managing director may be attempting to manipulate the financial statements. The proposed treatment will overstate both revenue and assets which would improve the gearing ratio.

A governance issue arises from the behaviour of the managing director. It is important that no one individual is too powerful and domineering in running an entity's affairs. An intimidation threat arises from the managing director pressurising the accountant to overstate revenue from the contract. It was also the managing director who implemented the excessive revaluations on the property. It would appear that the managing director is exercising too much power over the financial statements.

Tutorial note

Outline specific actions that the accountant should take.

The accountant must not be influenced by the behaviour of the managing director and should produce financial statements which are transparent and free from bias. Instead, the managing director should be reminded of their ethical responsibilities. The accountant may need to consider professional advice should the managing director refuse to correct the financial statements.

			Marks
		Marking guide	
(a)	–	application of the following discussion to the scenario:	
		correct accounting treatment of the lease	3
		implications for the financial statements	2
		implications for the debt covenant	2
			———
			7
			———
(b)	–	consideration of whether it is performance satisfied over time or at a point in time and application to the scenario	3
	–	conclusion and implications for revenue	1
			———
			4
			———
(c)	–	application of the following discussion of ethical issues to the scenario:	
		classification of property as investment property	2
		revaluation and manipulation of the debt covenant	3
	–	consideration of the ethical implications and their resolution	2
			———
			7
			———
		Professional	2
			———
Total			**20**
			———

Examiner's comments

Many candidates felt that the investment property classification was justified. Where a candidate concluded, with some justification, that the property was an investment property, some marks were awarded. Where candidates made a reasonable attempt at calculations, then the Own Figure Rule was used to justify the conclusions reached by the candidate.

The second part of the question required a discussion as to whether revenue arising from a sales contract should be recognised on a stage of completion basis under IFRS 15. Any mention of IFRS 15 in a question seems to prompt a regurgitation of the five steps to revenue recognition. This type of answer gains very few marks as this level of exam requires candidate knowledge of the specific requirement in IFRS 15. Thus in this case, candidates should have stated that the entity should determine whether its promise to construct the asset is a performance obligation satisfied over time. Generally, candidates obtained at least half marks on this part.

The final part of the question was generally well answered and full marks were often awarded. The main issue was that some candidates simply quoted ethical guidance without applying it to the scenario. Also, the professional marks were awarded for the quality of ethical discussion and thus where candidates did not apply ethical guidance to the scenario, further marks were lost.

16   FARHAM (SEP 2018) *Walk in the footsteps of a top tutor*

Key answer tips

This question shows the marks available for each part. Use this to help you with timings. Almost half of the marks are for ethics, so make sure that you write enough. You will score one mark for each valid point that you make.

Ethical issues are never clear-cut. To score the two professional marks, your discussion must demonstrate an understanding of the reality of a problem.

(a)   Factory subsidence

Tutorial note

Use subheadings so that it is clear which issue you are addressing.

In accordance with IAS 36 *Impairment of Assets,* the subsidence is an indication of impairment in relation to the production facility.

The impairment review would be performed on a suitable cash generating unit as presumably the factory, as a standalone asset, would not independently generate cash flows for Farham.

Tutorial note

A cash generating unit is the smallest group of assets that generate cash flows that are independent from the rest of the business.

The recoverable amount of the unit would need to be assessed as the higher of fair value less costs to sell and value in use.

Reference to IFRS 13 *Fair Value Measurement* would be required in estimating the fair value of the facility. This may involve considering whether similar facilities have been on the market or recently sold.

Value in use would be calculated by estimating the present value of the cash flows generated from the production facility discounted at a suitable rate of interest to reflect the risks to the business.

Where the carrying amount exceeds the recoverable amount, impairment has occurred. Any impairment loss is allocated to reduce the carrying amount of the assets of the unit. This cannot be netted off the revaluation surplus as the surplus does not specifically relate to the facility impaired. As such the impairment should be recorded in profit or loss.

No provision should be recognised for the costs of repairing the factory. To recognise a provision, IAS 37 *Provisions, Contingent Liabilities and Contingent Assets* would require a legal or constructive obligation to repair the factory. No such obligation exists.

Sale of Newall

The disposal of Newall appears to meet the criteria to be held for sale as per IFRS 5 *Non-current Assets Held for Sale and Discontinued Operations*. Management has shown commitment to the sale by approving the plan and reporting it to the media. A probable acquirer has been found, the sale is highly probable, and it is expected to be completed six months after the year end (well within the 12-month criteria).

Tutorial note

A disposal group is a group of assets that will be disposed of in a single transaction.

Newall would be treated as a disposal group because a single equity transaction is the most likely form of disposal.

If Newall is deemed to be a separate major component of business or geographical area of the group, the losses of the group should be presented separately as a discontinued operation within the consolidated financial statements of Farham.

Assets held for sale are valued at the lower of carrying amount and fair value less costs to sell. The carrying amount consists of the net assets and goodwill relating to Newall less the non-controlling interest's share.

Assets within the disposal group which are not inside the scope of IFRS 5 are adjusted for in accordance with the relevant standard first. This includes leased assets. The right-of-use asset deemed surplus to requirements will most likely be written off with a corresponding expense recognised in profit or loss.

Any further impairment loss recognised to reduce Newall to fair value less costs to sell would be allocated first to goodwill and then on a pro rata basis across the other non-current assets of the group.

Tutorial note

A constructive obligation is where an entity's past behaviour and practice indicates to other parties that it will accept certain responsibilities.

The chief operating officer is wrong to exclude any form of restructuring provision from the consolidated financial statements. The disposal has been communicated to the media and a constructive obligation exists. However, only directly attributable costs of the restructuring should be included and not ongoing costs of the business. The legal fees and redundancy costs should be provided for. Future operating losses should not be provided for because no obligating event has arisen. No provision is required for the impairments of the owned assets as this would have been accounted for on remeasurement to fair value less costs to sell.

Tutorial note

If the lease will be terminated then the lease term has changed.

If the early termination penalty is likely to be paid then the lease term has changed. Per IFRS 16 *Leases*, the lease liability must be remeasured and should now include the present value of the penalty (but should exclude any payments scheduled after this date). When the lease liability is remeasured, a corresponding adjustment is posted against the right-of-use asset. If the right-of-use asset has been written down to zero an expense should instead be charged to profit or loss.

(b)   Ethics

Tutorial note

Financial statement errors are an ethical issue, even if they were accidental. Accountants have a responsibility to be professionally competent so that primary user groups are not misled.

Accountants have a duty to ensure that the financial statements are fair, transparent and comply with accounting standards. The accountant has made mistakes that would be unexpected from a professionally qualified accountant. In particular, the accountant appears unaware of which costs should be included within a restructuring provision and has failed to recognise that there is no obligating event in relation to future operating losses. Accountants must carry out their work with due care and attention for the financial statements to have credibility. They must therefore ensure that their knowledge is kept up to date and that they do carry out their work in accordance with the relevant ethical and professional standards. Failure to do so would be a breach of professional competence. The accountant must make sure that they address this issue through, for example, attending regular training and professional development courses.

Tutorial note

Discuss the specific impact of the errors on the financial statements.

There are a number of instances which suggest that the chief operating officer is happy to manipulate the financial statements for their own benefit. She is not willing to account for an impairment loss for the subsidence despite knowing that this is contrary to IFRS Standards. She is also unwilling to reduce the profits of the group by properly applying the assets held for sale criteria in relation to Newall nor to create a restructuring provision. All of the adjustments required to ensure the financial statements comply with IFRS and IAS Standards will reduce profitability. It is true that the directors do have a responsibility to run the group on behalf of their shareholders and to try to maximise their return. This must not be to the detriment, though, of producing financial statements which are objective and faithfully represent the performance of the group. It is likely that the chief operating officer is motivated by bonus targets and is therefore trying to misrepresent the results of the group. The chief operating officer must make sure that she is not unduly influenced by this self-interest threat to her objectivity.

The chief operating officer is also acting unethically by threatening to dismiss the accountant should they try to correct the financial statements. It is not clear whether the chief operating officer is a qualified accountant but the ethical principles should extend to all employees and not just qualified accountants. Threatening and intimidating behaviour is unacceptable and against all ethical principles. The accountant faces an ethical dilemma. They have a duty to produce financial statements which are objective and fair but to do so could mean losing their job.

Tutorial note

Remember to discuss actions that the accountant should take.

The accountant should approach the chief operating officer and remind them of the basic ethical principles and try to persuade them of the need to put the adjustments through the consolidated accounts so that they are fair and objective. Should the chief operating officer remain unmoved, the accountant may wish to contact the ACCA ethical helpline and take legal advice before undertaking any further action.

	Marking scheme	
		Marks
(a)	Subsidence as impairment indicator	2
	Fair value	2
	Allocation of impairment loss	1
	Held for sale criteria, valuation and impairment	3
	Required accounting treatment	3
		11
(b)	Discussion of ethical principles	2
	Application of ethical principles to scenario	5
		7
	Professional marks	2
Total		20

Examiner's comments

Candidates with good exam technique should briefly plan the content of their written answer to avoid repetition: writing the same point twice loses valuable time and certainly will not score marks twice. Good practice is to have separate headings for each 'situation', with lines left in between them for ease of marking.

Part (b) was well-answered in most cases, with better answers applying ethical principles to the scenario. It was pleasing to see fewer answers merely 'listing out' rote-learned ethical requirements in this sitting.

17 JONJON *Walk in the footsteps of a top tutor*

Key answer tips

This is an ethical case-study style question. You need to talk about the impact of the transactions on the financial statements and the ethical issues raised. There are two professional marks for the application of ethical principles. Make sure that your ethics answer is not too generic and that it relates to the specific circumstances and transactions in the question.

Intangible asset

IAS 38 *Intangible Assets* states that an intangible asset has an indefinite useful life only if there is no 'foreseeable' limit to its useful life. Difficulties in accurately determining an intangible asset's useful life do not provide a basis for regarding that useful life as indefinite.

In the case of JonJon, the customer relationship is with individuals so there is, is by definition, a time limit to that relationship. Therefore JonJon is contravening IAS 38.

Tutorial note

Make an explicit reference to the impact of the error on the financial statements.

Failing to amortise intangible assets will overstate profits and assets in the current period.

Fair value

IFRS 13 *Fair Value Measurement* defines the fair value of an asset as the price that would be received to sell an asset or paid to transfer a liability in an orderly transaction between market participants at the measurement date. Fair value is a market-based measurement, not an entity-specific measurement.

Tutorial note

IFRS 13 uses a three-level hierarchy that prioritises level 1 inputs when measuring fair value. Give a brief description of each level of the hierarchy.

In IFRS 13, fair value measurements are categorised into a three-level hierarchy based on the type of inputs. The hierarchy is defined as follows:

- Level 1 inputs are unadjusted quoted prices in active markets for items identical to the asset being measured.

- Level 2 inputs are quoted prices other than those included in level 1.

- Level 3 inputs are unobservable inputs that are usually determined based on management's assumptions.

Tutorial note

Now it is time to apply your knowledge to the scenario. What level of input has JonJon used? What level of input is available for them to use?

Due to the nature of investment property, which is often unique and not traded on a regular basis, and the subsequent lack of observable input data for identical assets, fair value measurements are likely to be categorised as Level 2 or Level 3 valuations.

Level 2 inputs are likely to be sale prices per square metre for similar properties in the same location, observable market rents and property yields from the latest transactions. Level 3 inputs may be yields based on management estimates, cash flow forecasts using the entity's own data, and assumptions about the future development of certain parameters such as rental income that are not derived from the market.

Management should maximise the use of relevant observable inputs and minimise the use of unobservable inputs. A valuation based on 'new-build value less obsolescence' does not reflect the level 2 inputs which are available, such as sale prices. As level 2 data is available, JonJon should have used this when valuing the industrial property.

Gains and losses on the revaluation of investment property are reported in the statement of profit or loss. Therefore, over-estimating the fair value of the property will over-state profits and assets in the current period.

Impairment test

IAS 36 *impairment of Assets* states that cash flow projections used in measuring value in use shall be based on reasonable and supportable assumptions which represent management's best estimate of the range of economic conditions which will exist over the remaining useful life of the asset. IAS 36 also states that management must assess the reasonableness of the assumptions by examining the causes of differences between past cash flow projections and actual cash. Management should ensure that the assumptions on which its current cash flow projections are based are consistent with past actual outcomes.

Despite the fact that the realised cash flows for 20X5 were negative and far below projected cash flows, the directors had significantly raised forecasted cash flows for 20X6 without justification. There are serious doubts about JonJon's ability produce realistic and reliable forecasts.

According to IAS 36, estimates of future cash flows should include:

- projections of cash inflows from the continuing use of the asset

- projections of cash outflows which are necessarily incurred to generate the cash inflows from continuing use of the asset; and

- net cash flows to be received (or paid) for the disposal of the asset at the end of its useful life.

IAS 36 states that projected cash outflows should include those required for the day-to-day servicing of the asset which includes future cash outflows to maintain the level of economic benefits expected to arise from the asset in its current condition. It is highly unlikely that no investments in working capital or operating assets would need to be made to maintain the assets of the CGUs in their current condition.

It would seem that the cash flow projections that the finance director of JonJon wants the accountant to use are not in compliance with IAS 36. These projections will most likely over-state the recoverable amount of the CGUs, potentially reducing (or eliminating) the amount of any impairment loss. This would overstate profits and assets in the current period.

Ethics

Tutorial note

Do not simply describe the ACCA Code of Ethics. Make sure that your answer is tailored to the question. You should make reference to the bank covenants, the fact that the errors over-state profits and assets, and the finance director's comments to the accountant.

JonJon has breached several accounting standards. All of these breaches over-state reported profits and assets. This will make the performance and position of JonJon appear much stronger to the users of its financial statements. In particular, it will reduce the likelihood that JonJon will breach its loan covenants.

The users of financial statements, such as banks and shareholders, trust accountants and rely on them to faithfully represent the effects of a company's transactions. IAS 1 *Presentation of Financial Statements* makes it clear that this will be obtained when accounting standards are correctly applied. Nonetheless, incentives might exist to depart from particular IFRS and IAS Standards. It is therefore vital that accountants comply with the ACCA's *Code of Ethics*.

It may be that the breaches of accounting standards are due to a lack of knowledge. Nonetheless, as per the *Code of Ethics,* accountants have a responsibility to ensure that they are technically competent. However, the number of errors and the fact that they consistently over-state assets and profits would suggest that the breaches of accounting standards are purposeful. If so the directors of JonJon lack integrity and objectivity.

It has been suggested that the accountant would suffer financially if the finance director's instructions are not followed. This is inappropriate as it creates a risk that the accountant will prioritise their own interests above those of JonJon's stakeholders. The accountant should discuss the matters with the finance director, and keep a record of these conversations. If disagreements still exist, then professional advice should be sought from ACCA. The accountant should also approach other company directors, including non-executive directors. If the matters cannot be resolved then the accountant should consider resignation.

Marking scheme	
	Marks
Accounting treatment of intangible – 1 mark per point	3
Investment property fair value – 1 mark per point	4
CGU impairment – 1 mark per point	5
Ethical implications – 1 mark per point	6
Professional marks	2
Total	**20**

18   CLOUD *Walk in the footsteps of a top tutor*

Key answer tips

There are two professional marks awarded for the application of ethical principles. Make sure that your discussion of ethics relates to the specific circumstances and transactions in the question. Do not just regurgitate the ACCA Code of Ethics, but do have a think about what ethical principles Cloud's directors and staff might be breaching.

Presentation of loan in statement of cash flows

Tutorial note

Begin by defining the relevant categories of cash flows. Use these definitions to decide whether the cash receipt has been appropriately presented.

IAS 7 *Statement of Cash Flows* says that cash flows from operating activities are those related to the revenue-producing activities of an entity, such as cash received from customers and cash paid to suppliers. Cash flows from financing activities are those that change the equity or borrowing structure of an entity.

The cash received from the bank is a borrowing. As such, it should be reported as a cash flow from financing activities.

The current treatment is over-stating Cloud's operating cash flows, which is likely to make Cloud look more liquid than it really is. It may also improve perceptions of its long-term sustainability.

Share sale

Tutorial note

A profit or loss on the sale of shares in a subsidiary arises in the consolidated financial statements only if control is lost.

If a share sale results in loss of control over a subsidiary then a profit or loss on disposal should be recorded. If there is no loss of control then there should be no profit or loss on disposal and no remeasurement of goodwill. Instead the transaction is accounted for in equity, as an increase to the non-controlling interest (NCI).

Cloud has incorrectly recorded a profit on disposal in the consolidated statement of profit of loss. This is over-stating profits and should be removed.

Tutorial note

Use the figures to calculate the adjustments required to equity.

Cloud should account for an increase to the NCI. This will be calculated as the percentage of the net assets and goodwill sold to the NCI. This amounts to $1.5 million (5% × ($5m + $25m)). The difference between the cash proceeds and the increase to the NCI is accounted for as an increase of $0.5 million ($2m – $1.5m) in other components of equity.

Revaluation of property, plant and equipment

IAS 16 *Property, Plant and Equipment* states that revaluation gains on property, plant and equipment are recorded in other comprehensive income (OCI) and held in a revaluation reserve in equity (other components of equity). Revaluation losses are charged to OCI to the extent that a revaluation reserve exists for that specific asset. Any revaluation loss in excess of the balance on the revaluation reserve is charged to profit or loss.

Tutorial note

You need to work out the revaluation reserve created by the prior year revaluation. Any revaluation loss in excess of the reserve balance is charged to profit or loss.

At 31 December 20X0, there was a revaluation gain of $4 million being the difference between the carrying amount of $8 million ($10m × 4/5) and the fair value of $12 million. This revaluation gain would have been recognised in other comprehensive income and held in a revaluation surplus in equity.

At 31 December 20X1 the carrying amount of the asset before the revaluation was $9 million ($12 million × 3/4).

The revaluation loss is $5 million ($9m – $4m). Of this, $4 million should be charged to other comprehensive income because that is the balance in the revaluation reserve. The remaining loss of $1 million should be charged against profit or loss. Cloud's error means that profits are currently over-stated by $1 million.

Tutorial note

Some entities perform a reserve transfer in respect of the excess depreciation arising from revaluations. This policy is optional. If you need to consider the impact of a reserve transfer then it will be explicitly mentioned in the question.

Ethics

The directors have a responsibility to faithfully represent the transactions that the entity has entered into during the year. This is because various user groups rely on the financial statements to make economic decisions. Accountants are trusted as professionals and it is important that this trust is not broken. Therefore, it is vital that the principles outlined in the ACCA *Code of Ethics* are understood and followed.

The directors receive a bonus based on profits and operating cash flows. This might impair their objectivity when accounting for transactions that have taken place during the year.

Tutorial note

Make specific reference to the accounting errors that Cloud has made. These errors increase cash flows from operating activities and profit – what does that suggest?

The error in the statement of cash flows increased cash flows from operating activities. The errors relating to the share sale and the downwards revaluation of property, plant and equipment have over-stated profit for the year. It seems likely that the misstatements were deliberate in order to meet the bonus target.

It is unclear if it was the finance director who processed these incorrect accounting entries, or if it was other members of the accounts department. However, the other accountants still have an ethical responsibility not to mislead the users of the financial statements. It may be that they are intimidated by the dominant finance director. They should consider reporting any concerns to the other directors, if possible, or they could highlight these issues to the audit committee or the external auditors.

Of course, it may be that the misstatements were legitimate mistakes rather than a deliberate attempt to meet profit and cash flow targets. Nonetheless, accountants have a responsibility to ensure that they are professionally competent. Thus, possessing insufficient knowledge of IFRS and IAS Standards constitutes an ethical issue. If this is the case then the finance director and/or relevant members of the accounts department need to actively seek out opportunities to continue their professional development.

Marking scheme	
	Marks
Cash flow classification – 1 mark per point	3
Share sale – 1 mark per point	4
Downwards revaluation – 1 mark per point	4
Ethical implications – 1 mark per point	7
Professional marks	2
	—
Total	**20**
	—

19 TILES *Walk in the footsteps of a top tutor*

Key answer tips

This is an ethical case-study style question.

Take each of the accounting issues in turn and explain, with reference to the relevant standard, how it should have been accounted for.

There are two professional marks for the application of ethical principles. You will not receive these marks if your answer is generic. Explain the ethical issues facing Tiles!

Deferred tax asset

Tutorial note

State the rules from IAS 12 Income Taxes about when a deferred tax asset can be recognised.

A deferred tax asset should be recognised for deductible temporary differences, unused tax losses and unused tax credits to the extent that it is probable that taxable profit will be available against which the deductible temporary differences can be utilised.

According to IAS 12 *Income Taxes* the existence of unused tax losses is strong evidence that future taxable profit may not be available against which to offset the losses. Therefore when an entity has a history of recent losses, the entity recognises deferred tax assets arising from unused tax losses only to the extent that the entity has sufficient taxable temporary differences or there is convincing other evidence that sufficient taxable profit will be available.

Tutorial note

Use the scenario to decide if Tiles' recognition of a deferred tax asset is in accordance with IAS 12 Income Taxes.

As Tiles has a history of recent losses it needs to provide convincing other evidence that sufficient taxable profit would be available against which the unused tax losses could be offset. The improved performance in 20X5 would not be indicative of future good performance as Tiles would have suffered a net loss before tax had it not been for the non-operating gains.

Tiles' anticipation of improved future trading could not alone be regarded as meeting the requirement for strong evidence of future profits. When assessing the use of carry-forward tax losses, weight should be given to revenues from existing orders or confirmed contracts rather than those that are merely expected from improved trading.

Thus at 30 April 20X5 it is unlikely that the entity would generate taxable profits before the unused tax losses expired. Tiles is not able to provide convincing evidence that sufficient taxable profits would be generated against which the unused tax losses could be offset and so the recognition of the deferred tax assets is not in accordance with IAS 12.

Discontinued Operation

Tutorial note

Remember, a subsidiary is a group of assets and liabilities and so is a 'disposal group'.

Start your answer to this issue by outlining the definition of a discontinued operation and the criteria in IFRS 5 concerning when a disposal group can be classified as held for sale.

A discontinued operation is a component of an entity that has been sold or which has been classified as held for sale.

According to IFRS 5 *Non-current Assets Held for Sale and Discontinued Operations*, an asset or disposal group is classified as held for sale where its carrying amount will be recovered principally through sale rather than continuing use.

To be classified as held for sale, the sale should be highly probable and expected to be complete within one year from the date of classification. The asset or disposal group should be available for sale in its immediate location and condition and actively marketed at a price reasonable in relation to its fair value.

A disposal group can, exceptionally, be classified as held for sale after a period of 12 months if certain criteria are met, such as circumstances arising that were previously considered unlikely and which prevented the sale from occurring.

Tutorial note

Apply your knowledge of IFRS 5 to the scenario. Does the subsidiary meet the criteria to be classified as held for sale? Make sure that you fully explain your answer.

Tiles made certain organisational changes during the year to 30 April 20X5, which resulted in additional activities being transferred to the subsidiary. This confirms that the subsidiary was not available for sale in its present condition as at the point of classification.

Furthermore, the shareholders' authorisation to sell the subsidiary was only granted for one year and there is no indication that this has been extended. This places doubt on whether the sale of the subsidiary is highly probable.

The subsidiary should therefore be treated as a continuing operation in the financial statements for both the years ended 30 April 20X5 and 30 April 20X4. This means that the subsidiary's loss will no longer be presented as a separate line within the statement of profit or loss, and will instead be held within profit from continuing operations. Some of the assets and liabilities of the subsidiary will also need to be reclassified from current to non-current.

Disclosure of bonuses

Tutorial note

Make sure that you explain why the bonus needs to be disclosed – it is a requirement of IAS 24 Related Party Disclosures.

According to IAS 24 *Related Party Disclosures*, a member of 'key management personnel' is related to a reporting entity. The standard explicitly states that directors are key management personnel.

IAS 24 states that entities must disclose all compensation paid or payable to members of key management personnel. Therefore Tiles must disclose the bonuses payable to the directors.

Ethical and professional issues

Users of an entity's financial statements, such as shareholders and employees, rely on the accountants to faithfully represent that entity's performance and position. Accountants are professionals, who are bestowed with status and are trusted. To ensure that this trust is not broken, accountants are bound by a *Code of Ethics and Conduct*. The ACCA code sets out the importance of the fundamental principles of confidentiality, objectivity, professional behaviour, integrity, and professional competence and due care.

Tutorial note

Specific reference to the scenario is needed otherwise you will not score the two professional marks that are available.

A faithful representation necessitates compliance with accounting standards, including IAS 12, IFRS 5 and IAS 24. The directors have not followed the rules in these accounting standards, and thus the performance and position of Tiles has been misrepresented.

For example the recognition of the deferred tax asset has boosted profit for the year. The incorrect classification of the subsidiary as a discontinued operation means that its loss is presented separately from the rest of Tiles' operations, and therefore is likely to be seen by the users as a non-recurring item. Such measures suggest that the directors lack integrity and objectivity.

Related party disclosures will impact the users' perception of an entity's past and future performance as well as the success or failure of those who govern it. After all, excessive director remuneration is unlikely to be in the best interests of shareholder wealth and is at odds with the directors' stewardship responsibilities. Director pay is an issue that the shareholders have explicitly raised concerns about and it would therefore seem that Tiles is trying to actively mislead its investors. This is in clear breach of the ethical code. Moreover, in some jurisdictions, disclosure of director remuneration is a legal requirement and so Tiles could also be breaching company law.

Therefore, despite the finance director's claim about the impact on shareholder wealth, she has a responsibility as a member of the accountancy profession to present the information in a fair and honest fashion.

Marking scheme	
	Marks
Deferred tax asset – 1 mark per point	5
Discontinued operation – 1 mark per point	4
Related parties – 1 mark per point	2
Ethical implications – 1 mark per point	7
Professional marks	2
	—
Total	**20**
	—

20 GARDEN *Walk in the footsteps of a top tutor*

Key answer tips

Your best chance of scoring well is to talk about each of the transactions in turn. However, without a mark allocation it can be difficult to manage your time and it would be easy to over-run. Remember that you will score one mark for each valid point that you make – set out your work neatly so that you can keep track of whether you've written enough (or too little or too much) for each issue. You may wish to discuss ethics as you work through each issue – if you do this be careful that your answer does not become overly repetitive.

Share-based payment

Tutorial note

Outline the rules regarding the accounting treatment of equity-settled share-based payments and then apply these to the information given.

The directors have been granted share-options so this is an equity-settled share-based payment transaction. According to IFRS 2 *Share-based Payment,* the expense should be based on the fair value of the options at the grant date, which is $4 per option. The expense should be spread over the three year vesting period, based on the number of options expected to vest. One third of the vesting period has passed so the finance director is incorrect in stating that no expense should be recognised in the current financial year.

Tutorial note

Always show full workings for any calculations. That way you may still score some marks, even if you make a mistake.

The expense that should be recognised in the year-ended 30 November 20X6 is:

5 directors × 600,000 options × $4 × 1/3 = $4 million.

An expense of $4 million should be recognised in profit or loss and a corresponding entry made to equity. This will reduce the reported profits of Garden.

Tutorial note

Don't forget that any transaction with a director is a related party transaction. Disclosures are therefore required.

IAS 24 *Related Party Disclosures* requires that key management personnel, which includes all directors, are related parties of the reporting entity. With regards to key management personnel, an entity is required to disclose employee benefits, including share-based payments.

The directors' son

Tutorial note

Do the payments to the son of the two directors need to be disclosed? Identify the relevant provisions of IAS 24 and use them to explain why disclosure is or is not required.

Directors are key management personnel and therefore are related parties of the reporting entity. IAS 24 also says that the close family members of key management personnel would be related parties of the reporting entity. The definition of close family members includes children.

The son of the finance and sales directors is therefore a related party of Garden. The salary paid to him would need to be disclosed in a note to the financial statements. A statement could be made that the transaction is on market value terms as long as this can be substantiated.

Operating segments

Tutorial note

The retail outlets have been aggregated with the rest of Garden's trading operations. Is this correct? State the rules regulating when aggregation of operating segments is appropriate and then apply these to the scenario.

According to IFRS 8 *Operating Segments*, an operating segment is a component of an entity that engages in business activities, and which has discrete financial information available that is monitored by the entity's chief decision maker. It would therefore seem that the retail outlets are an operating segment.

Operating segments can be aggregated if they have similar economic characteristics. Such segments would normally have similar long-term margins and also be similar in terms of the products that they sell, the customers that they sell to, and the distribution methods used.

The retail outlets have a different margin to the rest of Garden's activities. Furthermore, the retail stores sell to customers face-to-face, whereas the rest of Garden's businesses is conducted online with goods despatched to customers via couriers. This suggests that the retail outlets do not have economic characteristics similar to the other operating segments. As such, the retail outlets should be disclosed as a separate segment (assuming they exceed the quantitative thresholds outlined in IFRS 8).

IAS 24 *Related Party Disclosures* says that a close family member of a director is a related party of the reporting entity. However, the definition of a close family member does not include friends. This means that the purchase of the trade and assets of the retail business should not be disclosed as a related party transaction.

Ethical and professional issues

The purpose of financial statements is to give a fair representation of the company's position and performance to enable investors, lenders and other users to make economic decisions. Accountants have a social and ethical responsibility to issue financial statements which do not mislead the public. Deliberate falsification of financial statements is unethical. Any manipulation of the accounts will harm the credibility of the profession since the public assume that professional accountants will act in an ethical capacity.

A fair representation is normally deemed to have been provided if the financial statements are prepared in accordance with International Financial Reporting Standards. It would seem that the financial statements currently breach a number of key standards, such as IFRS 2 *Share-based Payments*, IAS 24 *Related Party Disclosures* and IFRS 8 *Operating Segments*.

Tutorial note

Make specific reference to the transactions in the question. What is the impact of the mistakes/omissions on the financial statements?

Omitting the share-based payment transaction from the financial statements has inflated profit for the year, which could impact shareholder perception of the underlying performance of Garden. Moreover, the shareholders have already been critical about director remuneration, so omitting the transaction may have been a tactic for deliberately concealing this additional benefit.

It would also seem that the recruitment and remuneration of the son of the finance and sales directors is being deliberately concealed. Although it is claimed that he is being paid a salary that is in line with market rates, questions may still be asked about the appointment, such as: Is this the best person for the job? Is this role really required? Is this the best use of company money? Some users of the financial statements might conclude that the directors are putting their own interests, and the interests of their family members, above those of the other company shareholders.

Garden's finance director has wrongly aggregated the entity's operating segments. This might be an attempt to hide the poor performance of the newly acquired retail outlets, thus avoiding further criticism and scrutiny of the transaction. Whilst the trade and assets were not purchased from a related party, the fact that the transaction took place with a close friend of one of the directors raises questions about integrity and the extent to which the directors more generally are effectively and efficiently using the entity's resources.

Tutorial note

Note that the question requires you to answer from the perspective of the accountant. Explicitly state the ethical principles that have been breached. Try and come up with practical steps that the accountant should take to resolve the ethical issues.

The accountant should remind the directors that professional ethics are an integral part of the framework from which professional accountants operate. They must adhere to ethical guidelines such as the ACCA's *Code of Ethics and Conduct*. It would appear that the financial statements are being deliberately manipulated, probably to avoid further criticism from shareholders about the running of the company and the stewardship of its assets. This would contravene the principles of integrity, objectivity and professional behaviour. Records of discussions between the accountant and the directors should be kept and, if disagreements remain, advice should be sought by the accountant from ACCA. If no effective channel for internal reporting of concerns exists then the accountant may need to consider resignation.

Marking scheme	
	Marks
Share-based payment – 1 mark per point	4
Son of directors – 1 mark per point	2
Operating segments – 1 mark per point	4
Ethical implications – 1 mark per point	8
Professional marks	2
	—
Total	**20**
	—

21 CHERRY *Walk in the footsteps of a top tutor*

Key answer tips

There are two marks available for the application of ethical principles. To get these you should tailor your answer to the specific transactions in the question.

Do not write everything that you know about each accounting standard or you will run out of time. Instead, jot down the rules and principles that are relevant to the scenario and then apply these.

Remember that one mark is awarded per valid point that you make. Make sure that you are writing enough to pass.

Change in accounting policy for pension scheme

Tutorial note

If an entity talks about changing its accounting policies then there will be marks available for referring to IAS 8 Accounting Policies, Changes in Accounting Estimates and Errors. Try and remember that entities can only depart from IFRS and IAS Standards if compliance would be misleading.

IAS 8 *Accounting Policies, Changes in Accounting Estimates and Errors* only permits a change in accounting policy if the change is:

* required by an IFRS Standard or

* results in the financial statements providing reliable and more relevant information.

A retrospective adjustment is required unless the change arises from a new accounting policy with transitional arrangements to account for the change.

It is possible to depart from the requirements of IFRS and IAS Standards but only in the extremely rare circumstances where compliance would be so misleading that it would conflict with the overall objectives of the financial statements. This override is rarely, if ever, invoked.

Tutorial note

Use the relevant accounting standard, IAS 19 Employee Benefits, to explain why the directors' policy change is not allowed.

IAS 19 *Employee Benefits* requires all gains and losses on a defined benefit scheme to be recognised in profit or loss except for the remeasurement component which must be recognised in other comprehensive income.

The amendment to the pension scheme is a past service cost and must be expensed to profit or loss. Additionally, it appears that the directors wish to manipulate other aspects of the pension scheme such as the current service cost and, since the scheme is in deficit, the net finance cost. The directors are deliberately manipulating the presentation of these items by recording them in OCI rather than in profit or loss.

Trademark

Tutorial note

Don't rush into calculations. Easy marks are available for using IAS 38 Intangible Assets to explain why Cherry's treatment of the brand is incorrect.

IAS 38 *Intangible Assets* states an intangible asset with a finite useful life should be amortised on a systematic basis over that life. The amortisation method should reflect the pattern of benefits and it should be reviewed at least annually. A change in amortisation method is adjusted prospectively as a change in estimate under IAS 8 *Accounting Policies, Changes in Accounting Estimates and Errors*.

Expected future reductions in sales could be indicative of a higher rate of consumption of the future economic benefits embodied in an asset. Hence, the trademark should have been amortised over a remaining 2.5 year period (from 1 December 20X5 until 31 May 20X8).

At the date of the estimate change the trademark had a carrying amount of $2.1 million ($3m × 7/10). The amortisation charge in the current period should have been $0.84 million ($2.1m/2.5 years). This means that Cherry's profits and intangible assets are currently overstated by $0.54 million ($0.84m – $0.3m).

The correcting entry required is:

Dr Amortisation expense (P/L) $0.54m

Cr Intangible assets $0.54m

Tutorial note

Reducing the expected useful economic life of an asset is an indication that it might be impaired. You should discuss impairment, even though you are not given enough information to calculate it.

IAS 36 *Impairment of Assets* states that an entity should assess annually whether there is any indication that an asset may be impaired. If any such indication exists, the entity should estimate the recoverable amount of the asset. Thus, Cherry should test the trademark for impairment by comparing its carrying amount to its recoverable amount. The recoverable amount is the higher of fair value less costs to sell, and value in use. If the trademark is impaired then the current over-statement of Cherry's profits and assets is even greater.

Sale and leaseback

Tutorial note

Remember that lessees are required to recognise a right-of-use asset and a lease liability. Cherry has not done this. Comment on this to score some easy marks. The calculation of the correct profit on disposal is trickier. Revisit the Study Text if you cannot remember how to do this.

Sale and leaseback transactions are accounted for under IFRS 16 *Leases*. If the transfer of the asset represents a sale then the seller-lessee measures the right-of-use asset at the proportion of the previous carrying amount that relates to the rights retained after the sale. This means that the seller-lessee recognises a profit or loss based only on the rights transferred.

If the transfer does not qualify as a sale then the seller-lessee continues to recognise the underlying asset and will also recognise a financial liability equal to the proceeds received.

It would seem that the transfer does represent a sale because Cherry is only leasing the asset back for a fraction of its remaining useful life and so the buyer-lessor seems to have obtained control of the underlying asset.

Cherry must initially measure the right-of-use asset at $1.26 million (($1.8m/$5m) × $3.5 million).

The lease liability will be initially measured at the present value of the lease payments, which is $1.80 million.

Cherry has recorded a profit on disposal of $1.5 million but this should have been $0.96 million ($1.5m × (($5m − $1.8m)/$5m)). Therefore, the profit on disposal must be reduced by $0.54 million.

The correcting entry required is as follows:

Dr Right of use asset $1.26m

Dr Profit or loss $0.54m

Cr Lease liability $1.80m

In the next reporting period, depreciation on the right-of-use asset and interest on the lease liability will be recorded in profit or loss.

Ethics

Tutorial note

Make sure that you discuss why the directors are behaving unethically.

The current accounting treatments cannot be justified. The directors have an ethical responsibility to produce financial statements which are a fair representation of the entity's performance and position and which comply with all accounting standards. The errors made by Cherry under-state its liabilities and over-state its assets and profits.

There is a clear self-interest threat arising from the bonus scheme. The directors' change in policy with regards to pensions appears to be motivated by an intention to overstate operating profit to maximise their bonus potential.

Tutorial note

State the specific principles from the ethical code that the directors are breaching.

Such treatment is against the ACCA ethical principles of objectivity, integrity and professional behaviour.

The objectivity of the financial controller is also being compromised. The implicit threat to reduce her bonus would seem to give rise to both self-interest and intimidation threats.

The financial controller should remind the directors of their ethical responsibilities and should persuade them to change the current accounting treatment of all three of the transactions. If she feels she cannot discuss this with the directors then she should discuss the matters with the audit committee. The financial controller should document her discussions.

Marking scheme	
	Marks
Change in pension policy – 1 mark per point	3
Intangible asset – 1 mark per point	4
Sale and leaseback – 1 mark per point	5
Ethical implications – 1 mark per point	6
Professional marks	2
	——
Total	**20**
	——

22   ANOUK *Online question assistance*

Key answer tips

This question requires knowledge of three key accounting standards – IFRS 9 *Financial Instruments*, IAS 32 *Financial Instruments: Presentation*, and IFRS 16 *Leases.* If you are unfamiliar with these, then you should revisit the Study Text. In Strategic Business Reporting, marks are awarded for demonstrating knowledge of the relevant accounting standards and also for applying this knowledge to the scenario.

When discussing the ethical implications remember that generic comments about the *Code of Ethics* will not score highly. You must explain the particular ethical issues facing Anouk and outline how the financial controller should address these.

Receivables

Tutorial note

Many students forget that receivables are a financial instrument and therefore make no reference to IFRS 9 Financial Instruments. However, you could still score well if you applied basic accounting principles to the scenario.

IFRS 9 *Financial Instruments* suggests that the trade receivables should be derecognised from the financial statements when the following conditions are met:

- There are no further rights to receive cash

- The risks and rewards of ownership have substantially transferred.

The factor has full recourse for a six-month period so Anouk still has the irrecoverable debt risk. Furthermore, Anouk has the right to receive further cash payments from the factor, the amounts to be received being dependent on when and if the customers pay the factor. Anouk therefore still has the risks associated with slow payment by their customers. As such, the receivables must not be derecognised from the financial statements on 31 December 20X1. Instead the proceeds of $8 million (20% × $40m) should be treated as a short-term liability.

Accounting for the legal form of the transaction will understate receivables and understate liabilities. This makes it less likely that Anouk will break its loan covenants.

Debt or equity

Tutorial note

This is a very popular exam topic. It is essential to memorise the definitions of equity and financial liabilities.

IAS 32 *Financial Instruments: Presentation* uses principles-based definitions of a financial liability (debt) and of equity. The key feature of debt is that the issuer is obliged to deliver either cash or another financial asset to the holder. The contractual obligation may arise from a requirement to repay principal or interest or dividends. Equity is any contract which evidences a residual interest in the entity's assets after deducting all of its liabilities. A financial instrument is normally an equity instrument if the instrument includes no contractual obligation to deliver cash or another financial asset to another entity (such as ordinary shares).

Anouk's decision to classify B-shares as non-controlling interests is incorrect. Anouk has a clear contractual obligation to buy B-shares from the non-controlling interest under agreed terms and does not have an unconditional right to avoid delivering cash to settle the obligation. The minority shareholders' B-shares should therefore be treated as a financial liability in the consolidated financial statements.

The current treatment of the B shares over-states Anouk's equity and understates its liabilities. This makes it less likely that Anouk will break its loan covenants.

Crane contract

Tutorial note

It is important that entities correctly identify a contract that contains a lease because lessees are required to recognise a liability and a right-of-use asset in respect of all leases (unless short-term or of low value).

IFRS 16 *Leases* says that a contract contains a lease if it '**conveys the right to control the use of an identified asset for a period of time in exchange for consideration**' (IFRS 16, para 9). To have control, the contract must give the customer the right, throughout the period of use, to:

- substantially all of the identified asset's economic benefits, and

- direct the identified asset's use.

Although the crane used by Anouk can be substituted, the supplier is unlikely to benefit from this due to the costs involved. Therefore it can be concluded that Anouk has the right to use an identified asset over the contract term.

Anouk has the right to direct the use of the crane because it decides how the crane will be used. The restriction on operating during high winds, as outlined in the contract, defines the scope of Anouk's use, rather than preventing Anouk from directing use. Therefore Anouk controls the Crane over the period of use.

Tutorial note

Do not stop once you have concluded that the contract contains a lease. You need to discuss the correct accounting treatment.

Based on the above discussion, it would seem that the contract contains a lease. A lease liability should have been recognised at the commencement of the lease for the present value of the payments to be made. A right-of-use asset should be recognised for the same value, plus any associated direct costs.

Anouk has posted no accounting entries and so is currently understating both its assets and liabilities. Once again, this makes it less likely that the loan covenants will be breached.

Ethics

It is important that stakeholders of a company can rely on financial statements to make informed and accurate decisions. The directors of Anouk have an ethical responsibility to produce financial statements which comply with accounting standards, are transparent, and are free from material error.

Tutorial note

Make specific reference to the errors in Anouk's financial statements.

The current accounting treatment of all three transactions understates Anouk's reported liabilities. The current accounting treatments, if uncorrected, may mislead Anouk's stakeholders. Any adverse publicity could lead to a loss of public trust in the accounting profession.

Tutorial note

Make specific reference to the ethical principles that the directors are breaching.

It would seem likely that the directors are deliberately circumventing the terms of the covenants, particularly as they have concealed documents from the financial controller. Such actions are a clear breach of the fundamental principles of objectivity and integrity as outlined in the ACCA *Code of Ethics and Conduct*.

Tutorial note

Outline practical steps that the financial controller should take to resolve the issues.

The financial controller should remind the directors of their ethical responsibilities and remind them that Anouk's financial statements must fully comply with accounting standards. Records of these discussions should be kept. If disagreements remain, the financial controller should seek advice from ACCA. The financial controller may need to consider resignation if no effective channel for internal reporting of concerns exists.

Marking scheme	
	Marks
Receivables and factoring – 1 mark per point	4
Debt or equity – 1 mark per point	4
Lease contract – 1 mark per point	4
Ethical implications – 1 mark per point	6
Professional marks	2
Total	**20**

SECTION B QUESTIONS

23   FILL (DEC 2018)

Key answer tips

Parts (a) and (c) both require reference to the *Conceptual Framework*. This is a key topic in SBR that is being tested heavily. Make sure that you read Chapter 1 in the Study Text thoroughly.

(a)   (i)   Conceptual Framework

The *Conceptual Framework* acknowledges two measurement bases: historical cost, and current value. Net realisable value (NRV) is a current value measurement. However, the *Conceptual Framework* is not an accounting standard and so, in order to determine NRV, the directors would need to refer to IAS 2 *Inventories*.

(ii)   Net realisable value

IAS 2 defines NRV as the estimated selling price in the ordinary course of business less the costs of completion and costs of sale. In this case, the NRV will be determined on the basis of conditions which existed at the date of the statement of financial position.

NRV will be based upon the most reliable estimate of the amounts which will be realised for the coal. The year-end spot price will provide good evidence of the realisable value of the inventories and where the company has an executory contract to sell coal at a future date, then the use of the forward contract price may be appropriate. However, if the contract is not executory but is a financial instrument under IFRS 9 *Financial Instruments* or an onerous contract recognised as a provision under IAS 37 *Provisions, Contingent Liabilities and Contingent Assets*, it is unlikely to be used to calculate NRV.

Fill should calculate the NRV of the low carbon coal using the forecast market price based upon when the inventory is expected to be processed and realised. Future changes in the forecast market price or the processing and sale of the low carbon coal may result in adjustments to the NRV. As these adjustments are changes in estimates, IAS 8 *Accounting Policies, Changes in Accounting Estimates and Errors* will apply with the result that such gains and losses will be recognised in the statement of profit or loss in the period in which they arise.

(b)   Replacement costs

IAS 16 *Property, Plant and Equipment* (PPE) requires an entity to recognise in the carrying amount of PPE, the cost of replacing part of such an item. When each major inspection is performed, its cost is recognised in the carrying amount of the item of PPE as a replacement if the recognition criteria are satisfied. Any remaining carrying amount of the cost of a previous inspection is derecognised. The costs of performing a major reconditioning are capitalised if it gives access to future economic benefits. Such costs will include the labour and materials costs ($3 million) of performing the reconditioning. However, costs which do not relate to the replacement of components or the installation of new assets, such as routine maintenance costs, should be expensed as incurred.

Provision

It is not acceptable to provide the costs of reconditioning equipment as there is no legal or apparent constructive obligation to undertake the reconditioning. As set out above, the cost of the reconditioning should be identified as a separate component of the mine asset at initial recognition and depreciated over a period of two years. This will result in the same amount of expense being recognised as the proposal to create a provision.

Impairment

IAS 36 *Impairment of Assets* says that at the end of each reporting period, an entity is required to assess whether there is any indication that an asset may be impaired. IAS 36 has a list of external and internal indicators of impairment. If there is an indication that an asset may be impaired, then the asset's recoverable amount must be calculated.

Past and future reductions in selling prices may indicate that the future economic benefits which relate to the asset have been reduced. Mining assets should be tested for impairment whenever indicators of impairment exist. Impairments are recognised if a mine's carrying amount exceeds its recoverable amount. However, the nature of mining assets is that they often have a long useful life. Commodity prices can be volatile but downward price movements are more significant if they are likely to persist for longer periods. In this case, there is evidence of a decline in forward prices. If the decline in prices is for a significant proportion of the remaining expected life of the mine, this is more likely to be an impairment indicator. It appears that forward contract prices for two years out of the three years of the mine's remaining life indicate a reduction in selling prices. Based on market information, Fill has also calculated that the three-year forecast price of coal will be 20% lower than the current spot price (part (a) of question).

Short-term market fluctuations may not be impairment indicators if prices are expected to return to higher levels. However, despite the difficulty in making such assessments, it would appear that the mining assets should be tested for impairment.

(c) **Control**

The *Conceptual Framework* states that an entity controls an economic resource if it has the present ability to direct the use of the economic resource and obtain the economic benefits which flow from it. An entity has the ability to direct the use of an economic resource if it has the right to deploy that economic resource in its activities. Although control of an economic resource usually arises from legal rights, it can also arise if an entity has the present ability to prevent all other parties from directing the use of it and obtaining the benefits from the economic resource. For an entity to control a resource, the economic benefits from the resource must flow to the entity instead of another party.

Although the *Conceptual Framework* gives some guidance on the definition of control, existing IFRS Standards should be used when making the assessment.

IFRS 10 *Consolidated Financial Statements* states that an investor controls an investee when it is exposed, or has rights, to variable returns from its involvement with the investee and has the ability to affect those returns through its power over the investee. Fill does not have control over the mine because its voting power is not sufficient for it to pass operating decisions that will affect the mine's relevant activities and thus its returns.

However, in accordance with IFRS 11 *Joint Arrangements*, it would seem that joint control exists. This is because two of the parties (Fill and the participant that owns 35%) share control and operating decisions require them to unanimously agree. The mine does not appear to be a separate entity and would therefore most likely be classified as a joint operation.

Business Combinations

A business combination is defined in IFRS 3 *Business Combinations* as a transaction or other event in which an acquirer obtains control of one or more businesses. A business is further defined as an integrated set of activities and assets capable of providing a return. Thus, the mine represents a business. However, the Fill's purchase of a 40% interest is not a business combination because Fill does not have control.

That said, IFRS 3 states that the accounting treatment of the acquisition of an interest in a joint operation that meets the definition of a business should apply the same principles as are applied to a business combination unless those principles contradict IFRS 11. In other words, the identifiable net assets of the joint operation should be measured at fair value. However, unlike with a business combination, Fill should not recognise any non-controlling interest. Instead, Fill should only recognise its share of the mine's assets and liabilities. Goodwill would be recognised for the difference between the consideration paid for the interest and Fill's share of the net assets acquired.

Marking guide			
			Marks
(a)	–	a discussion of potential measurement basis, NRV and relevant Standards	4
	–	application of IAS 2 to the scenario	3
			——
			7
			——
(b)	–	a discussion of IAS 16 and application to the scenario	4
	–	a discussion of IAS 36 and application to the scenario	4
			——
			8
			——
(c)	–	a discussion of control in the ED Conceptual Framework and other relevant Standards	4
	–	a discussion of a business combination per IFRS 3	2
	–	application of the above discussions to the scenario	4
			——
			10
			——
Total			**25**
			——

Examiner's comments

The key to answering the first part of the question (and most questions) was to use the information in the scenario. The scenario mentioned that the entity sells its coal on the spot and futures markets and that low quality coal is to be extracted in three years' time when the forecast price of coal is to be 20% lower than the current spot price. Candidates could gain marks by simply discussing how this information would impact on coal valuation. In addition, candidates could gain marks by discussing the variety of measurement bases set out in the Conceptual Framework and how these might be applied to inventory valuation.

This second part of the question was well answered by candidates. However, the same cannot be said for the third part of the question which tested joint control and whether the Conceptual Framework affected the decision over the control of the mine. The wording of the question was such that it gave candidates the scope for a wide discussion of the issues involved. For example, candidates could have discussed the Conceptual Framework and the guidance on the definition of control. Additionally, existing IFRS standards also provide help in determining control via IFRS 10 Consolidated Financial Statements. IFRS 3 Business Combinations discusses the situation where an acquirer obtains control of one or more businesses. Unfortunately most candidates took a narrow approach and discussed mainly IFRS 10 or IFRS 3. However, if a candidate concluded differently to the model answer, and substantiated this, then credit was given.

24 HOLLS (DEC 2018) *Walk in the footsteps of a top tutor*

Key answer tips

Many students who sat the December 2018 found this question difficult. No doubt there are some tricky elements within in. However, part of the problem no doubt resulted from issues with exam technique and exam preparation.

Part (a) is relatively straight forward. However, 'management commentary' is a current issue, and many students do not study this area of the syllabus adequately. Current issues feature in every SBR exam; do not neglect them.

Part (b) appears tricky but actually offers some very easy sources of marks. For example, all students sitting SBR should be able to 'provide an explanation of accounting for deferred taxation'. Make sure that you concentrate on the parts of the question that you are most comfortable with.

(a) (i) Management commentary

Tutorial note

Management commentary is listed as a 'current issue' within the SBR syllabus. Do not neglect this area of the syllabus when studying. Current issues feature in every SBR exam.

The IFRS Practice Statement *Management Commentary* provides a broad, non-binding framework for the presentation of management commentary. The Practice Statement is not an IFRS Standard. Consequently, entities applying IFRS Standards are not required to comply with the Practice Statement, unless specifically required by their jurisdiction. Furthermore, non-compliance with the Practice Statement will not prevent an entity's financial statements from complying with IFRS Standards.

Arguments against non-binding approach

Tutorial note

You should be able to generate some points here using common-sense.

A mandatory standard is more likely to guarantee a consistent application of its principles and practices. Some entities will not produce management commentary because its application is non-mandatory. It can therefore be argued that the Board's objectives of enhancing the comparability of financial information will not be achieved unless management commentary is mandatory.

Arguments for non-binding approach

Tutorial note

Remember that a non-binding approach will permit greater flexibility. Whilst this can be a drawback, it can also lead to the disclosure of more relevant information.

It is difficult to create a standard on the MC which is sufficiently detailed to cover the business models of every entity or be consistent with all IFRS Standards. The Practice Statement allows companies to adapt the information provided to particular aspects of their business. This flexible approach could help generate more meaningful disclosures about resources, risks and relationships which can affect an entity's value and how these resources are managed. It provides management with an opportunity to add context to the published financial information, and to explain their future strategy and objectives without being restricted by the constraints of a standard.

Some jurisdictions take little notice of non-mandatory guidance but the Practice Statement provides local regulators with a framework to develop more authoritative requirements.

If the MC were a full IFRS Standard, the integration of management commentaries and the information produced in accordance with IFRS Standards could be challenged on technical grounds, as well as its practical merits.

(ii) **Understandability**

The *Conceptual Framework* states that financial information should be readily understandable. The MC should therefore be written in plain language and a style appropriate to users' needs.

The form and content of the MC will vary between entities, reflecting the nature of their business, the strategies adopted and the regulatory environment in which they operate. Whatever the form and content, users should be able to locate information relevant to their needs.

Relevance

Tutorial note

Begin by defining 'relevance' as per the Conceptual Framework.

Information has the quality of relevance when it has the capacity to influence the economic decisions of users by helping them evaluate past, present or future events or confirming, or correcting, their past evaluations. Relevant financial information has predictive value, confirmatory value or both.

The onus is on management to determine what information is important enough to be included in the MC to enable users to 'understand' the financial statements and meet the objective of the MC. If the entity provides too much information, it could reduce its relevance and understandability. If material events or uncertainties are not disclosed, then users may have insufficient information to meet their needs.

However, unnecessary detail may obscure important information especially if entities adopt a boiler-plate approach. If management presents too much information about, for example, all the risks facing an organisation, this will conflict with the relevance objective. There is no single optimal number of disclosures but it is useful to convey their relative importance in a meaningful way.

Comparability

Tutorial note

Begin by defining comparability as per the Conceptual Framework.

Comparability is the qualitative characteristic which enables users to identify and understand similarities and differences amongst items. It is important for users to be able to compare information over time and between entities. Comparability between entities is problematic as the MC is designed to reflect the perspectives of management and the circumstances of individual entities. Thus, entities in the same industry may have different perceptions of what is important and how they measure and report it. There are some precedents on how to define and calculate non-financial measures and financial measures which are not produced in accordance with IFRS Standards but there are inconsistencies in the definition and calculation of these measures.

It is sometimes suggested that the effectiveness of the overall report may be enhanced by strengthening the links between financial statements and the MC. However, such suggestions raise concerns about maintaining a clear distinction between the financial statement information and other information.

An entity should ensure consistency in terms of wording, definitions, segment disclosures, etc. between the financial statements and the MC to improve the understanding of financial performance.

(b)   Current tax

Current tax is based on taxable profit for the year. Taxable profit is different from accounting profit due to temporary differences between accounting and tax treatments, and due to items which are never taxable or tax deductible. Tax benefits such as tax credits are not recognised unless it is probable that the tax positions are sustainable.

The Group is required to estimate the corporate tax in each of the many jurisdictions in which it operates. The Group is subject to tax audits in many jurisdictions; as a result, the Group may be required to make an adjustment in a subsequent period which could have a material impact on the Group's profit for the year.

Tax reconciliation

Tutorial note

Discuss the tax reconciliation, what it shows, and why it is useful.

The tax rate reconciliation is important for understanding the tax charge reported in the financial statements and why the effective tax rate differs from the statutory rate.

Most companies will reconcile the group's annual tax expense to the statutory rate in the country in which the parent is based. Hence the rate of 22% is used in the tax reconciliation. It is important that the reconciliation explains the reasons for the differences between the effective rate and the statutory rate.

Tutorial note

Remember to state the obvious. The 'other' category is vague and does not provide useful information to financial statement users.

There should be minimal use of the 'other' category. In this case, the other category is significant ($14 million) and there is no explanation of what 'other' constitutes. This makes it harder for investors to predict the Group's tax expense in future periods.

One-off and unusual items can have a significant effect on the effective tax rate, but financial statements and disclosure notes rarely include a detailed discussion of them. For example, the brand impairment and disposals of businesses should be explained to investors, as they are probably material items. The explanation should include any potential reversal of the treatment.

Some profits recognised in the financial statements are non-taxable. In some jurisdictions, gains on disposals of businesses are not taxable and impairment losses do not obtain tax relief. These issues should be explained to investors so that they understand the impact on the Group's effective tax rate.

Tax rates

Tutorial note

To make investment decisions, investors need information that will help them to assess an entity's future cash flows. Tax paid is a significant annual cash flow, so information about different tax rates is important.

As the Group is operating in multiple countries, the actual tax rates applicable to profits in those countries are different from the local tax rate. The overseas tax rates are higher than local rates, hence the increase in the taxation charge of $10 million. The local rate is different from the weighted average tax rate (27%) of the Group based on the different jurisdictions in which it operates. Investors may feel that using the weighted tax rate in the reconciliation gives a more meaningful number because it is a better estimate of the tax rate the Group expects to pay over the long term. Investors will wish to understand the company's expected long-term sustainable tax rate so they can prepare their cash flow or profit forecasts.

Information about the sustainability of the tax rate over the long term is more important than whether the rate is high or low compared to other jurisdictions. An adjustment can be made to an investor's financial model for a long-term sustainable rate, but not for a volatile rate where there is no certainty over future performance.

Tutorial note

Volatility in financial statements makes it harder for investors to predict an entity's future net cash flows.

For modelling purposes, an understanding of the actual cash taxes paid is critical and the cash paid of $95 million can be found in the statement of cash flows.

Deferred taxation

Tutorial note

Easy marks can be obtained for outlining the accounting treatment of deferred tax.

Provision for deferred tax is made for temporary differences between the carrying amount of assets and liabilities for financial reporting purposes and their value for tax purposes. The amount of deferred tax reflects the expected recoverable amount and is based on the expected manner of recovery or settlement of the carrying amount of assets and liabilities, using the basis of taxation enacted or substantively enacted by the financial statement date.

Deferred tax assets are not recognised where it is more likely than not that the assets will not be realised in the future. The evaluation of deferred tax assets' recoverability requires judgements to be made regarding the availability of future taxable income.

Management assesses the available evidence to estimate if sufficient future taxable income will be generated to use the existing deferred tax assets. A significant piece of objective negative evidence evaluated was the loss incurred in the period prior to the period ended 30 November 20X7. Such objective evidence may limit the ability to consider other subjective evidence such as projections for future growth.

Deferred taxes are one of the most difficult areas of the financial statements for investors to understand. Thus there is a need for a clear explanation of the deferred tax balances and an analysis of the expected timing of reversals. This would help investors see the time period over which deferred tax assets arising from losses might reverse. It would be helpful if the company provided a breakdown of which reversals would have a cash tax impact and which would not.

Application of deferred tax rules to Holls

As the proposed tax law was approved, it is considered to be enacted. Therefore, the rate of 25% should be used to calculate the deferred tax liability associated with the relevant items which affect deferred taxation.

Tutorial note

Use the information in the question to calculate the deferred tax balances.

At 30 November 20X7, Holls has deductible temporary differences of $4.5 million which are expected to reverse in the next year. In addition, Holls also has taxable temporary differences of $5 million which relate to the same taxable company and the tax authority. Holls expects $3 million of those taxable temporary differences to reverse in 20X8 and the remaining $2 million to reverse in 20X9. Thus a deferred tax liability of $1.25 million ($5 million × 25%) should be recognised and as $3 million of these taxable temporary differences are expected to reverse in the year in which the deductible temporary differences reverse, Holls can also recognise a deferred tax asset for $0.75 million ($3 million × 25%). The recognition of a deferred tax asset for the rest of the deductible temporary differences will depend on whether future taxable profits sufficient to cover the reversal of this deductible temporary difference are expected to arise. An entity is permitted to offset deferred tax assets and deferred tax liabilities if there is a legally enforceable right to offset the current tax assets against current tax liabilities as the amounts relate to income tax levied by the same taxation authority on the same taxable entity.

After the enactment of a new tax law, when material, Holls should consider disclosing the anticipated current and future impact on their results of operations, financial position, liquidity, and capital resources. In addition, Holls should consider disclosures in the critical accounting estimates section of the management commentary to the extent the changes could materially affect existing assumptions used in making estimates of tax-related balances. Changes in tax laws and rates may affect recorded deferred tax assets and liabilities and the effective tax rate in the future.

Marking guide				Marks
(a)	(i)	–	arguments for and against the non-binding framework	4
	(ii)	–	a discussion of understandability, relevance and comparability	3
		–	application of the above characteristics to MC	2
				—
				5
				—
(b)		–	an explanation of why taxable profits are different from accounting profit	2
		–	application of the following explanations to the scenario:	
			tax reconciliation	4
			tax rates	3
			deferred taxation	5
				—
				14
				—
		Professional marks		2
				—
Total				**25**
				—

Examiner's comments

There were a range of answers available to the first part of the question and candidates were given due credit if they were able to justify their conclusions. However for both parts of the question, many candidates did not actually answer the requirement but instead simply described a management commentary or defined the qualitative characteristics. They did this without applying their knowledge to the preparation of the management commentary. Due credit was given to this type of answer but of course, full marks cannot be awarded unless the question set is actually answered.

The second part of the question caused some candidates concern and yet it was well answered. It has been said on numerous occasions that SBR is an exam were candidates cannot rely on rote learned knowledge but that they need to understand principles and be able to apply the knowledge of these principles to the question scenario. In this part of the question, candidates needed to discuss and evaluate the facts in the question. The syllabus area requires candidates to demonstrate synthesis and evaluation and not simply factual knowledge. The model answer sets out significantly more than was required to gain a good mark. Likewise, candidates were also awarded marks for points raised which were not included in the model answer. By their nature, questions on an investor perspective are going to produce variations in answers because investors have many different perspectives and may even require different information from that provided in the financial statements.

25 SKIZER (SEP 2018) *Walk in the footsteps of a top tutor*

Key answer tips

The *Conceptual Framework* is an important topic in the SBR syllabus. You need to learn its contents but also practise applying it to each of the examinable IFRS and IAS Standards.

The SBR syllabus requires you to be able to discuss the current framework for integrated reporting, including the objectives, concepts, guiding principles and content of an integrated report. Do not neglect this popular exam topic.

(a) (i) IAS 38 recognition criteria

Tutorial note

You should know the recognition criteria in all of the examinable IFRS and IAS Standards. This is core knowledge.

IAS 38 *Intangible Assets* defines an intangible asset as a non-monetary asset without physical substance. It requires an entity to recognise an intangible asset if:

- it is probable that expected future economic benefits will flow to the entity, and

- the cost of the asset can be measured reliably.

This requirement applies whether an intangible asset is acquired externally or generated internally. The probability of future economic benefits must be based on reasonable and supportable assumptions about conditions which will exist over the life of the asset. The probability recognition criterion is always considered to be satisfied for intangible assets which are acquired separately or in a business combination.

If the recognition criteria are not met, IAS 38 requires the expenditure to be expensed when it is incurred.

Conceptual Framework

Tutorial note

The Conceptual Framework was revised in 2018. Make sure that your knowledge here is up-to-date. The current definitions of assets and liabilities make no reference to the probability of economic inflows or outflows.

According to the *Conceptual Framework,* items are only recognised if they meet the definition of an element. The definition of an asset is '**a present economic resource controlled by an entity as a result of a past event**' (para 4.3).

This does not mean that all items meeting the definition of an element are recognised. An element is only recognised if recognition provides users with useful financial information. In other words recognition must provide:

- relevant information

- a faithful representation of the asset or liability, and resulting income, expenses or equity movements.

Recognition might not provide relevant information if there is uncertainty over the existence of the element or if there is a low probability of an inflow or outflow of economic resources. Recognition of an element might not provide a faithful representation if there is a very high degree of measurement uncertainty.

Consistency

As can be seen, the recognition criteria in the *Conceptual Framework* and IAS 38 are different. This is because the recognition criteria in IAS 38 were based on previous versions of the *Conceptual Framework*, and have not been updated to reflect the 2018 *Conceptual Framework*.

Tutorial note

The recognition criteria in many other IFRS and IAS Standards are also based on the previous version of the Conceptual Framework. The Board may revise these standards in the future.

Both IAS 38 and the *Conceptual Framework* attempt to ensure that financial statements provide information that meets the qualitative characteristics of useful information but do this in different ways. IAS 38 uses practical filters of probability and reliability to exclude information that will not be useful. In contrast, the *Conceptual Framework* refers directly to the qualitative characteristics, and provides guidance on how to apply them.

The *Conceptual Framework* does not override IAS 38. The *Conceptual Framework* is only applied by preparers of financial statements when no standard applies to a particular transaction. Transactions involving intangible assets fall within the scope of IAS 38 and so the recognition criteria in this standard will be applied.

Tutorial note

Remember that one of the key purposes of the Conceptual Framework is to assist the Board when developing or revising an IFRS Standard.

(ii) **Implications if recognition criteria were met**

Tutorial note

Capitalisation is not optional. Expenditure that meets the criteria in IAS 38 must be recognised as an intangible asset, unless the effect is immaterial.

Skizer should have assessed whether the recognition criteria in IAS 38 were met at the time the entity capitalised the intangible assets. If the recognition criteria were met, then it was not appropriate to derecognise the intangible assets. According to IAS 38, an intangible asset should be derecognised only on disposal or when no future economic benefits are expected from its use or disposal.

If there were any doubts regarding the recoverability of the intangible asset, then Skizer should have assessed whether the intangible assets would be impaired. IAS 36 *Impairment of Assets* would be used to determine whether an intangible asset is impaired.

Further, the reclassification of intangible assets to research and development costs does not constitute a change in an accounting estimate. IAS 8 *Accounting Policies, Changes in Accounting Estimates and Errors* states that a change in accounting estimate is an adjustment of the carrying amount of an asset or liability, or related expense, resulting from reassessing the expected future benefits and obligations associated with that asset or liability. The costs of the stakes in the development projects can be determined and will not have been estimated.

Implications if recognition criteria were not met

Tutorial note

If a mistake was made on initial recognition, then this would constitute a prior period error.

If it is believed that the transactions never met the recognition criteria in IAS 38 then Skizer would have to recognise retrospectively a correction of an error, in accordance with IAS 8.

(iii) **Sale of intangible**

Revenue is defined in IFRS 15 *Revenue from Contracts with Customers* as income arising from a company's ordinary activities.

There is no indication that Skizer's business model is to sell development projects. Skizer's business model is to jointly develop a product, then leave the production to partners. Moreover, if the asset was for sale in the ordinary course of business then it would have been classified on acquisition as inventory. Skizer recognised an intangible asset, and fully impaired the asset, so it cannot argue that it has thereafter been held for sale in the ordinary course of business.

Tutorial note

Intangible assets are non-current assets. If an asset is held for sale in the ordinary course of business then, per IAS 1 Presentation of Financial Statements, it is presented as a current asset (most likely as inventories).

Furthermore, IAS 38 prohibits presenting the proceeds from the disposal of an intangible asset as revenue.

(b) (i) Issues with intangible assets acquired in a business combination

Tutorial note

This is a tricky requirement, but you are not expected to answer in the same level as detail as the model answer below. Seven separate points across the three issues would be sufficient to score full marks.

Under IFRS 3 *Business Combinations*, acquired intangible assets must be recognised and measured at fair value if they are separable or arise from other contractual rights. Once recognised, IAS 38 requires intangible assets with finite lives to be amortised over their useful lives and intangible assets with indefinite lives to be subject to an annual impairment review in accordance with IAS 36.

However, it is unlikely that all intangible assets acquired in a business combination will be homogeneous and investors may feel that there are different types of intangible assets which may be acquired. For example, a patent may only last for a finite period of time and may be thought as having an identifiable future revenue stream. In this case, amortisation of the patent would be logical. However, there are other intangible assets which are gradually replaced by the purchasing entity's own intangible assets, for example, customer lists, and it may make sense to account for these assets within goodwill. In such cases, investors may wish to reverse amortisation charges. In order to decide whether an amortisation charge makes sense, investors require greater detail about the nature of the identified intangible assets. IFRS Standards do not permit a different accounting treatment for this distinction.

Issues with choice in accounting policy

Tutorial note

Remember that measurement choices within IFRS Standards limit comparability because it is harder to compare one entity with another.

IAS 38 requires an entity to choose either the cost model or the revaluation model for each class of intangible asset. Under the cost model, after initial recognition intangible assets should be carried at cost less accumulated amortisation and impairment losses. Under the revaluation model, intangible assets may be carried at a revalued amount, based on fair value, less any subsequent amortisation and impairment losses.

The revaluation model can only be used if there is an active market for the intangible asset. Such active markets are not common for intangible assets.

Tutorial note

An active market is one where identical assets are regularly traded and prices are readily available.

If an intangible asset is reported using the cost model, the reported figures for intangible assets such as trademarks may be understated when compared to their fair values.

Moreover, the ability to choose the revaluation model or the cost model may limit comparability between different entities.

Capitalisation of development expenditure

Tutorial note

In real life, the distinction between 'research' and 'development' may not be clear cut. Moreover, performance related bonuses or stock market pressure may be incentives to classify research expenditure as development.

IAS 38 requires all research costs to be expensed. Development costs must be capitalised if the technical and commercial feasibility of the asset for sale or use has been established.

If an entity cannot distinguish the research phase of an internal project to create an intangible asset from the development phase, the entity treats the expenditure for that project as if it were incurred in the research phase only. This cautious approach ensures that assets are not overstated.

The problem for investors is that companies do not have a consistent approach to capitalisation. It is often unclear from disclosures how research expenditure was distinguished from development expenditure. It may be that entities allow bias to impact their decision-making in this area.

Intangible asset disclosure can help analysts understand the innovation capacity of companies. Investors can use the disclosure to identify companies with valuable development assets – once these launch in the market they should generate economic benefits, potentially increasing investment returns. However, preparers of financial statements are failing to adequately comply with the disclosure requirements of IAS 38, which limits their usefulness.

(ii)   **Integrated reporting**

Tutorial note

An integrated report communicates an entity's value creation in the short, medium, and long-term. It conceptualises value in terms of a range of capitals (stocks of value), rather than just in terms of financial capital.

Measuring the contribution of intangible assets to future cash flows is fundamental to integrated reporting. This helps explain the gap between the carrying amount of an entity's net assets and its market equity value.

As set out above, organisations are required to recognise intangible assets acquired in a business combination. Consequently, the intangible assets are only measured once for this purpose. However, organisations are likely to go further in their integrated report and disclose the impact on intangible assets as a result of sustainable growth strategies or specific initiatives. It is therefore very useful to communicate the value of intangible assets in an integrated report. For example, an entity may decide to disclose its assessment of the increase in brand value as a result of a corporate social responsibility initiative.

		Marking scheme	
			Marks
(a)	(i)	Discussion of recognition criteria	**5**
	(ii)	Derecognition criteria and impairment	2
		Reclassification and estimates	2
		If criteria not met	1
			5
	(iii)	Consideration of Skizer's business model	2
		Application of IFRS 15	2
			4
(b)	(i)	Different types of intangibles	3
		Cost or revaluation	2
		Development or research	2
			7
	(ii)	Measurement in financial statements	2
		Discussion of whether IR can supplement financial statements	2
			4
Total			25

Examiner's comments

Candidates should be able to discuss the consistency of the Conceptual Framework with each IFRS that is examined. Part (a)(i) is a good illustration of how candidates can be tested on this. Answers to this section were weak in general.

Answers to part (a)(ii) were generally weak. Some candidates missed that the question specifically referred to the recognition criteria being met, in which case derecognition would be inappropriate. Very few candidates identified the need for an impairment review under IAS 36 *Impairment of Assets* if there were doubts over recoverability from the intangible assets.

Answers to part (b) were generally good, where discussion included the accounting choices and subjective aspects of IAS 38 and IFRS 3. However, some answers limited opportunities for marks by not considering both standards. Part (b)(ii) asked for a discussion on whether integrated reporting can enhance reporting for intangible assets. Whilst many candidates were familiar with integrated reporting, fewer applied it to the situation (relating to intangible assets).

---

26 TABOOSCO (SEP 2018) *Walk in the footsteps of a top tutor*

Key answer tips

Additional performance measures (APMs) are increasingly prominent in the financial statements of public limited entities. The SBR syllabus states that students need to be able to discuss and apply APMs. Part (a) of this question should be a source of easy marks because lots of common-sense points can be made.

Part (b) is trickier. Many students dislike statements of cash flows and so would struggle to correct the errors made by Daveed. There are four marks available in part (b) (i) and part (b) (ii) – so you only need to post two correct adjustments on each to score a pass mark. Deal with the easiest adjustments first. If you don't understand an issue then leave it and move on.

(a)   APMs

(i)   APMs are not defined by International Financial Reporting Standards and therefore may not be directly comparable with other companies' APMs, including those in the same industry. If the same category of material items recurs each year and in similar amounts (in this example, restructuring costs and impairment losses) then the reporting entity should consider whether excluding these amounts from underlying profit provides a faithful representation of economic performance.

Under IFRS Standards, items cannot be presented as 'extraordinary items' in the financial statements or in the notes. Thus it may be confusing to users of the APMs to see this term used.

Tutorial note

Many entities are quick to classify expenses as non-recurring. Relatively few entities classify incomes as 'non-recurring'. Why do you think this is?

Items such as restructuring costs or impairment losses should not be labelled as non-recurring where it is misleading. The entity can make an adjustment for a charge or gain which they believe is appropriate, but they cannot describe such adjustments inaccurately.

(ii) The deduction of capital expenditure, purchase of own shares and the purchase of intangible assets from cash flows from operating activities is acceptable because free cash flow does not have a uniform definition.

A clear description of free cash flow and a reconciliation showing how this measure is calculated should be disclosed so that users can draw conclusions about the usefulness of the APM.

Entities should avoid misleading comments when describing APMs. Free cash flow does not normally represent the residual cash flow available as many entities have mandatory debt service requirements which are not normally deducted from the measure. It would also be misleading to show free cash flow per share in bold alongside earnings per share as they are not comparable.

(iii) When an entity presents an APM, it should present the most directly comparable measure calculated in accordance with IFRS Standards with equal or greater prominence. Whether an APM is more prominent would depend on the facts and circumstances. In this case, the entity has omitted comparable information calculated in accordance with IFRS Standards from an earnings release which includes APMs such as EBITDAR. Additionally, the entity has emphasised the APM measure by describing it as 'record performance' without an equally prominent description any measure calculated in accordance with IFRS Standards. Further, the entity has provided a discussion of the APM measure without a similar discussion and analysis of the IFRS Standards measure.

The entity has presented EBITDAR as a performance measure; such measures should be reconciled to profit for the year as presented in the statement of comprehensive income. Operating profit would not be considered the best starting point as EBITDAR makes adjustments for items which are not included in operating profit such as interest and tax.

Tutorial note

Comparability is an important characteristic of useful financial information. The users of financial statements should be able to compare the financial performance and position of one entity with another. They should also be able to compare the same entity year-on-year.

The entity has changed the way it calculates the APM because it has treated rent differently. However, if an entity chooses to change an APM, the change and the reason for the change should be explained and any comparatives restated. A change would be appropriate only in exceptional circumstances where the new APM better achieves the same objectives, perhaps if there has been a change in the strategy. The revised APM should be reliable and more relevant.

(iv)   The entity should provide income tax effects on its APMs depending on the nature of the measures. The entity should include current and deferred income tax expense commensurate with the APM and the APM should not be presented net of tax as income taxes should be shown as a separate adjustment and explained.

(b)   (i)   **Adjustment of net cash generated from operating activities for errors in the statement**

Tutorial note

Label your workings so that the marker can understand the adjustments you have made.

	$m
Draft net cash generated from operations (per question)	278
Cash inflows relating to car disposals	30
Effects of changes in foreign exchange rates	28
Reclassification of interest paid	18
Tax credit not recorded	6
Associate's profit – incorrectly included	(12)
Share of associate's profit – non-cash item that should have been deducted from profit.	(4)
Net cash generated from operating activities	344

(ii)   **Free cash flow reconciliation**

Tutorial note

The question tells you how to calculate operating 'free cash flow'. Make sure you read note (vi) carefully.

In note (iv) we are told that the pension deficit payments are 'exceptional'. It is easy to miss this. Daveed excludes exceptional items when calculating free cash flow.

	$m
Net cash generated from operating activities (part (i))	344
Net capital expenditure	(46)
Purchase of associate (W1)	(20)
Dividend received from associate (25% × $4m)	1
Interest received	10
Interest paid	(18)
Pension deficit payments – add back to exclude	27
Free cash flow	298

(W1) Purchase of associate

	$m
Purchase cost (bal. fig.)	20
Share of profit of associate	4
Dividend received	(1)
Carrying amount as at 31 August 20X8	23

(iii)   Explanation of adjustments

Tutorial note

There is only one mark available for each issue. Keep your explanations brief.

Purchase and sale of cars

Daveed's presentation of cash flows from the sale of cars as being from investing activities is incorrect as cash flows from the sale of cars should have been presented as cash flows from operating activities ($30 million). IAS 16 *Property, Plant and Equipment* (PPE) states that an entity which normally sells items of PPE which are held for rental to others should transfer such assets to inventories at their carrying amount when they cease to be rented and become held for sale. Subsequent proceeds from the sale of such assets should be recognised as revenue in accordance with IFRS 15 *Revenue from Contracts with Customers* and thus shown as cash flows from operating activities.

Purchase of associate

Cash paid for the investment is $20 million, and cash received from the dividend is $1 million. In order to arrive at the correct figure for net cash generated from operating activities, the incorrect treatment of the profit for the year for the associate must be eliminated ($12 million) and the correct adjustment of $4 million shown in net cash generated by operating activities.

Foreign exchange losses

IAS 7 *Statement of Cash Flows* states that unrealised gains and losses arising from changes in foreign exchange rates are not cash flows. The amounts reported in the statement of cash flows included, in error, the effect of changes in foreign exchange rates arising on the retranslation of its overseas operations. As a consequence, cash generated from operating activities should be increased by $28 million. All exchange differences relating to the subsidiary are recorded in other comprehensive income and taken to a separate component of equity. On disposal of the foreign operation the gains (or losses) are reclassified to the statement of profit or loss.

Pension payments

The pension payments are correctly included in operating cash flows. However, Daveed excludes them when calculating free cash flow. As the tax cash benefit has not been included, net cash generated from operating activities will be adjusted for the $6 million and $27 million ($33m – $6m) will be excluded from the free cash flow calculation.

Interest paid

Interest paid which is capitalised as part of the cost of property, plant, and equipment should be treated as a cash flow from investing activities. Interest paid and capitalised as part of inventory should be classified within operating activities the statement of cash flows. Thus there should be a reclassification of interest paid of $18 million from the operating section to the investing activities section.

		Marking scheme	Marks
(a)		Discussion of comparability of APMs	1
		Extraordinary items	2
		Free cash flow	2
		EBITDAR	4
		Tax effects	1
			———
			10
			———
(b)	(i)	Adjustment schedule	4
			———
	(ii)	Free cash reconciliation	4
			———
	(iii)	Purchase of cars	1
		Purchase of associate	1
		Foreign exchange losses	1
		Pension payments	1
		Interest paid	1
			———
			5
			———
		Professional marks	2
			———
Total			25
			———

Examiner's comments

It was pleasing to see that part (a) was often well-described, reasoned and applied to the scenario. However, answers to part (b) were more varied.

27   PLAYER TWO

Key answer tips

Part (a) of this question tests additional performance measures (APMs). This is a new topic that appears in the SBR pilot paper. Make sure that you have read about their use and legitimacy. Marks are available for general points about APMs, as well as for raising specific issues with Player Two's APM.

Part (b) requires assessment of a financial statement disclosure. Users of the financial statements want information that is entity specific rather than generic. What else do you think Wrap's investors would want to know about the impairment review?

(a)   Additional Performance Measures

IAS 1 *Presentation of Financial Statements* permits entities to disclose additional information that is relevant to understanding an entity's performance and position. The *Conceptual Framework* notes that the primary users of financial statements are investors, lenders and other creditors.

Additional performance measures (APMs) are often used internally when assessing management performance. As such, they can help financial statement users to understand management's view about what is important to the entity

However, there are concerns about the use of APMs.

It is commonly argued that APMs are used by management to disguise weak financial performance, which may mislead financial statement users. This criticism might apply to Player Two. Basic earnings per share (EPS) is 2.0 cents per share ($2.5m/122.2m), whereas adjusted basic EPS is more than five times higher.

APMs can be particularly misleading if displayed prominently. This is because they may become indistinguishable from figures produced in accordance with IFRS Standards and therefore obtain unwarranted credibility. Although Player Two does not disclose this APM on the face of its primary statements the ordering of disclosure notes is important and the disclosure of this information may still mislead investors as to its nature.

Performance measures that use figures prepared in accordance with IFRS Standards are more likely to be comparable with other entities. Entities may differ markedly when calculating APMs. For example, the types of adjustments made by Player Two when calculating adjusted basic EPS may differ from those used by other entities, hindering comparability. One company's APMs may also not be comparable year-on-year.

Some entities do not reconcile their APMs back to the financial statements. However, this criticism does not apply to Player Two. As such, it is possible to assess the adequacy and reasonableness of the adjusting items.

Some users may question the appropriateness of the profit adjustments that Player Two has made to arrive at adjusted basic EPS:

- Although amortisation is a judgemental, non-cash expense, the business may need to replace its intangible assets. This will require investment. Moreover, amortisation of brands should reflect their pattern of use. If brands have a definite useful life then the business will need to incur costs in order to protect its brand positioning and market share.

- Restructuring costs were incurred in both the current and prior periods and so they are not a one-off cost. Excluding these amounts from underlying basic EPS ignores the fact that restructuring is a regular part of Player Two's business.

- The existence of impairment charges suggests that the retail stores have performed poorly and are under-utilised. It also suggests a poor outlook for the business in terms of its future net cash inflows. Eliminating this impairment charge when calculating adjusted basic EPS could be argued to provide an over-optimistic representation of Player Two's current and future performance.

As part of the Principles of Disclosure project, the International Accounting Standards Board is proposing to offer guidance on the calculation and presentation of APMs. This should help to alleviate some of the concerns expressed by financial statement users.

(b) Impairment disclosures

Impairment reviews involve judgement and therefore the users of the financial statements must be provided with enough information to assess whether the assumptions used were reliable.

The disclosure note is lacking key information about many of the judgements used. It is very generic and does not provide information that is specific to Wrap's impairment review.

Cash-generating unit

No information has been provided about how the cash generating unit was determined.

No information has been provided about how goodwill was allocated to the cash generating unit.

Value-in-use

The disclosure note does not describe key assumptions factored into the cash flow forecast and therefore the users cannot assess its reliability. Important assumptions might include estimates of future margins or, if relevant, foreign currency movements.

The disclosure does not say whether the forecasts represent past experience or future expectations. It also does not state whether there is any consistency with external sources of information.

The disclosure note does not say how many years the cash flow forecasts covered. This is important because forecasts that cover a longer period are less likely to be reliable.

The note does not say how many years' worth of cash flows have been extrapolated beyond the end of the budgeted period. The longer this period, the less likely it is that the growth rate will be maintained, due to obsolescence issues or the entrance of new competitors to the market.

The disclosure note does not justify the rate of growth used to extrapolate cash flows beyond the period covered by the cash flow forecasts. This is important because the growth rate used seems unrealistically high, particularly when compared to the current economic climate and the sluggish performance of the industry within which Wrap operates.

The disclosure does not state whether the growth rate used is specific to Unit D. Growth could therefore be over or under-stated.

Wrap have disclosed an average discount rate. They should instead disclose the specific rate used to discount the cash flows of Unit D so that users can assess whether it appears reasonable. The discount rate used should reflect the time value of money and the risks specific to the CGU for which future cash flow estimates have not been adjusted.

Sensitivity

The market capitalisation of Wrap is below its net asset value, suggesting that the market is expecting impairment in value. This would contradict the disclosure, which says that a 'reasonably possible change' would not cause impairment.

Sensitivity analysis would therefore be of use to the users so that they assess the likelihood and impact of potential future impairments.

Marking scheme		Marks
(a)	Additional performance measures – 1 mark per point	15
(b)	Impairment disclosures – 1 mark per point	8
	Professional marks	2
Total		**25**

28 ZACK *Walk in the footsteps of a top tutor*

Key answer tips

This question mainly tests two accounting standards: IAS 37 *Provisions, Contingent Liabilities and Contingent Assets* and IAS 8 *Accounting Policies, Changes in Accounting Estimates and Errors*. You should be familiar with these from prior studies although the level of application and engagement required here is much higher.

The SBR syllabus identifies accounting policies as a current issue, and an exposure draft relating to IAS 8 is an examinable document. If you lack familiarity with this then revisit Chapter 23 in the Study Text.

(a)   **Provisions**

Tutorial note

Provisions are a core accounting standard. Make sure that you know the basic criteria for recognising, measuring and derecognising provisions.

Under IAS 37 *Provisions, Contingent Liabilities and Contingent Assets*, an entity must recognise a provision if, and only if:

- a present obligation (legal or constructive) has arisen as a result of a past event (the obligating event),

- payment is probable, and

- the amount can be estimated reliably.

A provision should be made on the date of the obligating event, which is the date on which the event takes place that results in an entity having no realistic alternative to settling the legal or constructive obligation.

The obligating event took place in the year to 31 March 20X2. However, it is reasonable at 31 March 20X2 to assess the need for a provision to be immaterial because the damage to the building seemed superficial.

In the year to 31 March 20X3, as a result of the legal arguments supporting the action, Zack must reassess its estimate of the likely damages and a provision is needed, based on the advice that it has regarding the likely settlement. Provisions should be reviewed at each year end for material changes to the best estimate.

Dr Profit or loss	$800,000
Cr Provision	$800,000

The potential for reimbursements (e.g. insurance payments) to cover some of the expenditure required to settle a provision can be recognised, but only if receipt is virtually certain if the entity settles the obligation. IAS 37 requires that the reimbursement be treated as a separate asset. The company seems confident that it will satisfy the terms of the insurance policy and should accrue for the reimbursement:

Dr Other receivables	$200,000
Cr Profit or loss	$200,000

The court case was found against Zack but as this was after the authorisation of the financial statements. As such it is not, per IAS 10 *Events After the Reporting Period*, an adjusting event.

(b) (i) **Accruals error**

Tutorial note

A prior period error results from misuse of information that was available, or which could reasonably be expected to be available, when the financial statements were authorised.

The systems error has resulted in a prior period error. IAS 8 *Accounting Policies, Changes in Accounting Estimates and Errors* requires prior period errors to be amended retrospectively by restating the comparatives as if the error had never occurred.

In order to correct this error, Zack should restate the prior year information for the year ended 31 March 20X2. As such, expenses in the statement of profit or loss and other comprehensive income must be reduced by $2 million. As a result, brought forward retained earnings in the current year statement of changes in equity will increase by $2 million. Additionally, the trade payables figure in the prior year statement of financial position should be reduced by $2 million.

(ii) **Selection of accounting policies**

Entities should follow the requirements of IAS 8 *Accounting Policies, Changes in Accounting Estimates and Errors*, when selecting or changing accounting policies. An entity should determine the accounting policy to be applied to an item with direct reference to IFRS Standards. However, an accounting policy need not be applied if the effect of applying them would be immaterial.

Tutorial note

An item is material if its omission or misstatement would influence the economic decisions of financial statement user groups.

The Practice Statement on materiality is an examinable document.

Materiality is judgemental, but the Board have issued a Practice Statement that provides guidance in this area.

Tutorial note

Some accounting standards offer a choice of accounting policy, such as IAS 40 Investment Property.

Entities should select and apply their accounting policies consistently for similar transactions. If a specific IFRS Standard permits different accounting policies for categories of similar items, an entity should apply an appropriate policy for each of the categories in question and apply these accounting policies consistently for each category. For example, for different classes of property, plant and equipment, some may be carried at fair value and some at historical cost.

The *Conceptual Framework* provides guidance when an accounting standard offers a choice of measurement base. Preparers should ensure that the resulting financial information is useful to primary user groups. In other words, the measurement base selected should provide relevant information and offer a faithful representation of the underlying transaction. To provide relevant information, preparers should consider the nature of the asset or liability being measured, and how it generates cash flows for the reporting entity. A measurement base that has a very high level of measurement uncertainty may not provide a faithful representation. Such decisions clearly involve the exercise of judgement and consideration must be given to the information requirements of the entity's user groups. These will vary from one entity to another.

Tutorial note

IAS 8 provides guidance if no accounting standard applies to a transaction. Remember that this will be a rare occurrence.

Where IFRS Standards do not specifically apply to a transaction, judgement should be used in developing or applying an accounting policy which will result in useful financial information. In making that judgement, entities must refer to guidance in specific IFRS Standards that deal with similar issues and then, subsequently, to definitions, and criteria in the *Conceptual Framework*. Additionally, entities can refer to recent pronouncements of other standard setters who use similar conceptual frameworks.

(iii)   Criticisms of IAS 8

IAS 8 requires prior period errors to be amended retrospectively by restating the comparatives as if the error had never occurred. Hence, the impact of any prior period errors is shown through retained earnings rather than being included in the current period's profit or loss. Prepares of financial statements could use this treatment for prior period errors as a method for manipulating current period earnings.

Tutorial note

Entities should only change an accounting policy if required to do so by an IFRS Standard, or because the resulting financial information is more useful.

A change in accounting policy, per IAS 8, is also dealt with retrospectively. However, this can prove time consuming and costly. Entities may decide to retain their current accounting policy, even though a change might result in more useful information for user groups.

A key issue with IAS 8 is that the definitions of 'accounting policies' and 'accounting estimates' are not clear enough and so distinguishing an accounting policy from an accounting estimate can be difficult. Changes in accounting policy are dealt with retrospectively whereas changes in accounting estimates are dealt with prospectively so being able to distinguish policies and estimates is important. The lack of clarity here leads to inconsistency in practice, which may impact comparability.

Exposure Draft – ED/2018/1

Tutorial note

Current issues are tested in every SBR exam.

The IFRS Interpretations Committee's role is to respond to questions about the application of IFRS Standards that are submitted by stakeholders. If the Committee concludes that the existing IFRS Standard is adequate then they publish an agenda decision. This details the reasons why the IFRS Standard does not require revision, but also explains how best to apply that standard. Agenda decisions therefore provide helpful guidance and best-practice.

As a result of an agenda decision, an entity may wish to change an accounting policy but be deterred by the time and cost involved in retrospective application. In *ED/2018/1 Accounting Policy Changes* the Board proposes that an accounting policy change resulting from an agenda decision made by the IFRS Interpretations Committee should be implemented retrospectively unless:

- it is impracticable to do so (due to a lack of data), or

- the cost of working out the effect of the change exceeds the benefits to the users of the financial statements.

Marking scheme		Marks
(a)	Provision discussion – 1 mark per point	7
(b)	(i) Accruals error – 1 mark per point	4
	(ii) Accounting policies – 1 mark per point	7
	(iii) Criticisms of IAS 8 – 1 mark per point	7
Total		25

29 MCVEIGH (DEC 18)

Key answer tips

Part (a) examines financial assets. It is worth seven marks. You will not be able to score a pass mark from calculations and journals alone. Remember to discuss why the loan is a financial asset and how it should be initially and subsequently measured. Don't forget about impairment issues.

Part (b) of the question tests knowledge of IAS 19 *Employee Benefits* as well as its consistency with the *Conceptual Framework*. Requirement (b) (iii) largely examines recent amendments to IAS 19 that are covered in Chapter 23 of the Study Text. Without knowledge of these amendments you will find this tricky. However, there are easy marks available. The accounting treatment of the remeasurement component is clearly incorrect. Beginning your discussion with this issue would be the easiest and quickest way to score marks.

(a)   Interest Free Loan

Tutorial note

Make sure that you talk about the initial recognition of the financial asset, and the subsequent treatment up to the reporting date.

The loan to the employee is a financial asset. This is because McVeigh has a contractual right to receive cash from its employees.

IFRS 9 *Financial Instruments* requires financial assets to be initially measured at fair value (plus transaction costs in certain situations). Normally the fair value is the price paid. However, an interest free loan is not taking place on the same terms as would exist between market participants. In this case, the fair value should be estimated as the present value of future receipts using the market interest rate.

The difference between the fair value of the loan and the face value of the loan will be treated as employee remuneration under IAS 19 *Employee Benefits*.

	$m
Fair value of loan at 1 June 20X2 ($10m × 1/1.06^2)	8.9
Employee compensation (bal. fig.)	1.1

Cash paid	10.0

The following entries are required:

Dr Financial asset	$8.9m
Dr Employee compensation	$1.1m
Cr Cost of sales	$10.0m

The employee compensation would be charged to profit or loss over the two-year period. Recognising it on a straight line basis would lead to half being charged to profit or loss in the current period, whereas the other half would be recognised as a prepayment on the statement of financial position.

The loan asset will then be measured at amortised cost. These loans with employees cannot be traded so are held within a business model which has the aim of collecting contractual cash flows. Interest income will be calculated using the effective interest method. In this case the effective interest rate is 6% and the carrying amount of the loan in the statement of financial position at 31 May 20X3 will be $9.43 million ($8.9 million × 1.06). Interest of $0.53 million will be credited to profit or loss.

Dr Financial asset	$0.53m
Cr Profit or loss	$0.53m

IFRS 9 requires that a loss allowance is calculated for financial assets measured at amortised cost and fair value through other comprehensive income (unless the financial asset is an equity investment). McVeigh must calculate a loss allowance equal to 12-month expected credit losses. This is because credit risk at the reporting date is low and therefore there has not been a significant increase in credit risk since inception of the loans. The loss allowance will be charged to profit or loss and will reduce the net carrying amount of the financial asset.

(b) (i) Plan A

Tutorial note

Start with the definition of a defined contribution plan and a defined benefit plan.

A defined contribution plan is one where an entity has no legal or constructive obligation to pay further contributions if the fund does not have sufficient assets to pay all employee benefits relating to employee service in the current and prior periods.

A constructive obligation arises when past behaviour creates an expectation that the entity will discharge certain responsibilities in the future.

All post-employment benefit plans that do not qualify as a defined contribution plan are, by definition, defined benefit plans.

Tutorial note

The key feature that distinguishes a defined benefit plan from a defined contribution plan is whether or not the entity has an obligation to contribute further assets to the scheme. Try and pull out the reasons why McVeigh is obliged to make these payments.

There are various indications that Plan A should be accounted for as a defined benefit plan:

- McVeigh has a history of paying pension benefits and has therefore created a constructive obligation that it will continue to do so.

- The benefits payable are linked to final salaries, thus potentially creating a plan deficit. Due to its constructive obligation, McVeigh will need to increase its contributions if there are insufficient plan assets to pay for the promised benefits.

- If McVeigh terminates the plan then it has a legal obligation to pay further contributions in order to purchase lifetime annuities for retired scheme members.

McVeigh clearly has legal and constructive obligations to pay further amounts into Plan A. Hence Plan A was correctly classified as a defined benefit plan.

(ii) **Conceptual Framework**

Tutorial note

The SBR examining team have said that students should be able to discuss the consistency of any issued IFRS Standard with the Conceptual Framework.

A good starting point would be to state the recognition criteria from the Conceptual Framework.

The *Conceptual Framework* states that an item should only be recognised if it meets the definition of an element. The definition of a liability is that it is a present obligation from a past event to transfer an economic resource. However, the *Conceptual Framework* notes that not all elements are recognised. Instead an element is recognised if it provides useful financial information – i.e. relevant information and a faithful representation of the underlying transaction.

A defined benefit deficit meets the definition of a liability. It represents a legal or constructive obligation to transfer cash or other assets (economic resources). This is because an entity must pay additional assets into the scheme in order to fund the post-retirement benefits promised to employees.

The defined benefit deficit is reduced by the fair value of the plan assets. This is because the plan assets reduce the entity's obligation, resulting in a single net obligation – essentially, the promised benefits not yet funded which the reporting entity is liable for.

Recognising a defined benefit deficit provides relevant information to users of the financial statements. The net deficit represents the present value of unfunded but promised pension obligations. This deficit will need to be funded – most likely through increased cash contributions into the scheme. Such contributions reduce the cash available for investment and for dividend payments. A company with a large defined benefit deficit may be viewed by some potential shareholders as risky, and they may choose to invest their money elsewhere.

The plan obligation is complex to measure because it involves making a number of assumptions – such as about employee life expectancy and final/average salaries. These assumptions also involve a lot of subjectivity, and thus are liable to error and bias. However, IAS 19 recommends the use of a qualified actuary so that the assets and obligations of the underlying scheme are faithfully represented. Moreover, IAS 19 requires extensive disclosures to enable users to understand the estimation techniques used and the sensitivity of the deficit to wider economic change.

(iii)   **Plan B**

Tutorial note

This question largely tests recent amendments to IAS 19 relating to past service costs, settlements and curtailments. These are covered in the current issues chapter of the Study Text.

Recent amendments to IAS 19 specify that the calculation of a past service cost or a gain or loss on settlement or curtailment requires the recalculation of the defined benefit deficit using the latest assumptions. These updated assumptions should be used when calculating the net interest component and current service cost for the remainder of the reporting period.

The settlement happened after 9 months. The net interest component for the first nine months of the year should therefore be based on the $125 million brought forward deficit and the interest rate of 4% i.e. $3.75 million ($125m × 4% × 9/12). However, the net interest component for the final three months should be based on the recalculated deficit and the interest rate on the date this was recalculated – i.e. 3%.

The current service cost has been calculated using assumptions at the start of the year. However, the current service cost for the final three months of the year should have been determined using the assumptions used when remeasuring the deficit post-settlement.

Tutorial note

McVeigh has incorrectly accounted and presented the remeasurement component. This should be the easiest part of the question to address.

IAS 19 does not allow the remeasurement component to be deferred. This must be recognised immediately in other comprehensive income. McVeigh has also misclassified the loss – the remeasurement component is an item that will not be reclassified to profit or loss in the future.

Marking scheme		Marks
(a)	Financial asset – 1 mark per point	7
(b)	(i) Plan A – 1 mark per point	7
	(ii) Conceptual Framework – 1 mark per point	5
	(iii) Plan B – 1 mark per point	6
		───
Total		**25**
		───

30   MEHRAN (SEP 18) *Walk in the footsteps of a top tutor*

Key answer tips

Part (a) requires an in-depth knowledge of IFRS 13 *Fair Value Measurement*. As with all narrative based questions, you need to demonstrate both your knowledge of the standard and your ability to apply it to real-life scenarios.

(a)   (i)   IFRS 13 and non-financial assets

Tutorial note

IFRS 13 Fair Value Measurement says that the fair value of a non-financial asset is based on its 'highest and best use'. This is an important concept. Fair value is also a market-based measurement, rather than one which is entity specific.

IFRS 13 *Fair Value Measurement* requires the fair value of a non-financial asset to be measured based on its highest and best use. This is determined from the perspective of market participants. It does not matter whether the entity intends to use the asset differently.

The highest and best use takes into account the use of the asset which is physically possible, legally permissible and financially feasible. IFRS 13 allows management to presume that the current use of an asset is the highest and best use unless factors suggest otherwise.

Land

If the land zoned for agricultural use is currently used for farming, the fair value should reflect the cost structure to continue operating the land for farming, including any tax credits which could be realised by market participants. Thus the fair value of the land if used for farming would be $5.1 million ($5m + $0.1m).

The agricultural land appears to have an alternative use as market participants have considered its use for residential purposes instead. A use of an asset need not be legal at the measurement date, but it must not be legally prohibited in the jurisdiction.

If used for residential purposes, the value should include all costs associated with changing the land to the market participant's intended use. In addition, demolition and other costs associated with preparing the land for a different use should be included in the valuation. These costs would include the uncertainty related to whether the approval needed for changing the usage would be obtained, because market participants would take that into account when pricing value of the land if it had a different use. Thus the fair value of the land if used for residential purposes would be $5.44 million (($7.4m − $0.2m − $0.3m − $0.1m) × 80%).

In this situation, the presumption that the current use is the highest and best use of the land has been overridden by the market factors which indicate that residential development is the highest and best use. Therefore the fair value of the land would be $5.44 million.

Brand

In the absence of any evidence to the contrary, Mehran should value the brand on the basis of the highest and best use by market participants, even if Mehran intends a different use.

Market participants would not discontinue the brand, because their existing brands are less strong. Instead market participants would continue to use the brand in order to obtain the direct benefits.

Mehran's decision to discontinue the brand is therefore not relevant in determining fair value. As such, the fair value of the brand is $17 million.

(ii)   IFRS 13 and financial assets

Tutorial note

This part of the question can be answered well using common-sense. How do Mehran's ordinary shares differ from the preferred shares? What impact will these differences have on their fair value?

IFRS 13 *Fair Value Measurement* states that fair value is a market-based measurement, although it acknowledges that observable market transactions might not be available. Whether or not observable information is available, the aim of IFRS 13 is to estimate the price at which an asset would be sold at in an orderly transaction between market participants at the measurement date.

The market approach takes a transaction price paid for an identical or a similar instrument and adjusts it. Using a market approach, Mehran could take the transaction price for the preferred shares and adjust it to reflect certain differences between the preferred shares and the ordinary shares. For example:

- There would be an adjustment to reflect the priority of the preferred shares upon liquidation.

- Mehran should acknowledge the benefit associated with control. This adjustment relates to the fact that Mehran's individual ordinary shares represent a non-controlling interest whereas the preferred shares issued reflect a controlling interest.

- There will be an adjustment for the lack of liquidity of the investment which reflects the lesser ability of the ordinary shareholder to initiate a sale of Erham relative to the preferred shareholder.

- There will be an adjustment for the cumulative dividend entitlement of the preferred shares. This would be calculated as the present value of the expected future dividend receipts on the preferred shares, less the present value of any expected dividend receipts on the ordinary shares.

Mehran should review the circumstances of the issue of the preferred shares to ensure that its price was a valid benchmark. In addition, Mehran should consider whether there have been changes in market conditions between the issue of the preferred shares and the measurement date.

(b)   **Accounting for provisions**

Tutorial note

The question requires you to explain the accounting treatment of provisions. This should be a source of easy marks.

Provisions are defined in IAS 37 *Provisions, Contingent Liabilities, and Contingent Assets* as liabilities where the timing or the amount of the future outflow is uncertain. A provision is recognised if all of the following criteria are met:

- there is an obligation from a past event

- an outflow of economic resources to settle the obligation is probable

- the outflow of economic resources can be measured reliably.

Provisions should be measured at the best estimate of the economic resources required to settle the obligation. They should be remeasured at each reporting date using the best available information. If the time value of money is material then the provision should be discounted to present value. The discount rate used should reflect risks specific to the liability.

Benefits and limitations

Tutorial note

Imagine you are an investor. What useful information about future cash flows and risks can you get from the disclosure? What other information would you like to know?

Provisions involve uncertainty. Disclosures should provide important information to help users understand the nature of the obligation, the timing of any outflow of economic benefits, uncertainties about the amounts or timing involved, and major assumptions made.

The disclosure note splits the provision between current and non-current liabilities. This helps users of the financial statements assess the timing of the cash outflows and the potential impact on Mehran's overall net cash inflows. It would be useful to provide further information about the expected timing of the outflows classified as a non-current liability.

Financial reporting focusses on past events, but provisions disclosures also provide important information about the future. This disclosure note informs investors about restructuring activities within stores, but also in Finance and IT. Whilst this restructuring will incur costs, investors may value Mehran's efforts to streamline its operations and improve efficiency.

The disclosure shows that provisions, as a total balance, increased year on year. Liabilities always entail risk because there is an obligation to make payments to settle the obligation even if the company has insufficient liquid resources to do so. Provisions might be viewed as particularly risky, because they are estimated and therefore the actual cash outflows required might be significantly higher than estimated. Some investors may be deterred from investing in companies with substantial provisions.

With regards to the refund provision, the amount utilised in the reporting period is less than the provision at the start of the year. This suggests that, in the prior year, management had over-estimated the refund provision. This information may cast doubt on management's ability to accurately estimate its provisions and increase uncertainty regarding Mehran's future cash flows.

Further information could be provided to help users assess the adequacy of the provisions made. Part of the restructuring provision is classified as non-current but no information is provided about discount rates. Very little information is provided about any uncertainties that would impact the measurement of the provision, or the assumptions made. This hinders the ability of the users to assess the adequacy of the estimates made by management.

Marking scheme		Marks
(a)	(i) Non-financial assets and fair value – 1 mark per point	9
	(ii) Financial assets and fair value – 1 mark per point	6
(b)	Provisions accounting – 1 mark per point	3
	Benefits and limitations – 1 mark per point	5
	Professional marks	2
Total		25

31 CARSOON

Key answer tips

Part (a) of this question requires a good knowledge of IFRS 9 *Financial Instruments* and IFRS 15 *Revenue from Contracts with Customers.* Part (b) requires knowledge of the Practice Statement on management commentary – refer to the Study Text if needed.

(a) (i) Financial asset

According to IFRS 9 *Financial Instruments,* debt instruments measured at FVOCI are measured at fair value in the statement of financial position. Interest income is calculated using the effective interest rate. Fair value gains and losses on these financial assets are recognised in other comprehensive income (OCI).

Expected credit losses (ECLs) do not reduce the carrying amount of the financial assets, which remains at fair value. Instead, an amount equal to the ECL allowance is recognised in OCI.

When these financial assets are derecognised, the cumulative gains and losses previously recognised in OCI are reclassified from equity to profit or loss.

The fair value of the debt instrument therefore needs to be ascertained at 28 February 20X7. IFRS 13 *Fair Value Measurement* states that Level 1 inputs are unadjusted quoted prices in active markets for identical assets or liabilities which the entity can access at the measurement date. The standard sets out that adjustment to Level 1 prices should not be made except in certain circumstances. It would seem that a Level 1 input is available so there is no reason to use the 'in house' model.

Therefore the accounting for the instrument should be as follows:

- The bonds will be initially recorded at $6 million

- Interest of $0.24 million will be received and credited to profit or loss.

- At 28 February 20X7, the bonds will be valued at $5.3 million. The loss of $0.7 million will be charged as an impairment loss of $0.4 million to profit or loss and $0.3 million to OCI.

- When the bond is sold for $5.3 million on 1 March 20X7, the financial asset is derecognised and the loss in OCI ($0.3 million) is reclassified to profit or loss.

(ii)   Revenue recognition

IFRS 15 *Revenue from Contracts with Customers* specifies how to account for costs incurred in fulfilling a contract which are not in the scope of another standard. These are divided into those which give rise to an asset and those which are expensed as incurred. Entities will recognise an asset when costs incurred to fulfil a contract meet certain criteria, one of which is that the costs are expected to be recovered. For costs to meet the 'expected to be recovered' criterion, they need to be either explicitly reimbursable under the contract or reflected through the pricing of the contract and recoverable through the margin.

General and administrative costs cannot be capitalised unless these costs are specifically chargeable to the customer under the contract. Similarly, wasted material costs are expensed where they are not chargeable to the customer. Therefore a total expense of $15 million will be charged to profit or loss and not shown as assets.

A penalty is a form of variable consideration. The penalty payable should be estimated and deducted from the transaction price if it is highly probable that a significant reversal in the amount of revenue recognised will not occur when the uncertainty is resolved.

The construction of the separate storage facility is a distinct performance obligation; the contract modification for the additional storage facility would be, in effect, a new contract which does not affect the accounting for the existing contract. When the contract is modified for the construction of the storage facility, an additional $7 million is added to the consideration which Carsoon will receive. The performance obligation has been satisfied so this revenue can be recognised in full.

(b)   Management commentary

Management commentary is a narrative report in which management provide context and background against which stakeholders can assess the financial position and performance of a company. It is not mandatory to produce a management commentary. However, if entities produce a management commentary then it should include information that is essential to an understanding of:

- the nature of the business

- management's objectives and its strategies for meeting those objectives

- the entity's resources, risks and relationships

- the results of operations and prospects, and

- the key performance measures that management use to evaluate the entity's performance.

Management commentary should include forward-looking information. The commentary should be entity-specific, rather than generic.

Link to *Conceptual Framework*

The Practice Statement states that management commentary should include information that possesses the qualitative characteristics of useful financial information. The fundamental qualitative characteristics are relevance and faithful representation. The enhancing qualitative characteristics are understandability, verifiability, comparability and timeliness.

Management commentary provides users with information about risk management, as well as the extent to which current performance may be indicative of future performance. This forward-looking information is relevant because it helps users to make decisions about whether to hold or sell investments in an entity.

To enhance relevance, management commentary should include material information and should focus on the most important information. Generic information is not relevant and should be avoided.

To maximise understandability, management commentary should be presented in a clear and straightforward manner.

When selecting key performance measures, management should use those that are accepted and used widely within the industry. This will enable users to draw comparisons between entities. Management should calculate and report performance measures consistently over time, thus enabling users to compare the performance of the entity year-on-year.

If information from the financial statements is adjusted for inclusion in management commentary then this fact should be disclosed. Financial performance measures should be reconciled to the figures in the financial statements. Users are therefore able to verify the nature of the calculations. They can also assess whether the performance measures included offer a faithful presentation of the entity's financial performance and position.

Marking scheme			Marks
(a)	(i)	Financial asset – 1 mark per point	8
	(ii)	Revenue – 1 mark per point	7
(b)		Management commentary – 1 mark per point	10
Total			25

32 SKYE *Online question assistance*

Key answer tips

Part (a) requires a good knowledge of two key topics: classifying a financial instrument as debt or equity, and deferred tax. Part (b) is about the *Conceptual Framework*, which is a fundamental part of the SBR syllabus.

(a) (i) Debt or equity

Tutorial note

This is a very common exam topic. Make sure that you know the definition of a financial liability and are able to apply it. Revisit the Study Text if your knowledge is lacking.

IAS 32 *Financial Instruments: Presentation* states that a liability is a contractual obligation to deliver cash or another financial asset to another entity. Equity is any contract which evidences a residual interest in the assets of an entity after deducting all of its liabilities.

In the case of the B shares, Skye has no obligation to transfer cash or another asset to the holders of the instruments. Therefore the B shares should be classed as equity. The fact that Skye has not refused redemption in the past does not cause the B shares to be classified as a liability since this does not create a contractual obligation on Skye.

The preference shares create an obligation for Skye because of the put option clause in the agreement. The fact that Skye may not be in a position to satisfy the put option feature because of insufficient distributable reserves does not negate the fact that Skye has an obligation.

(ii) **Deferred tax**

Tutorial note

Deferred tax is calculated by comparing the carrying amount of an asset or liability with its tax base. An important first step is therefore to calculate the carrying amount of the property at the reporting date. Remember that the overseas property is a non-monetary item and so is initially translated into the functional currency of Skye at the historic rate and is not retranslated.

According to IAS 12 *Income Taxes*, deferred tax is accounted for on temporary differences between the financial reporting treatment of a transaction and the tax treatment.

The property of the overseas branch is written down at different rates in the financial statements than it is for tax purposes, giving rise to a temporary difference. A temporary difference may also arise if the carrying amounts of the non-monetary assets of the overseas branch are translated at different rates to the tax base.

The property is a non-monetary asset and so, according to IAS 21 *The Effects of Changes in Foreign Exchange Rates*, is translated into Skye's functional currency using the historic rate and is not retranslated. This means that the asset would initially be recorded at $1.2 million (D6m/5).

IAS 16 *Property, Plant and Equipment* requires that the asset is depreciated over its useful life. The carrying amount of the asset at the reporting date is therefore $1.1 million ($1.2m × 11/12).

The tax base of the property at the reporting date is D5.25 million (D6m × 7/8). If translated at the closing rate, this gives $0.875 million (D5.25m/6).

There is a taxable temporary difference of $0.225 million ($1.1m – $0.875m). The deferred tax balance will be calculated using the tax rate in the overseas country. The deferred tax liability arising is $45,000 ($0.225m × 20%), which will increase the tax charge in profit or loss.

(b) **(i)** **Prudence**

Tutorial note

You should be able to give a definition of prudence for some easy marks.

Prudence is the inclusion of a degree of caution in the exercise of the judgements needed in making the estimates. Prudence is generally taken to mean that assets or income are not overstated and liabilities or expenses are not understated.

Exercising prudence can lead to increased subjectivity in the financial statements, which will affect the evaluation of the entity's performance. Deliberate understatement or deliberate overstatement of the financial statements, even in the name of prudence, is not neutral. Overstating liabilities and expenses in the current period will lead to higher reported profits in the next reporting period. As such, this would not offer a faithful representation of an entity's financial performance and position.

However, to offer a faithful representation, financial statements should be free from bias. Preparers of financial statements have a natural bias towards optimism – often as a result of incentives to report higher profits and/or assets – and therefore prudence might counteract this. Investors are often concerned about financial risk relating to potential losses and so some form of conservatism certainly has a role to play in financial reporting.

(ii) **Measurement**

Tutorial note

The purpose of financial reporting is to provide information to users that will help them to make decisions about advancing economic resources to an entity. To be useful, the information must embody the fundamental qualitative characteristics.

The *Conceptual Framework* identifies two broad measurement bases: historical cost and current value.

When selecting a measurement base, preparers of the financial statements should ensure that the resulting financial information is as useful as possible to primary user groups. To be useful, financial information must be relevant and it must faithfully represent an entity's underlying transactions.

To maximise relevance, preparers of financial statements should consider the characteristics of the asset or liability they are measuring. In particular, they should consider how the asset contributes to future cash flows, and whether those cash flows are sensitive to market factors.

Depreciated cost is unlikely to provide relevant information about an asset with a volatile market value that will be traded in the short-term. Similarly, reporting an asset or liability at fair value will not provide relevant information if the item is held to collect contractual cash flows.

In order to faithfully represent an entity's transactions, consideration must be given to measurement uncertainty. This arises when estimation techniques are used. If measurement uncertainty is too high then information provided by that measurement basis is unlikely to be useful.

When selecting a measurement basis, preparers of financial statements should consider whether the benefits of the information it provides to the users of the financial statements outweigh the costs providing that information.

Tutorial note

Don't forget about the enhancing qualitative characteristics of useful financial information. These should be maximised where possible.

Consideration should also be given to the enhancing qualitative characteristics of useful financial information. Using the same measurement basis as other entities in the same sector would enhance comparability. Using many difference measurement bases in a set of financial statements reduces understandability. Verifiability is maximised by using measurement bases that can be corroborated.

		Marking scheme	Marks
(a)	(i)	Debt or equity – 1 mark per point	6
	(ii)	Deferred tax – 1 mark per point	7
(b)	(i)	Prudence – 1 mark per point	6
	(ii)	Selecting a measurement base – 1 mark per point	6
Total			25

33 WHITEBIRK

Key answer tips

Part (a) (i) should be relatively straight forward because it tests knowledge from the Financial Reporting paper. However, part (a) (ii) requires knowledge of the differences between full International Financial Reporting Standards and the IFRS for SMEs Standard. Many students neglect this area of the syllabus. All of the examinable content can be found in the Study Text.

You can score relatively well on the practical considerations in part (b) using common sense. The financial statement implications, however, are trickier. Try and refer to specific accounting standards, otherwise your answer is likely to be too generic.

(a) **(i)** **Borrowing costs**

IAS 23 *Borrowing Costs* requires borrowing costs incurred when acquiring or constructing an asset to be capitalised if the asset takes a substantial period of time to be prepared for its intended use or sale.

The definition of borrowing costs includes interest expense calculated by the effective interest method, finance charges on leases and exchange differences arising from foreign currency borrowings relating to interest costs.

Borrowing costs should be capitalised during construction and include the costs of funds borrowed for the purpose of financing the construction of the asset, and general borrowings which would have been avoided if the expenditure on the asset had not occurred. The general borrowing costs are determined by applying a capitalisation rate to the expenditure on that asset.

The weighted-average carrying amount of the machine during the period is $3.5 million ($2m + $3m + $4m + $5m) / 4). The capitalisation rate of the borrowings of Whitebirk during the period of construction is 9% per annum. The total amount of borrowing costs to be capitalised is the weighted-average carrying amount of the stadium multiplied by the capitalisation rate. This amounts to $0.1 million ($3.5 million × 9% × 4/12).

(ii) **Research and development**

According to IAS 38 *Intangible Assets*, research expenditure does not give rise to probable economic benefits and therefore no intangible asset should be recognised. The $1 million research expenditure should be written off to profit or loss.

IAS 38 requires development expenditure to be capitalised as long as certain criteria are met. The project must give rise to probable economic benefits, the entity must have sufficient resources to complete development, and the expenditure incurred must be able to be measurable. Assuming the criteria are met, the $0.5 million expenditure should be capitalised as an intangible asset. The asset should be amortised to profit or loss to reflect its pattern of use by the entity.

SMEs Standard

Borrowing costs

In accordance with the SMEs Standard, borrowing costs are always expensed to the statement of profit or loss. Therefore, none of the borrowing costs incurred as a result of the construction of the machine can be capitalised.

Research and development expenditure

The SMEs Standard states that an entity must recognise expenditure incurred internally on an intangible item, including all expenditure on both research and development activities, as an expense when it is incurred. Thus the expenditure of $1.5 million on research and development would all be written off to profit or loss.

(b)   (i)   Practical considerations

When implementing a new accounting standard, an entity should prepare an impact assessment and project plan. The entity may need to spend money on training staff, or on updating or replacing its systems. New processes and controls may need to be developed and documented.

New accounting standards will most likely contain new recognition, measurement and disclosure requirements. If the impact of these is not communicated then investors' assessments of how management has discharged its stewardship responsibilities may change and this could affect their investment decisions. As such, management should communicate the impact of a new standard to investors and other stakeholders – particularly if it will result in lower profits or increased liabilities.

Banking agreements often specify maximum debt levels or financial ratios based on figures reported in the financial statements. New financial reporting requirements can affect those ratios, causing potential covenant breaches.

Dividends could be affected. Many jurisdictions have regulations, which restrict the amount which can be paid out in dividends. This restriction is normally based on accounting profits.

The impact of adopting a new IFRS Standard should be communicated to analysts. Some governments use information prepared under IFRS standards for statistical and economic planning purposes.

Competitive advantage could be lost if a new financial reporting standard requires extensive disclosures.

Bonus schemes may need to be re-assessed because the new standard could affect the calculation of performance-related pay.

Financial statement implications

Where there is the introduction of a new accounting standard, the financial statements will need to reflect the new recognition, measurement and disclosure requirements which, in turn, will mean that entities will need to consider the requirements of IAS 8 *Accounting Policies, Changes in Accounting Estimates and Errors*. IAS 8 contains a requirement that changes in accounting policies are fully applied retrospectively unless there are specific transitional provisions contained in the new IFRS Standard being implemented.

IAS 1 *Presentation of Financial Statements* requires a third statement of financial position to be presented if the entity retrospectively applies an accounting policy, restates items, or reclassifies items, and those adjustments had a material effect on the information in the statement of financial position at the beginning of the comparative period.

IAS 33 *Earnings per Share* requires basic and diluted EPS to be adjusted for the impacts of adjustments resulting from changes in accounting policies accounted for retrospectively and IAS 8 requires the disclosure of the amount of any such adjustments.

A change in an accounting standard can change the carrying amounts of assets and liabilities, which will have deferred tax consequences.

(ii)   First time adoption of IFRS Standards

IFRS 1 *First-time Adoption of IFRS* says that an entity must produce an opening statement of financial position in accordance with IFRS Standards as at the date of transition. The date of transition is the beginning of the earliest period for which an entity presents full comparative information under IFRS Standards in its first financial statements produced using IFRS Standards.

At the date of transition, the entity must:

• recognise all assets and liabilities required by IFRS Standards

• derecognise assets and liabilities not permitted by IFRS Standards

• reclassify assets, liabilities and equity in accordance with IFRS Standards

• measure assets and liabilities in accordance with IFRS Standards.

Gains or losses arising on the adoption of IFRS Standards at the date of transition should be recognised directly in retained earnings.

Marking scheme		
		Marks
(a)	(i) IAS 23 and IAS 38 – 1 mark per point	8
	(ii) IFRS Standards vs. IFRS for SMEs Standard – 1 mark per point	4
(b)	(i) Practicalities of implementing new IFRS Standards – 1 mark per point	10
	(ii) IFRS 1	3
		—
Total		**25**
		—

34   ASPIRE *Walk in the footsteps of a top tutor*

Key answer tips

This question primarily tests the accounting treatment of overseas transactions. If you struggle with the calculations, make sure you revisit the relevant chapters from the Study Text.

(a)   (i)

Tutorial note

In discursive questions, it is important to state the relevant rules from the accounting standard before applying them to the scenario. Make sure you begin your answer by identifying the factors that an entity should consider when determining a functional currency. If you do not know these rules, then you must learn them.

Functional currency

IAS 21 *The Effects of Changes in Foreign Exchange Rates* defines functional currency as the currency of the primary economic environment in which the entity operates.

Primary indicators

An entity's management considers the following primary indicators in determining its functional currency:

(i)   the currency which mainly influences sales prices for goods and services

(ii)   the currency of the country whose competitive forces and regulations mainly determine the sales prices of goods and services; and

(iii)   the currency which mainly influences labour, material and other costs of providing goods and services.

Secondary factors and group factors

Further secondary indicators which may also provide evidence of an entity's functional currency are the currency in which funds from financing activities are generated and in which receipts from operating activities are retained.

Additional factors are considered in determining the functional currency of a foreign operation and whether its functional currency is the same as that of the reporting entity. These are:

(a)   the autonomy of a foreign operation from the reporting entity

(b)   the level of transactions between the two

(c)   whether the foreign operation generates sufficient cash flows to meet its cash needs; and

(d)   whether its cash flows directly affect those of the reporting entity.

When the functional currency is not obvious, management uses its judgement to determine the functional currency which most faithfully represents the economic effects of the underlying transactions, events and conditions.

Application to scenario

Tutorial note

Apply the rules to the scenario and reach a conclusion. If your discussion is educated and balanced then you will still scores marks, even if your answer is incorrect.

The operating costs are incurred in dollars. However, they are not material to any decision as to the functional currency. Therefore it is important to look at secondary factors to determine the functional currency.

The subsidiary has issued 2 million dinars of equity capital to Aspire. The subsidiary has also raised 100,000 dinars of equity capital from external sources. It therefore seems that dinar represents the currency in which the economic activities of the subsidiary are primarily carried out.

However, the subsidiary seems to operate with little autonomy. The income from investments is either remitted to Aspire or reinvested on instruction from Aspire. The subsidiary has a minimal number of staff and does not have any independent management. It would therefore seem that the subsidiary is simply a vehicle for the parent entity to invest in dinar related investments.

In conclusion, the subsidiary appears to be merely an extension of Aspire's activities. Therefore the functional currency of the subsidiary is the same as its parent's: the dollar.

(ii) **Overseas loan**

Tutorial note

There are two issues implicit in part (ii): how to account for the loan, and how to translate the figures from dinars into dollars. Make sure that you address both of these issues.

The loan is a financial liability because it contains a contractual obligation to transfer cash. In accordance with IFRS 9 *Financial Instruments*, most financial liabilities are measured at amortised cost. Liabilities at amortised cost should be initially recognised at fair value less transaction costs. The finance cost is calculated using the effective rate of interest and charged to profit or loss.

This loan is denominated in an overseas currency and so must be translated using the rules in IAS 21 *The Effects of Changes in Foreign Exchange Rates*. The overseas loan should initially be translated into the functional currency using the historic (spot) rate. The finance cost is translated at the average rate because it approximates to the actual rate. The cash payment should be translated at the historic (spot) rate (which, because the payment occurs at the reporting date, is the year-end rate). A loan is a monetary liability so is retranslated at the reporting date using the closing rate. Any exchange gain or loss is recognised in profit or loss.

Tutorial note

Complete the amortised cost working in dinars, and then translate each figure into dollars using the appropriate exchange rate.

	Dm	Rate	$m
1 May 2013	5.0	5	1.000
Finance cost (8%)	0.4	5.6	0.071
Payment	(0.4)	6	(0.067)
Foreign exchange gain (bal. fig.)			(0.171)
30 April 2014	5.0	6	0.833

The loan is initially recorded at $1 million. The finance cost recorded in the statement of profit or loss is $0.071 million, whilst the cash payment is recorded at $0.067 million. A foreign exchange gain of $0.171 million is recorded in the statement of profit or loss. The liability at the reporting date has a carrying amount of $0.833 million.

(b)   APM

Tutorial note

*Have a think about **why** Aspire wants to disclose the APM.*

Advantages

Foreign exchange gains and losses are volatile. Eliminating these may give the stakeholders a better understanding of Aspire's underlying performance. This is particularly true if the foreign exchange gains and losses are likely to reverse before the transaction is settled.

Eliminating foreign exchange gains and losses may make Aspire's performance more comparable with entities that do not trade so heavily overseas.

Disadvantages

It would seem that Aspire is trying to disguise its weak performance in the current year. Adding back the foreign exchange losses turns the $2 million operating loss of Aspire into a $1 million profit.

Aspire's exposure to foreign exchange losses is not wholly outside of management control. Management could, for instance, enter into hedging arrangements to reduce their foreign currency risk exposure. Eliminating foreign exchange losses may disguise management inactivity with regards to foreign exchange risk management.

Whilst foreign exchange movements on long-term items (such as loans) are likely to reverse over time, this is not the case on short-term items. A foreign exchange loss on a relatively short term receivable means that the entity has received, or will receive, less money from their customers than the value at which the sale was originally recorded. This is a real loss to Aspire that will affect their cash flows and liquidity. Eliminating these foreign exchange losses is therefore inflating the economic performance of Aspire.

It would also seem that Aspire intends to disclose this APM prominently. This might cause users of the financial statements to wrongly believe that it is a subtotal identified within IFRS and IAS Standards. This could have a material, and potentially misleading, impact on current and potential investors.

Marking scheme			
			Marks
(a)	(i)	Functional currency – 1 mark per point	7
	(ii)	Overseas loan – 1 mark per point	7
(b)		APM – 1 mark per point	9
		Professional marks	2
			—
Total			**25**
			—

35 BUSINESS COMBINATIONS *Walk in the footsteps of a top tutor*

Key answer tips

The two requirements in part (a) are worth a lot of marks. Broadly speaking, you will be awarded one mark for every valid point that you make. Ensure that you are making enough points to achieve at least a pass mark.

Always thoroughly read the model answer and learn from any mistakes that you made. If you lack the required technical knowledge then revisit the Study Text.

(a)   (i)   Business combinations and Ceemone

Tutorial note

Should Ceemone have been accounted for as a business combination or an asset acquisition? This requires knowledge of the definition of a business per IFRS 3 Business Combinations. State this definition, and then apply it to the information provided in the question.

An entity should determine whether a transaction is a business combination by applying IFRS 3 *Business Combinations*.

IFRS 3 defines a business as an integrated set of activities and assets which is capable of being conducted and managed for the purpose of providing a return in the form of dividends, lower costs or other economic benefits directly to investors or other owners, members or participants. A business consists of inputs and processes applied to those inputs which have the ability to create outputs.

When analysing the transaction, the following elements are relevant:

- Inputs: Shares in vessel owning companies, charter arrangements, outsourcing arrangements with a management company, and relationships with a shipping broker.

- Processes: Activities regarding chartering and operating the vessels, financing the business, purchase and sales of vessels.

- Outputs: Ceemone would generate revenue from charter agreements and has the ability to gain economic benefit from the vessels.

IFRS 3 states that whether a seller operated a set of assets and activities as a business or intends to operate it as a business is not relevant in evaluating whether it is a business. It is not relevant therefore that some activities were outsourced as Ceemone could choose to conduct and manage the integrated set of assets and activities as a business.

The accounting for the transaction as an asset acquisition does not comply with the requirements of IFRS 3 because the acquisition included all the elements which constitute a business. This would mean that transaction costs should be expensed. The vessels should be consolidated at fair value. A goodwill asset should be recognised for the difference between the consideration transferred and the fair value of the net assets at acquisition.

(ii) **Bimbi and Lental**

Tutorial note

Remember that the acquirer in a business combination is the entity that exercises control. Easy marks can be obtained for stating the definition of control in IFRS 10.

IFRS 3 *Business Combinations* requires an acquirer to be identified in all business combinations. The acquirer is the combining entity which obtains control of the other combined entity.

IFRS 10 *Consolidated Financial Statements* says that an investor controls an investee when it is exposed, or has rights, to variable returns from its involvement with the investee and has the ability to affect those returns through its power over the investee.

Sometimes it is straightforward to assess power by looking at the voting rights obtained. When the parent acquires more than half of the voting rights of the entity, it normally has power if the relevant activities of the investee are directed by a vote.

There is a presumption that an entity achieves control over another entity by acquiring more than one half of the voting rights, unless it can be demonstrated that such ownership does not constitute control.

Tutorial note

In more complicated scenarios, like the one in this question, IFRS 3 sets out further rules for determining the acquirer in a business combination.

You may struggle to remember the rules off by heart. If this is the case, then use your common sense. Which company issued equity in the transaction? Which company is the bigger of the two? Which company seems to control the other? As always, try and reach a justified conclusion.

If the guidance in IFRS 10 does not clearly indicate which of the combining entities is the acquirer then the indicators listed in IFRS 3 should be considered.

The acquirer is usually the entity which transfers cash or other assets. In this scenario, as Bimbi is the entity giving up a cash amount corresponding to 45% of the purchase price, this represents a significant share of the total purchase consideration.

When there is an exchange of equity interests in a business combination, the entity which issues the equity interests is normally the acquirer. In this case, as the majority of the purchase consideration is settled in equity instruments, Bimbi would appear to be the acquirer.

The acquirer is usually the combining entities whose shareholders retain or receive the largest portion of the voting rights in the combined entity. The shareholders of Bimbi, the smaller of the two combining entities, appear to have obtained control since their share amounts to 51% of the voting rights after the transaction. A controlling ownership, however, does not necessarily mean that the entity has the power to govern the combined entity's financial and operating policies so as to obtain benefits from its activities.

Additionally, the acquirer could be deemed to be the entity whose owners have the ability to appoint or remove a majority of the members of the governing body of the combined entity. Five out of six members of the board here are former board members of Bimbi, which again suggests that Bimbi is the acquirer.

Additionally, the acquirer could be deemed the entity whose former management dominates the management of the combined entity. However, the management team consists of the COO plus two former employees of Lental as compared to two former employees of Bimbi. Therefore, the former management of Lental has a greater representation. Although the board nominates the management team, the COO will have significant influence through his share ownership and the selection of the team.

IFRS 3 also says that the acquirer is often the larger entity. As the fair value of Lental ($90 million) is significantly greater than Bimbi ($70 million), this would point towards Lental as the acquirer.

The arguments supporting Bimbi or Lental as the acquirer are finely balanced and therefore it is difficult to identify an acquirer in this case. It can be argued that Bimbi can be identified as the acquirer, on the basis that:

- Bimbi issued the equity interest

- Bimbi is the entity transferring the cash or other assets and

- Bimbi has the marginal controlling interest (51%).

(b) **Kata**

Tutorial note

You have enough information to calculate the impact that consolidating Kata, or using the equity method, would have on the consolidated financial statements.

Subsidiary

If accounted for as a subsidiary:

- The assets, liabilities, incomes and expenses of Kata would be consolidated in full.

- Goodwill of $1.92 million (W1) would be recognised.

- The group would recognise its share of Kata's post-acquisition retained earnings. This amounts to $0.27 million (45% × ($2m – ($2.4m – $1.0m)).

- The group would recognise a non-controlling interest in respect of Kata of $1.65 million (W2).

Associate

If accounted for as an associate, the investment in Kata at the year-end would be carried at $3.27 million (W3).

In the statement of profit or loss, the group would show its share of Kata's profit of $0.27 million (W3).

Comparison of impact

Tutorial note

Don't just calculate figures. Make sure that you explain and compare the likely impact of the classification decision on the users' perceptions of the consolidated financial statements.

Assets

Consolidating Kata would lead to a higher non-current asset position than if equity accounting was used (PPE of $14 million and goodwill of $1.92 million compared with an investment in the associate of $3.27 million).

This will make the group look more asset rich, which may help it to raise finance in the future.

However, consolidating Kata's large PPE balance may have a detrimental impact on the group's non-current asset turnover, thus making the group look less efficient at generating profits.

Liabilities

Consolidating the loans of Kata may have a negative impact on the group's gearing ratio. This may have the effect of making the group look riskier than if equity accounting was used. A higher gearing ratio may make it harder for the group to raise finance in the future.

Profit or loss

Consolidating the incomes and expenses of Kata line by line will impact key profit or loss figures, such as revenue, gross profit and profit from operations. Increased revenues will make the group's market share look more impressive.

Kata is profitable so consolidating its results will improve the group's profit from operations. This may have a positive impact on investor perception.

If Kata was accounted for using the equity method, the group would simply shows its share of Kata's profits as a single line below profit from operations. This would therefore have no impact (positive or negative) on the group's operating profit.

Workings

Tutorial note

Always show your workings.

(W1) Goodwill

	$m
Consideration	3.0
NCI at acquisition (55% × $2.4m)	1.32
Fair value of net assets at acquisition	(2.40)
Goodwill	1.92

(W2) Non-controlling interest

	$m
NCI at acquisition	1.32
NCI % of post-acq'n net assets 55% × ($3m – $2.4m)	0.33
	1.65

(W3) Investment in associate

	$m
Cost	3.0
Group % of post-acq'n P/L 45% × ($2m – ($2.4m – $1.0m))	0.27
	3.27

Note: The same answer could be obtained by taking the group's share of the post-acquisition movement in the associate's net assets (equivalent to the movement in its share capital and retained earnings).

Marking scheme			Marks
(a)	(i)	Business combinations – 1 mark per point	7
	(ii)	Identifying the acquirer – 1 mark per point	8
(b)		Comparison of consolidation and equity accounting – 1 mark per point	8
		Professional marks	2
Total			**25**

36 MARGIE *Walk in the footsteps of a top tutor*

Key answer tips

This is a multi-part question which focuses upon application of IFRS 2 *Share-based Payment*. Each part is self-contained, so can be answered in the order you prefer. Remember to clearly identify which part you are answering, particularly if you are answering them out of order. The marks attributable for each part of the question give a good indication of how to allocate your time.

(a) (i) Share-appreciation rights

Tutorial note

There are key differences between the accounting treatment of cash-settled share-based payments and equity-settled share-based payments. Make sure that you learn the rules thoroughly.

The scope of IFRS 13

IFRS 13 *Fair Value Measurement* applies when another IFRS or IAS Standard requires or permits fair value measurements or disclosures about fair value measurements. IFRS 13 specifically excludes transactions covered by certain other standards including share-based payment transactions within the scope of IFRS 2 *Share-based Payment*.

Thus share-based payment transactions are scoped out of IFRS 13.

Accounting for the SARs

Tutorial note

The question asks you to 'advise'. Lots of students jump straight into calculations – don't forget the words!

For cash settled share-based payment transactions, the entity should recognise an expense and liability as service is rendered. The fair value of the liability is measured at each reporting date. Any changes in fair value are recognised in profit or loss in the period.

Tutorial note

Show all workings. This will help you to score marks even if you make a mistake.

The SARs would have been accounted for during the vesting period as follows:

Year	Expense	Liability	Calculation
	$	$	
30 April 20X3	641,250	641,250	(300 × 95%) × 500 × $9 × ½
30 April 20X4	926,250	1,567,500	(300 × 95%) × 500 × $11

Until the liability is settled, the entity must re-measure the fair value of the liability at the end of each reporting period and at the date of settlement, with any changes in fair value recognised in profit or loss for the period.

	$
Liability 1 May 20X4	1,567,500
Cash paid (60 × 500 × $10.50)	(315,000)
Expense (bal. fig.)	97,500
Liability 30 April 20X5 ((285 – 60) × 500 × $12)	1,350,000

The fair value of the liability would be $1,350,000 at 30 April 20X5 and the expense for the year would be $97,500.

(ii)   Share transactions

Tutorial note

This part of the question contains two separate transactions – one with shareholders and one with a supplier. Ensure that you address both issues in turn.

A share-based payment is when an entity receives goods or services in exchange for equity instruments or cash based on the value of equity instruments

The shares issued to the employees were issued in their capacity as shareholders and not in exchange for their services. The employees were not required to complete a period of service in exchange for the shares. Thus the transaction is outside the scope of IFRS 2 *Share-based Payment*.

As regards to Grief, Margie approached the company with the proposal to buy the building in exchange for shares. As such the transaction comes under IFRS 2. Grief is not an employee so the transaction will be recorded at the value of the goods received. This means that the building is recognised at its fair value and equity will be credited with the same amount.

(iii)   **Wheat contract**

Tutorial note

Determine whether or not the transaction falls within the scope of IFRS 2. If not, explain why not and then continue by discussing the required accounting treatment.

The arrangement is not within the scope of IFRS 2 *Share-based Payment* because Margie is not expecting to take delivery of the wheat.

This contract is within the scope of IFRS 9 *Financial Instruments* because it can be settled net and was not entered into for the purpose of the receipt or delivery of the item in accordance with the entity's expected purchase, sale, or usage requirements.

The contract is a derivative because it meets the following criteria:

*   Its value changes compared to an underlying item

*   It required no, or a low, initial investment

*   It is settled in the future

Tutorial note

Don't stop your answer once you've concluded that the contract is a derivative. Make sure that you explain how derivatives are initially and subsequently measured.

IFRS 9 *Financial Instruments* requires derivatives to be measured at fair value through profit or loss, unless the entity applies hedge accounting.

The contract will be initially recognised at fair value. This will probably be nil as, under the terms of a commercial contract, the value of 2,500 shares should equate to the value of 350 tonnes of wheat.

Derivatives are remeasured to fair value at each reporting date, with the gain or loss reported in the statement of profit or loss. The fair value will be based on the values of wheat and Margie shares. The fair value gain or loss should be recorded in the statement of profit or loss.

(b)   **Recent developments**

A sustainability report details the entity's economic, social and environmental effects. It ensures that entities consider their wider impacts, and enables them to be transparent about the risks and opportunities they face. This increased transparency means that stakeholders can make better decisions.

A number of sustainable reporting initiatives have emerged in recent years. These include:

*   The United Nations Global Compact (UNGC), which is a voluntary initiative that encourages companies to report actions taken to implement UN principles in respect of human rights, labour, the environment, and anti-corruption.

- The Global Reporting Initiative (GRI), which encourages entities to produce a balanced report that represents their positive and negative impacts on society and the environment.

- The International Integrated Reporting Framework, which encourages entities to report on how they create value in the short, medium and long term by discussing their impact on a range of capitals. Amongst others, the capitals include financial, social, human, and natural.

It should also be noted that laws are being passed around the world that make certain sustainability disclosures mandatory. For instance, large companies in the European Union are required to disclose information about diversity on a 'comply or explain' basis.

As can be seen, there are no worldwide agreed standards on sustainability reporting. There are many initiatives and entities can comply with a range of 'standards'. This leads to diversity, which limits the ability of stakeholders to compare one company's sustainability reporting with another.

Advantages of reporting environmental impact

Tutorial note

Keep your answer concise. You will score one mark per valid point.

The following are advantages that may arise when an entity discloses its impact on the environment:

- Traditional financial reporting makes limited reference to environmental issues. Filling this information gap may meet the needs of certain stakeholders.

- Providing more information to stakeholders increases an entity's accountability, as it is more difficult to conceal information.

- Reports that demonstrate an entity is managing environmental risks will improve perception of its sustainability and therefore its prospects in the medium to long-term.

- Good quality reporting may make an entity more attractive to investors, particularly if they can see that risks to sustainability are being managed.

- Non-financial reporting is increasingly regarded as best practice and may improve an entity's corporate image.

- 'Green' consumers are more likely to buy from entities that are open and transparent about their environmental impact.

- Entities are increasingly concerned about the ethical stance of other entities within their supply chain. Disclosing quality environmental information may make an entity a more attractive supplier.

- Environmental reporting might increase community support for an entity.

- The process of evaluating environmental performance might highlight inefficiencies in operating activities, enabling management to improve the entity's systems.

		Marking scheme	
			Marks
(a)	(i)	Share appreciation rights – 1 mark per point	6
	(ii)	Share transactions – 1 mark per point	5
	(iii)	Wheat contract – 1 mark per point	7
(b)		Sustainability – 1 mark per point	7
			———
Total			**25**
			———

37 KAYTE   *Online question assistance*

Key answer tips

Broadly speaking, you will be awarded one mark for every valid point that you make. Ensure that you are making enough points to achieve at least a pass mark.

As always, make sure that you thoroughly debrief the answer and learn from any mistakes that you made.

(a) Vessels

Residual values

IAS 16 *Property, Plant and Equipment* defines residual value as the estimated amount which an entity would currently obtain from disposal of the asset, after deducting the estimated costs of disposal, if the asset were already at the age and in the condition expected at the end of its useful life. IAS 16 requires the residual value to be reviewed at least at the end of each financial year end. If the estimated residual value is higher than an asset's carrying amount then no depreciation is charged.

Vessels with 10 year useful life

Kayte's calculation of the residual value of the vessels with a 10-year useful life is not acceptable under IAS 16 *Property, Plant and Equipment*. Undesirable volatility is not a convincing argument to support the use of a residual value equivalent to half of the acquisition cost. The residual value should be the value at the reporting date as if the vessel were already of the age and in the condition expected at the end of its useful life. Kayte should prepare a new model to determine residual value which would take account of broker valuations at the end of each reporting period.

Vessels with 30 year useful life

As regards the vessels which are kept for the whole of their economic life, a residual value based upon the scrap value of steel is acceptable. Therefore the vessels should be depreciated based upon the cost less the scrap value of steel over the 30-year period.

When major planned maintenance work is to be undertaken, the cost should be capitalised. The engine overhaul will be capitalised as a new asset which will then be depreciated over the 10-year period to the next overhaul. The depreciation of the original capitalised amount will typically be calculated such that it had a carrying amount of nil when the overhaul is undertaken.

This is not the case with one vessel, because work was required earlier than expected. In this case, any remaining carrying amount of the old engine and overhaul cost should be expensed immediately.

Funnels

The initial carve out of components should include all major maintenance events which are likely to occur over the economic life of the vessel. Sometimes, it may subsequently be found that the initial allocation was insufficiently detailed, in that not all components were identified. This is the case with the funnels. In this situation it is necessary to determine what the carrying amount of the component would currently be had it been initially identified. This will sometimes require the initial cost to be determined by reference to the replacement cost and the associated accumulated depreciation charge determined using the rate used for the vessel. This is likely to leave a significant carrying amount in the component being replaced, which will need to be written off at the time the replacement is capitalised.

(b) (i) Selection of KPIs

The Integrated Reporting Framework does not specify which KPIs should be disclosed, or how they should be disclosed, but instead leaves this to management judgement. However, the Integrated Reporting Framework does identify characteristics of useful quantitative indicators.

KPIs should be focussed on matters that management have identified as material. They should be consistent with the KPIs used internally by management.

KPIs should be presented with comparative figures so that users of the <IR> can appreciate trends. Targets should also be disclosed, as well as projections for future periods.

The KPIs selected should be consistent with those used within the industry in which the entity operates.

The same KPIs should be reported each period, unless they are no longer material. KPIs should be calculated in a consistent manner in each reporting period.

Qualitative information and discussion is required to add context to KPIs, such as the assumptions used and the reasons for significant trends.

(ii) Interpretation of KPIs

Tutorial note

Imagine that you are a user of Kayte's <IR> – what conclusions might you draw? There are no right or wrong answers here. You will score one mark for every sensible point that you make. Make sure that you say at least seven different things.

The average employee salary has risen by 1.2%. This is less than the rate of inflation. Although the statistic could be skewed by high earners, it suggests that employees are earning less in real terms than they were a year ago.

Despite this, revenue per employee has increased by 14%. This suggests that there have been large scale measures to improve efficiency. There may be many reasons for this increase, such as technological changes, or new contracts. However, when combined with the small year-on-year pay increase, this extra workload could cause employee dissatisfaction.

The KPIs on sick days corroborate the above. Sick days per employee have increased by 133.3%. This may be suggestive of high levels of stress, potentially caused by the dramatic rise in efficiency, or simply the fact that many employees are not enjoying their jobs. Employee turnover has increased, and it is now in excess of the industry average. Once again, this may suggest dissatisfaction with pay or working conditions. It may be that Kayte's competitors offer more attractive employment terms.

Kayte is reliant on a skilled workforce, but the KPIs suggest that it needs to take measures to reduce absenteeism and to improve employee retention. Kayte appears to be losing a large number of its staff, which is ultimately not sustainable. A lack of experienced staff in the business will have a detrimental impact on the quality of the service provided by Kayte and a negative impact on its reputation. Users of the <IR> may therefore be pessimistic about Kayte's long-term prospects.

Marking scheme			
			Marks
(a)	Vessels– 1 mark per point		11
(b)	(i)	Selection of KPIs – 1 mark per point	4
	(ii)	Interpretation of KPIs – 1 mark per point	8
	Professional marks		2
			—
Total			**25**
			—

38   VERGE *Walk in the footsteps of a top tutor*

Key answer tips

This question covers a number of different standards that are commonly examined. It is vital that you learn these thoroughly. Make sure that you state the relevant accounting rules for easy marks, before applying them to the information in the scenario.

(a)   (i)   **Operating segments**

Tutorial note

IFRS 8 Operating Segments is a standard applicable to listed entities. Its aim is to increase the usefulness of the information provided to the users by disaggregating the highly summarised information provided in the primary financial statements.

Even if you do not have a detailed knowledge of this standard, you should still be able to reach a sensible conclusion as to whether or not segments 1 and 2 should be aggregated.

IFRS *8 Operating Segments* states that reportable segments are those operating segments or aggregations of operating segments for which segment information must be separately reported. Aggregation of one or more operating segments into a single reportable segment is permitted (but not required) where certain conditions are met, the principal condition being that the operating segments should have similar economic characteristics. The segments must be similar in each of the following respects:

- the nature of the products and services

- the nature of the production processes

- the type or class of customer

- the methods used to distribute their products or provide their services

- the nature of the regulatory environment.

Segments 1 and 2 have different customers. The decision to award or withdraw a local train contract rests with the transport authority and not with the end customer, the passenger. In contrast, the decision to withdraw from a route in the inter-city train market would normally rest with Verge but would be largely influenced by the passengers' actions that would lead to the route becoming economically unviable. In view of the fact that the segments have different customers, the two segments do not satisfy the aggregation criteria above.

In the local train market, contracts are awarded following a competitive tender process, and, consequently, there is no exposure to passenger revenue risk. The ticket prices paid by passengers are set by a transport authority and not Verge. By contrast, in the inter-city train market, ticket prices are set by Verge and its revenues are, therefore, the fares paid by the passengers travelling on the trains. In this set of circumstances, the company is exposed to passenger revenue risk. This risk would affect the two segments in different ways but generally through the action of the operating segment's customer.

Therefore the economic characteristics of the two segments are different and so they should be reported as separate segments.

(ii)   **Revenue recognition**

Tutorial note

If a customer is provided with a significant financing benefit, revenue is calculated by discounting the consideration receivable to present value.

Make sure that you pay careful attention to dates in this question. This is important for the discounting calculations as well as for determining that a prior period error has occurred.

Maintenance services are simultaneously received and consumed. According to IFRS 15 *Revenue from Contracts with Customers,* this means that revenue should be recognised over time based on progress towards the satisfaction of the performance obligation. Thus Verge must recognise revenue as work is performed throughout the contract life.

The length of time between the transfer of the promised services and the payment date suggests that there is a significant financing component. The consideration should be discounted to present value using the rate at which the customer could borrow.

In the year ended 31 March 20X2, Verge should have recorded revenue of $2.6 million ($1 million + ($1.8 million × $(1/1.06^2)$)). Since Verge has received $1 million cash, a receivable of $1.6 million should have been recognised.

In the year ended 31 March 20X3, revenue should be recorded at $1.13 million ($1.2 million × (1/1.06)). In addition, the discount on the receivable recognised in the year ended 31 March 20X2 must be unwound. Consequently, there will be interest income of $96,000 ($1.6 million × 6%).

Prior period error

Prior period errors are omissions from, and misstatements in, the entity's financial statements for one or more prior periods arising from a failure to use, or misuse of, reliable information that:

• was available when financial statements for those periods were authorised for issue, and

• could reasonably be expected to have been obtained and taken into account in the preparation and presentation of those financial statements.

Such errors include mathematical mistakes, mistakes in applying accounting policies and fraud. The fact that Verge only included $1 million of the revenue in the financial statements for the year ended 31 March 20X2 is a prior period error.

Verge should correct the prior period error retrospectively. In the financial statements for the year ended 31 March 20X3, the comparative amounts for the prior period should be restated.

(b)   **Proposed financing**

Tutorial note

Start of by explaining the accounting treatment of these transactions. Will they impact profit? Will these instruments be classified as debt, or equity, or both?

Ordinary shares

Ordinary shares do not create a contractual obligation to deliver cash or another financial asset. As such, per IAS 32 *Financial Instruments: Presentation*, they are classified as equity on the statement of financial position. If equity increases then the gearing ratio will improve, which may make Verge's financing structure look less risky to its investors.

Dividends paid on equity shares have no impact on profits because they are charged directly to retained earnings. Dividends are, in substance, the distribution of the entity's profits to its shareholders.

Issuing equity shares will increase the number of ordinary shares in the basic earnings per share calculation. If the entity is not able to grow its profits then basic earnings per share may fall year-on-year. Investors might perceive this negatively because it is an indication that their future dividend returns will fall.

Convertible bonds

A bond that is redeemed in the form of cash or a fixed number of the entity's own equity shares has characteristics of debt and equity. According to IAS 32 *Financial Instruments: Presentation,* the issuer should 'split' the bond into a liability component and an equity component. The liability component is calculated by taking the cash repayments and discounting them to present value using the rate on a similar non-convertible bond. The difference between the cash proceeds and the liability component on the issue date is classified as equity.

The liability component is normally much larger than the equity component. As such, the issue of the bond is likely to make the gearing ratio deteriorate, increasing investors' perception of risk. This is because liabilities necessitate mandatory repayments, whereas equity does not.

If the convertible bond is issued then an annual interest expense will be charged to profit or loss. This interest is calculated by applying the effective rate of interest to the liability component. Interest expenses are charged to the statement of profit or loss and so will reduce profits and basic earnings per share. However, whilst in issue, the convertible bonds have no impact on the number of shares used in the basic earnings per share calculation.

Most convertible bonds are dilutive instruments. This is because the entity has a commitment to issue ordinary shares in the future. The maximum number of shares that Verge may issue to redeem the convertible bonds should be included in the diluted earnings per share calculation. Moreover, the earnings figure used in the calculation should be increased by the current year interest on the bond because this will not be charged after redemption.

The disclosure of diluted earnings per share warns current and potential investors that earnings per share will fall when the convertible bond is redeemed. If investors are concerned about the potential drop, and the impact this may have on their investment returns, then they may decide to invest in other companies.

Marking scheme			
			Marks
(a)	(i)	Segment reporting – 1 mark per point	7
	(ii)	Revenue explanation and calculation – 1 mark per point	7
(b)		Finance and impact on financial statements	9
		Professional marks	2
			—
Total			25
			—

39   ARON

Key answer tips

This question deals with recognition and measurement of financial instruments. Part (a) is concerned with the use of fair values, particularly if there is no reliable or active market to help determine fair value. Part (b) of the requirement deals with accounting for four financial instruments, including a convertible bond and an interest-free loan, together with supporting calculations, comment and explanation. Accounting for one of the financial instruments also required knowledge of accounting for foreign currency transactions.

(a)   (i)   Convertible bond

Some financial instruments have both a liability and an equity component. In this case, IAS 32 *Financial Instruments: Presentation* requires that the component parts be accounted for and presented separately according to their substance. The split is made on the issue date.

A convertible bond contains two components:

- a financial liability – the issuer's contractual obligation to pay cash in the form of interest or capital

- an equity instrument – the contract to issue a fixed number of equity shares.

The liability component will be determined by discounting the future cash flows. The discount rate used will be 9%, which is the market rate for similar bonds without the conversion right. The difference between cash received and the liability component is the value of the equity.

	$m
Present value of cash flows	
Year 1 (31 May 20X7) ($100m × 6%) ÷ 1.09	5.50
Year 2 (31 May 20X8) ($100m × 6%) ÷ 1.09^2	5.05
Year 3 (31 May 20X9) ($100m + ($100m × 6%)) ÷ 1.09^3	81.85
Total liability component	92.40
Total equity element	7.60
Proceeds of issue	100.0

The entries required to account for this are:

Dr Cash	$100m
Cr Liability	$92.40m
Cr Equity	$7.60m

The issue cost will have to be allocated between the liability and equity. The entries required are:

Dr Liability	$0.92m
Dr Equity	$0.08m
Cr Cash	$1.00m

After posting the above entries, the liability and equity would have carrying amounts as follows:

	$m Liability	$m Equity
Proceeds	92.40	7.60
Issue cost	(0.92)	(0.08)
	91.48	7.52

The equity of $7.52 million will not be re-measured.

The liability component of $91.48 million would be measured at amortised cost. This means that interest is charged at the effective rate of 9.38%. The cash payments reduce the liability.

1 June X6 $m	Interest (9.38%) $m	Cash paid (6% × $100m) $m	31 May X7 $m
91.48	8.58	(6.0)	94.06

The finance cost in profit or loss will be $8.58 million. The liability will have a carrying amount on 31 May 20X7 of $94.06 million.

(ii) **Shares in Smart**

Aron has to determine if the transfer of shares in Smart qualifies for derecognition. If substantially all the risks and rewards have been transferred, the asset is derecognised. If substantially all the risks and rewards have been retained, the asset is not derecognised. In this case the transfer of shares in Smart qualifies for derecognition as Aron no longer retains any risks and rewards of ownership.

Aron has obtained a new financial asset which is the shares in Given. Financial assets are initially recognised at fair value. The shares in Given should therefore be initially recognised at $5.5 million. If not held for trading, a designation could be made upon initial recognition to account for this new financial asset at fair value through other comprehensive income.

A profit on disposal of $0.5 million will be recorded in the statement of profit or loss. This is the difference between the initial carrying amount of the Shares in Given and the carrying amount of the shares in Smart that have been derecognised.

The entries required are:

Dr Financial asset (shares in Given)	$5.5m
Cr Financial asset (shares in Smart)	$5.0m
Cr Profit on disposal	$0.5m

In addition, Aron may choose to make a transfer within equity of the cumulative gain recognised up to the disposal date of $400,000.

(iii) **Investment in bonds**

Financial assets are initially measured at fair value, so the investment in the bond will be initially recognised at $10 million.

The entity's business model involves both holding debt instruments to collect their contractual cash flows and also selling the assets. As a debt instrument, it would appear that the contractual terms of the asset comprise the repayment of the principal and interest on the principal amount outstanding. Therefore, the asset should be measured at fair value through other comprehensive income.

Interest income should be recognised in profit or loss using the effective rate of interest. At the reporting date, the asset should be revalued to fair value with the gain or loss recognised in other comprehensive income. These gains or losses will be recycled to profit or loss if the asset is disposed of.

Interest income of $1.5 million (W1) should be recognised in profit or loss. Revaluing the asset to its fair value of $9.0 million will lead to a loss of $2.0 million (W1) being recorded in other comprehensive income.

Loss allowance

IFRS 9 *Financial Instruments* requires a loss allowance to be recognised on investments in debt that are measured at amortised cost or fair value through other comprehensive income.

If credit risk has not increased significantly since initial recognition, the loss allowance should be equal to 12-month expected credit losses. If credit risk has increased significantly, the loss allowance must be equal to lifetime expected credit losses.

The credit risk of Winston's bonds remains low at the reporting date, suggesting that there has not been a significant increase in credit risk. The loss allowance should therefore be equal to the 12-month expected credit losses of $0.2 million.

When the financial asset is measured at fair value though other comprehensive income, the loss allowance is not adjusted against the asset's carrying amount (otherwise the asset will be held below fair value). Therefore, the loss allowance is charged to profit or loss, with the credit entry being recorded in other comprehensive income (essentially, this adjustment reclassifies $0.2 million of the earlier downwards revaluation from other comprehensive income to profit or loss).

Working

(W1) Financial asset

	1/12/X3	Interest (15%)	Cash received	Total	Loss.	30/11/X4
	$m	$m	$m	$m	$m	$m
	10.0	1.5	(0.5)	11.0	(2.0)	9.0

(b) Financial instruments and fair value

Financial assets and liabilities are initially recognised at fair value (plus or minus transaction costs in certain circumstances). However, it is incorrect to state that all financial instruments are subsequently measured at fair value.

Many financial liabilities, except for those held for trading or those designated to be measured at fair value to reduce an accounting mismatch, are measured at amortised cost. An entity will also measure financial assets at amortised cost if:

- Its business model is to hold financial assets to collect the contractual cash flows

- The contractual cash flows represent solely receipt of the principal amount and interest on the principal amount outstanding.

Fair value measurement

When financial instruments are measured at fair value then the fair value will be determined by reference to IFRS 13 *Fair Value Measurement*. IFRS 13 defines fair value as the price at which an orderly transaction would take place between market participants at the measurement date. When determining the transaction price, IFRS 13 prioritises level 1 inputs into valuation techniques – quoted prices for identical assets or liabilities in active markets. This increases consistency and comparability both within and between entities, and reduces subjectivity and bias.

If level 1 inputs do not exist then Level 2 inputs should be used – quoted prices not included within level 1. However, for financial assets that are not publicly traded, level 3 inputs may need to be used – unquoted inputs using the best information available. Level 3 inputs should only be used for fair value measurement if observable inputs do not exist. However, there is clearly some scope for the manipulation of these prices.

The *Conceptual Framework* notes that a faithful representation of an asset or liability might not be achieved if measurement involves a very high degree of uncertainty. However, a faithful representation may still be possible if disclosures are adequate with regards to the nature of the financial instrument, and the techniques used to estimate its fair value.

Volatility

Measuring assets and liabilities at fair value can lead to greater financial statement volatility than measurements based on historical cost. If an investment in ordinary shares is measured at fair value through profit or loss then the asset and profit position of an entity will be subject to a year-on-year fluctuation.

With the exception of investments in equity, financial assets and liabilities are generally only held at fair value when the entity does not intend to hold them until maturity. Thus, many financial assets are held at fair value when the entity's business model involves realising cash flows from a sale.

Since most sales of financial instruments will occur at fair value then this is a timely and transparent approach to measurement that informs stakeholders about the gains and losses that the entity is exposed to and the variability of the cash flows that may ultimately be received. Delaying the recognition of gains and losses until the eventual disposal of a financial asset will instead lead to volatility on the disposal date and increase uncertainty amongst financial statement user groups.

Moreover if an entity is worried about the financial statement volatility produced by its financial instruments then it could hedge this risk through the use of derivative contracts. If the derivatives were designated as hedging instruments within a fair value or cash flow hedge arrangement then financial statement volatility would be greatly minimised. If an entity does not hedge its risk exposure through derivative contracts then it is leaving itself open to the possibility of volatile losses (or gains) – the financial reporting requirements of IFRS 9 *Financial Instruments* ensure this is clearly communicated to the entity's stakeholders.

Marking scheme			Marks
(a)	(i)	Convertible bond – 1 mark per point	6
	(ii)	Share acquisition and sale – 1 mark per point	4
	(iii)	Investment in bonds – 1 mark per point	7
(b)		Fair value measurement and stakeholders – 1 mark per point	8
Total			25

40 ALEXANDRA

Key answer tips

This is a mixed-standards question. Do not be put off by the level of detail in the answer as this would not be expected from even the most prepared students. Solid marks can be obtained by stating your knowledge of the relevant standards, even if you then reach an incorrect conclusion about the accounting treatment.

(a)   (i)   **Current/Non-current liabilities**

According to IAS 1 *Presentation of Financial Statements* a liability should be classified as current if it is due to be settled within 12 months after the reporting date.

If an issuer breaches a long-term loan agreement on or before the reporting date but the lender agrees after the reporting date to not demand repayment then the liability should still be classified as current.

The default on the interest payment in November represented an event that could have led to a claim from the bondholders to repay the whole of the loan immediately, inclusive of incurred interest and expenses. The waiver was issued after the date of the statement of financial position. As such, the loan should have been classified as a current liability.

Going concern issues

Alexandra should also consider the impact that a recall of the borrowing would have on the going concern status. If the going concern status is questionable then Alexandra would need to provide additional disclosure surrounding the uncertainty and the possible outcomes if waivers are not renewed. If Alexandra ceases to be a going concern then the financial statements would need to be prepared on a break-up basis.

   (ii)   **Disclosure of the impact of fair value uplifts**

IAS 2 *Inventories* requires the carrying amount of inventories sold to be recognised as an expense in the period in which the related revenue is recognised. Cost of sales are costs previously included in the measurement of inventory which has now been sold plus unallocated production overheads and abnormal amounts of production costs of inventories.

IFRS 3 *Business Combinations* requires an acquirer to measure the identifiable assets acquired in a business combination at their fair values at the date of acquisition. Therefore, the carrying amount of the inventories originating from the acquisition of the subsidiary is their acquisition-date fair value. Consequently, the entire carrying amount of inventory, including the effects of the fair value step-up, should be presented as cost of sales.

IAS 1 *Presentation of Financial Statements* sets out minimum levels of required items in the financial statements by requiring certain items to be presented on the face of, or in the notes to, the financial statements and in other required disclosures.

IAS 1 provides little further guidance on the presentation of line items in financial statements, such as the level of detail or number of line items that should be presented in the financial statements. The absence of specific requirements arises from the fact that the guidance in IAS 1 relies on management's judgement about which additional line items, headings and subtotals:

(a)   are relevant to an understanding of the entity's financial position/ financial performance; and

(b)   should be presented in a manner which provides relevant, reliable, comparable and understandable information.

IAS 1 allows entities to include additional line items, amend descriptions and the ordering of items in order to explain the elements of financial performance due to various activities, which may differ in frequency and predictability.

Transactions like business combinations may have a significant impact on profit or loss and these transactions are not necessarily frequent or regular. However, the practice of presenting non-recurring items may be interpreted as a way to present 'extraordinary items' in the financial statements despite the fact that 'extraordinary items' are not allowed under IAS 1. It can also be argued that additional lines and subtotals, as permitted by IAS 1, may add complexity to the analysis of the financial statements, which may become difficult to understand if entities use sub-totals and additional headings to isolate the effects of non-recurring transactions from classes of expense or income.

To conclude, the cost of the inventories sold should be presented as a cost of sale and not split in the manner proposed by Alexandra.

(iii) **Contingent liabilities**

IAS 37 *Provisions, Contingent Liabilities and Contingent Assets* describes contingent liabilities in two ways:

- Firstly, as reliably possible obligations whose existence will be confirmed only on the occurrence or non-occurrence of uncertain future events outside the entity's control, and

- Secondly, as present obligations that are not recognised because:

    - it is not probable that an outflow of economic benefits will be required to settle the obligation, or

    - the amount cannot be measured reliably.

Treatment in the individual financial statements

In Chrissy's financial statements contingent liabilities are not recognised but are disclosed and described in the notes to the financial statements. The disclosure should include an estimate of their potential financial effect and uncertainties relating to the amount or timing of any outflow, unless the possibility of settlement is remote.

Treatment in the consolidated financial statements

In a business combination, a contingent liability is recognised at the acquisition date if it meets the definition of a liability and if it can be measured.

This means Alexandra would recognise a liability of $4 million in the consolidated accounts. This will increase the goodwill arising on the acquisition of Chrissy.

(b) **Principles and key components of the IIRC's Framework**

The International Integrated Reporting Council (IIRC) has released a framework for integrated reporting. The Framework establishes principles and concepts which govern the overall content of an integrated report. The IIRC has set out a principles-based framework rather than specifying a detailed disclosure and measurement standard. This enables each company to set out its own report rather than adopting a checklist approach.

An integrated report sets out how the organisation's strategy, governance, performance and prospects can lead to the creation of value. The integrated report aims to provide an insight into the company's resources and relationships, which are known as the capitals and how the company interacts with the external environment and the capitals to create value. These capitals can be financial, manufactured, intellectual, human, social and relationship, and natural capital but companies need not adopt these classifications. Integrated reporting is built around the following key components:

(i)   Organisational overview and the external environment under which it operates

(ii)   Governance structure and how this supports its ability to create value

(iii)   Business model

(iv)   Risks and opportunities and how they are dealing with them and how they affect the company's ability to create value

(v)   Strategy and resource allocation

(vi)   Performance and achievement of strategic objectives for the period and outcomes

(vii)   Outlook and challenges facing the company and their implications.

(viii) The basis of presentation needs to be determined including what matters are to be included in the integrated report and how the elements are quantified or evaluated.

The Framework does not require discrete sections to be compiled in the report but there should be a high level review to ensure that all relevant aspects are included. An integrated report should provide insight into the nature and quality of the organisation's relationships with its key stakeholders, including how and to what extent the organisation understands, takes into account and responds to their needs and interests. Further, the report should be consistent over time to enable comparison with other entities.

The IIRC considered the nature of value and value creation. These terms can include the total of all the capitals, the benefit captured by the company, the market value or cash flows of the organisation and the successful achievement of the company's objectives. However, the conclusion reached was that the Framework should not define value from any one particular perspective because value depends upon the individual company's own perspective. It can be shown through movement of capital and can be defined as value created for the company or for others. An integrated report should not attempt to quantify value as assessments of value are left to those using the report.

The IIRC has stated that the prescription of specific measurement methods is beyond the scope of a principles-based framework. The Framework contains information on the principles-based approach and indicates that there is a need to include quantitative indicators whenever practicable and possible. Additionally, consistency of measurement methods across different reports is of paramount importance. There is outline guidance on the selection of suitable quantitative indicators.

Concerns

There are concerns over the ability to assess future disclosures, and there may be a need for confidence intervals to be disclosed. The preparation of an integrated report requires judgement but there is a requirement for the report to describe its basis of preparation and presentation, including the significant frameworks and methods used to quantify or evaluate material matters. Also included is the disclosure of a summary of how the company determined the materiality limits and a description of the reporting boundaries.

A company should consider how to describe the disclosures without causing a significant loss of competitive advantage. The entity will consider what advantage a competitor could actually gain from information in the integrated report, and will balance this against the need for disclosure.

The report does not contain a statement from those 'charged with governance' acknowledging their responsibility for the integrated report. This may undermine the reliability and credibility of the integrated report.

Marking scheme			
			Marks
(a)	(i)	Loan – 1 mark per point	5
	(ii)	Presentation of financial statements – 1 mark per point	6
	(iii)	Contingency – 1 mark per point	4
(b)		IIRC Framework – 1 mark per point	8
		Professional marks	2
			—
Total			**25**
			—

41 KLANCET *Walk in the footsteps of a top tutor*

Key answer tips

Part (a) requires no calculations. To score well, it is important to be able to apply your accounting knowledge to the specific transactions. Do not simply knowledge dump. Instead, state the recognition and measurement rules from the relevant accounting standards before applying them to the scenario. If you struggle to identify which standards are relevant then think about the items involved. What accounting standard is used to account for an investment in shares? What accounting standard is used for purchases when consideration is in the form of shares?

(a) (i) IFRS 8 *Operating Segments*

Tutorial note

Students often neglect IFRS 8 when studying but it is a popular exam topic. Make sure that you are familiar with the definition of an operating segment as well as the rules governing which operating segments must be disclosed.

IFRS 8 *Operating Segments* states that an operating segment is a component of an entity which engages in business activities from which it may earn revenues and incur costs. In addition, discrete financial information should be available for the segment and these results should be regularly reviewed by the entity's chief operating decision maker (CODM) when making decisions about resource allocation to the segment and assessing its performance.

If a function is an integral part of the business, it may be disclosed as a segment even though it may not earn revenue.

According to IFRS 8, an operating segment should be reported if it meets one of the following quantitative thresholds:

1   Its reported revenue, including both sales to external customers and intersegment sales or transfers, is 10% or more of the combined revenue, internal and external, of all operating segments.

2   The absolute amount of its reported profit or loss is 10% or more of the greater, in absolute amount, of (i) the combined reported profit of all operating segments which did not report a loss and (ii) the combined reported loss of all operating segments which reported a loss.

3   Its assets are 10% or more of the combined assets of all operating segments.

The research and development laboratories

Tutorial note

Apply the rules to each of the laboratories in turn. Make sure that you reach an explicit conclusion about whether or not they constitute operating segments.

The first laboratory is not an operating segment. This is because:

•   The laboratory does not have a separate segment manager and the existence of a segment manager is normally an important factor in determining operating segments.

•   The laboratory is responsible to the divisions themselves, which would seem to indicate that it is simply supporting the existing divisions and not a separate segment.

•   There does not seem to be any discrete performance information, which is reviewed by the CODM.

The second laboratory is an operating segment. This is because:

•   It has a separate segment manager

•   It engages in activities which earn revenues and incurs costs

•   Its operating results are reviewed by the CODM and discrete information is available for the laboratory's activities.

The second laboratory should be separately disclosed because its revenues make up more than 10% of the revenues of all operating segments.

(ii)   **Share transactions**

> *Tutorial note*
>
> *Take your time and think through which accounting standards are relevant to these transactions. Marks will only be given for discussion of the relevant accounting standards.*

Sale of patent

The shares received are in the scope of IFRS 9 *Financial Instruments* and are to be initially measured at fair value. Klancet should derecognise the patent which is transferred to Jancy. Any gain or loss on disposal is recorded in the statement of profit or loss.

The shares should be remeasured to fair value at the year end. Fair value changes are recognised in profit or loss, except for those equity investments for which the entity has elected to report value changes in 'other comprehensive income'.

Klancet should not yet recognise any asset relating to the future royalty stream from the potential sales of the drug, because this stream of royalties is contingent upon the successful development of the drug.

Purchase of patent

Klancet has received a patent in exchange for issuing its own shares. This transaction is within the scope of IFRS 2 *Share-based Payment*.

The transaction is with a supplier, rather than an employee, so Klancet should measure the patent purchased at its fair value and make a corresponding entry to equity (share capital). If Klancet cannot estimate reliably the fair value of the patent then it should measure the transaction at the fair value of the equity instruments granted.

(b)   (i)   **Financial instrument**

According to IFRS 9 *Financial Instruments* the financial asset should be initially recognised at its fair value of $5 million. Klancet's business model means that the asset will be measured at fair value through other comprehensive income. Interest income should be calculated using the effective rate of interest. Gains and losses on revaluation to fair value are recorded in OCI.

Bfd	Interest 10%	Receipt*	Subtotal	Loss	Fair value
$m	$m	$m	$m	$m	$m
5.0	0.5	(0.2)	5.3	(0.8)	4.5

* = $5m × 4%

Interest income of $0.5 million is recorded in profit or loss. The asset is revalued to its fair value of $4.5 million, with a loss of $0.8 million recorded in OCI. This revaluation loss will be presented as an item that may be reclassified to profit or loss in the future.

(ii)   **Conceptual Framework**

The *Conceptual Framework* defines an asset as a resource of an entity that has the potential to produce economic benefits. The financial instrument meets the definition of an asset because Klancet has a contractual right to receive cash.

According to the *Conceptual Framework*, an element is recognised in the financial statements if recognition provides relevant financial information, and a faithful representation of the underlying transaction. This would seem to be the case because primary users of the financial statements are interested in the future cash flows that an entity will generate, and this financial instrument gives the entity a contractual right to future cash flows. Moreover, the cost of the asset can be measured reliably. As such, recognition of the asset would appear to be in accordance with the *Conceptual Framework*.

The *Conceptual Framework* states that the statement of profit or loss is the primary source of information about an entity's performance. This statement should enable investors to understand the entity's returns for the period, to assess future cash flows, and to assess stewardship of the entity's resources.

When developing or revising standards, the Board notes that it might require an income or expense to be presented in other comprehensive if it results from remeasuring an item to current value and if this means that:

- profit or loss provides more relevant information, or

- a more faithful representation is provided of an entity's performance.

Klancet's business model involves holding the asset to maturity in order to collect the contractual cash flows unless a better investment becomes available. It does not intend to trade the asset in the short-term and so fair value gains and losses on the instrument are largely irrelevant when assessing Klancet's performance. Presenting the fair value loss of $0.8 million in other comprehensive income therefore ensures that the statement of profit or loss best presents the entity's economic returns during the period. This is consistent with the *Conceptual Framework*.

The *Conceptual Framework* states that income and expenditure included in other comprehensive income should be reclassified to profit or loss when doing so results in profit or loss providing more relevant information. In accordance with IFRS 9, the gains and losses on Klancet's debt instrument will be reclassified to profit or loss when the asset is derecognised. In this regard, the treatment of the debt instrument is, once again, consistent with the *Conceptual Framework*.

Marking scheme			
			Marks
(a)	(i)	Operating segments – 1 mark per point	8
	(ii)	Share transactions – 1 mark per point	6
(b)	(i)	Financial instrument – 1 mark per point	4
	(ii)	Conceptual Framework – 1 mark per point	7
Total			25

42   EMCEE *Walk in the footsteps of a top tutor*

Key answer tips

This question tests a wide variety of standards. Moreover, part (a) (i) requires students to be able to apply those standards to scenarios that they may not have previously considered. This can be difficult at first but you will improve with practice.

(a)   (i)   Sports teams

Tutorial note

To score well in part (a)(i) it is important to pick up on certain 'trigger' words within the scenario – 'purchasing registrations' suggests that Emcee is buying intangible assets, 'deciding to sell' suggests that assets may need to be classified as 'held for sale', whereas 'player injuries' suggests there could be impairment issues. Many accounting standards can be examined within a single part of the question.

Purchase of player registrations

IAS 38 *Intangible Assets* states that an entity should recognise an intangible asset where it is probable that future economic benefits will flow to the entity and the cost of the asset can be measured reliably.

Tutorial note

If you are unaware of the detail of IAS 38 Intangible Assets, then use your knowledge of the Conceptual Framework instead. The examiner has said that using the Framework to answers questions will score marks.

Therefore, the costs associated with the acquisition of players' registrations should be capitalised at cost. Cost would include transfer fees, league levy fees, agents' fees incurred by the club and other directly attributable costs.

The cost of player registrations would be amortised over the period covered by the player's contract.

Where a playing contract is extended, any costs associated with securing the extension are added to the unamortised balance at the date of the extension and the revised carrying amount is amortised over the remaining revised contract life.

Decisions to sell

Player registrations would be classified as assets held for sale under IFRS 5 *Non-current Assets Held for Sale and Discontinued Operations* when their carrying amount is expected to be recovered principally through a sale transaction and a sale is considered to be highly probable. To qualify, the registrations should be actively marketed by Emcee, which it appears that they are. It would also appear that management commits itself to a plan to sell the registrations and that the assets are available for immediate sale. IFRS 5 requires that it is unlikely that the plan to sell the registrations will be significantly changed or withdrawn.

If classified as held for sale, the player registrations would be measured at the lower of their carrying amount and fair value less costs to sell.

Gains and losses on disposal of players' registrations would be determined by comparing the fair value of the consideration receivable, net of any transaction costs, with the carrying amount and would be recognised in profit or loss. Where a part of the consideration receivable is contingent on specified performance conditions, this amount is recognised in profit or loss when the conditions are met.

Impairment issues

Tutorial note

The question refers to players who are injured, or who will not play again. This is an indication that the registration rights for these players might be impaired.

IAS 36 *Impairment of Assets* states an asset is impaired if its carrying amount exceeds its recoverable amount. Recoverable amount is the higher of the asset's fair value less costs of disposal, and its value in use.

It will be difficult to determine the value in use of an individual player in isolation as that player cannot generate cash flows on their own (unless in a sale transaction). As such, impairments may need to be performed on the cash generating unit to which the player belongs. This is likely to be the team as a whole.

There may be some circumstances where a player is taken out of the team, such as if they sustain a career threatening injury. If such circumstances arise, the carrying amount of the player should be assessed against the best estimate of the player's fair value less any costs to sell.

Any impairment losses would be charged to profit or loss.

The playing registrations which were disposed of subsequent to the year-end for $25 million would be disclosed as an event after the reporting period.

(ii)   **Deferred tax assets**

Tutorial note

This is a common exam scenario. Use the information in the question to decide whether Emcee will receive probable benefits from its unused tax losses.

IAS 12 *Income Taxes* states that a deferred tax asset shall be recognised for the carry-forward of unused tax losses to the extent that it is probable that future taxable profit will be available against which unused tax losses can be utilised.

IAS 12 explains that the existence of unused tax losses is strong evidence that future taxable profit may not be available. Therefore, when an entity has a history of recent losses, the entity recognises a deferred tax asset arising from unused tax losses only to the extent that the entity has sufficient taxable temporary differences or when there is convincing other evidence that sufficient taxable profit will be available against which the unused tax losses can be utilised by the entity.

Emcee recognised losses during the previous five years. In order to use the deferred tax asset of $16 million, Emcee would have to recognise a profit of $53.3 million at the existing tax rate of 30%. In comparison, the entity recognised an average loss of $19 million per year during the five previous years.

Tutorial note

Do Emcee's budgets seem accurate and reliable?

Emcee's budgets and assumptions are not convincing other evidence because the entity does not appear to have been capable of making accurate forecasts in the past and there were material differences between the amounts budgeted and realised for the previous two years. Emcee had presented future budgets primarily based on general assumptions about economic improvement indicators, rather than what was expected to influence the future income and therefore enable the use of the deferred tax asset.

Tutorial note

Are Emcee's losses one-off events, or are they likely to recur?

IAS 12 states that in assessing the probability that taxable profit will be available against which the unused tax losses or unused tax credits can be utilised, a consideration is whether the unused tax losses result from identifiable causes which are unlikely to recur (i.e. one off events). However, Emcee has continued to recognise impairment losses in excess of budget. This places doubts on the likelihood of future profits arising.

Finally, in its financial statements, Emcee disclosed a material uncertainty about its ability to continue as a going concern. This, again, places doubts on the likelihood of future profits and suggests that recognition of a deferred tax asset for unused tax losses would be inappropriate.

In conclusion the liability of $3 million relating to temporary differences can be offset against $3 million of unused tax losses. No further deferred tax asset relating to tax losses should be recognised.

(b)

Tutorial note

There are some fairly common-sense points to be made in part (b) of the question. What problems arise if disclosures are insufficient? What problems arise if there are too many lengthy disclosures?

Importance of optimal level of disclosure

It is important that financial statements are relevant and understandable. Excessive disclosure can obscure relevant information. This makes it harder for users to find the key points about the performance of the business and its prospects for long-term success

Materiality

An item is material if its omission or misstatement will influence the economic decisions of the users of financial statements.

The Board feels that the poor application of materiality contributes to too much irrelevant information in financial statements and not enough relevant information. As such, they have issued a Practice Statement called *Making Materiality Judgements*.

In the Practice Statement, the Board re-iterate that an entity only needs to apply the disclosure requirements in an IFRS Standard if the resulting information is material. When making such decisions, an entity must consider the common information needs of the primary user groups of its financial statements.

When organising disclosure notes, entities should:

- Emphasise material matters

- Ensure material information is not obscured by immaterial information

- Ensure information is entity-specific

- Aim for simplicity and conciseness without omitting material detail

- Ensure formats are appropriate and understandable (e.g. tables, lists, narrative)

- Provide comparable information

- Avoid duplication

Entities may sometimes need to provide additional disclosures, not required by an IFRS Standard, if necessary to help financial statement users understand the financial impact of its transactions during the period.

Marking scheme			Marks
(a)	(i)	Player registrations – 1 mark per point	9
	(ii)	Deferred tax assets and losses – 1 mark per point	8
(b)		Disclosure – 1 mark per point	8
Total			25

43 GASNATURE *Walk in the footsteps of a top tutor*

Key answer tips

Use the mark allocation to help you plan your timings. Leaving parts of a question un-attempted is one of the main reasons why students fail exams.

Broadly speaking, you will be awarded one mark for every valid point that you make. If you have not written very much then think about whether there are any key principles from the relevant accounting standard that you haven't written down. Or, alternatively, try and use the *Conceptual Framework* to help you to develop your answer.

As always, thoroughly debrief the model answer and learn from your mistakes. Write down the things you did not know as this will help you to remember them for next time.

(a) (i) Joint arrangements

Tutorial note

In exam questions watch out for scenarios where decision making requires 'unanimous' consent of the parties that share control. This is usually an indication of joint control, suggesting that there is a joint arrangement.

Joint arrangements take two forms: joint operations or joint ventures. Make sure that you are clear on the difference between the two.

A joint arrangement occurs where two or more parties have joint control. Joint control exists when decisions about the relevant activities require the unanimous consent of the parties sharing control.

The classification of a joint arrangement as a joint operation or a joint venture depends upon the rights and obligations of the parties to the arrangement. A joint arrangement which is not structured through a separate vehicle is normally a joint operation. A joint operator accounts for the assets, liabilities, revenues and expenses relating to its involvement in a joint operation.

The arrangement with Gogas is a joint arrangement, because decisions regarding the platform require unanimous agreement of both parties. The joint arrangement with Gogas should be classified as a joint operation because there is no separate vehicle involved. Gasnature should recognise 55% of the asset's cost as property, plant and equipment.

Dismantling

Under IAS 16 *Property, Plant and Equipment* (PPE), the cost of an item of property, plant and equipment must include the initial estimate of the costs of dismantling and removing the item and restoring the site on which it is located.

IAS 37 *Provisions, Contingent Liabilities and Contingent Assets* stipulates how to measure decommissioning and restoration costs and similar liabilities. Where the effect of the time value of money is material, the amount of a provision should be the present value of the expected expenditure required to settle the obligation.

Tutorial note

In their financial statements, joint operators recognise their interest in the assets and liabilities of the joint operation.

Thus Gasnature should account for 55% of the present value of the estimated decommissioning costs. Gasnature will include this in PPE and will also recognise a provision for the same amount.

Because Gasnature is a joint operator, there is also a contingent liability for 45% of the decommissioning costs as there is a potential obligation if some uncertain future event occurs (such as if Gogas goes into liquidation and cannot fund the decommissioning costs). Therefore Gasnature should disclose a contingent liability to the extent that it is potentially liable for Gogas's share of the decommissioning costs.

(ii)   **Financial instruments**

Tutorial note

The answer below uses a lot of technical detail from IFRS 9 Financial Instruments. However, you could reach the same conclusion by using simple accounting principles. Gasnature is buying gas to use in its business – it is therefore a purchase contract.

IFRS 9 *Financial Instruments* applies to contracts to buy or sell a non-financial item that are settled net in cash Such contracts are accounted for as derivatives.

However, contracts which are for an entity's 'own use' of a non-financial asset are exempt from the requirements of IFRS 9.

There are various ways in which a contract to buy or sell a non-financial item can be settled net in cash. These include:

- when the terms of the contract permit either party to settle it net in cash

- when the entity has a practice of settling similar contracts net in cash

- when the entity has a practice of taking delivery of the non-financial asset and selling it in the short-term to generate a profit

- when the non-financial item is readily convertible to cash.

It could be argued that the contract is net settled because the penalty mechanism requires Agas to compensate Gasnature at the current prevailing market price. Further, if natural gas is readily convertible into cash in the location where the delivery takes place, the contract could be considered net settled.

However, the contract will probably still qualify as 'own use' as long as it has been entered into and continues to be held for Gasnature's usage requirements. This means that it falls outside IFRS 9 and should be treated as an executory contract. The gas will be recorded at cost on the purchase date.

(b) **Accounting policy choices**

Tutorial note

Take time to think about the choices allowed by each standard. This is your gateway into the rest of the question.

IAS 16 *Property, Plant and Equipment*

After initial recognition, IAS 16 allows property, plant and equipment (PPE) to be measured using either:

- the cost model – cost less accumulated depreciation and impairment losses

- the revaluation model – fair value less accumulated depreciation and impairment losses.

Tutorial note

*First of all think about the impact on the statement of profit or loss. Remember that revaluation gains on property, plant and equipment are **not** recorded in the statement of profit or loss.*

Assuming that property prices are increasing, an entity that revalues its PPE to fair value will record lower profits than one that uses the cost model. Although the gains arising from the revaluation of PPE are recognised outside of profit, in other comprehensive income, the depreciation charge on the revalued asset will be higher than if the cost model was used. As such, using the revaluation model may have a detrimental impact on stakeholders' assessment of an entity's financial performance.

Moreover, the higher asset value recorded in the statement of financial position under the revaluation model might also make the entity look less efficient than one which uses the cost model.

Tutorial note

Think about the impact on the statement of financial position.

However, on the positive side revaluation gains will increase equity which will improve the gearing ratio. This may make the entity look like a less risky investment. Moreover, some stakeholders may place importance on an entity's asset base, as this could be used as security for obtaining new finance. Thus, a higher PPE value in the statement of financial position could be viewed positively.

Another thing to note is that the revaluation model will make the asset position of an entity more volatile than an entity that uses the cost model. Volatility can increase the perception of risk. However, the statement of profit or loss will be much less volatile than the statement of financial position because revaluation gains are recorded in other comprehensive income.

It should be noted that entities using the revaluation model for PPE are required to disclose the carrying amounts that would be recognised if the cost model had been used. Such disclosures enable better comparison with entities that account for PPE using different measurement models.

IAS 20 *Accounting for Government Grants and Disclosure of Government Assistance*

Tutorial note

Your answer does not need to be as detailed as the one presented below.

With regards to asset related grants, two methods of presentation are allowed in the statement of financial position:

- recognise the grant as deferred income and release to profit or loss over the useful life of the asset

- deduct the grant from the carrying amount of the asset and then depreciate the asset over its useful life.

The overall net assets and profit of an entity will not be affected by this choice. However, it could still have an impact on an investor's analysis of the financial statements.

An entity that uses the deferred income method to present asset-related grants will report higher non-current asset assets and higher liabilities than an entity that uses the 'netting off' method.

Reporting a higher level of liabilities may have a detrimental impact on certain ratios, such as the current ratio. More generally, higher liabilities may increase the perception of financial risk, potentially deterring investment.

Reporting higher levels of non-current assets could be viewed positively (as a sign of a strong asset base), or negatively (it may make the entity look less efficient at generating its profit).

With regards to income related grants, two methods of presentation are allowed in the statement of profit or loss:

- present the grant as 'other income'

- present the grant as a reduction in the related expense.

The overall profit of an entity will not be affected by this choice. However, it could still have an impact when analysing financial statements. For instance, an entity that presents grant income by reducing its expenses may be perceived as having better cost control and as operating with greater efficiency than an entity that records its grants within 'other income'.

Cash flows

Accounting policy choices have no impact on the operating, investing or financing cash flows reported in the statement of cash flows.

Marking scheme			Marks
(a)	(i)	Joint operation – 1 mark per point	7
	(ii)	Gas contract – 1 mark per point	6
(b)		Accounting choices – 1 mark per point	10
		Professional	2
Total			**25**

44 JANNE *Walk in the footsteps of a top tutor*

Key answer tips

Part (a) (i) is a test of the difference between an operating lease and a finance lease. Make sure that you state the definition and indicators of a finance lease before applying these to the question. Explain why each factor is suggestive of a finance or operating lease, rather than just copying out the scenario.

Part (a) (ii) tests the calculation of a loss allowance for trade receivables. Remember that you are 'advising' Janne's directors – this requires more than just calculations.

Part (b) is about the *Conceptual Framework*. The examining team have regularly noted the importance of this topic to the SBR exam. If you lack familiarity then revisit the Study Text.

(a) **(i)** **Leases**

Tutorial note

IFRS 16 lists many factors that should be considered by a lessor when determining whether a lease is a finance lease or an operating lease. You should begin your answer by stating as many of these as you can remember.

If a lease transfers substantially all the risks and rewards incidental to ownership to the lessee, then the lease is a finance lease, otherwise it is an operating lease.

IFRS 16 *Leases* says that the key indications of a finance lease include:

- the lease transfers ownership of the asset to the lessee by the end of the lease term

- the lease term is for the major part of the economic life of the asset, even if title is not transferred

- at the inception of the lease, the present value of the minimum lease payments amounts to at least substantially all of the fair value of the leased asset

- the lessee has the ability to continue to lease for a secondary period at a rent that is substantially lower than market rent.

Tutorial note

You should now apply these criteria to the question. Do not worry if some parts of the scenario are suggestive of a finance lease whilst others are suggestive of an operating lease. However, do try and reach a conclusion at the end as to what type of lease you think it is and therefore what the accounting treatment should be.

The fact that land normally has an indefinite economic life may suggest that the lease is an operating lease. However, a lease of land could still be classified as a finance lease if other criteria are met.

The presence of an option to extend the lease at substantially less than a market rent or purchase it at a discount of 90% on the market value implies that the lessor expects to achieve its return on investment mainly through the lease payments and therefore is content to continue the lease for a secondary period at an immaterial rental or sell it at a substantial discount to the market value. This is an indicator of a finance lease. It is reasonable to assume that the lessee will extend the lease or purchase the land in these circumstances.

It would appear that the minimum lease payments would equate to the fair value of the asset, given the fact that the lease premium is 70% of the current fair value and the rent is 4% of the fair value for 30 years.

Tutorial note

Make sure that you reach a conclusion.

As a result of the above, the lease is a finance lease. At the inception of the lease, the land should be derecognised and a lease receivable should be recognised.

(ii) **Receivables**

Tutorial note

Start your answer with a discussion of the rules around the impairment of financial assets.

Trade receivables are financial assets and are normally measured at amortised cost in accordance with IFRS 9 *Financial Instruments*.

Tutorial note

IFRS 9 Financial Instruments permits a simplification for trade receivables.

A loss allowance is required for investments in debt instruments that are measured at amortised cost. For trade receivables that do not have a significant financing component, this loss allowance should always be equal to lifetime expected credit losses.

A credit loss is the difference between the contractual cash flows from an asset and what the entity expects to receive. These credit losses should be discounted to present value and weighted by the risks of a default occurring. Lifetime losses are the expected credit losses that arise from all possible default events over the life of the instrument.

Janne's expected credit losses can be calculated by multiplying the carrying amount of its receivables with the expected risk of default over their life. Calculation of credit losses must use information about past events and current economic conditions as well as forecasts of future economic conditions and therefore Janne is correct to have adjusted its historical default rates for future estimates. Discounting will not be required as the receivables are short-term.

Tutorial note

Remember to show all of your workings.

The lifetime expected credit losses on the trade receivables are:

	Lifetime expected credit losses $m
Not overdue ($10.1m × 0.5%)	0.05
1 – 30 days overdue ($4.3m × 1.5%)	0.06
31 – 60 days overdue ($1.6m × 6.1%)	0.10
More than 60 days overdue ($1.0m × 16.5%)	0.17
	0.38

Tutorial note

Remember that entities account for the movement in the loss allowance. This movement is charged (or credited) to the statement of profit or loss.

The allowance required is therefore $0.38 million. The current allowance of $0.2 million must be increased by $0.18 million and this will be charged as an impairment loss to the statement of profit or loss.

(iii)   **Fair value through profit or loss**

Tutorial note

*Read the question very carefully. Janne has **issued** bonds and so has a **financial liability**. Discussions of business models and contractual cash flows are irrelevant (they relate to the classification of financial assets).*

IFRS 9 requires gains and losses on financial liabilities designated to be measured at fair value through profit or loss to be split into the amount of change in the fair value which is attributable to changes in the credit risk of the liability, which is shown in other comprehensive income, and the remaining amount of change in the fair value of the liability which is shown in profit or loss.

IFRS 9 allows the recognition of the full amount of change in the fair value in the profit or loss only if the recognition of changes in the liability's credit risk in other comprehensive income would create an accounting mismatch in profit or loss.

Amounts presented in other comprehensive income are not subsequently transferred to profit or loss.

Application to Coatmin

Janne should reduce the carrying amount of the liability by $50 million. They should record $5 million of the gain in OCI and the other $45 million in profit or loss.

(b) Share-based payment

Tutorial note

Start with the definition of an 'expense'.

The *Conceptual Framework* defines an expense as a decrease in economic benefits that result in decreases in equity (other than those related to distributions to equity participants).

In the case of a cash-settled share-based payment, the entity has an obligation to pay cash in the future. This therefore meets the definition of an expense.

However, in the case of an equity-settled share-based payment, the entity is providing equity as payment for the good or service received. There is no apparent reduction in an asset or increase in a liability in accordance with the definition of an expense. In fact, an equity-settled share-based payment has no net impact on equity (expenses reduce retained earnings, but the other side of the transaction increases other components of equity). Although IFRS 2 *Share-based Payment* requires the recognition of an expense for equity-settled schemes, it can be argued that this is not in accordance with the definitions in the *Conceptual Framework*.

The Board refute the above. They argue that employee service is an asset that is received by the reporting entity but then simultaneously consumed. In other words, in accordance with the definition of an expense, there is a decrease in the assets of the reporting entity.

Non-refundable deposits

Tutorial note

Start with the definition of a 'liability'.

The *Conceptual Framework* defines a liability as a present obligation from a past event to transfer an economic resource.

In this example, there is no obligation to repay the cash because the deposit is non-refundable. Some commentators believe that the deposit amount should therefore be recognised immediately as income.

Nonetheless, the seller has an obligation to transfer the related goods or services to the customer. These goods or services are economic resources because they have the potential to produce economic benefits. As such, a non-refundable deposit received would seem to meet the definition of a liability.

That said, it can be argued that the liability to transfer goods or services should be recognised at the cost to the entity of providing these, rather than the price that was charged to the customer.

Internally generated brands

Tutorial note

This part is about the recognition of an asset. Therefore state the definition of an asset and the principles that govern the recognition of elements in the financial statements.

The *Conceptual Framework* defines an asset as a resource controlled by an entity as a result of a past event. Brands, whether internally generated or purchased, meet the definition of an asset. This is because they are controlled by the entity, normally through trademarks, and they have the potential to bring economic resources.

The *Conceptual Framework* says that items are recognised in the financial statements if recognition provides relevant information and a faithful representation of the underlying transaction. Recognition of a brand in the financial statements would most likely provide relevant information. Non-recognition arguably understates the financial value of the reporting entity to the primary users of the financial statements. However, the cost of an internally generated brand cannot be measured reliably because brand expenditure cannot be differentiated from the day-to-day operating costs of the business. This measurement uncertainty means that it is not possible to represent the brand faithfully in the financial statements.

The prohibition in IAS 38 on recognising internally generated brands would appear to be consistent with the *Conceptual Framework*.

Marking scheme			Marks
(a)	(i)	Lease classification – 1 mark per point	7
	(ii)	Gas contract – 1 mark per point	6
	(iii)	Financial liability at FVPL – 1 mark per point	4
(b)	Framework		8
Total			**25**

45 EVOLVE *Walk in the footsteps of a top tutor*

Key answer tips

This question tests core accounting standards in quite unusual scenarios. As such, good application skills are required to score well. Make sure that you get the easiest marks by stating your knowledge of the principles from each relevant accounting standard. Many students leave parts of these questions blank – there is no negative marking so you might as well give it your best attempt!

(a) (i) Non-current assets held for sale

IFRS 5 *Non-current Assets Held for Sale and Discontinued Operations* says that an asset should be held for sale if its carrying amount will be recovered primarily through a sale and the sale is highly probable to occur.

IFRS 5 does not require the existence of a binding sales agreement in order to classify a non-current asset as held for sale but only a high probability of its occurrence. IFRS 5 states that the appropriate level of management must be committed to a plan to sell the asset for the sale to be probable. Evolve's acceptance of a binding offer in August 20X6 and the publication of this information thus indicated a high probability of sale. Despite the uncertainties surrounding the sale, the transaction remained highly probable at 31 August 20X6.

Other criteria which indicate that the non-current assets should be shown as held for sale include the fact that a buyer for the non-current assets has been found, the sale occurred within 12 months of classification as held for sale, the asset was actively marketed for sale at a price which has been accepted. Despite the uncertainties at 31 August 20X6, events after the reporting period indicate that the contract was not significantly changed or withdrawn. The fact that the information regarding the uncertainties was not publicly disclosed is irrelevant.

Evolve cannot apply IFRS 5 measurement criteria without classifying the item as held for sale in its statement of financial position particularly as impairment may arise when using such criteria.

Thus as the non-current assets met the criteria to be classified as held for sale, they should have been measured and presented as such in the financial statements. Assets classified as held for sale are presented separately within current assets on the face of the statement of financial position.

(ii) Business combinations

IFRS 3 *Business Combinations* must be applied when accounting for business combinations, but does not apply where the acquisition is not of a business. In this case, the acquisition was essentially that of an asset and therefore the measurement requirements of IFRS 3 would not apply.

Investment property

IAS 40 *Investment Property* states that the cost of an investment property comprises its purchase price and any directly attributable expenditure, such as professional fees for legal services. Hence if Evolve wishes to use the cost basis for accounting for the investment property, the potential gain should not have been recorded in profit or loss or added to the cost of the asset.

The specific fiscal treatment and the tax to be paid were not linked to bringing the asset to the condition necessary for its operations, as the asset would have been operational without the tax. As such, the tax is a cost linked to the activity of Evolve and should be accounted for as an expense in accordance with IAS 12 *Income Taxes* and included in profit or loss for the period.

(b) **Materiality**

Definition

An item is material if its omission or misstatement might influence the economic decisions of the users of the financial statements.

When an entity is assessing materiality, it is considering whether information is relevant to the readers of its own financial statements – in other words, materiality is entity specific. An entity should assume that the users of its financial statements have a reasonable knowledge of business and accounting

The materiality Practice Statement emphasises that materiality judgements are not just quantitative – transactions that trigger non-compliance with laws, or which impact future operations, may affect user decisions even if the monetary amounts involved are small.

Importance of materiality to financial reporting

The purpose of financial reporting is to provide information that will help investors, lenders and other creditors to make economic decisions about providing an entity with resources.

It is important that management consider materiality throughout the process of preparing financial statements. This should ensure that relevant information is not omitted or misstated. The Practice Statement details a four step process:

- Identify information that might be material

- Assess whether that information is material

- Organise the information in draft financial statements

- Review the draft financial statements.

Management should produce financial statements that are free from error. However the impact of certain transactions might be omitted or simplified as long as the resulting errors are immaterial. The materiality Practice Statement recognises that simplified accounting procedures, such as writing off all capital expenditure below $1,000 to profit or loss, can greatly reduce the burden of financial reporting without causing material misstatements.

The concept of materiality does not just help to determine whether transactions are recognised in the financial statements, but also how they are presented. Management may decide to present some material transactions as separate line items in its financial statements, whereas the effects of other immaterial transactions might be aggregated. The Practice Statement emphasises the importance of these decisions: too much detail can obscure important information, whereas over-aggregation leads to a loss of relevant detail.

Materiality assessments also impact disclosure notes. Guidance in this area is important because financial statements have become increasingly cluttered in recent years as the disclosure requirements in IFRS Standards have expanded. However, as IAS 1 *Presentation of Financial Statements* states, an entity need not provide a specific disclosure required by an IFRS Standard if the information is immaterial. The Practice Statement emphasises that the common information needs of primary user groups should always be considered and that the disclosure requirements in IFRS Standards should not be treated as a simple checklist.

Marking scheme			Marks
(a)	(i)	Assets held for sale – 1 mark per point	7
	(ii)	Investment property – 1 mark per point	6
(b)		Materiality – 1 mark per point	10
		Professional marks	2
Total			**25**

46 ARTWRIGHT

Key answer tips

This question tests hedge accounting, which is a topic that students struggle with. The transactions in part (a) (ii) are relatively simple. If you struggle, it is important that you revisit the Study Text.

Part (b) tests the impact of errors on stakeholder perception. Analysis of financial information is a core topic in SBR that will feature in every exam.

(a) (i) Intangible assets

IAS *38 Intangible Assets* requires an entity to recognise an intangible asset if:

- It is probable that the future economic benefits which are attributable to the asset will flow to the entity, and

- the cost of the asset can be measured reliably.

This requirement applies whether an intangible asset is acquired externally or generated internally.

The probability of future economic benefits must be based on reasonable and supportable assumptions about conditions which will exist over the life of the asset. The price an entity pays to acquire an intangible asset reflects expectations about the probability that the expected future economic benefits from the asset will flow to the entity. This means that the effect of probability is reflected in the cost of the asset and so the probability recognition criterion is always considered to be satisfied for intangible assets that are acquired separately or in a business combination.

In this case, Artwright should recognise an intangible asset for the use of Jomaster's technology. The right should be measured at its cost of $4 million. The intangible asset should be amortised from the date it is available for use. The technology is available for use when the manufacturing of the compound begins. At the end of each reporting period, Artwright is required to assess whether there is any indication that the asset may be impaired.

Due to the nature of intangible assets, subsequent expenditure will rarely meet the criteria for being recognised in the carrying amount of an asset. Thus Artwright continues to expense its own internal development expenditure until the criteria for capitalisation are met and economic benefits are expected to flow to the entity from the capitalised asset. When the drug is sold, the royalty payments are presented in profit or loss.

Business combinations

IFRS 10 *Consolidated Financial Statements* says that: 'An investor controls an investee when the investor is exposed, or has rights, to variable returns from its involvement with the investee and has the ability to affect those returns through its power over the investee'. Therefore it appears that Artwright will control Conew.

Any transaction in which an entity obtains control of one or more businesses qualifies as a business combination and is subject to the measurement and recognition requirements of IFRS 3 *Business Combinations*.

IFRS 3 defines a 'business' as 'an integrated set of activities and assets that is capable of being conducted and managed for the purpose of providing a return in the form of dividends, lower costs or other economic benefits directly to investors or other owners, members or participants'. A business consists of inputs and processes applied to those inputs which have the ability to create outputs. Processes are included in the acquired group when intellectual property (IP) is accompanied by other resources such as assets or employees or other elements such as protocols and plans which will further help develop the IP to the next phase.

Conew does not meet the definition of a business. This means that the acquisition of an interest in Conew should be accounted for as an asset acquisition in accordance with IAS 38 *Intangible Assets*.

(ii)   **Hedge effectiveness**

If an entity chooses to hedge account then it must assess at inception and at each reporting date whether the hedge effectiveness criteria have been met.

These criteria are as follows:

- **'There is an economic relationship between the hedged item and the hedging instrument**

- **The effect of credit risk does not dominate the value changes that arise from that relationship**

- **The hedged ratio should be the same as that resulting from the quantity of the hedged item that the entity actually hedges and the quantity of the hedging instrument that the entity actually uses.'**

(IFRS 9, para 6.4.1)

IFRS 9 *Financial Instruments* says that the assessment of effectiveness must be forwards-looking.

Derivatives

All derivatives have to be initially recognised at fair value, i.e. at the consideration given or received at inception of the contract. Derivatives A and C appear to have no purchase price, so are initially recognised at nil. Derivative B will be initially recognised at its fair value of $1m.

Derivative A: Artwright has entered into this derivative for speculative purposes. IFRS 9 requires that all derivatives not designated as part of a hedge accounting arrangement are accounted for at fair value through profit or loss. The loss of $20 million that has been incurred has to be immediately recognised profit or loss.

Dr Profit or loss	$20m
Cr Derivative	$20m

Derivative B: If a fair value hedge is effective, then the movement in the fair value of the item and the instrument since the inception of the hedge are normally recognised in profit or loss. However, if the hedged item is an investment in shares that has been designated to be measured at fair value through other comprehensive income (FVOCI), then the fair value movement on the hedged item and the hedging instrument are recognised in other comprehensive income.

The hedged item is an investment of shares designated to be measured at FVOCI. Therefore, the following entries are required at the reporting date:

Dr Financial asset	$8.5m
Cr Other comprehensive income	$8.5m
Dr Other comprehensive income	$10m
Cr Derivative	$10m

Derivative C: If a cash flow hedge is effective, then the movement in the fair value of the instrument is accounted for through other comprehensive income. However, if the movement on the instrument exceeds the movement on the item, then the excess is recognised in profit or loss.

The following entry is required:

Dr Derivative	$25m
Cr Other comprehensive income	$24m
Cr Profit or loss	$1m

When the raw materials are purchased, the gains recognised in other comprehensive income can be reclassified against the carrying amount of the inventory.

(b) Reporting a financial instrument as debt rather than equity would lead to a deterioration in the gearing ratio. This may make the company appear more risky to potential investors or lenders, potentially creating problems when raising further finance.

Liability classification normally results in the servicing of the finance being treated as an interest expense, which is charged to profit or loss. Finance costs in profit or loss will reduce earnings per share, which may lower investor confidence in the entity. Lower profits could also lead to a breach of loan covenants, potentially triggering the need to repay borrowings.

Equity classification may avoid these impacts, but could be perceived negatively if seen to be diluting existing equity interests.

Marking scheme			Marks
(a)	(i)	Intangibles and business combinations – 1 mark per point	8
	(ii)	Derivatives and hedge accounting – 1 mark per point	9
(b)		Impact of debt/equity classification – 1 mark per point	6
		Professional marks	2
			___
Total			**25**
			___

47 LUCKY DAIRY

Key answer tips

Part (a) (i) of this question tests IAS 41 *Agriculture*. This is a relatively simple accounting standard, albeit one that is not examined frequently. As such, you may lack familiarity with the core principles of the standard.

Part (b) examines integrated reporting. This is an important area of the syllabus so do not neglect it.

(a) (i) Biological assets

According to IAS 41 *Agriculture* a biological asset, such as a dairy cow, is initially measured at fair value less costs to sell. It should be remeasured at each reporting date to its fair value less estimated costs to sell. Gains or losses on remeasurement are recorded in the statement of profit or loss.

As at 31 May 20X1, the herd would have been carried in the statement of financial position at $3.5 million. The heifers purchased in the current year should have been recognised at $1.15 million. At year end, the herd is revalued to its fair value less costs to sell of $5.58 million. A revaluation gain of $0.93 million is recognised in profit or loss (W1).

(W1) Biological assets

	Fair value less costs to sell
	$m
Carrying amount at 31 May 20X1 (70,000 × $50)	3.50
Purchase (25,000 × $46)	1.15
Fair value gain (bal. fig.)	0.93
Carrying amount at 31 May 20X2	5.58
(70,000 × 60) + (25,000 × $55)	

(ii)   Financial assets

According to IFRS 9 *Financial Instruments*, a loss allowance should be recognised on financial assets that are debt instruments and which are measured at amortised cost or fair value through other comprehensive income.

If the credit risk of a financial asset has not increased significantly since inception, the loss allowance should equal 12-month expected credit losses. If the credit risk of a financial asset has increased significantly since inception, the loss allowance should equal lifetime expected credit losses. An entity must use reasonable forward-looking information when assessing the level of credit risk.

The bonds had a low credit risk at inception. It would seem that credit risk has increased significantly since inception. This is because of the following:

- The financial performance and cash generation of Jags have been poor and this will have impaired its ability to service its financing obligations.

- The entity was close to breaching loan covenants at year end. A breach of covenants would potentially make loans repayable, thus having a detrimental impact on cash flow.

- The decreased bond price appears to be entity specific and therefore reflective of market concerns about Jags and its credit risk

- External agencies are reviewing the credit rating of Jags, suggesting that credit risk has increased since the publication of its latest financial results.

Due to the increase in credit risk, the loss allowance should be equal to lifetime expected credit losses. Increases or decreases in the allowance will be charged to profit or loss.

(b)   Statements of cash flows

Statements of cash flows provide valuable information to stakeholders:

- Cash flows are objective and verifiable and so are more easily understood than profits. In contrast, profits can be manipulated through the use of judgement or choice of a particular accounting policy.

- Cash generated from operations is a useful indication of the quality of the profits generated by a business. Good quality profits will generate cash and increase the financial adaptability of an entity.

- Cash flow information has some predictive value. It may assist stakeholders in making judgements on the amount, timing and degree of certainty on future cash flows.

However, the adjustment of non-cash flow items within operating activities is complex and may not be easily understood. Moreover, the classification of cash flows can be manipulated between operating, investing and financing activities. As such, it is only through an analysis of the statement of financial position, statement of comprehensive income and notes, together with cash flow, that a comprehensive understanding of the entity's position and performance can develop.

Integrated reporting

It is true that International Financial Reporting Standards are extensive and their required disclosures very comprehensive. This has led to criticism that the most relevant information can become obscured by immaterial disclosures. An integrated report would increase disclosure as well as imposing additional time and cost constraints on the reporting entity.

However, integrated reporting will provide stakeholders with valuable information which would not be immediately accessible from an entity's financial statements.

Financial statements are based on historical information and may lack predictive value. They are essential in corporate reporting, particularly for compliance purposes but do not provide meaningful information regarding business value. The primary purpose of an integrated report is to explain to providers of capital how the organisation generates value over time.

This is summarised through an examination of the key activities and outputs of the organisation whether they be financial, manufactured, intellectual, human, social or natural.

An integrated report seeks to examine the external environment which the entity operates within and to provide an insight into the entity's resources and relationships to generate value. It is principles based and should be driven by materiality, including how and to what extent the entity understands and responds to the needs of its stakeholders. This would include an analysis of how the entity has performed within its business environment, together with a description of prospects and challenges for the future. It is this strategic direction which is lacking from a traditional set of financial statements and will be invaluable to stakeholders to make a more informed assessment of the organisation and its prospects.

Marking scheme			
			Marks
(a)	(i)	Biological assets – 1 mark per point	6
	(ii)	Financial assets – 1 mark per point	8
(b)		Cash flows and integrated reports – 1 mark per point	9
		Professional marks	2
Total			**25**

UK GAAP FOCUS

48 FILL (DEC 2018)

Key answer tips

Students sitting SBR UK might be asked to discuss the accounting treatment of a transaction in accordance with FRS 102. If you know the treatment under IFRS Standards, and you know the differences between IFRS Standards and FRS 102, then you should be able to make a good attempt.

(a) **Borrowing costs**

Under FRS 102 *The Financial Reporting Standard Applicable in the UK and Republic of Ireland*, an entity **may** adopt a policy of capitalising borrowing costs which are directly attributable to the acquisition, construction or production of a qualifying asset as part of the cost of that asset. A qualifying asset is an asset which necessarily takes a substantial period of time to get ready for its intended use. Fill can capitalise the borrowing costs which relate to the licence. However, as the equipment will be used for other construction projects throughout the UK, the borrowing costs relating to it cannot be capitalised.

Impairment

FRS 102 specifies that a recoverable amount need not be determined unless there are indicators of impairment. There is evidence of a decline in forward prices. Short-term market fluctuations may not be impairment indicators if prices are expected to return to higher levels. However, if the decline in prices is for a significant proportion of the remaining expected life of the mine then it is more likely to be an impairment indicator. It appears that forward contract prices for two years out of the four years of the mine's remaining life indicate a reduction in selling prices and so it would appear that the mining assets should be tested for impairment, especially as the entity wishes to sell the mine. Impairment would be recognised if a mine's carrying amount exceeds its recoverable amount.

Decision to sell

As far as the decision to sell the mine is concerned, FRS 102 does not address assets held for sale; the decision to sell an asset is considered an impairment indicator although continuing and discontinued activities must be analysed. FRS 102 states that an internal indicator of impairment occurs when significant changes with an adverse effect on the entity have taken place during the period, or are expected to take place in the near future, in the extent to which, or manner in which, an asset is used or is expected to be used. These changes include plans to dispose of an asset before the previously expected date. If there is an indication that an asset may be impaired, this may indicate that the entity should review the remaining useful life, the depreciation method or the residual value for the asset.

(b) **Business combinations**

Under FRS 102, the cost of a business combination includes any costs directly attributable to the business combination, for example, any advisory and legal fees. However, IFRS 3 *Business Combinations* explicitly excludes such costs from the cost of a business combination. Thus, such costs generally form part of goodwill under FRS 102, whereas under IFRS 3, they are recognised as expenses in the period.

If a business combination is acquired in stages, IFRS 3 states that the consideration paid is all measured at the acquisition date fair value in accordance with full IFRS Standards whereas FRS 102 states that the consideration given for each stage is measured at its fair value at the date when the stage was recognised in the financial statements.

Under FRS 102, contingent consideration is included in the cost of a business combination, if its payment is probable and the amount can be measured reliably. IFRS 3 requires the fair value of contingent consideration to be included in the cost of a business combination regardless of whether payment is probable; its fair value is determined by considering the different possible outcomes and estimating the probability of each outcome. Under FRS 102, if the contingent consideration subsequently becomes probable and can be measured reliably, the amount is treated as an adjustment to the cost of the business combination.

Under FRS 102, non-controlling interest (NCI) is measured at its proportionate share of the group carrying amounts of the subsidiary's identifiable net assets. Using this method, goodwill is not included in the carrying amount of non-controlling interest. Under IFRS 3, non-controlling interest is measured using either the fair value method or the proportionate share method. With the fair value method, the NCI's stake in the entity is valued at fair value with the result that all of the entity's goodwill is recognised. The part of the goodwill which is attributable to the equity owned by the NCI is included in the measurement of the non-controlling interest. If the fair value method is used, both goodwill and non-controlling interest are different from those calculated under FRS 102.

Marking scheme		Marks
(a)	Borrowing costs	2
	Impairment and decision to sell	5
		───
		7
		───
(b)	Costs	2
	Consideration and stage payments	3
	NCI	3
		───
		8
		───
Total		**15**
		───

49   SKIZER (SEP 2018)

Key answer tips

Students sitting SBR UK might be asked to discuss the accounting treatment of a transaction in accordance with FRS 102. If you know the treatment under IFRS Standards, and you know the differences between IFRS Standards and FRS 102, then you should be able to make a good attempt.

(a)   FRS 102 recognition criteria

FRS 102 requires an entity to recognise an intangible asset if:

- it is probable that expected future economic benefits will flow to the entity, and

- the cost of the asset can be measured reliably.

This requirement applies whether an intangible asset is acquired externally or generated internally. The probability of future economic benefits must be based on reasonable and supportable assumptions about conditions which will exist over the life of the asset. The probability recognition criterion is always considered to be satisfied for intangible assets which are acquired separately or in a business combination.

If the recognition criteria are not met, FRS 102 requires the expenditure to be expensed when it is incurred.

Conceptual Framework

According to the *Conceptual Framework,* items are only recognised if they meet the definition of an element. The definition of an asset is '**a present economic resource controlled by an entity as a result of a past event**' (para 4.3).

This does not mean that all items meeting the definition of an element are recognised. An element is only recognised if recognition provides users with useful financial information. In other words recognition must provide:

- relevant information

- a faithful representation of the asset or liability, and resulting income, expenses or equity movements.

Recognition might not provide relevant information if there is uncertainty over the existence of the element or if there is a low probability of an inflow or outflow of economic resources. Recognition of an element might not provide a faithful representation if there is a very high degree of measurement uncertainty.

Consistency

As can be seen, the recognition criteria in the *Conceptual Framework* and FRS 102 are different.

Both FRS 102 and the *Conceptual Framework* attempt to ensure that financial statements provide information that meets the qualitative characteristics of useful information but do this in different ways. FRS 102 uses practical filters of probability and reliability to exclude information that will not be useful. In contrast, the *Conceptual Framework* refers directly to the qualitative characteristics, and provides guidance on how to apply them.

(b)   Development projects

Skizer should have assessed whether the recognition criteria in FRS 102 were met at the time the entity capitalised the intangible assets. If the recognition criteria were met, then it was not appropriate to derecognise the intangible assets. According to FRS 102, an intangible asset should be derecognised only on disposal or when no future economic benefits are expected from its use or disposal.

If there were any doubts regarding the recoverability of the intangible asset, then Skizer should have assessed whether the intangible assets would be impaired. Prior to the current year, Skizer was unable to make a reliable estimate of the useful life of the intangible assets. However, FRS 102 states that the life should not exceed 10 years.

Further, the reclassification of intangible assets to research and development costs does not constitute a change in an accounting estimate. Under FRS 102, a change in accounting estimate is an adjustment of the carrying amount of an asset or liability, or related expense, resulting from the assessment of the present status of, and expected future benefits associated with, that asset or liability.

If the directors of Skizer decide that the recognition criteria were not initially met, then Skizer would have to recognise retrospectively a correction of an error.

(c)   Differences between UK GAAP and IFRS Standards

Under UK GAAP, an entity may capitalise development expenditure where certain criteria are met. Under IAS 38 *Intangible Assets*, an intangible asset arising from the development phase of an internal project must be capitalised if certain criteria are met.

If an intangible asset is acquired through a business combination and arises from legal or contractual rights, then FRS 102 allows recognition if there is evidence of exchange transactions for similar assets. Under IFRS 3 *Business Combinations*, intangible assets acquired through a business combination are recognised if they are separable, or if they arise from legal or contractual rights.

Under FRS 102, goodwill is amortised over its useful life. If the useful economic life cannot be reliably determined, then the estimate used should not exceed ten years. Under International Financial Reporting Standards, amortisation of goodwill is not permitted. Instead annual impairment testing is required.

Marking scheme		
		Marks
(a)	Recognition criteria – 1 mark per point	6
(b)	Development – 1 mark per point	5
(c)	UK GAAP differences	4
		—
Total		**15**
		—

50 BOBARRA

Key answer tips

Students sitting the UK paper are expected to know Companies Act requirements concerning the preparation of consolidated financial statements. This needs to be learned. However, you would not be expected to reproduce the detail below.

There are not many differences between International Financial Reporting Standards and UK GAAP with regards to related party transactions. There are a couple of marks available for talking about FRS 102 exemptions and whether they apply in this scenario.

(a) Companies Act

The requirements in the Companies Act to prepare group accounts are largely mirrored in FRS 102, which states that consolidated financial statements (group accounts in the Companies Act) are prepared by all parent entities unless one of the following exemptions, which are derived from the Companies Act, applies:

- The parent company is subject to the small companies' regime (see ss.383 to 384 of the Companies Act).

- The parent company is a subsidiary included in a larger group which prepares consolidated financial statements and meets the requirements of ss.400 or 401 of the Companies Act, including:

    - The parent is itself a subsidiary whose immediate parent is established in an EEA state, and whose results are consolidated into the group financial statements of an undertaking established in an EEA state (not necessarily the immediate parent). Companies Act sets out further conditions for this exemption, including that a company, which has any of its securities admitted to trading on a regulated market in an EEA state, is not eligible for this exemption.

    - The parent is itself a subsidiary, its immediate parent is not established in an EEA state, and its results are consolidated into the group accounts of an undertaking (either the same parent or another) drawn up in accordance with the EU Seventh Directive or in an equivalent manner (for example, EU-IFRS accounts). Companies Act sets out further conditions for this exemption, including that a company, which has any of its securities admitted to trading on a regulated market in an EEA state, is not eligible for this exemption.

- All of the parent's subsidiaries are excluded from consolidation under FRS 102.

If an entity is not a parent at the year end, then it is not required to prepare consolidated accounts.

Exclusion of subsidiaries from consolidation

Consolidated financial statements provide information about the group as a single economic entity. They include all subsidiaries of the parent except those excluded on one of the following grounds:

- severe long-term restrictions substantially hinder the exercise of the rights of the parent over the assets or management of the subsidiary. These rights are the rights held by or attributed to the company in the absence of which it would not be the parent company; or

- the subsidiary is held exclusively for resale and has not previously been included in the consolidation.

Companies Act states that a subsidiary may be excluded from consolidation if the necessary information to prepare the group accounts cannot be obtained without disproportionate expense or undue delay. FRS 102, however, states that this does not justify non-consolidation, effectively closing off the statutory option. Subsidiaries are not excluded from consolidation simply because the subsidiary has dissimilar business activities to the rest of the group.

(b) **Related parties**

The objective of both IAS 24 *Related Party Disclosures* and FRS 102 *The Financial Reporting Standard applicable in the UK and Republic of Ireland* as regards related party disclosures is to ensure that an entity's financial statements contain the disclosures necessary to draw attention to the possibility that its financial position and profit or loss may have been affected by the existence of related parties and by transactions and outstanding balances with such parties.

Individuals

A person or a close member of that person's family is related to a reporting entity if that person:

- has control or joint control over the reporting entity;

- has significant influence over the reporting entity; or

- is a member of the key management personnel of the reporting entity or of a parent of the reporting entity.

As regards Bobarra, the finance director is a related party because he controls Bobarra and is a member of the key management personnel. The sales director is also a related party of Bobarra as she is a member of the key management personnel and is a close member (spouse) of the family of the finance director. Their son is a related party of Bobarra as he is a close member (son) of their family. The operations director is also a related party as he is a member of key management personnel and has significant influence (more than 20% of the voting power) over Bobarra.

IAS 24 requires that the disclosure of key management personnel remuneration is broken down into the following categories:

- short-term benefits

- post-employment benefits

- other long-term benefits

- termination benefits

- share-based payments.

FRS 102 simply requires the disclosure of management personnel remuneration in total.

Entities

An entity is related to a reporting entity if the entity is controlled or jointly controlled by a person identified as a related party. Hence, the family trust is a related party of Bobarra. The family trust is controlled by related parties, the finance and sales directors, for the benefit of a close member of their family, i.e. their son. In the absence of evidence to the contrary, the third owner of the shares is not a related party. The person is a passive investor who does not appear to exert significant influence over Bobarra.

A related party relationship exists where the entity and the reporting entity are members of the same group, which means that each parent, subsidiary and fellow subsidiary is related to the others. However, FRS 102 states that disclosures need not be given of transactions entered into between two or more members of a group if any subsidiary which is a party to the transaction is wholly owned by such a member.

The transactions between Bobarra and Drumby would be disclosed as related party disclosures under both IAS 24 and FRS 102. Drumby is not wholly owned by any member of the group and hence the FRS 102 exemption does not apply. However, any transactions between Bobarra, Alucant and Cantor would be covered by the exemption from disclosure in FRS 102 even though the three entities are related parties.

Marking scheme		Marks
(a)	Companies Act – 1 mark per point	9
(b)	Related parties – 1 mark per point	7
Total		**16**

51 HARRIS

Key answer tips

One area where there are still large differences between International Financial Reporting Standards and UK GAAP is business combinations. Make sure that you memorise the examinable differences.

Deferred tax is a popular topic for UK specific questions because this section of FRS 102 is worded very differently from IAS 12.

(a)   Goodwill

Consideration

IFRS 3 *Business Combinations* requires that contingent consideration is included in the calculation of goodwill at its fair value at the acquisition date. This fair value will incorporate the probability of payment. In contrast FRS 102 says that contingent consideration is only included in the calculation of goodwill if payment is probable.

IFRS 3 requires that any acquisition fees are expensed, whereas FRS 102 states that these should be included in the calculation of goodwill.

Non-controlling interest

Under IFRS 3, the non-controlling interest at the acquisition date can be measured at fair value or at its proportionate share of the fair value of the subsidiary's identifiable net assets. This decision is made on an acquisition by acquisition basis. FRS 102 only allows the proportionate method to be used.

Bargain purchase/negative goodwill

Under IFRS 3 *Business Combinations*, a gain on a bargain purchase is recognised immediately in the statement of profit or loss.

If a bargain purchase arises, FRS 102 requires the entity to:

- Reassess the identification and measurement of the acquiree's assets, liabilities and provisions for contingent liabilities and the measurement of the cost of the combination (this condition is the same as IFRS 3).

- Recognise and separately disclose the resulting excess on the face of the statement of financial position on the acquisition date (i.e. as a negative asset), immediately below goodwill, and followed by a subtotal of the net amount of goodwill and the excess.

- Recognise subsequently the excess up to the fair value of non-monetary assets acquired in profit or loss in the periods in which the non-monetary assets are recovered. Any excess exceeding the fair value of non-monetary assets acquired should be recognised in profit or loss in the periods expected to benefit.

(b) **Deferred tax**

Under IAS 12 *Income Taxes*, an entity recognises a deferred tax asset or liability for tax recoverable or payable in future periods as a result of past transactions or events. Such tax arises from the difference between the amounts recognised for the entity's assets and liabilities in the statement of financial position and the recognition of those assets and liabilities by the tax authorities plus the carry forward of currently unused tax losses and tax credits.

Under FRS 102, deferred tax is recognised in respect timing differences at the reporting date. Timing differences are differences between taxable profits and total comprehensive income as stated in the financial statements which arise from the inclusion of income and expenses in tax assessments in periods different from those in which they are recognised in financial statements. In addition, FRS 102 states that deferred tax should be recognised on the differences between the tax value and fair value of assets and liabilities acquired in a business combination, even though this impacts neither taxable profits nor total comprehensive income. As such, FRS 102 is said to adopt a 'timing difference plus' approach.

FRS 102 uses the term 'permanent difference', whereas IAS 12 does not use this term.

In practice it is unlikely that the differences between FRS 102 and IAS 12 will cause a significant difference in terms of the recognition and measurement of deferred tax assets and liabilities.

Marking scheme		Marks
(a)	Goodwill – 1 mark per point	9
(b)	Deferred tax – 1 mark per point	6
Total		**15**

52   ROWLING

Key answer tips

The UK specific syllabus content is very factual and needs to be learned by students sitting the UK exam. This question concerns the scope of the UK standards FRS 100, FRS 101, FRS 102 and FRS 105. This is core knowledge. If you struggled with this question, revisit the UK content in the Study Text.

The UK Standards

The Financial Reporting Council in the UK has published:

1   FRS 100 *Application of Financial Reporting Requirements*

2   FRS 101 *Reduced Disclosure Framework*

3   FRS 102 *The Financial Reporting Standard applicable in the UK and Republic of Ireland*

4   FRS 105 *The Financial Reporting Standard applicable to the Micro-entities Regime.*

FRS 100

FRS 100 sets out the overall financial reporting requirements, giving many entities a choice depending on factors such as size, and whether or not they are part of a listed group.

FRS 100 identifies whether entities need to produce their consolidated or individual financial statements in accordance with EU approved IFRS Standards or FRS 102.

FRS 101

FRS 101 provides companies with an opportunity to take advantage of reduced disclosures.

FRS 101 permits UK subsidiaries to adopt EU approved IFRS Standards for their individual financial statements but within the reduced disclosure framework. This option is also available for the parent company's individual financial statements.

FRS 102

FRS 102 adopts an IFRS Standard-based framework with proportionate disclosure requirements. It is based on the IFRS for SMEs Standard but with significant changes in order to address company law and to include extra accounting options.

FRS 105

Micro-entities can choose to prepare their financial statements in accordance with FRS 105.

FRS 105 is based on FRS 102 but with some amendments to satisfy legal requirements and to reflect the simpler nature of micro-entities.

For example, FRS 105:

- Prohibits accounting for deferred tax

- Prohibits accounting for equity-settled share-based payments before the issue of the shares

- Simplifies the rules around classifying a financial instrument as debt or equity

- Removes the distinction between functional and presentation currencies.

Intangible assets

Under UK GAAP, where certain criteria are met, an entity **may** capitalise development expenditure. Under IAS 38 *Intangible Assets*, an intangible asset arising from the development phase of an internal project **must** be capitalised if certain criteria are met.

If an intangible is acquired through a business combination and arises from legal or contractual rights then FRS 102 only permits its recognition if there is evidence of exchange transactions for similar assets. Under IFRS 3 *Business Combinations*, intangible assets acquired through a business combination are recognised if they are separable, or if they arise from legal or contractual rights.

Under FRS 102, goodwill is amortised over its useful economic life. If the useful economic life cannot be reliably determined then the estimate used should not exceed ten years. Under International Financial Reporting Standards, amortisation of goodwill is not permitted. Instead annual impairment testing is required.

Marking scheme	
	Marks
1 mark per valid point	15
	—
Total	**15**
	—

53 TOTO

Key answer tips

The recent issue of IFRS 16 *Leases* means that there are now significant differences between International Financial Reporting Standards and UK GAAP with regards to lessee accounting.

IFRS 16 *Leases*

With regards to lessee accounting, IFRS 16 *Leases* says that a lease liability and a right-of-use asset should be recognised at the inception of all leases (unless they are short-term or of low value). The lease liability will be measured at the present value of the lease payments yet to be made – the discount rate used should be the interest rate implicit in the lease. As there are no other costs or payments, the right-of-use asset will be measured at the same value.

Interest on the lease liability will be charged to profit or loss based on the rate implicit in the lease. The right-of-use asset will be depreciated over the three year lease term and this will be recorded in the statement of profit or loss.

FRS 102 *The Financial Reporting Standard applicable in the UK and Republic of Ireland*

FRS 102 classifies leases as finance leases or operating leases. A finance lease is a lease where the risks and rewards of ownership transfer to the lessee. It would seem that the lease is an operating lease, because ownership of the asset does not transfer to Toto at the end of the lease term, and the lease term is much shorter than the asset's useful life.

As such, no asset or liability is would be recognised at the inception of the lease. Instead, lease rentals would be charged to profit or loss on a straight line basis.

Comparison of impact

Liabilities will be higher if the financial statements are prepared using IFRS Standards rather than FRS 102. This will make the entity look more highly geared and, potentially, riskier to investors. Under IFRS 16, some of the lease liability would be classified as current on the statement of financial position, having an adverse impact on the current ratio.

Non-current assets will be higher under IFRS Standards. This could be viewed positively because Toto will appear more asset rich. However, users may conclude that Toto is inefficient at generating returns from its assets, and so invest their money elsewhere.

The total lease expense over the three year period will be the same under both IFRS 16 and FRS 102. However, under IFRS 16, the lease expense is likely to be split between operating expenses (the depreciation on the right-of-use asset) and finance costs (the interest on the lease liability). Under FRS 102 it is likely that the full lease expense will be recorded against operating expenses. As such, IFRS 16 might result in Toto recording higher operating profits.

In the first year of the lease it is likely that IFRS 16 will result in lower profits than FRS 102. This is because IFRS 16 requires recognition of a lease liability and a larger interest expense will be recognised in the first year of the lease when the liability is highest. Lower profits will lead to lower earnings per share, which is a key ratio for assessing company performance and for deriving company valuations.

Marking scheme	
	Marks
1 mark per valid point	15
	—
Total	**15**
	—

54   HOWEY

Key answer tips

Remember you will score one mark per valid point that you make. This means that you would not be expected to reproduce the detail below. However, do try and memorise the key differences between International Financial Reporting Standards and UK GAAP. In particular, it is important to remember that there is no concept of 'held for sale' in FRS 102.

(a) **Held for sale and discontinued operations**

Held for sale

IFRS 5 *Non-current Assets Held for Sale and Discontinued Operations* sets out requirements for the classification, measurement and presentation of non-current assets held for sale. Under IFRS 5, a non-current asset should be classified held for sale if its carrying amount will be recovered primarily through a sales transaction. At the date of meeting the criteria, such an asset will be measured at the lower of its carrying amount and fair value less costs to sell. Depreciation on the asset ceases.

FRS 102 does not refer to the concept of 'held for sale'. As such the asset will be depreciated or amortised until the disposal date. However, the decision to sell an asset does trigger an impairment review.

Discontinued operations

Under IFRS 5, an operation is classified as discontinued at the date the operation meets the criteria to be classified as held for sale or when the entity has disposed of the operation.

Because the concept of 'held for sale' is absent from FRS 102, an operation is classified as discontinued only if it has been disposed of.

With regards to discontinued operations, IFRS 5 requires a single number to be disclosed on the face of the statement of profit or loss, being the total of (i) the discontinued operations' post-tax profit/loss and (ii) the post-tax gain/loss recognised in the measurement of the fair value less costs to sell or on the disposal of the discontinued operations' assets. A breakdown of this number is required to be given either on the face of the statement of profit or loss or in the notes.

FRS 102 requires disclosure of the results of continuing operations and discontinued operations in separate columns on the face of the income statement.

Subsidiaries acquired exclusively for resale

Under IFRS 5, subsidiaries acquired exclusively with a view to resale that meet the conditions to be classified as held for sale are consolidated. However, their results are presented within the single line item for discontinued operations. In the statement of financial position they are presented as two separate items – assets, including goodwill, and liabilities.

Under FRS 102, subsidiaries acquired exclusively with a view to sell must be measured at either:

- Cost less impairment, or

- Fair value, with gains and losses recognised in profit or loss, or

- Fair value, with gains and losses recognised in other comprehensive income.

(b) **Reasons for adopting FRS 102**

There are various reasons why an entity might choose to prepare its financial statements in accordance with FRS 102 rather than IFRS Standards:

- FRS 102 is more accessibly worded than IFRS Standards.

- FRS 102 is a single accounting standard that is split into sections (such as 'revenue', 'leases' etc). This means that it is quicker and easier to navigate than IFRS Standards.

- Some accounting concepts are absent from FRS 102, such as 'assets held for sale'. Reducing the number of rules that entities must apply reduces the burden of financial reporting.

- FRS 102 permits some accounting policy choices that will help entities to simplify their financial reporting. For example, entities can choose to write off development expenditure and borrowing costs to profit or loss.

- Some FRS 102 rules are less time-consuming than their IFRS Standard equivalents. For instance, FRS 102 does not require the useful lives of property, plant and equipment to be reassessed annually.

- If other entities in the same sector also prepare financial statements in accordance with FRS 102 then it will make it easier to benchmark performance against them.

- There are far fewer disclosure requirements in FRS 102 than in full IFRS Standards.

Marking scheme		
		Marks
(a)	Held for sale and disc. operations – 1 mark per point	9
(b)	Reasons for adopting FRS 102 – 1 mark per point	6
		——
Total		**15**
		——

55 LOKI

Key answer tips

Although this question requires knowledge of the differences between IFRS Standards and UK GAAP, it also requires a thorough understanding of the impact of different ways of measuring the non-controlling interest. Students often struggle with this area. If you found this question difficult then revisit the chapter on 'basic groups' in the Study Text.

(a)   International Financial Reporting Standards

IFRS 3 *Business Combinations* permits the NCI at acquisition to be measured at its fair value or at its proportionate share of the fair value of the subsidiary's identifiable net assets. This choice is made on an acquisition-by-acquisition basis.

Loki opts to measure the NCI at fair value so the calculation of goodwill arising at acquisition is as follows:

	$m
Fair value of consideration	300
Fair value of non-controlling interest	120
Fair value of identifiable net assets acquired	(280)
Goodwill at acquisition	140

Under IFRS Standards, goodwill is not amortised. Instead, IAS 36 *Impairment of Assets* stipulates that it is subject to annual impairment review. An asset, or cash generating unit, is impaired if its carrying amount exceeds its recoverable amount. The calculation of the impairment loss is as follows:

	$m
Goodwill	140
Net assets	260
Total	400
Recoverable amount	(350)
Impairment	50

IAS 36 requires that the impairment is firstly allocated against goodwill. The impairment will be charged to the statement of profit or loss:

Dr Profit or loss	$50m
Cr Goodwill	$50m

The carrying mount of goodwill will therefore be reduced to $90 million ($140m – $50m). The expense will be allocated to the owners of the parent ($35m) and the NCI ($15m) in proportion to their shareholdings.

(b) **FRS 102**

FRS 102 does not permit the NCI at acquisition to be measured at fair value. As such, the proportionate method must be used. The calculation of goodwill would be as follows:

	$m
Fair value of consideration	300
Non-controlling interest (30% × $280m)	84
Fair value of identifiable net assets acquired	(280)
Goodwill at acquisition	104

In accordance with FRS 102, goodwill is amortised over its estimated useful economic life. By the year ended 31 December 20X2, the goodwill would have a carrying amount of $83.2 million ($104m × 8/10).

When performing an impairment review under FRS 102 (and under IAS 36 if the proportionate method for valuing the NCI has been used), goodwill will need to be notionally grossed up to include the NCI share.

The impairment will be calculated as follows:

	$m	$m
Goodwill	83.2	
Notional NCI ($83.2m × 30/70)	35.7	
Total notional goodwill		118.9
Net assets at reporting date		260.0
Total carrying amount of assets		378.9
Recoverable amount		(350.0)
Impairment		28.9

The impairment is allocated to the total notional goodwill. However, only 70% of the total notional goodwill was recognised and so only 70% of the impairment should be recognised. Therefore, the charge in profit or loss will be $20.2 million ($28.9m × 70%) and goodwill will be reduced to $63 million ($83.2 – $20.2m). All of the charge is attributable to the owners of the parent company.

Marking scheme		
		Marks
(a)	IFRS Standards and impairment – 1 mark per point	6
(b)	FRS 102 and impairment – 1 mark per point	9
Total		**15**

Section 3

SPECIMEN 1 EXAM QUESTIONS

1 KUTCHEN

Background and financial statements

The following group financial statements relate to the Kutchen Group which comprised Kutchen, House and Mach, all public limited companies.

Group statement of financial position as at 31 December 20X6

	$m
Assets:	
Non-current assets	
Property, plant and equipment	365
Goodwill	–
Intangible assets	23
	388
Current assets	133
Total assets	521
Equity and liabilities	
Share capital of $1 each	63
Retained earnings	56
Other components of equity	26
Non-controlling interest	3
	148
Non-current liabilities	101
Current liabilities	
Trade payables	272
Total liabilities	373
Total equity and liabilities	521

Acquisition of 70% of House

On 1 June 20X6, Kutchen acquired 70% of the equity interests of House. The purchase consideration comprised 20 million shares of $1 of Kutchen at the acquisition date and a further 5 million shares on 31 December 20X7 if House's net profit after taxation was at least $4 million for the year ending on that date.

The market price of Kutchen's shares on 1 June 20X6 was $2 per share and that of House was $4.20 per share. It is felt that there is a 20% chance of the profit target being met.

In accounting for the acquisition of House, the finance director did not take into account the non-controlling interest in the goodwill calculation. He determined that a bargain purchase of $8 million arose on the acquisition of House, being the purchase consideration of $40 million less the fair value of the identifiable net assets of House acquired on 1 June 20X6 of $48 million. This valuation was included in the group financial statements above.

After the directors of Kutchen discovered the error, they decided to measure the non-controlling interest at fair value at the date of acquisition. The fair value of the non-controlling interest (NCI) in House was to be based upon quoted market prices at acquisition. House had issued share capital of $1 each, totalling $13 million at 1 June 20X6 and there has been no change in this amount since acquisition.

Initial acquisition of 80% of Mach

On 1 January 20X6, Kutchen acquired 80% of the equity interests of Mach, a privately owned entity, for a consideration of $57 million. The consideration comprised cash of $52 million and the transfer of non-depreciable land with a fair value of $5 million. The carrying amount of the land at the acquisition date was $3 million and the land has only recently been transferred to the seller of the shares in Mach and is still carried at $3 million in the group financial statements at 31 December 20X6.

At the date of acquisition, the identifiable net assets of Mach had a fair value of $55 million. Mach had made a net profit attributable to ordinary shareholders of $3.6 million for the year to 31 December 20X5.

The directors of Kutchen wish to measure the non-controlling interest at fair value at the date of acquisition but had again omitted NCI from the goodwill calculation. The NCI is to be fair valued using a public entity market multiple method. The directors of Kutchen have identified two companies who are comparable to Mach and who are trading at an average price to earnings ratio (P/E ratio) of 21. The directors have adjusted the P/E ratio to 19 for differences between the entities and Mach, for the purpose of fair valuing the NCI. The finance director has determined that a bargain purchase of $3 million arose on the acquisition of Mach being the cash consideration of $52 million less the fair value of the net assets of Mach of $55 million. This gain on the bargain purchase had been included in the group financial statements above.

Acquisition and disposal of 80% of Niche

Kutchen purchased an 80% interest in Niche for $40 million on 1 January 20X6 when the fair value of the identifiable net assets was $44 million. The partial goodwill method had been used and an impairment of $2 million had arisen in the year ended 31 December 20X6. The holding in Niche was sold for $50 million on 31 December 20X6. The carrying amount of Niche's identifiable net assets other than goodwill was $60 million at the date of sale. Kutchen had carried the investment in Niche at cost in its separate financial statements. The finance director calculated that a gain arose of $2 million on the sale of Niche in the group financial statements being the sale proceeds of $50 million less $48 million being their share of the identifiable net assets at the date of sale (80% of $60 million). This was credited to retained earnings.

Business segment restructure

Kutchen has decided to restructure one of its business segments. The plan was agreed by the board of directors on 1 October 20X6 and affects employees in two locations. In the first location, half of the factory units have been closed by 31 December 20X6 and the affected employees' pension benefits have been frozen. Any new employees will not be eligible to join the defined benefit plan. After the restructuring, the present value of the defined benefit obligation in this location is $8 million. The following table relates to location 1.

	$m
Value before restructuring:	
Present value of defined benefit obligation	(10)
Fair value of plan assets	7
Net pension liability	(3)

In the second location, all activities have been discontinued. It has been agreed that employees will receive a payment of $4 million in exchange for the pension liability of $2.4 million in the unfunded pension scheme.

Kutchen estimates that the costs of the above restructuring excluding pension costs will be $6 million. Kutchen has not accounted for the effects of the restructuring in its financial statements because it is planning a rights issue and does not wish to depress the share price. Therefore there has been no formal announcement of the restructuring.

Subsequent acquisition of 20% of Mach

When Kutchen acquired the majority shareholding in Mach, there was an option on the remaining 20% non-controlling interest (NCI), which could be exercised at any time up to 31 March 20X7. On 31 January 20X7, Kutchen acquired the remaining NCI in Mach. The payment for the NCI was structured so that it contained a fixed initial payment and a series of contingent amounts payable over the following two years.

The contingent payments were to be based on the future profits of Mach up to a maximum amount. Kutchen felt that the fixed initial payment was an equity transaction. Additionally, Kutchen was unsure as to whether the contingent payments were equity, financial liabilities or contingent liabilities.

After a board discussion which contained disagreement as to the accounting treatment, Kutchen is preparing to disclose the contingent payments in accordance with IAS 37 *Provisions, Contingent Liabilities and Contingent Assets*. The disclosure will include the estimated timing of the payments and the directors' estimate of the amounts to be settled.

Required:

(a) (i) Explain to the directors of Kutchen, with suitable workings, how goodwill should have been calculated on the acquisition of House and Mach showing the adjustments which need to be made to the consolidated financial statements to correct any errors by the finance director. **(10 marks)**

(ii) Explain, with suitable calculations, how the gain or loss on the sale of Niche should have been recorded in the group financial statements. **(5 marks)**

(iii) Discuss, with suitable workings, how the pension scheme should be dealt with after the restructuring of the business segment and whether a provision for restructuring should have been made in the financial statements for the year ended 31 December 20X6. **(7 marks)**

Note: Marks will be allocated in (a) for a suitable discussion of the principles involved as well as the accounting treatment.

(b) Advise Kutchen on the difference between equity and liabilities, and on the proposed accounting treatment of the contingent payments on the subsequent acquisition of 20% of Mach. **(8 marks)**

(Total: 30 marks)

2 ABBY

Abby is a company which conducts business in several parts of the world.

Related party transactions

The accountant has discovered that the finance director of Abby has purchased goods from a company, Arwight, which the director jointly owns with his wife and the accountant believes that this purchase should be disclosed. However, the director refuses to disclose the transaction as in his opinion it is an 'arm's length' transaction. He feels that if the transaction is disclosed, it will be harmful to business and feels that the information asymmetry caused by such non-disclosure is irrelevant as most entities undertake related party transactions without disclosing them. Similarly, the director felt that competitive harm would occur if disclosure of operating segment profit or loss was made. As a result, the entity only disclosed a measure of total assets and total liabilities for each reportable segment.

When preparing the financial statements for the recent year end, the accountant noticed that Arwight has not paid an invoice for several million dollars and it is significantly overdue for payment. It appears that the entity has liquidity problems and it is unlikely that Arwight will pay. The accountant believes that a loss allowance for trade receivables is required. The finance director has refused to make such an allowance and has told the accountant that the issue must not be discussed with anyone within the trade because of possible repercussions for the credit worthiness of Arwight.

Subsidiary fair value adjustments

Additionally, when completing the consolidated financial statements, the director has suggested that there should be no positive fair value adjustments for a recently acquired subsidiary and has stated that the accountant's current position is dependent upon following these instructions. The fair value of the subsidiary is $50 million above the carrying amount in the financial records. The reason given for not fair valuing the subsidiary's net assets is that goodwill is an arbitrary calculation which is meaningless in the context of the performance evaluation of an entity.

Goodwill impairment calculation

Finally, when preparing the annual impairment tests of goodwill arising on other subsidiaries, the director has suggested that the accountant is flexible in the assumptions used in calculating future expected cash flows, so that no impairment of goodwill arises and that the accountant should use a discount rate which reflects risks for which future cash flows have been adjusted. He has indicated that he will support a salary increase for the accountant if he follows his suggestions.

Required:

Discuss the ethical and accounting implications of the above situations from the perspective of the reporting accountant. **(18 marks)**

Professional marks will be awarded in question 2 for the application of ethical principles.

(2 marks)

(Total: 20 marks)

3 AFRICANT

(a) Africant owns several farms and also owns a division which sells agricultural vehicles. It is considering selling this agricultural retail division and wishes to measure the fair value of the inventory of vehicles for the purpose of the sale. Three markets currently exist for the vehicles. Africant has transacted regularly in all three markets.

At 31 December 20X5, Africant wishes to find the fair value of 150 new vehicles, which are identical. The current volume and prices in the three markets are as follows:

Market	Sales price per vehicle $	Historical volume – vehicles sold by Africant	Total volume of vehicles sold in the market	Transaction costs per vehicle $	Transport cost to market per vehicle $
Europe	40,000	6,000	150,000	500	400
Asia	38,000	2,500	750,000	400	700
Africa	34,000	1,500	100,000	300	600

Africant wishes to value the vehicles at $39,100 per vehicle as these are the highest net proceeds per vehicle, and Europe is the largest market for Africant's product.

(i) Africant wishes to understand the principles behind the valuation of the new vehicles and also whether their valuation would be acceptable under IFRS 13 *Fair Value Measurement*. **(8 marks)**

(ii) Africant uses the revaluation model for its non-current assets. Africant has several plots of farmland which are unproductive. The company feels that the land would have more value if it were used for residential purposes. There are several potential purchasers for the land but planning permission has not yet been granted for use of the land for residential purposes. However, preliminary enquiries with the regulatory authorities seem to indicate that planning permission may be granted. Additionally, the government has recently indicated that more agricultural land should be used for residential purposes.

Africant has also been approached to sell the land for commercial development at a higher price than that for residential purposes and understands that fair value measurement of a non-financial asset takes into account a market perspective.

Africant would like an explanation of what is meant by a 'market perspective' and advice on how to measure the fair value of the land in its financial statements. **(7 marks)**

Required:

Advise Africant on the matters set out above (in (i) and (ii)) with reference to relevant IFRS Standards.

Note: The mark allocation is shown against each of the two issues above.

(b) Africant is about to hold its annual general meeting with shareholders and the directors wish to prepare for any potential questions which may be raised at the meeting. There have been discussions in the media over the fact that the most relevant measurement method should be selected for each category of assets and liabilities. This 'mixed measurement approach' is used by many entities when preparing financial statements. There have also been comments in the media about the impact that measurement uncertainty and price volatility can have on the quality of financial information.

Required:

Discuss the impact which the above matters may have on the analysis of financial statements by investors in Africant. **(8 marks)**

Professional marks will be awarded in part (b) for clarity and quality of presentation. **(2 marks)**

(Total: 25 marks)

4 RATIONALE

The directors of Rationale are reviewing the published financial statements of the group. The following is an extract of information to be found in the financial statements.

Year ended		31 December 20X6 $m	31 December 20X5 $m
Net profit/(loss) before taxation and after the items set out below		(5)	38
Net interest expense		10	4
Depreciation		9	8
Amortisation of intangible assets		3	2
Impairment of property	10		
Insurance proceeds	(7)	3	
Debt issue costs		2	
Share-based payment		3	1
Restructuring charges		4	
Impairment of acquired intangible assets		6	8

The directors use 'underlying profit' to comment on its financial performance. Underlying profit is a measure normally based on earnings before interest, tax, depreciation and amortisation (EBITDA). However, the effects of events which are not part of the usual business activity are also excluded when evaluating performance.

The following items were excluded from net profit to arrive at 'underlying profit'. In 20X6, the entity had to write off a property due to subsidence and the insurance proceeds recovered for this property was recorded but not approved until 20X7, when the company's insurer concluded that the claim was valid. In 20X6, the entity considered issuing loan notes to finance an asset purchase, however, the purchase did not go ahead. The entity incurred costs associated with the potential issue and so these costs were expensed as part of net profit before taxation. The entity felt that the share-based payment was not a cash expense and that the value of the options was subjective. Therefore, the directors wished to exclude the item from 'underlying profit'. Similarly, the directors wish to exclude restructuring charges incurred in the year, and impairments of acquired intangible assets.

Required:

(a) **(i)** Discuss the possible concerns where an entity may wish to disclose additional information in its financial statements. **(8 marks)**

(ii) Discuss the use and the limitations of the proposed calculation of 'underlying profit' by Rationale. Your answer should include a comparative calculation of underlying profit for the years ended 31 December 20X5 and 20X6. **(9 marks)**

(b) The directors of Rationale are confused over the nature of a reclassification adjustment and understand that the Board has recently revised the *Conceptual Framework* to cover this issue.

Required:

(i) Discuss, with examples and reference to the *Conceptual Framework*, the nature of a reclassification adjustment **(5 marks)**

(ii) Discuss arguments against allowing reclassification of items from other comprehensive income to profit or loss. **(3 marks)**

(Total: 25 marks)

Section 4

SPECIMEN 1 EXAM ANSWERS

1   KUTCHEN

(a)   (i)   Goodwill

Goodwill on the acquisition of House and Mach should have been calculated as follows:

House

	$m
Fair value of consideration for 70% interest	42.00
Fair value of non-controlling interest (see below)	16.38
Fair value of identifiable net assets acquired	(48.00)
Goodwill	10.38

Contingent consideration should be valued at fair value and will have to take into account the various milestones set under the agreement. The expected value is (20% × 5 million shares) 1 million shares × $2, i.e. $2 million. This is equity so there will be no remeasurement of the fair value in subsequent periods. The contingent consideration will be recorded in other components of equity. The fair value of the consideration is therefore 20 million shares at $2 plus $2 million (above), i.e. $42 million.

The fair value of the NCI is 30% × 13 million × $4.20 = $16.38 million.

The finance director has not taken into account the fair value of the NCI in the valuation of goodwill or the contingent consideration. If the difference between the fair value of the consideration, NCI and the identifiable net assets is negative, the resulting gain is a bargain purchase in profit or loss, which may arise in circumstances such as a forced seller acting under compulsion. However, before any bargain purchase gain is recognised in profit or loss, and hence in retained earnings in the group statement of financial position, the finance director should have undertaken a review to ensure the identification of assets and liabilities is complete, and that measurements appropriately reflect consideration of all available information.

The adjustment to the group financial statements would be as follows:

Dr Goodwill	$10.38 million
Dr Profit or loss	$8 million
Cr NCI	$16.38 million
Cr OCE	$2 million

Mach

Net profit of Mach for the year to 31 December 20X5 is $3.6 million. The P/E ratio (adjusted) is 19. Therefore the fair value of Mach is 19 × $3.6 million, i.e. $68.4 million. The NCI has a 20% holding, so the fair value of the NCI is $13.68 million.

	$m
Fair value of consideration for 80% interest ($52m + $5m)	57
Fair value of non-controlling interest	13.68
Fair value of identifiable net assets acquired	(55)
	———
Goodwill	15.68
	———

The land transferred as part of the purchase consideration should be valued at its acquisition date fair value of $5 million and included in the goodwill calculation. Therefore the increase of $2 million over the carrying amount should be shown in retained earnings.

Dr PPE	$2 million
Cr Retained earnings	$2 million

The adjustment to the group financial statements would be as follows:

Dr Goodwill	$15.68 million
Dr Retained earnings	$3 million
Cr NCI	$13.68 million
Cr PPE	$5 million

Total goodwill is therefore $26.06 million ($15.68m + $10.38m).

(ii) **Niche**

The gain or loss on sale should have been calculated as the difference between the proceeds received of $50 million and the carrying amount of the subsidiary in the consolidated financial statements at the date of disposal.

The correct calculation is as follows:

	$m
Sale proceeds	50.0
Goodwill at disposal (W1)	(2.8)
Net assets at disposal	(60.0)
NCI at disposal (W2)	12.0
	———
Loss on sale of Niche in group profit or loss	(0.8)
	———

(W1) Goodwill

	$m
Fair value of consideration for 70% interest	40.0
Non-controlling interest ($44m × 20%)	8.8
Fair value of identifiable net assets acquired	(44.0)
Goodwill at acquisition	4.8
Impairment	(2.0)
Goodwill at disposal	2.8

(W2) NCI at disposal

	$m
NCI at acquisition	8.8
NCI share of post-acquisition net assets	3.2
20% × ($60m – $44m)	
NCI at disposal	12.0

(iii) After restructuring, the present value of the pension liability in location 1 is reduced to $8 million. Thus there will be a negative past service cost in this location of $2 million ($10m – $8m). As regards location 2, there is a settlement and a curtailment as all liability will be extinguished by the payment of $4 million. Therefore there is a loss of $1.6 million ($2.4m – $4m). The changes to the pension scheme in locations 1 and 2 will both affect profit or loss as follows:

Location 1

Dr Pension obligation	$2m
Cr Retained earnings	$2m

Location 2

Dr Pension obligation	$2.4m
Dr Retained earnings	$1.6m
Cr Current liabilities	$4m

IAS 37 *Provisions, Contingent Liabilities and Contingent Assets* states that a provision for restructuring should be made only when a detailed formal plan is in place and the entity has started to implement the plan, or announced its main features to those affected. A board decision is insufficient. Even though there has been no formal announcement of the restructuring, Kutchen has started implementing it and therefore it must be accounted for under IAS 37.

A provision of $6 million should also be made at the year end.

(b) The *Conceptual Framework* defines a liability as a present obligation, arising from past events, to transfer an economic resource. IAS 32 *Financial Instruments: Presentation* establishes principles for presenting financial instruments as liabilities or equity. The key feature of a financial liability is that the issuer has a contractual obligation to deliver either cash or another financial asset to the holder. An obligation may arise from a requirement to repay principal or interest or dividends.

In contrast, equity has a residual interest in the entity's assets after deducting all of its liabilities. An equity instrument includes no obligation to deliver cash or another financial asset to another entity. A contract which will be settled by the entity delivering a fixed number of its own equity instruments in exchange for cash or another financial asset is an equity instrument. However, if there is any variability in the amount of equity instruments which will be delivered then such a contract is a financial liability.

Contingent consideration for a business must be recognised at the time of acquisition, in accordance with IFRS 3 *Business Combinations*. IFRS Standards do not contain any guidance when accounting for contingent consideration for the acquisition of a NCI in a subsidiary but the contract for contingent payments does meet the definition of a financial liability under IAS 32. Kutchen has an obligation to pay cash to the vendor of the NCI under the terms of a contract. It is not within Kutchen's control to be able to avoid that obligation. The amount of the contingent payments depends on the profitability of Mach, which itself depends on a number of factors which are uncontrollable. IAS 32 states that a contingent obligation to pay cash which is outside the control of both parties to a contract meets the definition of a financial liability which shall be initially measured at fair value. Since the contingent payments relate to the acquisition of the NCI, the offsetting entry would be recognised directly in equity.

Marking scheme				
				Marks
(a)	(i)	– application of the following discussion to the scenario:		
			contingent consideration	2
			NCI	2
			fair value of assets acquired	2
		– goodwill calculations and corrections required		4
	(ii)	– application of the following discussion to the scenario:		
			proceeds	1
			carrying amount of the assets disposed of	1
		– calculation of the gain/loss on disposal of Niche		3
	(iii)	– application of the following discussion to the scenario:		
			present value and past service cost	2
		– calculation of SOPL effect		3
		– consideration of a restructuring provision		2
(b)		– application of the following discussion to the scenario:		
		definition of a liability and IAS 32 (liability v equity)		2
		definition of equity		2
		consideration of contingent payments of Mach		4
Total				30

2   ABBY

Related party transaction

The objective of IAS 24 *Related Party Disclosures* is to ensure that an entity's financial statements contain the disclosures necessary to draw attention to the possibility that its financial position and profit or loss may have been affected by the existence of related parties and by transactions and outstanding balances with such parties. If there have been transactions between related parties, there should be disclosure of the nature of the related party relationship as well as information about the transactions and outstanding balances necessary for an understanding of the potential effect of the relationship on the financial statements. The director is a member of the key management personnel of the reporting entity and the entity from whom the goods were purchased is jointly controlled by that director. Therefore a related party relationship exists and should be disclosed.

IFRS 8 *Operating Segments* requires an entity to report financial and descriptive information about its reportable segments. Reportable segments are operating segments or aggregations of operating segments which meet specified criteria. IFRS 8 does not contain a 'competitive harm' exemption and requires entities to disclose the financial information which is provided by the chief operating decision maker (CODM). The management accounts reviewed by the CODM may contain commercially sensitive information, and IFRS 8 might require that information to be disclosed externally. Under IFRS 8, firms should provide financial segment disclosures which enable investors to assess the different sources of risk and income as management does. This sensitive information would also be available for competitors. The potential competitive harm may encourage firms to withhold segment information. However, this is contrary to IFRS 8 which requires information about the profit or loss for each reportable segment, including certain specified revenues and expenses such as revenue from external customers and from transactions with other segments, interest revenue and expense, depreciation and amortisation, income tax expense or income and material non-cash items.

Areas such as impairments of financial assets often involve the application of professional judgement. The director may have received additional information, which has allowed him to form a different opinion to that of the accountant. The matter should be discussed with the director to ascertain why no allowance is required and to ask whether there is additional information available. However, suspicion is raised by the fact that the accountant has been told not to discuss the matter. Whilst there may be valid reasons for this, it appears again that the related party relationship is affecting the judgement of the director.

Subsidiary fair value adjustments

Positive fair value adjustments increase the assets of the acquired company and as such reduce the goodwill recognised on consolidation. However, the majority of positive fair value adjustments usually relate to items of property, plant and equipment. As a result, extra depreciation based on the net fair value adjustment reduces the post-acquisition profits of the subsidiary. This has a negative impact on important financial performance measures such as EPS. Therefore, by reducing fair value adjustments it will improve the apparent performance of new acquisitions and the consolidated financial statements. Accountants should act ethically and ignore undue pressure to undertake creative accounting in preparing such adjustments. Guidance such as IFRS 3 *Business Combinations* and IFRS 13 *Fair Value Measurement* should be used in preparing adjustments and professional valuers should be engaged where necessary.

Goodwill impairment calculation

In measuring value in use, the discount rate used should be the pre-tax rate which reflects current market assessments of the time value of money and the risks specific to the asset. The discount rate should not reflect risks for which future cash flows have been adjusted and should equal the rate of return which investors would require if they were to choose an investment which would generate cash flows equivalent to those expected from the asset. By reducing the impairment, it would have a positive impact on the financial statements. The offer of a salary increase is inappropriate and no action should be taken until the situation is clarified. Inappropriate financial reporting raises issues and risks for those involved and others associated with the company. Whilst financial reporting involves judgement, it would appear that this situation is related to judgement.

Ethics

There are several potential breaches of accounting standards and unethical practices being used by the director. The director is trying to coerce the accountant into acting unethically. IAS 1 *Presentation of Financial Statements* requires all standards to be applied if fair presentation is to be obtained. Directors cannot choose which standards they do or do not apply. It is important that accountants identify issues of unethical practice and act appropriately in accordance with ACCA's *Codes of Ethics*. The accountant should discuss the matters with the director. The technical issues should be explained and the risks of non-compliance explained to the director. If the director refuses to comply with accounting standards, then it would be appropriate to discuss the matter with others affected such as other directors and seek professional advice from ACCA. Legal advice should be considered if necessary.

An accountant who comes under pressure from senior colleagues to make inappropriate valuations and disclosures should discuss the matter with the person suggesting this. The discussion should try to confirm the facts and the reporting guidance which needs to be followed. Financial reporting does involve judgement but the cases above seem to be more than just differences in opinion. The accountant should keep a record of conversations and actions and discuss the matters with others affected by the decision, such as directors. Additionally, resignation should be considered if the matters cannot be satisfactorily resolved.

Marking scheme	
	Marks
– application of the following discussion of accounting issues to the scenario:	
related party transactions	2
competitive harm exemptions	2
impairment of financial assets	2
fair value adjustments	2
goodwill impairment review	2
– application of the following discussion of ethical issues to the scenario:	
potential breaches	4
advice to accountant	4
Professional	2
Total	**20**

3 AFRICANT

(a) (i) Vehicle valuation

IFRS 13 *Fair Value Measurement* says that fair value is an exit price in the principal market, which is the market with the highest volume and level of activity. It is not determined based on the volume or level of activity of the reporting entity's transactions in a particular market. Once the accessible markets are identified, market-based volume and activity determines the principal market. There is a presumption that the principal market is the one in which the entity would normally enter into a transaction to sell the asset or transfer the liability, unless there is evidence to the contrary. In practice, an entity would first consider the markets it can access. In the absence of a principal market, it is assumed that the transaction would occur in the most advantageous market. This is the market which would maximise the amount which would be received to sell an asset or minimise the amount which would be paid to transfer a liability, taking into consideration transport and transaction costs. In either case, the entity must have access to the market on the measurement date. Although an entity must be able to access the market at the measurement date, IFRS 13 does not require an entity to be able to sell the particular asset or transfer the particular liability on that date. If there is a principal market for the asset or liability, the fair value measurement represents the price in that market at the measurement date regardless of whether that price is directly observable or estimated using another valuation technique and even if the price in a different market is potentially more advantageous.

In Africant's case, Asia is the principal market as this is the market in which the majority of transactions for the vehicles occur. The most advantageous market would be Europe where a net price of $39,100 (after all costs) would be gained by selling there and the number of vehicles sold in this market is at its highest. Africant would therefore utilise the fair value calculated by reference to the Asian market as this is the principal market.

IFRS 13 makes it clear that the price used to measure fair value must not be adjusted for transaction costs, but should consider transportation costs. Transaction costs are not deemed to be a characteristic of an asset or a liability but they are specific to a transaction and will differ depending on how an entity enters into a transaction.

As such, the fair value of the 150 vehicles would be $5,595,000 ($38,000 − $700 = $37,300 × 150).

(ii) Fair value of land

A fair value measurement of a non-financial asset takes into account a market participant's ability to generate economic benefits by using the asset in its highest and best use or by selling it to another market participant who would use the asset in its highest and best use. The maximum value of a non-financial asset may arise from its use in combination with other assets or by itself. IFRS 13 requires the entity to consider uses which are physically possible, legally permissible and financially feasible. The use must not be legally prohibited. For example, if the land is protected in some way by law and a change of law is required, then it cannot be the highest and best use of the land.

In this case, Africant's land for residential development would only require approval from the regulatory authority and as that approval seems to be possible, then this alternative use could be deemed to be legally permissible. Market participants would consider the probability, extent and timing of the approval which may be required in assessing whether a change in the legal use of the non-financial asset could be obtained.

Africant would need to have sufficient evidence to support its assumption about the potential for an alternative use, particularly in light of IFRS 13's presumption that the highest and best use is an asset's current use. Africant's belief that planning permission was possible is unlikely to be sufficient evidence that the change of use is legally permissible. However, the fact the government has indicated that more agricultural land should be released for residential purposes may provide additional evidence as to the likelihood that the land being measured should be based upon residential value. Africant would need to prove that market participants would consider residential use of the land to be legally permissible. Provided there is sufficient evidence to support these assertions, alternative uses, for example, commercial development which would enable market participants to maximise value, should be considered, but a search for potential alternative uses need not be exhaustive. In addition, any costs to transform the land, for example, obtaining planning permission or converting the land to its alternative use, and profit expectations from a market participant's perspective should also be considered in the fair value measurement.

If there are multiple types of market participants who would use the asset differently, these alternative scenarios must be considered before concluding on the asset's highest and best use. It appears that Africant is not certain about what constitutes the highest and best use and therefore IFRS 13's presumption that the highest and best use is an asset's current use appears to be valid at this stage.

(b)   Mixed measurement

Some investors might argue in favour of a single measurement basis for all recognised assets and liabilities as the resulting totals and subtotals can have little meaning if different measurement methods are used. Similarly, profit or loss may lack relevance if it reflects a combination of flows based on historical cost and of value changes for items measured on a current value basis.

However, the majority of investors would tend to favour a mixed measurement approach, whereby the most relevant measurement method is selected for each category of assets and liabilities. This approach is consistent with how investors analyse financial statements. The problems of mixed measurement are outweighed by the greater relevance achieved if the most relevant measurement basis is used for each class of assets and liabilities. The mixed measurement approach is reflected in recent standards; for example, IFRS 9 *Financial Instruments* and IFRS 15 *Revenue from Contracts* with Customers. Historical cost would not have been relevant for all financial assets and has severe limitations for many liabilities; hence, the only viable single measurement method would have been fair value. The *Conceptual Framework* does not propose a single measurement method for assets and liabilities, and instead supports the continued use of a mixed measurement approach.

Most accounting measures of assets and liabilities are uncertain and require estimation. While some measures of historical cost are straightforward as it is the amount paid or received, there are many occasions when the measurement of cost can be uncertain – particularly recoverable cost, for which impairment and depreciation estimates are required. In a similar vein, while some measures of fair value can be easily observed because of the availability of prices in an actively traded market (a so-called 'Level 1' fair value), others inevitably rely on management estimates and judgements ('Level 2' and 'Level 3').

High measurement uncertainty might reduce the quality of information available to investors. High price volatility may make analysing an investment in that entity more challenging. If a relevant measure of an asset or liability value is volatile, this should not be hidden from investors. To conceal its volatility would decrease the usefulness of the financial statements. Of course, such volatile gains and losses do need to be clearly presented and disclosed, because their predictive value may differ from that provided by other components of performance.

Marking scheme			Marks
(a)	(i)	– discussion of the principles of IFRS 13	4
		– application of the IFRS 13 principles to Africant	4
	(ii)	– market perspective and highest and best use	4
		– application of highest and best use to Africant	3
(b)		– single v mixed measurement and investor issues	2
		– examples	2
		– investor issues re uncertainty	2
		– investor issues re price volatility	2
		Professional	2
Total			25

4   RATIONALE

(a)   (i)   There is no specific guidance on information which is not required by an IFRS being disclosed in financial statements. IFRS requires an entity to disclose additional information which is relevant to an understanding of the entity's financial position and financial performance.

A company may disclose additional information where it is felt that an entity's performance may not be apparent from accounts prepared under IFRS. A single standardised set of accounting practices can never be sufficient information to understand an entity's position or performance. Additional information can help users understand management's view of what is important to the entity and the nature of management's decisions.

There are concerns relating to the disclosure of additional information. Such information may not readily be derived or reconciled back to financial statements. There is also difficulty comparing information across periods and between entities because of the lack of standardised approaches. Also the presentation of additional information may be inconsistent with that defined or specified in IFRS and the entity may present an excessively optimistic picture of an entity's financial performance. Non-IFRS information may make it difficult to identify the complete set of financial statements, including whether the information is audited or not. Additionally, the information may be given undue prominence or credibility merely because of its location within the financial statements. Non-IFRS financial information should be clearly labelled in a way that distinguishes it from the corresponding IFRS financial information. Any term used to describe the information should be appropriate having regard to the nature of the information. The term or label should not cause confusion with IFRS information and should accurately describe the measure.

(ii) The directors of Rationale are utilising a controversial figure for evaluating a company's earnings. Depreciation and amortisation are non-cash expenses related to assets which have already been purchased and they are expenses which are subject to judgement or estimates based on experience and projections. The company, by using EBITDA, is attempting to show operating cash flow since the non-cash expenses are added back.

However, EBITDA can also be misused and manipulated. It can be argued that because the estimation of depreciation, amortisation and other non-cash items is vulnerable to judgement error, the profit figure can be distorted but by focusing on profits before these elements are deducted, a truer estimation of cash flow can be given. However, the substitution of EBITDA for conventional profit fails to take into account the need for investment in fixed capital items.

There can be an argument for excluding non-recurring items from the net profit figure. Therefore, it is understandable that the deductions for the impairment of property, the insurance recovery and the debt issue costs are made to arrive at 'underlying profit'. However, IAS 1 *Presentation of Financial Statements* states 'An entity shall present additional line items, headings and subtotals in the statements presenting profit and loss and other comprehensive income when such presentation is relevant to an understanding of the entity's financial performance.' This paragraph should not be used to justify presentation of underlying, adjusted and pre-exceptional measures of performance on the face of the income statement. The measures proposed are entity specific and could obscure performance and poor management.

Share-based compensation may not represent cash but if an entity chooses to pay equity to an employee, that affects the value of equity, no matter what form that payment is in and therefore it should be charged as employee compensation. It is an outlay in the form of equity. There is therefore little justification in excluding this expense from net profit. Restructuring charges are a feature of an entity's business and they can be volatile. They should not be excluded from net profit because they are part of corporate life. Severance costs and legal fees are not non-cash items.

Impairments of acquired intangible assets usually reflect a weaker outlook for an acquired business than was expected at the time of the acquisition, and could be considered to be non-recurring. However, the impairment charges are a useful way of holding management accountable for its acquisitions. In this case, it seems as though Rationale has not purchased wisely in 20X6.

It appears as though Rationale wishes to disguise a weak performance in 20X6 by adding back a series of expense items. EBITDA, although reduced significantly from 20X5, is now a positive figure and there is an underlying profit created as opposed to a loss. However, users will still be faced with a significant decline in profit whichever measure is disclosed by Rationale. The logic for the increase in profit is flawed in many cases but there is a lack of authoritative guidance in the area. Many companies adopt non-financial measures without articulating the relationship between the measures and the financial statements.

Year ended	31 December 20X6	31 December 20X5
	$m	$m
Net profit/(loss) before taxation and after the items set out below	(5)	38
Net interest expense	10	4
Depreciation	9	8
Amortisation of intangible assets	3	2
	—	—
EBITDA	17	52
Impairment of property	10	
Insurance recovery	(7)	–
Debt issue costs	2	
	—	—
EBITDA after non-recurring items	22	52
Share-based payment	3	1
Restructuring charges	4	
Impairment of acquired intangible assets	6	8
	—	—
Underlying profit	35	61
	—	—

(b)   (i)   The nature of reclassification adjustments

Reclassification adjustments are amounts recorded in profit or loss in the current period which were recognised in OCI in the current or previous periods.

According to the *Conceptual Framework*, income and expenditure included in other comprehensive income should be reclassified to profit or loss when doing so results in profit or loss providing more relevant information. However, when developing or revising an IFRS Standard, the Board may decide that reclassification is not appropriate if there is no clear basis for identifying the amount or timing of the reclassification.

Examples of items recognised in OCI which may be reclassified to profit or loss are foreign currency gains on the disposal of a foreign operation and realised gains or losses on cash flow hedges.

Items which are not reclassified include changes in a revaluation surplus under IAS 16 *Property, Plant and Equipment*, and remeasurement gains and losses on a defined benefit plan under IAS 19 *Employee Benefits*.

(ii)   **Arguments against reclassification**

Those against reclassification believe that it adds complexity to financial reporting because it is not fully understood by user groups. It is also argued that reclassification adjustments do not meet the definitions of income or expense in the *Conceptual Framework* because the change in the asset or liability may have occurred in a previous period.

The lack of a consistent basis in the 2010 *Conceptual Framework* for determining how items should be presented has led to an inconsistent use of OCI across IFRS Standards. Opinions vary but there is a feeling that OCI has become a place where the Board decide to put controversial gains or losses. Many users are thought to ignore OCI, as the changes reported are not caused by recurring trade activities and are therefore irrelevant to predicting future performance.

Marking scheme			
			Marks
(a)	(i)	– discussion of additional disclosure issues	4
		– Conceptual Framework ED and general financial statements	4
	(ii)	– the potential use, misuse and manipulation of EBITDA	3
		– application of use/misuse of EBITDA by Rationale	2
		– calculation of underlying profit of Rationale	4
(b)	(i)	– nature of reclassification adjustment	5
	(ii)	– arguments against reclassification	3
			–––
			25
Total			–––

Section 5

SPECIMEN 2 EXAM QUESTIONS

1   HILL

Background

Hill is a public limited company which has investments in a number of other entities. All of these entities prepare their financial statements in accordance with International Financial Reporting Standards. Extracts from the draft individual statements of profit or loss for Hill, Chandler and Doyle for the year ended 30 September 20X6 are presented below.

	Hill $m	Chandler $m	Doyle $m
Profit/(loss) before taxation	(45)	67	154
Taxation	9	(15)	(31)
Profit/(loss) for the period	(36)	52	123

Acquisition of 80% of Chandler

Hill purchased 80% of the ordinary shares of Chandler on 1 October 20X5. Cash consideration of $150 million has been included when calculating goodwill in the consolidated financial statements. The purchase agreement specified that a further cash payment of $32 million becomes payable on 1 October 20X7 but no entries have been posted in the consolidated financial statements in respect of this. A discount rate of 5% should be used.

In the goodwill calculation, the fair value of Chandler's identifiable net assets was assessed as $170 million. Of this, $30 million related to Chandler's non-depreciable land. However, on 31 December 20X5, a survey was received which revealed that the fair value of this land was actually only $20 million as at the acquisition date. No adjustments have been made to the goodwill calculation in respect of the results of the survey. The non-controlling interest at acquisition was measured using the proportionate method as $34 million ($170m × 20%).

As at 30 September 20X6, the recoverable amount of Chandler was calculated as $250 million. No impairment has been calculated or accounted for in the consolidated financial statements.

Disposal of 20% holding in Doyle

On 1 October 20X4, Hill purchased 60% of the ordinary shares of Doyle. At this date, the fair value of Doyle's identifiable net assets was $510 million. The non-controlling interest at acquisition was measured at its fair value of $215 million. Goodwill arising on the acquisition of Doyle was $50 million and had not been impaired prior to the disposal date. On 1 April 20X6, Hill disposed of a 20% holding in the shares of Doyle for cash consideration of $140 million. At this date, the net assets of Doyle, excluding goodwill, were carried in the consolidated financial statements at $590 million.

From 1 April 20X6, Hill has the ability to appoint two of the six members of Doyle's board of directors. The fair value of Hill's 40% shareholding was $300 million at that date.

Issue of convertible bond

On 1 October 20X5, Hill issued a convertible bond at par value of $20 million and has recorded it as a non-current liability. The bond is redeemable for cash on 30 September 20X7 at par. Bondholders can instead opt for conversion in the form of a fixed number of shares. Interest on the bond is payable at a rate of 4% a year in arrears. The interest paid in the year has been presented in finance costs. The interest rate on similar debt without a conversion option is 10%.

Discount factors

Year	Discount rate 5%	Discount rate 10%
1	0.952	0.909
2	0.907	0.826

Required

(a) (i)   In respect of the investment in Chandler, explain, with suitable calculations, how goodwill should have been calculated, and show the adjustments which need to be made to the consolidated financial statements for this as well as any implications of the recoverable amount calculated at 30 September 20X6. **(13 marks)**

(ii)   Discuss, with suitable calculations, how the investment in Doyle should be dealt with in the consolidated financial statements for the year ended 30 September 20X6. **(7 marks)**

(iii)   Discuss, with suitable calculations, how the convertible bond should be dealt with in the consolidated financial statements for the year ended 30 September 20X6, showing any adjustments required. **(6 marks)**

(b) Hill has made a loss in the year ended 30 September 20X6, as well as in the previous two financial years. In the consolidated statement of financial position it has recognised a material deferred tax asset in respect of the carry-forward of unused tax losses. These losses cannot be surrendered to other group companies. On 30 September 20X6, Hill breached a covenant attached to a bank loan which is due for repayment in 20X9. The loan is presented in non-current liabilities on the statement of financial position. The loan agreement terms state that a breach in loan covenants entitles the bank to demand immediate repayment of the loan. Hill and its subsidiaries do not have sufficient liquid assets to repay the loan in full. However, on 1 November 20X6 the bank confirmed that repayment of the loan would not be required until the original due date.

Hill has produced a business plan which forecasts significant improvement in its financial situation over the next three years as a result of the launch of new products which are currently being developed.

Required:

Discuss the proposed treatment of Hill's deferred tax asset and the financial reporting issues raised by its loan covenant breach. **(9 marks)**

(Total: 35 marks)

2 GUSTOSO

Gustoso is a public limited company which produces a range of luxury Italian food products which are sold to restaurants, shops and supermarkets. It prepares its financial statements in accordance with International Financial Reporting Standards. The directors of Gustoso receive a cash bonus each year if reported profits for the period exceed a pre-determined target. Gustoso has performed in excess of targets in the year ended 31 December 20X7. Forecasts for 20X8 are, however, pessimistic due to economic uncertainty and stagnant nationwide wage growth.

Provisions

A new accountant has recently started work at Gustoso. She noticed that the provisions balance as at 31 December 20X7 is significantly higher than in the prior year. She made enquiries of the finance director, who explained that the increase was due to substantial changes in food safety and hygiene laws which become effective during 20X8. As a result, Gustoso must retrain a large proportion of its workforce. This retraining has yet to occur, so a provision has been recognised for the estimated cost of $2 million. The finance director then told the accountant that such enquiries were a waste of time and would not be looked at favourably when deciding on her future pay rise and bonuses.

Wheat contract

Gustoso purchases significant quantities of wheat for use in its bread and pasta products. These are high-value products on which Gustoso records significant profit margins. Nonetheless, the price of wheat is volatile and so, on 1 November 20X7, Gustoso entered into a contract with a supplier to purchase 500,000 bushels of wheat in June 20X8 for $5 a bushel. The contract can be settled net in cash. Gustoso has entered into similar contracts in the past and has always taken delivery of the wheat. By 31 December 20X7 the price of wheat had fallen. The finance director recorded a derivative liability of $0.5 million on the statement of financial position and a loss of $0.5 million in the statement of profit or loss. Wheat prices may rise again before June 20X8. The accountant is unsure if the current accounting treatment is correct but feels uncomfortable approaching the finance director again.

Required:

Discuss the ethical and accounting implications of the above situations from the perspective of the accountant. **(13 marks)**

Professional marks will be awarded in question 2 for the application of ethical principles. **(2 marks)**

(Total: 15 marks)

3   CALENDAR

Calendar has a reporting date of 31 December 20X7. It prepares its financial statements in accordance with International Financial Reporting Standards. Calendar develops biotech products for pharmaceutical companies. These pharmaceutical companies then manufacture and sell the products. Calendar receives stage payments during product development and a share of royalties when the final product is sold to consumers. A new accountant has recently joined Calendar's finance department and has raised a number of queries.

(a)   (i)   During 20X6 Calendar acquired a development project through a business combination and recognised it as an intangible asset. The commercial director decided that the return made from the completion of this specific development project would be sub-optimal. As such, in October 20X7, the project was sold to a competitor. The gain arising on derecognition of the intangible asset was presented as revenue in the financial statements for the year ended 31 December 20X7 on the grounds that development of new products is one of Calendar's ordinary activities. Calendar has made two similar sales of development projects in the past, but none since 20X0.

The accountant requires advice about whether the accounting treatment of this sale is correct.   **(6 marks)**

(ii)   While searching for some invoices, the accountant found a contract which Calendar had entered into on 1 January 20X7 with Diary, another entity. The contract allows Calendar to use a specific aircraft owned by Diary for a period of three years. Calendar is required to make annual payments.

On 1 January 20X7, costs were incurred negotiating the contract. The first annual payment was made on 31 December 20X7. Both of these amounts have been expensed to the statement of profit or loss.

There are contractual restrictions concerning where the aircraft can fly. Subject to those restrictions, Calendar determines where and when the aircraft will fly, and the cargo and passengers which will be transported.

Diary is permitted to substitute the aircraft at any time during the three-year period for an alternative model and must replace the aircraft if it is not working. Any substitute aircraft must meet strict interior and exterior specifications outlined in the contract. There are significant costs involved in outfitting an aircraft to meet Calendar's specifications.

The accountant requires advice as to the correct accounting treatment of this contract.   **(9 marks)**

Required:

Advise the accountant on the matters set out above with reference to International Financial Reporting Standards.

Note: The split of the mark allocation is shown against each of the two issues above.

(b) The new accountant has been reviewing Calendar's financial reporting processes. She has recommended the following:

– All purchases of property, plant and equipment below $500 should be written off to profit or loss. The accountant believes that this will significantly reduce the time and cost involved in maintaining detailed financial records and producing the annual financial statements.

– A checklist should be used when finalising the annual financial statements to ensure that all disclosure notes required by specific IFRS and IAS Standards are included.

Required:

With reference to the concept of materiality, discuss the acceptability of the above two proposals.

Note: Your answer should refer to IFRS Practice Statement: *Making Materiality Judgements.* (10 marks)

(Total: 25 marks)

4   KIKI

(a)   Kiki is a public limited entity. It designs and manufactures children's toys. It has a reporting date of 31 December 20X7 and prepares its financial statements in accordance with International Financial Reporting Standards. The directors require advice about the following situations.

(i)   Kiki sells $50 gift cards. These can be used when purchasing any of Kiki's products through its website. The gift cards expire after 12 months. Based on significant past experience, Kiki estimates that its customers will redeem 70% of the value of the gift card and that 30% of the value will expire unused. Kiki has no requirement to remit any unused funds to the customer when the gift card expires unused.

The directors are unsure about how the gift cards should be accounted for.

(6 marks)

(ii)   Kiki's best-selling range of toys is called Scarimon. In 20X6 Colour, another listed company, entered into a contract with Kiki for the rights to use Scarimon characters and imagery in a monthly comic book. The contract terms state that Colour must pay Kiki a royalty fee for every issue of the comic book which is sold. Before signing the contract, Kiki determined that Colour had a strong credit rating. Throughout 20X6, Colour provided Kiki with monthly sales figures and paid all amounts due in the agreed-upon period. At the beginning of 20X7, Colour experienced cash flow problems. These were expected to be short term. Colour made nominal payments to Kiki in relation to comic sales for the first half of the year. At the beginning of July 20X7, Colour lost access to credit facilities and several major customers. Colour continued to sell Scarimon comics online and through specialist retailers but made no further payments to Kiki.

The directors are unsure how to deal with the above issues in the financial statements for the year ended 31 December 20X7. (6 marks)

Required:

Advise the accountant on the matters set out above with reference to International Financial Reporting Standards.

Note: The split of the mark allocation is shown against each of the two issues above.

(b)   As a result of rising property prices, Kiki purchased five buildings during the current period in order to benefit from further capital appreciation. Kiki has never owned an investment property before. In accordance with IAS 40 *Investment Property*, the directors are aware that they can measure the buildings using either the fair value model or the cost model. However, they are concerned about the impact that this choice will have on the analysis of Kiki's financial performance, position and cash flows by current and potential investors.

Required:

Discuss the potential impact which this choice in accounting policy will have on investors' analysis of Kiki's financial statements. Your answer should refer to key financial ratios. **(11 marks)**

Professional marks will be awarded in part (b) for clarity and quality of presentation. **(2 marks)**

(Total: 25 marks)

Section 6

SPECIMEN 2 EXAM ANSWERS

1   HILL

(a)   (i)   Deferred consideration

When calculating goodwill, IFRS 3 *Business Combinations* states that purchase consideration should be measured at fair value. For deferred cash consideration, this will be the present value of the cash flows. This amounts to $29 million ($32m × 0.907). Goodwill arising on acquisition should be increased by $29 million and a corresponding liability should be recognised:

Dr Goodwill	$29 million
Cr Liability	$29 million

Interest of $1.5 million ($29m × 5%) should be recorded. This is charged to the statement of profit or loss and increases the carrying amount of the liability:

Dr Finance costs	$1.5 million
Cr Liability	$1.5 million

Property, plant and equipment (PPE)

During the measurement period IFRS 3 states that adjustments should be made retrospectively if new information is determined about the value of consideration transferred, the subsidiary's identifiable net assets, or the non-controlling interest. The measurement period ends no later than 12 months after the acquisition date.

The survey detailed that Chandler's PPE was overvalued by $10 million as at the acquisition date. It was received four months after the acquisition date and so this revised valuation was received during the measurement period. As such, goodwill at acquisition should be recalculated. As at the acquisition date, the carrying amount of PPE should be reduced by $10 million and the carrying amount of goodwill increased by $10 million:

Dr Goodwill	$10 million
Cr PPE	$10 million

NCI

The NCI at acquisition was valued at $34 million but it should have been valued at $32 million (($170m − $10m PPE adjustment) × 20%). Both NCI at acquisition and goodwill at acquisition should be reduced by $2 million:

Dr NCI	$2 million
Cr Goodwill	$2 million

Goodwill

Goodwill arising on the acquisition of Chandler should have been calculated as follows:

	$m
Fair value of consideration ($150m + $29m)	179
NCI at acquisition	32
Fair value of identifiable net assets acquired	(160)
	____
Goodwill at acquisition	51
	____

Goodwill impairment

According to IAS 36 *Impairment of Assets*, a cash generating unit to which goodwill is allocated should be tested for impairment annually by comparing its carrying amount to its recoverable amount. As goodwill has been calculated using the proportionate method, then this must be grossed up to include the goodwill attributable to the NCI.

	$m	$m
Goodwill	51	
Notional NCI ($51m × 20/80)	12.8	
	____	
Total notional goodwill		63.8
Net assets at reporting date:		
Fair value at start of period	160	
Profit for period	52	
	____	
		212
		____
Total carrying amount of assets		275.8
Recoverable amount		(250.0)
		____
Impairment		25.8
		____

The impairment is allocated against the total notional goodwill. The NCI share of the goodwill has not been recognised in the consolidated financial statements and so the NCI share of the impairment is also not recognised. The impairment charged to profit or loss is therefore $20.6 million ($25.8m × 80%) and this expense is all attributable to the equity holders of the parent company.

Dr Operating expenses	$20.6 million
Cr Goodwill	$20.6 million

The carrying amount of the goodwill relating to Chandler at the reporting date will be $30.4 million ($51m acquisition –$20.6m impairment).

(ii)   Doyle

The share sale results in Hill losing control over Doyle. The goodwill, net assets and NCI of Doyle must be derecognised from the consolidated statement of financial position. The difference between the proceeds from the disposal (including the fair value of the shares retained) and these amounts will give rise to a $47 million profit on disposal. This is calculated as follows:

	$m	$m
Proceeds		140
Fair value of remaining interest		300
		———
		440
Goodwill at disposal		(50)
Net assets at disposal		(590)
NCI:		
At acquisition	215	
NCI % of post-acquisition profit	32	
(40% × ($590m – $510m))		
	———	
NCI at disposal		247
		———
Profit on disposal		47
		———

After the share sale, Hill owns 40% of Doyle's shares and has the ability to appoint two of the six members of Doyle's board of directors. IAS 28 *Investments in Associates and Joint Ventures* states that an associate is an entity over which an investor has significant influence. Significant influence is presumed when the investor has a shareholding of between 20 and 50%. Representation on the board of directors provides further evidence that significant influence exists.

Therefore, the remaining 40% shareholding in Doyle should be accounted for as an associate. It will be initially recognised at its fair value of $300 million and accounted for using the equity method. This means that the group recognises its share of the associate's profit after tax, which equates to $24.6 million ($123m × 6/12 × 40%). As at the reporting date, the associate will be carried at $324.6 million ($300m + $24.6m) in the consolidated statement of financial position.

(iii)   Convertible bond

Hill has issued a compound instrument because the bond has characteristics of both a financial liability (an obligation to repay cash) and equity (an obligation to issue a fixed number of Hill's own shares). IAS 32 *Financial Instruments: Presentation* specifies that compound instruments must be split into:

–   a liability component (the obligation to repay cash)

–   an equity component (the obligation to issue a fixed number of shares).

The split of the liability component and the equity component at the issue date is calculated as follows:

- the liability component is the present value of the cash repayments, discounted using the market rate on non-convertible bonds

- the equity component is the difference between the cash received and the liability component at the issue date.

The initial carrying amount of the liability should have been measured at $17.9 million, calculated as follows:

Date	Cash flow $m	Discount rate	Present value $m
30 September 20X6	0.8	0.909	0.73
30 September 20X7	20.8	0.826	17.18
			17.91

The equity component should have been initially measured at $2.1 million ($20m – $17.9m).

The adjustment required is:

Dr Non-current liabilities $2.1m

Cr Equity $2.1m

The equity component remains unchanged. After initial recognition, the liability is measured at amortised cost, as follows:

1 October 20X5 $m	Finance charge (10%) $m	Cash paid $m	30 September 20X6 $m
17.9	1.8	(0.8)	18.9

The finance cost recorded for the year was $0.8 million and so must be increased by $1.0 million ($1.8m – $0.8m).

Dr Finance costs $1.0m

Cr Non-current liabilities $1.0m

The liability has a carrying amount of $18.9 million as at the reporting date.

(b)   **Deferred tax**

According to IAS 12 *Income Taxes*, an entity should recognise a deferred tax asset in respect of the carry-forward of unused tax losses to the extent that it is probable that future taxable profit will be available against which the losses can be utilised. IAS 12 stresses that the existence of unused losses is strong evidence that future taxable profit may not be available. For this reason, convincing evidence is required about the existence of future taxable profits.

IAS 12 says that entities should consider whether the tax losses result from identifiable causes which are unlikely to recur. Hill has now made losses in three consecutive financial years, and therefore significant doubt exists about the likelihood of future profits being generated.

Although Hill is forecasting an improvement in its trading performance, this is a result of new products which are currently under development. It will be difficult to reliably forecast the performance of these products. More emphasis should be placed on the performance of existing products and existing customers when assessing the likelihood of future trading profits.

Finally, Hill breached a bank loan covenant and some uncertainty exists about its ability to continue as a going concern. This, again, places doubts on the likelihood of future profits and suggests that recognition of a deferred tax asset for unused tax losses would be inappropriate.

Based on the above, it would seem that Hill is incorrect to recognise a deferred tax asset in respect of its unused tax losses.

Covenant breach

Hill is currently presenting the loan as a non-current liability. IAS 1 *Presentation of Financial Statements* states that a liability should be presented as current if the entity:

- settles it as part of its operating cycle, or

- is due to settle the liability within 12 months of the reporting date, or

- does not have an unconditional right to defer settlement for at least 12 months after the reporting date.

Hill breached the loan covenants before the reporting date but only received confirmation after the reporting date that the loan was not immediately repayable. As per IAS 10 *Events after the Reporting Period*, the bank confirmation is a non-adjusting event because, as at the reporting date, Hill did not have an unconditional right to defer settlement of the loan for at least 12 months. In the statement of financial position as at 30 September 20X6 the loan should be reclassified as a current liability.

Going concern

Although positive forecasts of future performance exist, management must consider whether the breach of the loan covenant and the recent trading losses place doubt on Hill's ability to continue as a going concern. If material uncertainties exist, then disclosures should be made in accordance with IAS 1.

Marking scheme			
			Marks
(a)	(i)	Discussion 1 mark per point to a maximum	8
		Calculation	5
	(ii)	Discussion 1 mark per point to a maximum	3
		Calculation	4
	(iii)	1 mark for each point to a maximum	6
(b)		1 mark for each point to a maximum	9
Total			**35**

2 GUSTOSO

Provision

IAS 37 *Provisions, Contingent Liabilities and Contingent Assets* states that a provision should only be recognised if:

- there is a present obligation from a past event

- an outflow of economic resources is probable, and

- the obligation can be measured reliably.

No provision should be recognised because Gustoso does not have an obligation to incur the training costs. The expenditure could be avoided by changing the nature of Gustoso's operations and so it has no present obligation for the future expenditure.

The provision should be derecognised. This will reduce liabilities by $2 million and increase profits by the same amount.

Contract

IFRS 9 *Financial Instruments* applies to contracts to buy or sell a non-financial item which are settled net in cash. Such contracts are usually accounted for as derivatives. However, contracts which are for an entity's 'own use' of a non-financial asset are exempt from the requirements of IFRS 9. The contract will qualify as 'own use' because Gustoso always takes delivery of the wheat. This means that it falls outside IFRS 9 and so the recognition of a derivative is incorrect.

The contract is an executory contract. Executory contracts are not initially recognised in the financial statements unless they are onerous, in which case a provision is required. This particular contract is unlikely to be onerous because wheat prices may rise again. Moreover, the finished goods which the wheat forms a part of will be sold at a profit. As such, no provision is required. The contract will therefore remain unrecognised until Gustoso takes delivery of the wheat.

The derivative liability should be derecognised, meaning that profits will increase by $0.5 million.

Ethical implications

The users of Gustoso's financial statements, such as banks and shareholders, trust accountants and rely on them to faithfully represent the effects of a company's transactions. IAS 1 *Presentation of Financial Statements* makes it clear that this will be obtained when accounting standards are correctly applied.

Both of the errors made by Gustoso overstate liabilities and understate profits. It is possible that these are unintentional errors. However, incentives exist to depart from particular IFRS and IAS standards: most notably the bonus scheme. The bonus target in 20X7 has been exceeded, and so the finance director may be attempting to shift 'excess' profits into the next year in order to increase the chance of meeting 20X8's bonus target. In this respect, the finance director has a clear self-interest threat to objectivity and may be in breach of ACCA's *Code of Ethics and Conduct*.

The accountant is correct to challenge the finance director and has an ethical responsibility to do so. Despite the fact that the finance director is acting in an intimidating manner, the accountant should explain the technical issues to the director. If the director refuses to comply with accounting standards, then it would be appropriate to discuss the matter with other directors and to seek professional advice from ACCA. Legal advice should be considered if necessary. The accountant should keep a record of conversations and actions. Resignation should be considered if the matters cannot be satisfactorily resolved.

Marking scheme	
	Marks
Accounting issues – 1 mark per point up to maximum	6
Ethical issues – 1 mark per point up to maximum	7
Professional	2
Total	**15**

3   CALENDAR

(a)   (i)   Sale of intangible

IFRS 15 *Revenue from Contracts with Customers* defines revenue as income arising from an entity's ordinary activities. Calendar's ordinary activities do not involve selling development projects. In fact, Calendar has made no such sales since 20X0. It would seem that Calendar's business model instead involves developing products for its customers, who then take over its production, marketing and sale. Stage payments and royalties are the incomes which arise from Calendar's ordinary activities and should be treated as revenue.

Based on the above, Calendar is incorrect to recognise the gain as revenue. In fact, IAS 38 *Intangible Assets* explicitly prohibits the classification of a gain on derecognition of an intangible asset as revenue.

IAS 38 defines an intangible asset as an identifiable non-monetary asset without physical substance. Intangible assets held for sale in the ordinary course of business are outside the scope of IAS 38 and are instead accounted for in accordance with IAS 2 *Inventories*. The fact that the development project was classified as an intangible asset upon initial recognition further suggests that it was not held for sale in the ordinary course of business.

If the development was incorrectly categorised in the prior year financial statements as an intangible asset, then, as per IAS 8 *Accounting Policies, Changes in Accounting Estimates and Errors,* this should be corrected retrospectively. However, based on the infrequency of such sales, it seems unlikely that the development was misclassified.

(ii)   Contract

IFRS 16 *Leases* says that a contract contains a lease if it conveys the right to control the use of an identified asset for a period of time in exchange for consideration. When deciding if a contract involves the right to control an asset, the customer must assess whether they have:

–   The right to substantially all of the identified asset's economic benefits

–   The right to direct the asset's use.

Calendar has the right to use a specified aircraft for three years in exchange for annual payments. Although Diary can substitute the aircraft for an alternative, the costs of doing so would be prohibitive because of the strict specifications outlined in the contract.

Calendar appears to have control over the aircraft during the three-year period because no other parties can use the aircraft during this time, and Calendar makes key decisions about the aircraft's destinations and the cargo and passengers which it transports. There are some legal and contractual restrictions which limit the aircraft's use. These protective rights define the scope of Calendar's right of use but do not prevent it from having the right to direct the use of the aircraft.

Based on the above, the contract contains a lease. IFRS 16 permits exemptions for leases of less than 12 months or leases of low value. However, this lease contract is for three years, so is not short term, and is for a high value asset so a lease liability should have been recognised at contract inception. The lease liability should equal the present value of the payments yet to be made, using the discount rate implicit in the lease. A finance cost accrues over the year, which is charged to profit or loss and added to the carrying amount of the lease liability. The year-end cash payment should be removed from profit or loss and deducted from the carrying amount of the liability.

A right-of-use asset should have been recognised at the contract inception at an amount equal to the initial value of the lease liability plus the initial costs to Calendar of negotiating the lease. The right-of-use asset should be depreciated over the lease term of three years and so one year's depreciation should be charged to profit or loss.

(b)   Materiality

Calendar's financial statements should help investors, lenders and other creditors to make economic decisions about providing it with resources. An item is material if its omission or misstatement might influence the economic decisions of the users of the financial statements. Materiality is not a purely quantitative consideration; an item can be material if it triggers non-compliance with laws and regulations, or bank covenants. Calendar should consider materiality throughout the process of preparing its financial statements to ensure that relevant information is not omitted, misstated or obscured.

Property, plant and equipment (PPE)

IAS 16 *Property, Plant and Equipment* states that expenditure on PPE should be recognised as an asset and initially measured at the cost of purchase. Writing off such expenditure to profit or loss is therefore not in accordance with IAS 16.

According to IAS 8 *Accounting Policies, Changes in Accounting Estimates and Errors,* financial statements do not comply with International Financial Reporting Standards if they contain material errors, or errors made intentionally in order to present the entity's financial performance and position in a particular way. However, assuming that the aggregate impact of writing off small PPE purchases to profit or loss is not material, then the financial statements would still comply with International Financial Reporting Standards. Moreover, this decision seems to be a practical expedient which will reduce the time and cost involved in producing financial statements, rather than a decision made to achieve a particular financial statement presentation.

If implemented, this policy must be regularly reassessed to ensure that PPE and the statement of profit or loss are not materially misstated.

Disclosure notes

IAS 1 *Presentation of Financial Statements* states that application of IFRS Standards in an entity's financial statements will result in a fair presentation. As such, the use of a checklist may help to ensure that all disclosure requirements within IFRS Standards are fulfilled. However, IAS 1 and the Practice Statement *Making Materiality Judgements* both specify that the disclosures required by IFRS Standards are only required if the information presented is material.

The aim of disclosure notes is to further explain items included in the primary financial statements as well as unrecognised items (such as contingent liabilities) and other events which might influence the decisions of financial statement users (such as events after the reporting period). As such, Calendar should exercise judgement about the disclosures which it prepares, taking into account the information needs of its specific stakeholders. This is because the disclosure of immaterial information clutters the financial statements and makes relevant information harder to find.

Calendar may also need to disclose information in addition to that specified in IFRS Standards if relevant to helping users understand its financial statements.

Marking scheme			
			Marks
(a)	(i)	1 mark per point up to maximum	6
	(ii)	1 mark per point up to maximum	9
(b)		1 mark per point up to maximum	10
Total			**25**

4 KIKI

(a) (i) Gift cards

IFRS 15 *Revenue from Contracts with Customers* says that revenue should be recognised when or as a performance obligation is satisfied by transferring the promised good or service to the customer. When a customer buys a gift card they are pre-paying for a product. Revenue cannot be recognised because the entity has not yet transferred control over an asset and so has not satisfied a performance obligation. As such, cash received in respect of gift cards should be initially recognised as a contract liability.

IFRS 15 refers to a customer's unexercised rights as breakage. The guidance for variable consideration is followed when estimating breakage. In other words, the expected breakage is included in the transaction price if it is highly probable that a significant reversal in the amount of cumulative revenue recognised will not occur once the uncertainty is subsequently resolved. This means that if the company is unable to reliably estimate the breakage amount, then revenue for the unused portion of the gift card is recognised when the likelihood of the customer exercising their remaining rights becomes remote. However, if an entity is able to reliably estimate the breakage amount, then it recognises the expected breakage amount as revenue in proportion to the pattern of rights exercised by the customer.

In relation to Kiki, it appears that the amount of breakage can be reliably determined and so this should be recognised in revenue as the gift card is redeemed. For every $1 redeemed, Kiki should recognise $1.43 ($1 × 100/70) in revenue.

(ii) **Royalty**

According to IFRS 15, an entity should only account for revenue from a contract with a customer when it meets the following criteria:

- The contract has been approved

- Rights regarding goods and services can be identified

- Payment terms can be identified

- It is probable the seller will collect the consideration it is entitled to.

At inception of the agreement, Kiki and Colour entered an explicit contract which specified payment terms and conditions. Moreover, Colour had a strong credit rating and so payment was probable. As such, it would seem that the above criteria were met. IFRS 15 says that revenue from a usage-based royalty should be recognised as the usage occurs.

Whether a contract with a customer meets the above criteria is only reassessed if there is a significant change in facts and circumstances. In July 20X7, Colour lost major customers and sources of finance. As such, it was no longer probable that Kiki would collect the consideration it was entitled to. From July 20X7, no further revenue from the contract should be recognised.

According to IFRS 9 *Financial Instruments*, non-payment is an indicator that the outstanding receivables are credit impaired. A loss allowance should be recognised equivalent to the difference between the gross carrying amount of the receivables and the present value of the expected future cash flows receivable from Colour. Any increase or decrease in the loss allowance is charged to profit or loss.

(b) **Investment properties**

In accordance with IAS 40 *Investment Properties,* the buildings should be initially measured at cost.

If the cost model is applied, then the buildings will be measured at cost less accumulated depreciation and impairment losses.

If the fair value model is applied, then the buildings will be remeasured to fair value at each reporting date. Gains and losses on remeasurement are recognised in the statement of profit or loss. No depreciation is charged.

Statement of financial position

Assuming that property prices rise, the fair value model will lead to an increase in reported assets on the statement of financial position. In contrast, investment property measured using the cost model is depreciated, which reduces its carrying amount. This means that the fair value model may make Kiki appear more asset-rich. Some stakeholders may place importance on an entity's asset base, as it can be used as security for obtaining new finance. Moreover investors would expect that the carrying amount of the asset will be recovered in the form of future cash flows, whether directly or indirectly.

As such, a higher carrying amount may increase investor optimism about future returns. However, reporting higher assets can sometimes be perceived negatively. For example, asset turnover ratios will deteriorate, and so Kiki may appear less efficient.

If assets increase, then equity also increases. As such, the fair value model may lead to Kiki reporting a more optimistic gearing ratio. This may reduce the perception of risk, encouraging further investment.

Statement of profit or loss

In times of rising prices, the use of the fair value model will lead to gains being reported in the statement of profit or loss. This will increase profits for the period. In contrast, the depreciation charged under the cost model will reduce profits for the period. Therefore, earnings per share, a key stock market and investor ratio, is likely to be higher if the fair value model is adopted.

However, it should be noted that fair values are volatile. In some years, fair value gains may be much larger than in other years. If property prices decline, then the fair value model will result in losses. As such, reported profits are subject to more volatility if the fair value model is adopted. This may increase stakeholders' perception of risk because it becomes harder to predict future profits. In contrast, the depreciation expense recorded in accordance with the cost model will be much more predictable, meaning that investors will be better able to predict Kiki's future results.

Many entities now present alternative performance measures (APMs), such as EBITDA (earnings before interest, tax, depreciation and amortisation). Other entities present 'underlying profit' indicators, which strip out the impact of non-operating or non-recurring gains or losses (such as the remeasurement of investment properties). Although the use of APMs has been criticised, Kiki may consider them to be useful in helping investors to assess underlying business performance through the eyes of management and to eliminate the impact of certain accounting policy choices.

Statement of cash flows

Accounting policy choices have no impact on the operating, investing or financing cash flows reported in the statement of cash flows.

Disclosure

It should be noted that entities using the cost model for investment properties are required to disclose the fair value. Such disclosures enable better comparisons to be drawn between entities which account for investment property under different models.

Marking scheme			
			Marks
(a)	(i)	1 mark per point up to maximum	6
	(ii)	1 mark per point up to maximum	6
(b)		1 mark per point up to maximum	11
		Professional	2
Total			**25**

Section 7

REFERENCES

This document references IFRS Standards and IAS Standards, which are authored by the International Accounting Standards Board (the Board), and published in the 2018 IFRS Standards Red Book.

The Board (2018) *Conceptual Framework for Financial Reporting*. London: IFRS Foundation.

The Board (2018) *Discussion Paper: Financial Instruments with Characteristics of Equity*. London: IFRS Foundation.

The Board (2016) *ED/2016/1 Definition of a Business and Accounting for Previously Held Interests*. London: IFRS Foundation.

The Board (2018) *ED/2018/1 Accounting Policy Changes*. London: IFRS Foundation.

The Board (2018) *IAS 1 Presentation of Financial Statements*. London: IFRS Foundation.

The Board (2018) *IAS 2 Inventories*. London: IFRS Foundation.

The Board (2018) *IAS 7 Statement of Cash Flows*. London: IFRS Foundation.

The Board (2018) *IAS 8 Accounting Policies, Changes in Accounting Estimates and Errors*. London: IFRS Foundation.

The Board (2018) *IAS 10 Events after the Reporting Period*. London: IFRS Foundation.

The Board (2018) *IAS 12 Income Taxes*. London: IFRS Foundation.

The Board (2018) *IAS 16 Property, Plant and Equipment*. London: IFRS Foundation.

The Board (2018) *IAS 19 Employee Benefits*. London: IFRS Foundation.

The Board (2018) *IAS 20 Accounting for Government Grants and Disclosure of Government Assistance*. London: IFRS Foundation.

The Board (2018) *IAS 21 The Effects of Changes in Foreign Exchange Rates*. London: IFRS Foundation.

The Board (2018) *IAS 23 Borrowing Costs*. London: IFRS Foundation.

The Board (2018) *IAS 24 Related Party Disclosures*. London: IFRS Foundation.

The Board (2018) *IAS 27 Separate Financial Statements*. London: IFRS Foundation.

The Board (2018) *IAS 28 Investments in Associates and Joint Ventures*. London: IFRS Foundation.

The Board (2018) *IAS 32 Financial Instruments: Presentation*. London: IFRS Foundation.

The Board (2018) *IAS 33 Earnings per Share*. London: IFRS Foundation.

The Board (2018) *IAS 34 Interim Financial Reporting*. London: IFRS Foundation.

The Board (2018) *IAS 36 Impairment of Assets*. London: IFRS Foundation.

The Board (2018) *IAS 37 Provisions, Contingent Liabilities and Contingent Assets*. London: IFRS Foundation.

The Board (2018) *IAS 38 Intangible Assets*. London: IFRS Foundation.

The Board (2018) *IAS 40 Investment Property*. London: IFRS Foundation.

The Board (2018) *IAS 41 Agriculture*. London: IFRS Foundation.

The Board (2018) *IFRS 1 First-time Adoption of International Financial Reporting Standards*. London: IFRS Foundation.

The Board (2018) *IFRS 2 Share-based Payment*. London: IFRS Foundation.

The Board (2018) *IFRS 3 Business Combinations*. London: IFRS Foundation.

The Board (2018) *IFRS 5 Non-current Assets Held for Sale and Discontinued Operations*. London: IFRS Foundation.

The Board (2018) *IFRS 7 Financial Instruments: Disclosure*. London: IFRS Foundation.

The Board (2018) *IFRS 8 Operating Segments*. London: IFRS Foundation.

The Board (2018) *IFRS 9 Financial Instruments*. London: IFRS Foundation.

The Board (2018) *IFRS 10 Consolidated Financial Statements*. London: IFRS Foundation.

The Board (2018) *IFRS 11 Joint Arrangements*. London: IFRS Foundation.

The Board (2018) *IFRS 12 Disclosure of Interests in Other Entities*. London: IFRS Foundation.

The Board (2018) *IFRS 13 Fair Value Measurement*. London: IFRS Foundation.

The Board (2018) *IFRS 15 Revenue from Contracts with Customers*. London: IFRS Foundation.

The Board (2018) *IFRS 16 Leases*. London: IFRS Foundation.

The Board (2015) *IFRS for SMEs Standard*. London: IFRS Foundation.

The Board (2018) *IFRS Practice Statement: Management Commentary*. London: IFRS Foundation.

The Board (2018) *IFRS Practice Statement: Making Materiality Judgements*. London: IFRS Foundation.

KAPLAN PUBLISHING